Out of War

# Out of War

Violence, Trauma, and the Political Imagination
in Sierra Leone

## Mariane C. Ferme

UNIVERSITY OF CALIFORNIA PRESS

University of California Press, one of the most distinguished university presses in the United States, enriches
lives around the world by advancing scholarship in the
humanities, social sciences, and natural sciences. Its
activities are supported by the UC Press Foundation and
by philanthropic contributions from individuals and
institutions. For more information, visit www.ucpress.edu.

University of California Press
Oakland, California

Library of Congress Cataloging-in-Publication Data
Names: Ferme, Mariane C. (Mariane Conchita),
    1959– author.
Title: Out of war : violence, trauma, and the political
    imagination in Sierra Leone / Mariane C. Ferme.
Description: Oakland, California : University of
    California Press, [2018] | Includes bibliographical
    references and index. |
Identifiers: LCCN 2017041374 (print) | LCCN 2017043315
    (ebook) | ISBN 9780520967526 (ebook) |
    ISBN 9780520294370 (unjacketed cloth : alk. paper)
    ISBN 9780520294387 (pbk. : alk. paper)
Subjects: LCSH: Sierra Leone—History—Civil War,
    1991–2002. | War—Psychological aspects.
Classification: LCC DT516.826 (ebook) | LCC DT516.826
    .F47 2018 (print) | DDC 966.4/05—dc23
LC record available at https://lccn.loc.gov/2017041374

Manufactured in the United States of America

26  25  24  23  22  21  20  19  18
10  9  8  7  6  5  4  3  2  1

*Ai miei genitori, Roberto Ferme e Patricia Cicogna Mozzoni, ed a mio figlio, Gilo Ferme-D'Isanto, con riconoscenza ed amore*

# Contents

# Illustrations

# Acknowledgments

In *Elogio Dell'imperfezione* (2010), Rita Levi Montalcini, one of the great Italian women scientists of the twentieth century and winner of the 1986 Nobel Prize in medicine, inverted the line in William Butler Yeats's poem about the necessity of a choice between "perfection of the life or of the work." Instead, she argued for a kind of methodological choice for *imperfection* in scientific research. Her masterfully narrated autobiography reads also as a window into intellectual and daily life in twentieth-century, pre–World War II northern Italy, secular Jewish Turin, and the post-Victorian gender barriers she overcame to become a world-renowned scientist. Her observation during a very long life in science, working with teams of colleagues from all over the world over the years, was that,

> neither the degree of intelligence nor the capacity to execute and complete perfectly a planned project are essential to success and personal satisfaction. In both, what counts most is a total dedication and closing one's eyes in front of difficulties: this way we can face problems that others, more critical and more insightful, might not face. (Levi Montalcini 2010, 76; my translation)

Trustful collaborations, "closing one's eyes in front of difficulties" and making the leap, despite the conviction that something more perfect may come from deferral to others, are essential to completing any project, but especially a book that has taken many years to come to fruition, amid other smaller projects, ongoing research, teaching, and family life. I would especially like to thank the institutions that at various points along the way have supported me with funding or residencies while I worked through or presented some of this material: the Université Catholique de Louvain-la-Neuve (Belgium), where in 2008, as the "Chaire Jacques Leclerq," I first presented early versions of some of the following chapters; the Upper Guinea Coast research group at the Max Planck Institute for Social Anthropology (Halle), directed by Jacqueline Knörr; the Laboratoire d'Anthropologie des Mondes Contemporains at the Universitè Libre de Bruxelles, where I held the "International Chair" in fall 2014, especially department head Joel Noret and the much missed and prematurely deceased Mathieu Hilgers; the Development Economics Group at the Wageningen University School of Social Science (the Netherlands), particularly Erwin Bulte, Maarten Voors, and Paul Richards; and the Collège d'études mondiales at the Fondation de la Maison des Sciences de l'Homme (Paris), where my residency as "Directeur d'ètudes associèe" was made possible by the support of Vinh-Kim Nguyen. Funding for field research is acknowledged from Cambridge University (2002), the University of California, Berkeley Committee on Research (2008 and 2012) and Mellon Project Grant (2014–16), and the National Science Foundation (grant #BCS 1430959, 2014–16). An Abigail Reynolds Hogden publication grant and an Institute for International Studies Manuscript miniconference grant from the University of California, Berkeley, helped advance the project toward publication.

The following students have provided research assistance or technical assistance with images: Brittany Birberick, Heather Mellquist, Rebecca Small, Brittany Young, and Adrian Van Allen. Cheryl Mei-ting Schmitz collaborated in joint research and writing on the Chinese presence in Sierra Leone, which is partially included in chapter 8. The following individuals have provided feedback on earlier iterations of various chapters: Joseph Bangura, Özlem Biner, Erwin Bulte, Annie Bunting, Kamari Clarke, Lawrence Cohen, Jean Comaroff, John Comaroff, Don Donham, Sam Dubal, Monica Eppinger, Thomas Blom Hansen, Benjamin Lawrance, Louisa Lombard, Marda Mustapha, Charlie Piot, Paul Richards, Richard Roberts, and Sharika Thiranagama. A special thanks to two anonymous reviewers for the University of California Press, to Joe Hellweg, and to Luca d'Isanto for close readings of the whole manuscript.

In Sierra Leone, I benefited from the hospitality or logistical support of the Boima, Dabo, Kpagoi, and Lumeh families over the years, as well as from the paramount chief and elders of Wunde Chiefdom. The staff at the Sierra Leone Red Cross Society, headed by Emmanuel Tommy, and Mr. Ibrahim George—then of the International Committee of the Red Cross—were welcoming and generous with their time during a research visit in 2012. At the Special Court for Sierra Leone, my work was greatly facilitated by the support and introductions provided by Saleem Vahidy, head of the Victims and Witness Protection Unit (2008 and 2012), and by Alessandro Calderone at the International Criminal Court for Rwanda (2008). More recent research on the "legal empowerment" NGO environment in postconflict Sierra Leone was facilitated by Vivek Maru, Sonkita Conteh, and Dan Sesay of Namati and by Simeon Koroma of Timap for Justice. Green Scenery and its director, Joseph Rahall, have been welcoming during more recent research in the country. Thanking all these people, however, does not necessarily imply that they would agree with the analysis that follows.

Part of chapter 4 appeared as "Paramount Chiefs, Land, and Local-National Politics in Sierra Leone," in *The Politics of Custom: Chiefship, Capital, and the State in Contemporary Africa,* edited by John L. and Jean Comaroff (Chicago: University of Chicago Press, 2018); a version of chapter 5 appeared as "Diasporic States," in *Democratization and Human Security in Postwar Sierra Leone,* edited by Marda Mustapha and Joseph J. Bangura (New York: Palgrave Macmillan, 2016); chapters 6 and 7 are revised versions of material previously published in *Humanity: An International Journal of Human Rights, Humanitarianism, and Development* 4, no. 1 (Spring 2013), and in *Marriage by Force? Contestation over Consent and Coercion in Africa,* edited by Annie Bunting, Benjamin N. Lawrance, and Richard Roberts (Athens: Ohio University Press, 2016). Parts of chapter 8 appeared in "Writings on the Wall: Chinese Material Traces in an African Landscape," *Journal of Material Culture* 19, no. 4 (2014). Permission from these publishers and journals to reproduce these materials is gratefully acknowledged. Finally, I thank DMJ and AJ for supporting me in many practical ways during the later stages of manuscript revision.

# Introduction

## War Times and Forms of Life

"Peace" in military mouths today is a synonym for "war expected." The word has become a pure provocative, and no government wishing peace sincerely should allow it ever to be printed in a newspaper. Every up-to-date dictionary should say that "peace" and "war" mean the same thing, now *in posse,* now *in actu.* It may even reasonably be said that the intensely sharp *preparation* for war by the nations *is the real war,* permanent, unceasing; and that the battles are only a sort of public verification of the mastery gained during the "peace"-interval.

—William James, "The Moral Equivalence of War"

### DEFERRED HARMS

This book is about the lingering effects of war, for what comes out of conflict continues to pressure and disrupt the present long after it has taken place. It remains anchored in the institutions and in the collective awareness as a transcendental structure, as an open wound. The title of the book *Out of War* poses the question of which temporality can be attributed to the ubiquitous slogan *war don don* (the war is over), which was advertised in many signs in the Sierra Leonean Krio language at the close of the 1991–2002 civil war, both as an auspicious sign of hope for a peaceful future and one of restlessness for an event that is still deeply felt by the collective awareness (fig. 1).

As I will argue throughout the book, this temporality's articulation was similar to the structure of trauma, which is experienced as a delayed harm, unexpectedly, at a later time. Freud expressed this delayed effect

**FIGURE 1.** *War don don* (the war is over). Koidu, Kono District, 8 February 2005. Photo by Peter C. Andersen.

of trauma by means of the notion of *Nachträglichkeit* (after-the-factness), to account for the fact that his hysteric patients displayed symptoms that were owing to the reliving of an earlier traumatic event. As Cathy Caruth (1996, 151) has argued, the traumatic event, "does not simply serve as a record of the past, but precisely registers the force of an experience that is not yet fully owned." Caruth's emphasis on the disowning quality of trauma seems to be its distinctive component, insofar as a "traumatic event" is never fully appropriated by the subject who experiences it. My argument here is that it is this temporality of a past experience, which is never assimilated consciously and which returns to haunt the subject, that bears a similar relation to the temporality I observed in wartime Sierra Leone. This temporality was experienced anew after the war in the midst of ordinary and extraordinary events, often provoking more violent outcomes.

As Caruth suggests (1996, 151), the traumatic event does not operate as a "pathology of falsehood"—as a clinical symptomatology. Rather, it is a "symptom of history." Paradoxically, the traumatic erasure of the event is the condition of the possibility of history. For Caruth (5), "The traumatized, we might say, carry an impossible history within them, or they become themselves the symptom of a history that they cannot entirely possess." War trauma, I shall argue, operates at the same level of unfinished history and gives it the quality of open-endedness that can be lethal or provide closure. My ethnographic work shows how the material production of events and meanings is bounded with this traumatic structure, both at the level of individuality and of collective history. Rather than focusing on the impossible history at the level of the subject, as Caruth does, I locate the materiality of a history that cannot be fully appropriated by memory and awareness. As I discuss in later chapters, I focus on the material traces of (inappropriable) history left in agrarian practices, therapeutic approaches, and juridical interventions, which are at risk of being erased by the monumental projects of massive large-scale infrastructure rebuilding.

A second aspect of the temporality of trauma is the way in which it moves across generational lines, reproducing the original traumatic symptom and its return. In Freud's *Moses and Monotheism,* the link between individual trauma and (Jewish) history is made by demonstrating the latent effect of an earlier traumatic symptom, which is forgotten, and is experienced centuries later by new generations as if for the first time, with what Freud calls "the repetition compulsion." In a way, Freud demonstrated that the trauma of the father (his murder) is passed on as a forgotten event through successive generations of children until it is remembered and accounted for by means of religious ritual and public history. For the Jewish experience, this nexus between historical symptom and repetition compulsion was disclosed in the prophetic tradition's coming to terms with the link between the reality of exile and the guilt for having disobeyed the law of Moses. For the purposes of my discussion here, the fundamental nexus is that the trauma experienced by an individual can be experienced by another across generational lines. One's own forgotten, unfinished history always passes on to others, like one's immediate family, who lives in proximity. The devastating effect of inheriting somebody else's trauma is clearly illustrated by the pain experienced by survivors of Hiroshima and Nagasaki, long after the atomic explosions of August 1945. In those cases, the transmission of traumatic suffering was mediated by both extreme psychic and physico-epidemiological disruptions. The health damages caused by exposure to radiation when atomic bombs were dropped on Hiroshima and Nagasaki at the end of World War II emerged even in the survivors' descendants. In these cases, the threat of delayed harm was further concealed: it was in the genetic mutations that can cause lethal cancers and birth defects in individuals temporally removed from the events of August 1945 (Hiroshima Peace Museum)[1] and in the traumatic effects evoked in the personal memoirs of writers and other artists.

In Sierra Leone, the intergenerational transmission of trauma operated in a very powerful way at the level of knowledge, history, and individual existence. In particular, it embodied a different way of relating to one's own history and meting out deferred and unexpected casualties from the distance of more than a decade after the end of the civil war. The civil war had produced a generation of children who had lived in limbo. A decade-long conflict separated from the land those who were born and raised in camps for refugees or were displaced from relatives, who had remained in rural areas during the conflict. When I returned to the country in spring 2012—at the end of an unusually hot and long dry season—some of the fires set at this time of the year to clear plots for farming claimed several lives in rural areas across the country, as was reported on national radio news broadcasts. One of those lives was lost in Wunde Chiefdom, where I arrived at the end of April 2012 to hear that a farm-burning party had resulted in a fatality three days earlier. I was taken to see a large plot so thoroughly burnt that in some places the cut vegetation had gone beyond the normal transition from wood to charcoal and had left instead only outlines of the shapes of tree trunks and branches in white ash on the blackened ground.[2] Evidence that the fire had burned very hot and out of control was visible beyond the area where trees and brush had been cut, in the standing vegetation nearby. The fire had moved into a stand of mature trees, prompting local commentary about the unprecedented dry season and climate changes on a larger scale.

Figure 2 shows the cleared plot in the foreground, with the downed trees and stumps that would be harvested for cooking fires throughout the farming season. Evidence of the fire burning out of control is visible in the background—particularly in the upper left part of the picture—where fairly large standing trees, too, are completely or partially burned, well beyond the plot's boundaries. The fire had torn down the hill, burning right through the wet, muddy area at the foot of the hill, where a rice paddy had been planned, and jumped across into the mature tree stand on the opposite hill.

A molten lump of turquoise rubber marked the place where a young man who had died had lost one of his athletic shoes (fig. 3), and a short distance away I was shown the spot where his body had been found.

**FIGURE 2.** Burnt rice farm plot. Wunde Chiefdom, Bo District, 1 May 2012. Photo by author.

**FIGURE 3.** Burnt shoe of a rice farm fire casualty. Wunde Chiefdom, Bo District, 1 May 2012. Photo by author.

Two men who had been part of the burning party told me that Samuel had made a capital mistake he would have known not to make had he been raised there: the bundle of dry reeds he carried to start small fires as he descended the hilly plot had been extinguished, and instead of continuing downhill, or stepping out of the plot littered with dry, cut trees and vegetation so that one of the other men along the line could take his place, he had gone back up to where flames were already spreading and forming strong winds to reignite his bundle. Very quickly he was surrounded by the flames and became disoriented. By the time he tried to run downhill across the fire line, it had become too wide.

Samuel's charred body had been found in the lower part of the burned plot and taken to the chiefdom headquarters. I was told that after the accident, the paramount chief had come to the village, blaming the local population for not properly supervising the burn and imposing fines for this fatal infraction. He then held a sacrifice, for which the villagers had to bear the brunt of the expense of providing the sacrificial goat and other penalties. I was told that another man in a nearby village had barely escaped with his life from a farm fire and was recovering from third-degree burns on his back. People in the group that related these events underscored the great tragedy for Samuel's mother, who in a short span of time had lost both her husband and her eldest son, on whom she would normally count for support in her old age. Several of them stressed that Samuel had grown up in a camp for the war displaced, away from farmwork, and didn't know how to farm, let alone handle a proper burn. He also had ignored an omen: a woman had dreamed of a man falling in a fire, and the following morning Samuel was told to perform a sacrifice. He consulted a diviner, who told him to postpone the burn, which he did. That same night, the diviner again had a dream involving fire, and in the morning he had asked Samuel to perform another sacrifice. But Samuel was running out of money to buy the food, candles, and other items required for this, and people relating the event said they were not sure whether he ever performed the second sacrifice on the day in which he decided to go ahead with his farm burn.

This was the way in which rural people in the village made sense of the tragedy—by first pragmatically working through the possible occult reasons for the event, searching for clues in dreams and omens, and then offering a propitiatory sacrifice for Samuel's death. And the chief exercised the role of "arranger" and took responsibility for oversight, but in this case it was the war itself that was collectively seen as the (deferred) originary cause of this fatality, even though it had happened as long as ten years after its end. This story, then, had the unexpected effect of a delayed harm of war, suddenly bringing back for everyone the awareness of the epistemic effects of the war after such a long time, when they had already moved on, by and large, with their lives. In this case, the overpowering return of the war manifested itself in the experience of defamiliarization and loss of knowledge of farm life on the part of Samuel. He had forgotten or never learned—as a displaced child refugee—the farming know-how of his elders and of those who remained in the village, which could have saved him on this fatal day. But another peculiarity of this moment was that during earlier postwar returns to this rural area I had not heard so much concern with the issue of intergenerational loss of knowledge on farms, nor had I seen so much evidence of it in other ways. In a way, another effect of the war was the realization that not only had lives been affected, changed, and lost during the war but also knowledge, techniques, and ways of interpreting one's sense of place in the landscape had been altered. All this had not been transmitted intergenerationally because of isolation, displacement, and migration, and the consequences had been lethal.

The war had displaced large numbers of people toward camps or urban-based relief services, and in the afterwar many had remained in towns rather than taking advantage of opportunities to resettle in rural areas. Indeed, large-scale migrations from rural areas to urban ones are a common phenomenon in Africa, including in areas that have not seen recent conflicts. Land policy reforms aiming to make the agricultural sector more productive, and to meet food security benchmarks established by the "millennium development goals," have significantly accelerated the pace of urbanization all over the continent, in part through the implementation of large-scale land deals with private individuals or companies, which take the place of smallholder farms like the ones prevalent in Wunde Chiefdom. The most recent census available for Sierra Leone found that almost 23 percent of its population lived in the four largest urban centers, and in the two decades preceding 2004, the population of the capital city alone increased by more than 64 percent (Nabieu 2007, 3). But urban areas were not the only destinations of a population set in motion by the war—so, too, were the industrial zones in rural settings, where minerals and other resources are extracted on a large scale, as I mentioned above.

Regardless of where Sierra Leoneans live, however, the pull exercised by rural land, and the ways in which membership in landowning lineages is bundled with heterogeneous rights and claims—ranging from citizenship to political offices, to access to food, precious minerals, and even valuable construction materials for urban properties—keeps many tethered to agrarian settings, through regular visits and the circulation of gifts, favors, fosterage, and other social relations. The pull of familial obligations in their rural birthplaces had brought back Samuel and some of his peers for visits and work. This mobility between rural and urban areas or market centers was especially high, in areas and at times when the war "flared up," in the episodic, concentrated ways in which long-lasting, low intensity conflicts can do.[3] Cross border mobilities were also high during the war, though the flows changed depending on where the war was being fought with particular intensity.

I use as an example the border region where Guinea, Sierra Leone, and Liberia meet—a region known as "parrot's beak," but also as "Kissy triangle" for the language and ethnicity shared by people in the area (map 1). It was also an area with large markets even before the war, and the town of Guéckédou, in Guinea, was an especially large center.[4] Thus this was an area of particularly intense activities, but during the conflict, and at different stages, the direction of population movements changed among the three countries.

Thinking of war trauma across intergenerational lines and through temporal structures of deferment that cannot be fully possessed by the subject provides a different lens for exploring the relationship between an individual and a collective sense of traumatic loss. In a way, the war was never over for people like Samuel, because "closure" was impossible for them. War trauma (the loss of knowledge, the exposure to cruelty, and the encounters with those who unleashed the fury of death) meant both an impossibility of experiencing closure of the event (since the war continued to influence the present) and recovering any sense of selfhood.

The impossibility of experiencing closure in extreme situations can be caused by a deadly event, as it clearly was in Samuel's case. In fact, it can be directly linked to the impossibility of owning up to one's death, to the impossibility of making any sense of what is happening to the self. Being unable to deal with a traumatic history provokes a fracture within consciousness, which consigns the individual to an experience that cannot be understood or communicated. This has been the object of reflection by Italian philosopher Giorgio Agamben (1999) in the context of his work on the impossible structures of witnessing in the face of the dehumanizing violence experienced in World War II concentration camps. In *Remnants of Auschwitz,* Agamben shows that the radical

**MAP 1.** Sierra Leone with research areas and "Parrot's Beak" border region. Drawing by Gian Luca Ferme.

effect of the camp as a structure of death is the impossibility of holding on to the legal and ethical limit of dignity in death: "The *Musselmann,* as Levi describes him, is the site of an experiment in which morality and humanity themselves are called into question. The *Musselmann* is a limit figure of a special kind, in which not only categories such as dignity and respect but even the very idea of an ethical limit lose their meaning" (Agamben 1999, 63). Agamben's words point to a situation in which intimacy and exteriority are so completely inseparable in the concentration camps that they force the witnesses of self-degradation (the *Musselmanns,* or weakest of the Jewish internees, who are marked for death almost immediately upon their entrance in the camp) to give up any attempt to preserve some dignity. This is because the ethico-legal concept of *dignitas* is "something autonomous with respect to the existence of its bearer, an interior model or an external image to which he must conform, and which must be preserved at all costs. But in extreme situations . . . it is not possible to maintain even the slightest distance between real person and model, between life and norm. This is not because life or the norm, the internal or the external, in turn takes the upper hand. It is rather because they are inseparable at every point, because they no longer leave any space for the dignified compromise" (Agamben 1998, 69). Agamben bases this interpretation on Primo Levi's experience of the loss of dignity at Auschwitz as the discovery of a new form of the ethical. At Auschwitz—says Levi—maintaining one's own dignity was considered impossible for the living: "The good that the survivors were able to save from the camp—if there is any sense of speaking of a 'good' here—is therefore not dignity. On the contrary, the atrocious news that the survivors carry from the camp to the land of human beings is precisely that it is possible to lose dignity and decency beyond imagination, that there is still life in the most extreme degradation. And this new knowledge now becomes the touchstone by which to judge and measure all morality and all dignity" (69).

In a similar manner, the horrific practices of killing and mutilating that occurred during the 1991–2002 civil war in Sierra Leone did away with any ethical threshold between intimacy and exteriority, friend and enemy, combatants and civilians. And this was precisely when the horror of mutilation contained a veneer of intimacy because of the close nature of the event and the cruel logic of inflicting harm at arm's length. Mutilation is a form of violence that obliterates any appeal to the self, to the purported dignity of and respect for the victim. In other words—to use the language of Agamben—it is an event that disowns the self so thoroughly that it eclipses any conception of ethical limit. It is a form of violence meted out with the ordinary tool of domestic and farm labor—the machete—showing a horrific inversion of what was considered to be a domestic tool as a cruel weapon of war. This execution of violence was paradoxically experienced in sometimes ghoulish negotiations between perpetrator and victim, when the latter was given the "choice" of a long or short "sleeve" mutilation—amputation of the arm respectively below or above the elbow (Gberie 2005, 136–37; TRC 2004, 3A:476).[5] Thus the unique aspect of the Sierra Leonean situation was not only the loss of any threshold between intimacy and exteriority, friend and enemy, insider and outsider. It was also the fact that this threshold could be renegotiated as a sadistic death game, in multiple ways in extreme situations. One could lose one's dignity, as in Auschwitz, not only by being dehumanized, mutilated, or violated, but also by "choosing" to join the dehumanizing aggressor and therefore losing the possibility of returning immediately to one's own home. Physical mutilation was not the only form of loss. Betraying one's group, losing one's own relationship with the intimate group, was just as violent. This was another form of disowning the self by consigning the individual to an experience that could not be fully owned. A long process of atonement was involved before the victims who had chosen to join could return to their communities. Alternatively, when they were considered perennially suspect by both sides, they were killed.

Victims sometimes recognized those who mutilated and raped them in this conflict, as they could be neighbors and acquaintances, who were forced to harm them. However, they sometimes could also find support in shared captivity with other members of their own communities. Generally, Sierra Leone differed from the genocide in Rwanda, where the state and its media contributed to the spread of a general atmosphere of paranoia, which turned neighbors against each other. But in Sierra Leone, too, perpetrating atrocities on family members was adopted at one point as a special technique to impede and limit the possibilities of escape for new recruits to fighting factions, particularly young ones (TRC 2004, 2:96).

This recognition sometimes happened at a different level: relatives of enemies, or suspected spies, could be captured or abducted in retribution. In one case, a woman who testified at the Special Court for Sierra Leone (SCSL) was abducted as a teenager and was eventually given by force to a well-known "rebel" to become his "wife," as retribution for her father's alleged support for an opposing faction. The father could not be found, so the daughter was taken instead. Eventually, this woman escaped with the help of a fellow female captive.[6] Thus interventions even by a stranger, in the absence of individual recognition but in the name of a general principle of shared solidarity among captives, could spare someone more serious harms. As mentioned above, some captives chose to enter relationships with their captors by "choice"—even sexual ones, in the case of women—because this translated into better treatment in a situation of generalized hunger and neglect. Though often these commutations did not spare suffering, despite the appearance of a measure of choice, they are indicative of the complex nature of this conflict, which was characterized by different experiences and stories of wounded beings than those of other conflicts.

My argument is articulated by reconstructing a constellation of events that were frozen in time and inform the social imaginary of a community. I do so by using the term *war-scape,* which was repurposed by Carolyn Nordstrom (1997) from the work of Arjun Appadurai to convey the notion that a distinctive disjunctive setting is characteristic of particular modernities. I focus here on a constellation of practices that range from military tactics or technologies of war to the sociological imaginaries that inform collective representations (Castoriadis 1987). But I add special cases to this narrative mode of fixing in particular images the totality of a conflict by discussing more nuanced constellations of images frozen in the order of discourse, imagination, and narration. These "space-time" intersections and condensations are captured in a series of "chronotopes," which I discuss below.[7]

## WAR CHRONOTOPES

The disruptive nature of some events during the war could sometimes be captured only using neologisms, such as *sobel* (soldier-rebel), which gave voice to the need for new terminology to capture the uncanny blurring of distinctions between opposite fighting factions. This chronotope crystallized in figurative language the anxiety about the potential dissimulation of identities that in peace times was a known phenomenon but in war times had eroded the shared knowledge of events and interpretations to become completely unpredictable, thus generating confusion and anxiety about the real identities of those who were meant to protect the civilian population. It also generated figures of speech and of the social imaginary that became markers in narratives of war experience and of particular preoccupations at different points in time. Thus toward the end of the war, the expression "Rebel Cross" became a derogatory label for the well-known humanitarian organization, with its ubiquitous red emblem, after rumors of its purported collusion with rebels during the January 1999 attack on Freetown, the single bloodiest event of the war. But as I point out in the chapter devoted to this phenomenon, popular animosity against the International Committee of the Red Cross (ICRC)—and the political interests that fomented it—was amplified by the fact that it remained a resolutely "branded" organization at a time when changes in the humanitarian landscape had brought about, instead, a proliferation of interventions so bewildering to their target populations that they were lumped together in the generic, vernacularized word for NGOs (*NGOsisia* in Mende). At the same time, the circulation of *raiti,* the vernacularized word for "rights," in the context of often contentious debates over political and economic resources in the postconflict transition, pointed to the emerging awareness of, and exposure to, the discursive practices and forms of subjectivity mutually constitutive of humanitarian projects, their ethics and politics (see Fassin 2011; Redfield 2013). In this regard, the Sierra Leonean instances analyzed here are particular iterations of global phenomena.

During the first half of the 1991–2002 war in Sierra Leone, one could drive by "Foday Sankoh's garage"—a notorious tract of highway where Revolutionary United Front (RUF) rebels were purported to have ambushed a convoy of trucks, leaving their burned and destroyed wreckages strewn by the side of the road like a ghoulish parking lot, amid rural surroundings with no visible settlements (see Shepler 2014, 135).[8] Named for the RUF leader, Foday Sankoh, this site memorialized a time when the rebels controlled this tract of road and territory. Even though this was no longer the case in 2002, drivers mentioned this expression when the gutted, rusting vehicles came into view, and some still accelerated as though they were in danger of being attacked. The wreckage on the landscape triggered a compulsive automatism (Freud's repetition compulsion) linked to trauma. Now, some thirteen years after the end of the war, the wreckage is gone, and drivers may or may not accelerate to make it over the top. Whether they do so because they remember that wartime event, or its delayed transmission, depends on their age, but the moniker is fast receding in the popular collective memory. This book contributes to the archival retrieval of this and similar collective memories embedded in wartime neologisms.

In reflecting on the "explosion of neologisms" that occurred in Germany between the Enlightenment and the Industrial Revolution, Reinhart Koselleck argued that they were indices of a collective perception of accelerated change that had "not been adequately studied from the perspective of political and social change" (Koselleck 1996, 69). Drawing on language, dreams, and other unconventional sources for the historian is necessary, for Koselleck, in order to convey the facticity of historical events, or *res factae,* through the literary conventions of modern fiction and narration, or *res fictae:* "The historian . . . is fundamentally impelled to make use of the linguistic means of a fiction to render available a reality whose actuality has vanished" (Koselleck 2004, 208). Some of the linguistic expressions, popular stories, and figures of the political imagination in wartime Sierra Leone constitute veritable chronotopes: particular configurations of space-time that encapsulate and localize the conflict's events and the ways in which they were experienced. Chronotopes are inherently dialogical—they place particular narratives and what they represent "in their external material being" in dialogue with the larger world in which they are told, heard, and discussed, and in which they signify, and occupy "a certain specific place in space" (Bakhtin 1982, 252).[9] I use them in this book as short, focused pieces that move across space-time, to examine a particular aspect of war. Sometimes the chronotopes of war are marked not on the surrounding landscape, as in the case of Foday Sankoh's Garage, but on the body itself. During my postwar visit in April 2002, I was with a group walking from one village to another, when we crossed a clearing in the secondary forest growth for processing palm oil. This prompted one of the men to mention that this was the place where Foday Y, who had been a neighbor of mine, had been kidnapped by the rebels during the war. He had been at work with members of his family in this clearing, when rebels surprised them and took him off to one of their nearby bases, the large "Zogoda" camp, across the nearby Waanje river (see No Peace without Justice 2004, 299; TRC 2004, 3A:192). The story of this capture pointed to the cohabitation, or at least the contiguity in many wartime settings, between combatants and civilians, aggressors and their victims. This contiguity was consistent with the troubled boundaries between war and peace, and the causes of mortality in both, as fatalities owing to the structural violence of neglect and lack of access to food, security, and health care during the conflict could outnumber those attributable to combat or physical brutality.

The two men telling me Foday's story said that while he was in captivity, they regularly received news about him from a female relative, who knew someone with access to the rebel base. It was through this woman that they eventually learned of his death from an illness. They even received word from the rebel base that Foday had been given a proper burial. Then one man pointed to a boy in our group and said, "Ask him, he was there when Foday was captured by the rebels. He ran away and hid, so they didn't take him." Put on the spot in the clearing where all this had taken place, the boy began visibly to shake, stutter, and breathe heavily. He seemed to be having a panic attack and was clearly in distress.

Words failed the boy, but the place and the narrative of what happened there had brought back with full force the reality of events that were no longer actual—in Koselleck's terms—in ways that could still elicit a visceral response of fear. Too, the place had prompted the other members of our group, who had not witnessed the original event, to retell a story that they had heard from those who had escaped capture. The dialogical character of this particular chronotope had to do with our presence in the space where the *res factae* occurred, with the fact that among us was someone who had been a participant in the event told, and my presence as a listener who was well acquainted with some of the story's protagonists. In other words, my own past relationship with all those involved—the late Foday and his grandson, who saw him captured while hidden out of sight—and our shared familiarity with the place in which the event happened were among the dialogic elements that elicited and brought forth this story.

The microhistories, signifying practices, and experiences embedded in the civil war, but also, as this story suggests, in relationships that pre-dated the war and continued in its aftermath, are largely absent from the traditional ethnographic record of war. And yet they are important ele-ments in understanding its experience—the prevalent anxieties and obses-sions of particular phases—and its aftermath. On another occasion, and on a different path during that same postwar visit, I was shown a spot on the edge of a recently cleared and burned plot being readied for a new rice farm, where a few days earlier people had found the body of a man who had wandered into the village in a state of madness and confusion, bab-bling about having witnessed the murder of his wife and children. They took him in and fed him, because he seemed like a "city man" who had no familiarity with his rural surroundings—I was told this by the chief and a group of men—and would not have known how to survive. But he left at daybreak, and when they found his body, days later, by the side of the road to the chiefdom headquarters, they thought he probably had let himself die of hunger from a "ruined heart" (*ndi nyani,* the Mende expression for regret and sorrow)—a condition they remembered all too well from their own wartime experiences. His story was told as a limit case, as an unexplainable event, a case of madness induced by grief and trauma, of loss of the will to live inherited belatedly from the war.

Not all neologisms and popular coinages represented experiences of war events as they happened and after the fact: some turned out to be prognostic. In his analysis of two dreams reported by German Jews liv-ing under the Third Reich during the 1930s, Koselleck (2004, 210; emphasis added) argued that they were

> immeasurably outbid by the later reality of the Third Reich. Consequently these dreamed stories not only testify to terror and its victims, but they had at that time a prognostic content.... [They do] not report what has

happened but rather what could happen. Both dreams contain the probability that exceeds what appeared to be empirically feasible at the time they were dreamed. *They anticipate the empirical improbabilities that later, in the catastrophe of collapse, would take place.*

The fears elicited by the figure of the *sobel* that circulated in rumors during the first half of the war, and in the proverb "soldier by day, rebel by night," were rooted in the inability to tell rebels apart from soldiers who sporadically attacked the civilian population. In one instance, rebels hiding among civilians in a refugee camp donned military uniforms to launch a surprise attack on the town of Bo. In many other instances, soldiers took advantage of nighttime curfews to attack and plunder civilian properties. This blurring of boundaries among purported enemies caused a generalized paranoia and gave rise to rumors. The *sobel* is a chronotope—a dialogical condensation of the image of fear embodied in the unidentifiable aggressor—of an earlier phase of the war in Sierra Leone. However, it also had an "anticipatory" character similar to that observed by Koselleck in the dream life of certain Weimar subjects. An actual, formal alliance between elements of the Sierra Leone military and the rebels of the RUF came into being in 1997, four years after the popular expression had emerged in language and rumors.

The pidgin expression *sɔkiya* (suck air, empty stomach) was a neologism that spread through the country in the years leading up to the war, to convey the hardships of the structural adjustment programs of the 1980s, which left people with only air to eat. As things got worse, and three-digit inflation made imported goods prohibitively expensive, resulting in the chronic scarcity of food, fuel for transportation, and batteries for radios and lights, *sɔkiya* escalated to *sɔkdɔst* (suck dust).[10] Hunger and scarcity generated both these neologisms in popular expressions that were linked to particular commodities of war. The preferred staple, rice, was often scarce and replaced by, for instance, bulgur wheat, which was not deemed a proper food. Likewise, toward the end of the war, the flooding of local markets with food commodities associated with the massive intervention of UN peacekeeping troops produced a particular chronotope. "MREs," or "meals, ready to eat," became synonymous with foreign aid. These were twin packs of small, highly caloric energy bars, with a sesame flavor, wrapped in aluminum foil and distributed as emergency food rations by various intervening military forces, which intervened in large numbers to pacify the country after the year 2000. MREs could be found in abundance in local markets and became a chronotope for the period 2000–2002, but they disappeared from the local markets after that, and people no longer mentioned them in their daily parlance. Instead, they reverted to producing and consuming a local equivalent.

Thus the temporal specificity of chronotopes—in the case just mentioned, around the issue of food scarcity—and their lifespans make them markers of specific phases of the war, and of the ways in which these times were experienced and grasped in language by the collectivity. Their emergence and demise mark transitions to other dominant preoccupations. But in some cases, as in the case examined in the *sobel* chronotope, they also have the anticipatory aspect of the dreams discussed by Koselleck. What at the time was thought to be a case of imposture eventually became an actual collusion of rebels' and soldiers' interests.

In novels, according to Bakhtin (1982, 243), the chronotope of the road is often associated with that of chance encounters, where "people who are normally kept separate by social and spatial distance can accidentally meet." But in wartime Sierra Leone, a sinister valence was layered on this chronotope, as chance encounters on the road often took the form of rebel ambushes, such as those conducted at Foday Sankoh's garage, or of checkpoints, where travelers could be subject to arbitrary abuses. Far from igniting the imagination and the thirst for adventure and novelty, the road and travel were avoided if at all possible. In my own memories of the war, the proliferation of checkpoints was in itself a distinctive chronotope, a point made for other countries beset by violence and tensions between state and citizenry (e.g., Bazenguissa-Ganga 1998; Jaganathan 2004; Lombard 2013, 158; Roitman 2008). Already during the 1980s, amid the hardships brought about by structural adjustment programs, informal roadblocks—for instance, by unemployed youth charging fees from passersby for filling potholes and maintaining roads—were to be distinguished from checkpoints staffed by police, which had become sites for extracting bribes and imposing arbitrary discipline on passing traffic.

But the escalation during the war was noticeable: during a research trip to Sierra Leone in 1993, a trip that took a whole day on one of the daily buses that in those days plied that distance, I counted sixteen checkpoints along the highway separating Freetown from Blama. Manned variously by Nigerian ECOMOG (Economic Community of West African States Monitoring Group) soldiers, members of the Sierra Leone Armed Forces, and police, each stop entailed different modes of interaction, ranging from the threatening jabbing of loaded weapons in one's face by an ECOMOG soldier high on drugs and alcohol to shakedowns for money. At the other extreme, one hyperbureaucratic checkpoint required passengers to stand in single file to present their papers to uniformed military, who copied details by hand into overflowing notebooks and submitted the passengers to questions and luggage inspections.

Traveling the same route in 2002, at the end of the war, when a big push to improve police discipline, remuneration, and material conditions was under way,[11] I came across fewer, open checkpoints manned by uniformed police, who waved on most vehicles as they slowed down, saluting smartly. The same distance was covered in less than a handful of hours.[12] Temporality itself, then—the relative duration of travel, the quality of passing time, in the nervous anticipation of the next checkpoint, or of news about rebel movements, the split-second decisions about running or staying that could mark the difference between life and death—was one of the key dimensions of the wartime disruptions of the ordinary. Through the representational evocativeness of chronotopes, "Time becomes . . . palpable and visible; the chronotope makes narrative events concrete. . . . An event can be communicated, it becomes information, one can give precise data on place and time of its occurrence" (Bakhtin 1982, 250).

Checkpoints once again proliferated during the West African Ebola epidemic of 2013–15, though not in the same numbers as they had during the war, and their configurations were different. The Ebola virus disease struck in the same countries affected by the regional conflict that broke out in Liberia in 1989 and quickly spread into neighboring Sierra Leone (1991–2002) and parts of Guinea. The Ebola emergency and the interventions it triggered brought back memories of the relatively recent and unfinished war. From the deployment of military and police forces to contain contagion in the population considered at risk, to the proliferation of checkpoints and state regulation of commercial activities and cultural practices (such as care for the ill, mourning, and burial), this crisis resuscitated anxieties about true loyalties and intentions.

This border region still hosts large concentrations of refugees and internally displaced people from the conflict. Key factors in the scale of the Ebola virus disease crisis were the population mobility in this region—estimated by some to be among the highest in the world as a result of the conflict's disruptions (e.g., Alexander et al. 2015)—and the legacy of wartime destruction of health care infrastructures. This area also overlaps with one of the few remaining zones in the region of primary, mature forests, which have become the new frontiers of wealth creation for individuals displaced by the war. Here animals and humans are coming into closer contact than in the past. Epidemiologists have analyzed the correlation between conflict-related insecurity and the emergence or re-emergence of infectious diseases, due to factors ranging from environmental changes linked to large-scale population displacements to the collapse of health systems and the disruption of disease control programs (e.g., Gayer et al. 2007).

Now, too, there were stoppages by uniformed personnel, but they were wearing surgical gloves, and the "guns" they pointed were thermometers to gauge one's temperature. The procedures were different too: instead of having one's luggage checked, one might be asked to clean one's hands with sanitizer or descend from the vehicle to wash one's hands at buckets filled with chlorinated water.

This discussion of checkpoints or other stoppages on roads traveled in wartime and in the interwar period links Bakhtin's notion of the road as a place of chance encounters to the notion of chronotopes more generally. In wartime, fear was a key element in the material and affective experience of chance encounters on the road. Travelers could be trapped in ambushes in deserted parts of the road, which could entail not just delays but harms on a greater scale, like being killed or captured. But by the postwar period, these encounters displayed less life-threatening abuses.

My analysis of the predictive, anticipatory quality of chronotopes—popular expressions, events, and material commodities that came to signify particular periods in time during the civil war—comes to conclusions similar to those reached by Anna Simons in her account of the beginning of the Somali civil war in 1992. While official historiography established 1992 as the war's beginning, Simons shows that earlier events—recounted through the circulation of rumors and later forgotten—were crucial to reconstructing the history of the conflict. Further, the forgetting of these events raised problems for understanding the war's genealogy. On 14 July 1989, Simons found herself trapped in a Mogadishu compound during an outbreak of violence, in which government soldiers opened fire on worshipers leaving a mosque after Friday prayers. The topography of the part of the city where she was located, where compounds were surrounded by tall walls, made it possible to hear gunfire and other noises associated with conflict but not to see what was happening. The military cleared evidence and refused to make any public statement relating to several fatalities linked to this event, and these acts, coupled with another unexplained murder in the city some days earlier, triggered conflicting rumors about what had happened. The profound sense of insecurity among the city's residents after those killings and the regime of rumors they inaugurated was such that,

> In November 1988 Mogadishu was a safe place for most people although people felt safe expecting violence; by November 1989, Mogadishu felt dangerous because people had not yet settled their differences violently enough. In other words, nothing definitive had yet happened in the space of that year except that Mogadishu had definitely turned a corner. This was felt at the time—in the tensions spawned by rumor, in crime, in uncertainty, in heightened expectation. *Nevertheless, the proofs of such gut-level knowledge have already disappeared.* (Simons 1995, 57; emphasis added)

A palpable sense of insecurity permeated the city and became a kind of chronotope, which later was forgotten because it did not have an unambiguous referent on which to anchor this fear. There were rumors and heightened crime but no visible theater of war yet. The key element for Simons was that the history of the Somali conflict could only be understood authentically after the fact, because it was predominantly a matter of competing rumors about what had happened on that day. It was the substance of conversations, and government-controlled media communications, which was at odds with reports from the opposition. Even though all these rumors could not prove the truthfulness of what happened on 14 July 1989, they produced moods of anticipation and anxiety, as well as a general sense of not knowing: "Once these events become ordered for narrative, the tendency is to reduce, collapse, and edit out the very terror of not-knowing, which is at the heart and soul of every rumor. Consequently, the critical link—that all events are interpreted by nothing but rumors—gets missed, and this terror of not knowing comes to look hollow and tinny, even peripheral besides the blood, guts, and drama of physical violence" (Simon 1995, 56).

Writing in 1994, in the wake of the second US withdrawal from Somalia and in the uncertainty of the outcome of the conflict, Simons (1995, 56) noted that, though she was certain that at some point in the future 14 July 1989 would be written into the official history of the civil war because the day's events were so widely discussed and recorded in the local media, that day "did not exist in the foreground of consciousness in 1992 and 1993," or at the time of her writing. Once the rumors faded, and without the documentary evidence of historical records, the memory of the event was lost. Writing about rumors, then, operates in the realm of the dialogical imagination insofar as it follows dia-logues (the crossing and circulation of competing words and arguments from the one to the other) to capture the anticipatory awareness of a kind of not knowing. And what is captured by the imagination is the ability to reproduce images precisely when the event is not captured by the intellect, by an act of perception. In this case, the "anticipatory" aspect of Koselleck's dreams, which exceeded what appeared to be possible, was that year of suspended time in which "nothing definitive" had happened yet.

The circulation of rumors during the Sierra Leone civil war exhibited a similar dialogical structure and generalized sense of not-knowing, which was nevertheless captured in images and neologisms that I discuss in the following chapters. This book in part is about the ways in which the not-knowing of rumors articulate with historical narratives of the same events.

Adding facts to the historical archive is not an anodyne act but one with political and ethical implications. Writing about the ways in which "publicly known facts" can disappear from discussions by the very same public that once narrated them, to the point of becoming secrets, Hannah Arendt (1954, 236–39) noted that hostility to "factual truths" was precisely at the crux of many conflicts, because they can be much more inherently political than opinions in their mode of claiming authority. European politicians in the 1920s, she wrote, may very well have been right when they claimed that, regardless of how the future might interpret the causes of World War I, nobody would deny "the fact that on the night of August 4, 1914, German troops crossed the frontier of Belgium"—an invasion that precipitated the conflict. And yet, she points out, "it is not difficult to imagine what the fate of factual truth would be if power interests, national or social, had the last say in these matters. . . . [It is] in the nature of the political realm to be at war with truth in all its forms" (239), and therefore to condemn a commitment to factual truth as "anti-political" in order to easily dismiss it.

In my own analysis in the pages that follow of certain publicly debated and known events involving the Red Cross in 1992 Sierra Leone, which were all but forgotten by the time the organization was vilified as the "Rebel Cross" toward the end of the war, I explore the modalities of more or less deliberate erasure of aspects of the conflict's history. At the same time, I explore elsewhere in the book the productive ways in which selective histories—of chiefship, of hunting traditions—mobilized popular responses to the conflict and reshaped key figures of the political and practices in ways that continue to have implications for Sierra Leone's future.

## WARTIME WRITING

Since the 1990s, anthropologists have contributed in important ways to the scholarship on violence and warfare.[13] Africa, the continent that has seen the highest concentration of conflicts precipitated by the end of the Cold War (Fearon and Laitin 2003, 77), has also been a key site for humanitarian and transitional justice interventions that, along with violence, have attracted anthropological attention (e.g., Agier 2011; Englund 2006; Fassin 2011; Malkki 1995, 1996; Redfield 2013). Some scholars have pointed to continuities between, on the one hand, open conflict that metes out physical brutality and, on the other hand, forms of structural violence, such as neglect and arbitrary state abuses inflicted on the bodies of citizens, which characterized life in many African postcolonial nations, particularly during the taxing structural adjustment programs enacted from the 1980s onward (e.g., Ferme 1998; Mbembe 2001; Mbembe and Roitman 1995). Thanks in part to the work of anthropologists, who broadly framed social suffering in settings ranging from structural violence to physical brutality, the very notion of a clear distinction between war and peace has been challenged (e.g., Das, Kleinman, Ramphele, and Reynolds 2000; Hoffman 2011b; McGovern 2011; Nordstrom 2004, 45–54; Richards 2005; Scheper-Hughes and Bourgois 2003). This blurring of boundaries can be attributed to the fact that armed violence has become in some countries an avenue to wealth creation (e.g., Roitman 2004, 15–16), or a form of labor in the absence of alternative prospects, particularly for youth (Hoffman 2011a). For them the very incentives for peacemaking—such as political appointments or economic and educational resources offered in exchange for the disarmament and demobilization of combatants—can become a reason for engaging in warfare (e.g., Debos 2013, 132–33). Among other things, seeing violence as a form of labor, and the cessation of its overt expression as a time "between-wars" rather than of peace, helps explain why some conflicts—including the 1991–2002 civil war in Sierra Leone—were notable for collusions (Keen 2005; Richards 2005) and forms of masculine sociability between "brothers in arms" on opposing sides (Debos 2011, 414–16).

Though in conversation with this scholarship, the present work also underscores the ways in which knowledges and practices linked to "complex humanitarian emergencies" operate in more disrupted temporalities. They do this through mobile responses to crises deployed over limited time horizons, in which the focus on saving lives in the present displaces concerns with more fundamental and durable transitions to the war's aftermath (Redfield 2013). Seldom, however, do the kinds of delayed effects of war, such as those outlined in the previous section, fall within the purview of scholarship, even that focused on the complexity of wartimes whose relationship to peacetime violence is conceived as open-ended. By focusing on a broader and more complex temporal frame, one can arrive at a different understanding of what happens in conflict, of how it is experienced, and of its significance in the broader livelihoods of those living through it. And all of this has implications, not only for how we think about war, but how we intervene in it as well.

Disjunctive temporality has been central to studies of African experiences of modernity (e.g., Ferguson 1999; Gilroy 1993; Hanchard 1999), many of which have highlighted the notion "that inequalities visited on African and African-descended populations have often been understood temporally, as impositions on human time," for instance, through the experience of slavery, or of arbitrary exploitation by colonial and postcolonial autocratic regimes of labor (Hanchard 1999, 249; see also Mbembe 2001, 73).[14] But even against the backdrop of the discordant temporalities in the lives of Africans of different means and mobilities in the postcolony, and of mutual imbrications between wartimes and peacetimes, the experience of the 1991–2002 civil war in Sierra Leone was characterized by temporal disruptions on a new and different scale. This was in part owing to its timing between, on the one hand, the end of the Cold War and, on the other, a new era in humanitarian interventions, in which nongovernmental actors, private funding, and market approaches to "sustainable" development infused alliances with state actors and institutions with neoliberal principles in order to reach their target populations (see Ferguson 2009; Nordstrom 2004). This book takes a critical stance with respect to these humanitarian interventions.

The turn of the second millennium also saw a new race by foreign private and state interests to exploit Africa's mineral and natural resources. While some have dubbed these diverse phenomena "neoimperialist," others have noted that "nineteenth-century lessons" are being applied "to twenty-first century practices," in which new technologies and business models can yield enormous profits in highly insecure—even criminal— settings, where state institutions and regulatory environments are weak (Reno 2002; see also Ferguson 2006, 194–210; Comaroff and Comaroff 2006, 16ff.).

My first book was published during the concerted international intervention of the largest contingent of UN peacekeepers ever deployed to put an end to the civil war in Sierra Leone. It sought to put the 1991–2002 civil war in the context of "the broader sociocultural and historical" factors within which the conflict unfolded. It also examined "the ordinary conflicts that may erupt in times of peace" and the "institutions, values, and views of self and sociality that sometimes are associated with violent practices" (Ferme 2001b, 1). This effort to place the war in its broader historical and sociocultural context was in part because of the difficulty of analyzing a conflict that was still unfolding, and in part because the desire to counter widely discussed works that saw in the proliferation of post–Cold War conflicts and state criminality in Africa a harbinger of a "coming anarchy" that had consequences for the world at large (Kaplan 2001). In a similar manner, other anthropologists sought to situate "experience-near" accounts of conflict within broader politico-economic and cultural dynamics, in order to counter narratives that attributed the violence to African "savagery" (e.g., Geffray 1990; Hellweg 2011; Nordstrom 1997; Richards 1996).

In this book, I offer an account of salient aspects of the 1991–2002 civil war that is only possible after the fact, in part because I analyze events that were virtually forgotten within short-time spans—despite having been at the center of much popular and media commentary when they were taking place—and in part because I focus on the ways in which the conflict opened up a space for reimagining the political in ways that could only be assessed after the end of overt violence. Much of the burgeoning anthropological scholarship on war is based on research carried out sometimes during, but most commonly after, the end of hostilities, when the conflict has become narrative and where the anthropologist's observations cannot be placed in the context of more long-term relations with the ethnographic setting (e.g., Bolten 2012; Hoffman 2011b; Lubkemann 2007; for exceptions, see Henry 2006; Bourgois 2004, 425–34). A more long-term perspective—such as I offer here—is important in part for ethical reasons, for the particular truths it can offer about past events. But I also assess the ways in which the war's disruptions operated within longer time frames, through the axis of intergenerational trajectories and the temporal deferment of harms that are not examined elsewhere. The effects of war isolation, displacement, and migration have disproportionately impacted this small country in West Africa and have been experienced not only in the immediate context of the war but even more dramatically in its aftermath. An entire generation of youth—exemplified for me by the figure of "Kaikulo" in chapter 6—grew up away from the familiarity of the rural world beyond the border, in refugee camps, or in urban areas, completely rerouted and rerooted from its place and sense of belonging. These youths were cut off from the land, understood not only as a geographical area but also as a way of knowing, an embodied practice, an episteme. Once they returned to the rural areas after the war, some of these youth had lost the lessons of entire intergenerational transmissions and no longer knew how to inhabit the landscape without escaping from its dangers. For these youths, the landscape had become once again mysterious and unpredictable. The after effects of the war can only be understood in a broader *longue durèe,* a long-term perspective that shows instead that the war was only the latest of a long series of deferments, displacements, and neglectful treatments, which could make "reintegration" into rural life a highly dangerous and unpredictable process.

## ETHNOGRAPHY AND CIVIL WAR

The Sierra Leonean conflict has been the object of a number of studies, some devoted to understanding the history and motivations at play in the conflict overall (e.g., Abdullah 2004; Keen 2005; Richards 1996), others focused on one of the main parties to the conflict, particularly the RUF (e.g., Abdullah 2004; Gberie 2005; Peters 2011), and the Civil Defense Forces and the "Kamajor" militias from which they emerged (Ferme 2001a; Hoffman 2011b; Kelsall 2009; Muana 1997). By contrast, studies of the Sierra Leonean military, and its rogue splinter groups, such as the Armed Forces Revolutionary Council (AFRC) or the West Side Boys, during the civil war remain thin on the ground (cf. Dwyer 2012; Peters 2011; Riley 1997; Zack-Williams 1997), although Peters (2011) discussed the career paths of youths recruited by the National Provisional Military Council (NPRC), which held power between 1992 and 1996. Some scholars focused on practices such as sexual enslavement and the forced conscription of children as combatants in this conflict—the issue that helped mobilize a horrified international community, eventually bringing the conflict to a close and ensuring the presence in its aftermath of institutions focused on justice, accountability, demobilization, and reconciliation (e.g., Coulter 2009; Denov 2010; Shepler 2014). Indeed, as I discuss later in the book, the figures of "bush wives" and "child soldiers" that emerged from this conflict and the discursive practices surrounding them became veritable "archetypes" of humanitarian discourse, and featured prominently in the expansion of international humanitarian jurisprudence and institutions (see K. Clarke 2009; Ferme 2013; Rosen 2007).

These and other works have made important contributions to under-standing the Sierra Leone civil war in particular, and more generally the "new" post–Cold War conflicts it exemplified—conflicts unfolding in resource-rich regions where businesses can protect their interests through privatized security and maximize profits in the absence of state regulation (Reno 1996, 1998; Smillie, Gberie, Hazelton 2000), and where new military technologies and strategies are deployed (Duffield 2001; Hoffman 2011b). This scholarship offers, among other things, analytical chronologies and chronicles of the war (see Hoffman 2011b, 84–131) and innovative perspectives, especially for the first half of the war (Richards 1996).

In the pages that follow, I offer insights into the ways in which war-time disruptions to the lives of people and communities articulated with phenomena unfolding over a longer timespan, partly formed on the basis of research trips to Sierra Leone during the decade before and on the eve of the war (1984–87, 1990), as well as during (1993) and after the con-flict (2002, 2008, 2012, 2015–16), and partly based on exchanges through communication technologies, as these have evolved over the span of time. Some of the research on which this book is based was expe-rience-near, immersive fieldwork among a small cluster of networked rural communities over the span of three decades—particularly Wunde chiefdom—but in the country's urban areas as well. Memories of war (my own included) emerged in the course of daily shared activities and conversations that arose out of relationships established over time. In rural areas, these activities included weeding or harvesting together on rice farms, extracting palm oil in forest clearings, walking to the next vil-lage to buy something or for a meeting, while chatting along the way—Mende conversations with the give-and-take typical among old acquaint-ances. Information seldom emerged in the context of the classical interview format or through the mediation of interpreters or translators.

Other chapters, however, address research done on a different ana-lytical scale, in order to understand the emergence of political figures and temporalities linked to interventions in "complex humanitarian emergencies," as Sierra Leone was declared to be during the 1990s. In particular, work among war refugees in towns—with actors involved with humanitarian and human rights institutions—and among diasporic Sierra Leoneans in the United Kingdom, Egypt, and the United States spanned over the decades, and overlapped with other research. Partici-pation of Sierra Leoneans in their country's politics, and their critical role in shaping its modalities and horizons, has increased exponentially with access to personal computing and the Internet during the 1990s. During that decade, diasporic Sierra Leoneans began to connect through listservs like Leonenet and through publications like the UK-based *Focus on Sierra Leone,* so my research migrated to these platforms as well. There relations with my interlocutors were more intermittent, were more distant in space, and were mediated by email exchanges. Increasingly, diasporic Sierra Leoneans have returned to their home country to run for political office (as was the case for President Kabba, a retired UN official who held office for two terms in 1996–2008), or even for "traditional" roles, such as the paramount chieftaincy (see chapter 4)—a fact that, as we shall see, shapes political institutions and the bases of their sovereign rule.

Beginning in 2002, I began researching the ways in which transitional justice mechanisms and humanitarian interventions—and particularly the establishment of the hybrid SCSL—were in conversation with existing notions of rights and justice in different Sierra Leonean settings, as well as how they gave rise to particular figures of victimhood and criminality. The identification of crimes and specific legal definitions of abuses accounted for the creation of new subjects of jurisprudence, a process that revealed cultural misunderstandings of (marriage) practices and definitions of autonomy. I began my research at the SCSL with some comparative work on the International Criminal Tribunal for Rwanda in Arusha, Tanzania—attending trials and interviewing lawyers, judges, and interpreters in 2008, followed by several weeks in Sierra Leone in 2008 and 2012—and on the jurisprudence emerging from these settings. In particular, debates leading to the formulation of new crimes against humanity or of their application in novel ways—particularly regarding the forced conscription of child soldiers and forced marriage—pointed to the emergence of a focus on youth and gender in the context of post–Cold War conflicts increasingly perpetrated by and against civilians (see Ferme 2013, 2016; Kendall 2009). This work on the production of legal knowledge, on its use of anthropological evidence in the process, and on the figures of victimhood to which it gave rise shifted my focus to transnational institutions and the cadres of practitioners who move among the multiple ad hoc tribunals and courts established, not only for African conflicts, but also for the former Yugoslavia, East Timor, and Cambodia.

This book, then, displays the legal and humanitarian enterprise clash with incommensurable figures and events in ethnographic scale and temporalities, which are perhaps apt to understand the bewildering multiplicities of Sierra Leonean experiences of the recent decades. Indeed, some have argued that Africa more generally, and particularly with its recent history, needs to be understood in terms of the "cultural and social processes [that] produced their own commensuration and disjuncture," which diverge from the "ideal modernist type" of commensuration and disjuncture experienced elsewhere (Guyer 2004, 20). This, at any rate, is the meandering path of a long-term engagement of one scholar with one country through changes in her own interests—and those of her discipline—over time.

## OUTLINE OF CHAPTERS

The question of temporality both as temporal distance and as a structure of delay and deferment informs the first chapter, "Belatedness." Here I examine, through the analysis of parallel events in colonial history, and through my own experiences in Sierra Leone, the ways in which certain events can be fully understood only from a temporal distance. Not only is a kind of "belatedness" central to the ways in which the gap between experiencing and knowing traumatic events works, but the deferral of the ability of consciousness to describe and analyze violent events in the full force of the present is also accounted for by the shift between different registers of experience, in this case the visual and the textual. I analyze two parallel stories, separated by a century but connected by the fact that both featured performances by the same costumed performers whose attire, made up of human skulls and bones, and aggressive demeanor point to their engagement with violent forces. The first story involves T. J. Alldridge, a nineteenth-century British trader and, later, colonial officer, who was instrumental in the establishment of a protectorate over most of what is today Sierra Leone, and who wrote two books, some ten years apart, about the country. The role of *"Tasso* men," as Alldridge called them in the event he witnessed, point to the inherently political nature of this figure—its affiliation with the men's secret Poro Society in certain regions of the country—and of the threats it continues to perform in their postcolonial appearances. What is interesting is the difference time makes in Aldridge's narration of the violence that took place in his first encounter with the Tasso men. The first book (Alldridge 1901), as I will show, erases the violence of the encounter and treats it as normal. The second book (*A Transformed Colony: Sierra Leone, Its Progress, People, Native Customs, and Undeveloped Wealth,* 1910) written after he had left the protectorate, reinscribes the violence onto the Tasso event. This act of erasure is of fundamental importance for my own work, because it made me realize how vision and writing articulate with violence and trauma.

The second incident involved me and a performer who was introduced as a *soko,* who uncannily resembled the Tasso image in Alldridge's books. The incident happened only a few days after my arrival in Sierra Leone for the first time. A violent performance that also led to a threatening physical attack on me, the event left open the question of the relationship between entertainment (a costumed dance) and didactic, exemplary disciplining, which are often featured in rituals of power (see Comaroff and Comaroff 1993). At the time of the events, I left a gap in my own journal and eventually erased from memory the violence of the attack and its impression on me. It was only after viewing images of violence from the 1991–2002 civil war in Sierra Leone, and rereading Alldridge's book, that I realized the full extent of the potential harms to which I had been exposed as a young anthropologist during my first fieldwork. I also discuss the gendered dimensions of being exposed to the performances linked to a male secret society and "getting away" from dangerous situations, particularly in this conflict.

In Chronotope 1, I explore the issue of war chronotopes and the anxieties and obsessions that are captured as signposts for particular phases in the war. These include moments—like those Simons, discussed earlier, pointed out for the Somali case—that only in retrospect came into focus as turning points, after which things were no longer the same. In other words, I show the parallel between trauma and violence during the war. The structure of belatedness elucidates how a violent event captured only by rumors can be "revisited," after the fact, as a kind of anticipatory move. In a way, rumors capture the sense of direction of historical events without having the weight of historical records and documentality. Yet they can be seen after the fact as having grasped the directionality of the event, enabling the work of narrative historical reconstruction. They link time and narrative by configuring the event. In the days of the civil war, which, it bears recalling, took place before the advent of cell phones and social media and widespread access to the Internet, rumors, including ones about the purported identities of the rebels meting out violence, proliferated throughout the country. For the first two years of the war, the very identity of the leadership of the RUF was in doubt, and it was only after the capture of a satellite phone (one of the prized objects of loot in the early years of the war) that Foday Sankoh, their leader, called the BBC Africa service to announce his identity and demands on the air.

Later in the war, particular rumors became prognostic of disasters to come, in Koselleck's terms, as well as chronotopes for particular phases of the conflict. The first on which I focus is the *sobel* neologism, which circulated in popular parlance and media from about 1993 and which forecasted, in a way, the actual advent of the alliance it prefigured between rebels and soldiers. This was the May 1997 coup mounted jointly by the RUF and rogue elements of the military grouped into the AFRC. This chronotope explores, then, not only what accounted for the advent of this rumor, but also for its demise—a little-studied aspect in the scholarship on rumors.

Chapter 2 is devoted to rumors that circulated toward the end of the war about the ICRC's purported collusions with rebels, which earned it the moniker of Rebel Cross. The chapter argues that in some ways the suspicions circulating in Sierra Leone about the true motives and sympathies of the Red Cross have to do with the paradoxes of taking a neutral stance in the highly political and contentious context of conflicts. This problem has dogged this organization in many different war theaters where it has intervened since its founding in the nineteenth century. However, the chapter also analyzes parallels between the culture of secrecy required by the ICRC's diplomatic mandate, paired with the ubiquitous visibility of its emblem, and local practices of concealment behind public performances and masks, in which dissimulation of one's real intentions and knowledge is assumed. The multiplicity of entities, ranging from the Sierra Leone Red Cross Society to the ICRC and the Federation of Red Cross and Red Crescent societies, that adopted the same red cross emblem also introduces the possibility of discordant goals and messaging. The latter may have accounted for events that put these organizations at odds with the government at various critical stages of the civil war.

To revisit the question of the selectivity of historical memory in times of crisis and trauma, the chapter uses the analysis of one such event— the kidnapping in 1992 of Sierra Leone Red Cross personnel in rebel-held territory—which had been all but forgotten by the time the Rebel Cross rumor had begun to circulate But by analyzing the role of state actors and media in circulating both the 1992 rumors about purported "collusions" between one of the captives and his captors (reported in the day's news media) and the Rebel Cross rumor, the chapter also points to a key factor in the social life of this discursive form during times of uncertainty.

The transmogrifications of historical figures is revisited in chapter 3, which focuses on the "reinvention" of traditional hunters as warriors during the 1991–2002 civil war. Even in their traditional acception—the chapter argues—hunters were outwardly oriented innovators more than preservers and transmitters of the past, as their quest for firearms, expensive ammunition, and lighting materials for hunting at night kept them on the move in search of innovations and patronage. The chapter argues, too, that the slippage in accounts of the 1991–2002 civil war between hunting and warfare traditions—mostly based on the fact that both involve the skilled use of firearms—elides significant differences in the ways in which the figures of the hunter and the warrior deploy technologies, in the kinds of knowledge they require, and in their relations to the political.

While in the surrounding West African region there is a longer history of hunting guilds—which have increasingly taken on roles once associated with state functions, such as the provision of private security (Hellweg 2011) and the management of forests and their ecological habitats (Leach 2000)—hunting has been a more individual pursuit in the Mende-speaking southeast of Sierra Leone, where the *kamajo(r)* nomenclature and militias came to dominate during the 1991–2002 civil war.[15] The chapter contextualizes the consolidation of this phenomenon as a classic case of capture by the state apparatus of what had been a deterritorialized counterinsurgency more akin to a "war machine" (Ferme 2001a; Galy 1998; Hoffman 2011b), after the 1996 multiparty elections that brought to power the Sierra Leone People's Party. This was a party that had its historical roots in the Mende southeast, and in part for this reason it had been banned during a quarter century of single-party rule leading up to the civil war. While hunting with firearms has long been an individual activity in southeastern Sierra Leone, and required a mobility that is in tension with any deep engagement with local politics, historically the figure of the warrior or war chief has offered an alternative model of sovereignty to the land-centered models of chiefship standardized under British colonial rule. It was, therefore, a more apt antecedent of the *kamajɔ* militias than the hunter. The chapter also examines, however, the ways in which organized community hunts with nets, which are hierarchical, collective enterprises, are often connected to political projects.

The issue of alternative models of sovereignty in historical forms of rule, particularly those exemplified by war and land chiefs, is taken up again in chapter 4, which examines the impact of the decade-long war on chiefdom politics. There are contrasting views of the role of paramount chiefs—the highest political authority at the chiefdom level—during the

1991–2002 civil war that are consistent with historical perspectives on the institution since colonial times. On the one hand, the partly hereditary, lifelong office has been seen as a source of arbitrary abuses, generating popular resentment and the settling of scores that informed patterns of violence in particular local settings during the civil war. According to this view, abuses on the part of chiefs, particularly toward young men and nonnative dependents who have no direct access to the land, remain a potential source of future conflict (e.g., Mokuwa, Voors, Bulte, and Richards 2011). This position is consistent with the widely shared perspective that in Sierra Leone, more than elsewhere in Africa, the chieftaincy has been a mechanism for increasing social inequality, delivering votes to incumbent political parties and political regimes at election time, reinforcing links between local and national political office, and generally acting as an arm of the state (e.g., Bayart 1993; Kilson 1966). Partly for these reasons, at the end of the war, some international donors and scholars hoped "that the chiefdoms [could] wither on the vine" (Fanthorpe 2004, 43), arguing that the high vacancy rate offered a unique opportunity to do away with the office entirely.

On the other hand, during the civil war many chiefs resisted rebel incursions, sometimes by negotiating with or paying off potential attackers. They were instrumental in some cases in organizing local hunter militias to protect their subjects from abuses by all war factions. Indeed, their role in raising and holding accountable hunter militias, in concert with the civilian government of President Kabba, who was elected in 1996, was a key reason for the fact that, when a rebel junta took power in a coup the following year, "Sierra Leone People's Party chiefs" became targets for reprisals. But was this an instance of a chief siding with his people, or with the incumbent government, as the scholarship mentioned above argues? I follow the vicissitudes of the chieftaincy in historical perspective, and over the span of my engagement with a particular chiefdom as a lens through which to understand the ambivalence toward chiefs by the end of the 1991–2002 civil war, including the remarkable reach of kinship ties to politicians at all levels in large, expansive chiefly families. This reach of chiefly families across political office on different scales does not imply consensus, however. Indeed, intergenerational and factional conflicts sometimes play out in changing party affiliations of competing candidates from the same families. At the same time, I contextualize efforts to reform the chieftaincy— and the chiefly elections that unfolded over the decade after the end of the civil war—within a discourse of decentralization that donors saw as a way to address the corrupt, patrimonial politics of the state, with its centralizing tendencies.

The chapter then argues that developments in local governance reform since the end of the war, particularly the proliferation of regencies, of absentee officeholders, and of honorary titles, suggest in part new departures but also a return to precolonial models of chieftaincy, which were more heterogeneous and numerous in their political, fiscal, and military practices. A renewed emphasis by state authorities in the postwar period on symbols of office, coinciding with the fiftieth anniversary since independence from British rule, introduced an element of spectacle in performances of chiefly rule. While the justification for the revival of symbols was to erase traces of colonial rule, new legislation enshrined in these symbols the metonymic relationship between chiefs and their symbols of office, particularly their staffs.

Land—its allocation, stewardship over it, and the resolution of conflicts over boundaries—was central to the colonial standardization of chiefly office, and this is flagged by the fact that in Mende, paramount chiefs are known as "land chiefs." The chapter traces exemplary cases of territorial amalgamation and splits, and their relationship to competition and alliances among the ruling houses from which chiefs are elected, which help explain the stakes of the chieftaincy's relationship to land. Even before the war, paramount chiefs had the power to grant access to chiefdom mineral and natural resources and in exchange to exact rents. In the aftermath of war, economic liberalization has produced new government agencies to facilitate foreign investments, which encourage potential investors to directly approach chiefdom authorities. These in turn see their role as partners in extractive ventures enshrined in new legislation. At the same time, conflicts of interest are embedded in this legislation, providing for district councils to fix and benefit from revenues, while paramount chiefs are tasked with their collection.

One of the phenomena explored in the chieftaincy chapter is the relatively new emergence of diasporic Sierra Leoneans running for chiefly office—a phenomenon in evidence on the national scene as well. Chapter 5 explores the ways in which the 1991–2002 civil war marked a turning point in the weight of diasporic Sierra Leoneans in politics in their homeland, as a result of the large outflow of refugees from a relatively small country, which dramatically increased the numbers of residents abroad. Sierra Leonean emigration and displacements are placed within a broader context of African and global migration figures. But they are also viewed in the context of the increasing global focus—

in the era of "the humanitarian turn" and of the expansion of the reach of global humanitarian legal institutions—on the figure of the refugee of proliferating post–Cold War civil wars. Indeed, the chapter traces the transformation of migrants from Sierra Leone from an earlier era into "refugees" of the civil war, even though they were already living abroad. The chapter also takes up the new claims and mobilities made accessible to migrants by this designation. Through examples of Sierra Leoneans encountered in Cairo and in European cities during the 1990s, the chapter examines the ways in which even at its most weak and dysfunctional, and even under siege during the war, the state and its practices of documentation and identification can reterritorialize its most marginalized citizenry. Sometimes this takes place many years after they have left its territory, albeit through the agency of global humanitarian entities such as the ICRC and nongovernmental organizations.

The decade during which this civil war unfolded was also the decade when personal computers, the Internet, airline deregulation, and cheaper communication technologies gave Sierra Leoneans, particularly those residing in North American and European cities, the tools to form listservs and chat groups, start desktop publications focused on the war and peacemaking efforts, and to mobilize economic and political support for a broad range of initiatives—from humanitarian and development projects to electoral politics and candidacies.

Chapter 5 tracks the "Leonenet" listserv and some other publications that during the civil war began to take increasingly active roles in criticizing the government's handling of the war and in pushing for peace. The nature of these "cyber-publics," an increasingly global phenomenon, is examined in relation to particular electoral projects, and linked back to the political candidacies of diasporic Sierra Leoneans, which is an expanding phenomenon from the chiefdom to the national level.

Chapters 6 and 7 discuss in more depth the "archetypal" figures of interventions by international humanitarian legal institutions in the Sierra Leone civil war and its aftermath—the forced conscription of child soldiers and the juridical figure of "forced marriage" (and the "bush wife" the latter generated). This discussion takes place alongside the accelerated temporality and contracted horizons of "complex humanitarian emergencies." These chapters are based on research conducted in rural Sierra Leone on the impact of the discourse of rights that shaped interventions during the second half of the decade and also at the SCSL—the first of a new generation of "hybrid" tribunals set up to prosecute war crimes and crimes against humanity in the countries where these were committed, and applying some combination of national and international laws. These tribunals focus on the rights of the accused, on the rights of the victim, and on an increasingly narrow focus on perpetrators "bearing the greatest responsibility" for crimes in an evolving international humanitarian legal landscape. The move to identify and prosecute war criminals at the highest levels of chains of command was motivated in part to more rapidly deliver verdicts and therefore a sense of timely justice for victims and witnesses. This new generation of ad hoc tribunals were tasked with their own fundraising, as opposed to receiving support from the United Nations like the earlier generation of tribunals set up for the former Yugoslavia and for Rwanda. Completing its trials between 2004 and the end of 2013, the SCSL prosecuted thirteen defendants in three consolidated trials, with a separate trial dedicated to the key war criminal, former Liberian president Charles Taylor. First as a warlord and later as a head of state, Taylor harnessed the resources to make this a truly regional conflict, which at various stages involved Liberia, Guinée, and Sierra Leone.

Returning to the question of discordant temporalities, accelerations, and belated events, this chapter also traces the ways individual tribunals contribute to the advancement of international criminal jurisprudence, which is among the key goals of war crimes tribunals; of the humanitarian impulse animating them; and of the transnational careers they enable. These chapters also examine the role of these tribunals in creating historical archives of conflicts and injustices suffered, and in producing new figures of victimhood—in this case, that of the forcibly conscripted youth combatant, or "child soldier," and of the forcibly married, or "bush" wife. But the question of the ultimate fate of these victims is left open, as the chapter follows the different fates of war victims—both youth combatants and abducted and sexually enslaved women. In particular, it compares those who were given a forum in which to testify, or bear witness to their experiences—such as the SCSL, the Truth and Reconciliation Commission, or therapeutic venues—with those who did not.

In chapter 8, I discuss the material traces of Chinese-Sierra Leonean entanglements and the visual inscription on the landscape, as well as consumption and therapeutic practices. I start with the discussion of a historical photograph from my archive of a building in a small Sierra Leonean rural community, with a somewhat "colonial" iconography representing an aging patriarch surrounded by dependents, which bore the unexpected inscription, "Chinese Store." The label's novelty was owing to the fact that there were no Chinese residents in this community in the mid-1980s, when I took this picture. Instead, there were narratives of an encounter with a single agricultural technical advisor from "China," who had left behind agricultural inputs to be stored in the Chinese store.

At the time this image was taken, the only traces of "Chinese" passage in ordinary life in this rural community were in the scent of what was called "mentholatum" but was in fact contained in "Tiger Balm" tins marked with Chinese characters, as well as in other objects of daily domestic consumption (e.g., cheap enamelware or sheets). This was a relatively poor community, and those were the times when the key export from China to the continent were cheaply made goods. As I show in that chapter, colonial historical mediations showed a much more circuitous route for the arrival of these commodities on the Sierra Leonean and other African markets. At the same time, the only visible Chinese presence in those prewar days, apart from a couple of restaurants in the country's capital city, were insular groups that lived in walled compounds, had little contact with the surrounding population, and worked on major infrastructural projects such as the Dodo Hydro Electricity Dam, which eventually provided more reliable service in the two provincial towns of Kenema and Bo—at least during the rainy season—than in many parts of the country's capital city.

The vicissitudes of Chinese-Sierra Leonean relations, and the slippage over time between China as Taiwan and China as the People's Republic serve to contextualize "friend-enemy" relations, not only in colonial and postcolonial Sierra Leone, but on the global stage. The friend-enemy oppositional relationship between Taiwan and China was reproduced in rural Sierra Leone in a specular form. It deployed itself initially as an economic relationship between the Sierra Leonean government and Taiwan and later as a replacement of those same economic ties with an alliance with the Peoples' Republic of China, which sought to displace Taiwan on the global stage. The two strategic relationships left double inscriptions in the landscape as the People's Republic of China revisited agricultural schemes initiated by Taiwan, but they also saw an escalation as well, in the form of the monumental road, industrial, and construction projects that the former initiated in the early seventies. Despite these visible signs on the landscape, the physical presence of the workers responsible for them was elided by the fact that they lived in insular, walled compounds away from the local population. After a hiatus during the civil war, mainland Chinese returned in force to Sierra Leone, building new hospitals and a sports stadium, renovating earlier projects, and launching mining operations, as well as small-scale businesses that brought them into closer contact with the local population. During the Ebola epidemic, their interventions in the vaccination campaigns were at first met with suspicion from other international health actors because of their sui generis approach to healing and their development of an alternative vaccine, but they were well received among the local population, which had already begun to buy Chinese herbal remedies and attend their hospitals.

The conclusion addresses the question of survival in the light of the incipient West Africa Ebola epidemic. It fixes in time the "in-between of emergencies," or the critical period that provided the perspective from which this book was written, although from the Janus-faced perspective of past and future orientations (e.g., Munn [2003] 2013; Guyer 2007). It not only addresses the issue of "human" survivals but also those crystallized in places and objects, which in the face of new unstable times elicit narratives of previous ones, similar to the way the Ebola virus disease crisis does in relation to the 1991–2002 civil war. I use the example of checkpoints, their similar and yet different configurations and their increase in number with respect to "ordinary" times. But I also discuss the effects of decentralization at multiple levels in the postconflict reconfiguration of regulatory and other mechanisms, particularly insofar as they shape access to justice and the protection of rights in land matters. Though these phenomena may be shared with other postconflict settings, which are also the scene of "land grabs" on a larger scale than in Sierra Leone or elsewhere in Africa, they are only partially dependent on local framings. They also relate to global phenomena like the increased deployment of humanitarian interventions, or of humanitarian justice projects, with their discursive and material effects. And they relate to the articulation of different levels of narration and technologies, increasingly made possible in the current mediatized world, in which art is put to the purpose of development and humanitarian projects; film can be both "documentary" and partly staged (or photography differently "framed" for different purposes); and literary fictions can mimic or anticipate factual events, and vice versa. These phenomena are explored through the analysis of wartime documentary films and of colonial and postcolonial photographic material.

Finally, the book's narrative progression illustrates methodological issues raised by anthropological research over time and across different scales of analysis. It ranges in scope from intimate, first-person stories by the anthropologist, including some of her own direct experiences, in a limited geographical area and in a temporally intensive way early on, as well as during episodic shorter visits over time. But it moves also to the study of live and text-mediated court testimony, or to the study of the diasporic experience (in which participant observation was supplemented, for example, by monitoring electronic discussion groups that brought together people living far apart), beyond Sierra Leonean national boundaries. But it also demonstrates the advantages of contextualizing such experiences within phenomena on a broader scale, in more collaborative modes, and in multiple sites within the country. Finally, this book contributes to the growing archive that places a small, "out of the way" corner of Africa named Sierra Leone and the surrounding region on the map in a new, securitized world order, in which this civil war, successive peacemaking and justice-seeking interventions, and the regimes of care deployed since then have marked important turning points.

# 1

# Belatedness

## Vision, Writing, and the Labor of Time

In this chapter, I address the structure of the temporal deferrals and delays that characterize the translation of an experience of violence, or an instance of its witnessing, into ethnographic narrative. I examine the eyewitness accounts (official reports and two books published some ten years apart) by T. J. Alldridge, a British colonial officer in Sierra Leone, of an event that took place toward the end of the nineteenth century. A century later, I witnessed an event bearing some resemblance to what Alldridge had described in reports and manuscripts, and I explore Alldridge's and my experiences in parallel to shed light on the ways, over time, various displacements or refigurations—between image and textuality—make possible alternative representations of violence, and of their political implications. Work on trauma shows that the full impact of traumatic events cannot be assimilated in the present moment but is often experienced only after a period of latency, often by means of a second traumatic event (Freud 1939, 84; 1922, 34–40). Similarly, writing about violent and traumatic events that one has witnessed often can happen only in elliptical forms: "Traumatic experience, beyond the psychological dimension of suffering it involves, suggests a certain paradox: that the most direct seeing of a violent event may occur as an absolute inability to know it; that immediacy, paradoxically, may take the form of belatedness" (Caruth 1996, 91–92). The act of bearing witness to a violent event (often even in the context of staging performances) does not lead to cumulative knowledge of the event; on the contrary, it leads the subject into a state of not-knowing that is not far from the epistemic status of rumors mentioned earlier. What blocks the full assumption of "knowledge" is an excess of vision, the bursting into view of an aspect of experience that cannot be assimilated in the present. The more one "sees," the more knowledge of the event takes the form of deferral and delay, or what Caruth calls "belatedness." Thus trauma is a "double wound," because it "is experienced too soon, too unexpectedly to be fully known and is therefore not available to consciousness until it imposes itself again" (Caruth, 4). Bearing witness to violence is so shocking for consciousness that it cannot be subsumed under the categories of experience. This paradox within the structure of the traumatic event (even in performance) immediately presents the impasse of testimony: what one truly bears witness to cannot be fully "known," at least not immediately. What is apprehended in testimony is a gap, an impossibility to communicate. To reproduce the witnessed event for the clarity of consciousness, and for speech, needs the work of time. This belatedness also marks a critical shift from the register of vision—an excessive seeing, or witnessing, of a traumatic event—to that of voice and narrativity, which makes it communicable, transmissible. Deprived of transmission, bearing witness falls into the vacuum of self-reference and fails to produce knowledge. This shift is of special interest to me because T. J. Alldridge was an amateur photographer who, during his time in Sierra Leone, took many pictures, with which he illustrated reports to his superiors and his published work. Like Alldridge's, my own experience of bearing witness to a violent event, through its depiction in a performance in the same region involved a photographic camera and was also belatedly remembered in film footage of the most violent episode of the 1991–2002 civil war. In both cases, the movement from excessive vision to voice is critical to the possibility of speaking about the event and handing it over for ethnographic narration.

Claiming a traumatic experience—being able to assimilate it—according to Caruth (1996, 111), follows a kind of "awakening" that makes remembering and understanding possible, albeit sometimes in fragmented ways, or through reassembling the memories of a violent or shocking event in a different way (Williams 2006, 322–23). In what follows, I draw parallels between two different accounts of the same event in nineteenth-century Sierra Leone by T. J. Alldridge, and a frightening event I witnessed only a few days after arriving for the first time in Sierra Leone. The event I witnessed was similar to performances I was to see many times in the course of my fieldwork in Sierra Leone, in connection with the secret societies into which most rural Sierra Leoneans are initiated. Those initiations often involve painful ordeals, veritable forms of torture, in some cases, which are ways of unleashing and inscribing the full force of society's laws on the body (e.g., Clastres 1989, 177).

Until the outbreak of civil war, ordinary, ritualized forms of violence such as those performed during initiations were not discussed much in the contemporary scholarly literature. This was in part a reaction to exoticizing accounts and representations from earlier writings, primarily during Sierra Leone's colonial history, including T. J. Alldridge's and others' (e.g., Alldridge 1901, 124ff.; Thomas 1916, 145; Wallis 1903, 234–35). But during the civil war, the resistance in the scholarly literature to representations of violence in contemporary initiation rituals broke down. Thus the spectacularization and performance of bodily mutilations and other forms of inflicting pain in public, mostly carried out with cutlasses and other tools of ordinary farmwork during the civil war, were the most widely advertised types of harm. The reasons these mutilations were so powerful and shocking for the population at large must be loosely linked to the more routinized, ritualized, and staged forms of inflicting pain on the body during initiations, which they sometimes mimicked.

## WRITING, DOUBLING, AND THE STATUS OF IMAGES

T. J. Alldridge was an Englishman who spent almost two decades as a trader on the Atlantic coast adjacent to the Sierra Leone Colony, before being appointed traveling commissioner and being sent through the hinterland to sign "friendship treaties" with neighboring chiefs (Abraham 1978, 96, 99–101; Fyfe 1962, 486–87). Earlier that year, the British had settled a boundary dispute with the French, who were encroaching in this region of competing commercial interests in oil palm and other natural products. The colony administration was eager, therefore, to secure its influence in the region through alliances. In 1896, the relationship was formalized further with the establishment of a protectorate adjacent to the colony.

That same year, Alldridge had an opportunity to witness the installation of a new sokong of Imperri (a title later equated by the British administration with that of paramount chief), which bordered with the Sherbro coastal strip that had been part of the colony territory since 1825.[1] He reported observing "an important and exceptional meeting, the installation of a chief, after several years of interregnum" (Alldridge 1901, 131).[2] The new Imperri ruler was taking up a post that had been vacant since 1870 (Fyfe 1962, 556), a circumstance resulting from lingering conflicts fueled by competition over trade with European businesses from different countries, land disputes, and the suppression of the domestic slave trade. As we shall see, the 1991–2002 civil war similarly resulted in power vacuums and a decade or more of vacant chieftaincies throughout Sierra Leone. However, a reader of Alldridge's account might easily miss the fact that the twenty-six-year "interregnum" in Imperri had been the result of violent political conflict, including accusations of ritual murder. The latter provoked dozens of summary executions of those suspected of what the British referred to as acts of "cannibalism," because the killings aimed at securing human fat and body parts for making powerful secret societies' medicines. A few years before he witnessed the installation of the sokong, Alldridge himself had reported to the colonial secretary on the increasing incidence of "human sacrifice" in Imperri (quoted in Kalous 1974, 36–37).

But in his 1901 book, Alldridge mentions the "Human Leopard Society," which was associated with these murders, in a chapter devoted to secret societies, without linking it to the troubling narratives of rumors of murders during the long interregnum. He notes in a later chapter that "the Imperri was the great center of this institution," but he did not think it had been in existence for more than a few decades. In a 1894 report to the colonial secretary, Alldridge had suggested that assassinations by the Human Leopard Society had been practically unknown around 1871, when he first arrived in Sierra Leone as a trader. According to a local chief, however, the notion of a powerful "fetish" medicine that needed to be prepared with human substances took hold some five years later, in the midst of a conflict that broke out between Imperri and a neighboring chiefdom (cited in Kalous 1974, 36–37). In the 1880's, after a rapid increase in the incidence of ritual murders, British colonial courts began to investigate and bring these cases to trial (Fyfe 1962, 442). In 1898, in large parts of the protectorate territory, the "Hut Tax War" broke out against British control and fiscal regulation over the region, and its suppression also drove the Human Leopard Society into dormancy, though isolated, sporadic ritual murders were reported up to Alldridge's day (Alldridge 1901, 153–56; Governor Leslie Probyn, cited in Kalous 1974, 48).

The cycles of expanding violence were partly set in motion when a chief found evidence of human sacrifices in the territory under his or her control, by the practice of calling in "Tongo players" to expose the perpetrators. These were ritual specialists who carried divining objects with which they sought to identify the murderers, from a list drawn up with the help of local spies. The punishment for the individuals singled out by the Tongo staff was death, often by burning alive (Alldridge 1901, 158). In 1892, Alldridge had been sent to investigate an incident in Imperri, in which an estimated eighty people were burned to death as a result of Tongo players' "cannibal-finding" practices. "The pyramid of calcined bones that I saw at the junction of two roads just outside Bogo was about four feet high," he wrote, also noting that the very chief who had been responsible for calling in the Tongo players had been "one of the first to be condemned and burned by them" (Alldridge 1901, 159).

Thus ritual murder and its punishment displayed a circular chain of events similar to that of witchcraft crimes and accusations, and of witch-finding sessions in their aftermath, which also periodically traversed these areas: the very gesture of trying to put an end to the harm could bring suspicion upon the person calling for a remedy (e.g., Geschiere 1997, 57). It also shared with witchcraft the strange intimacy between victim and perpetrator: testimony and evidence collected by British medical examiners, district officers, and local chiefs in the wake of Leopard Society attacks often pointed to close kinship ties between them. Fathers "offered" one of their own children as sacrifice for their membership in the society (see Kalous 1974, 63), sometimes with the complicity of other relatives. This intimacy helped ensure that the phenomenon was slow in coming to the attention of British authorities when it first emerged, as it was easier to suppress knowledge of the disappearance of a family member when he or she was dispatched in secrecy, and with the collusion of other relatives. Finally, the events in Imperri of the 1890s also point to the links between the activities of human leopards—so called because they wore leopard skins and used a five-pronged metal contraption in attacking their victims that left marks similar to the claws of these wild animals—and times of heightened political insecurity and conflict (Pratten 2007, 9–14). Indeed, the phenomenon went beyond Sierra Leone: in 1945, Nigeria witnessed a similar case, which was investigated over the following three years by British colonial authorities (Pratten 2007).

More violence was to follow the 1896 chiefly installation witnessed by Alldridge, which put an end to the rampant insecurity and paranoia of the Leopard Society attacks and Tongo player raids. In 1898, after the Hut Tax War broke out across the protectorate in response to the imposition of British rule, the sokong was convicted and hanged by the British for an especially brutal murder that took place during that conflict and involved the mutilation of William Hughes, a British subject and native assistant district commissioner (Fyfe 1962, 574; Kalous 1974, 6). This was in Bogo, the very same location where the "Tongo player" sessions took place that had resulted in all those deaths six years earlier. Alldridge, who after the establishment of the protectorate had become district commissioner for the Sherbro, accompanied a punitive expedition to the area after Hughes's murder, burning and destroying several villages (cited in Kalous 1974, 44–45). Neighboring chiefs were also implicated in this and other massacres carried out during the war and were executed or exiled, thus leaving Imperri and the surrounding region once again without paramount chiefs, and in a state of insecurity.

One of my key concerns in some of the following chapters is to analyze analogous moments during the 1991–2002 civil war in Sierra Leone, when spates of violence linked to distinctive collective obsessions and anxieties about rumors of atrocities and violence began to take form and unfolded. Sometimes they faded away, while at other times they marked irreversible changes. It is a problem with which historians and anthropologists of war are familiar, particularly those focusing on the details of conflicts and their lived experiences as they unfold (e.g., Bloch 1921; Geffray 1990; Loëz 2010; Simons 1995). Some of the events and figures I examine in later chapters were grounded in a longer contested history of conflicts in the region, including the Human Leopard Society outbreaks of the late nineteenth century, which offered cultural blueprints and folk traditions that informed popular understandings of the civil war one century later.

Sierra Leoneans themselves, both past and present, in the press and in other public contexts, disagree about the extent to which ritual murders actually take place. This contrasts with the overpowering work staged by the frightening *discourse* about this form of violence—the suspicions, accusations, counteraccusations, rumors, and "confessions" that sometimes circulate during tense political conflicts. Scholars, too, have focused their attention on the political, cultural, and historical logic shaping the discourse and accusations of ritual murder (see Beattie 1915; MacCormack 1983; Kalous 1974; Richards 1996). Periodically, moral panics involving such cases have spread across the country, and in modern times these have been amplified by the national media and popular culture. One widely discussed case happened while I was in Sierra Leone in 1990 and involved the suspicious murder and mutilation of a young pregnant woman. The victim was the niece of one and the daughter of the other of two main defendants named and found guilty of her death: respectively, a prominent Muslim man seeking the speakership in Pan-guma Chiefdom, where the position could lead to wealth through licens-ing of diamonds and precious tropical wood extraction in the territory, and his sister. The case went to trial in Freetown and was the subject of popular songs by two of the best-known performers in Mende-speaking Sierra Leone, Amie Kallon and Salia Koroma. The songs were played daily on national radio and sold briskly at the many cassette-duplicating shops in the country's urban areas (see Ferme 2001b, 183–85). My point in bringing up these events is that, in the colonial and postcolonial histo-ries of Sierra Leone, times of great political insecurity and crucial succes-sion struggles for power in the chiefdoms sometimes saw outbreaks of ritual murders involving mutilations—or increased rumors about such events—and the fear they generated could set in motion moral panics and a climate of general paranoia (e.g., Ferme 1999). The panics were by no means rhetorical. People were put on trial, when named, and found guilty by the national courts as in the case of the candidate from the Panguma chiefdom. Traces of this history in the collective memory helped set the stage for similar events during the 1991–2002 civil war, during which the phantasm of colonial forms of inflicting pain returned more powerful than ever.

I now turn to the discrepancy between Alldridge's multiple accounts of the 1896 events, and his use of images in them, which points to the fragmented, nonlinear workings of individual and collective memories of violence. As pointed out earlier, there was a gap between Alldridge's professional reports and his first published book. His reports and letters to his superiors told of violent upheavals in Imperri during and after the "interregnum," when the area had no settled political leadership. In these reports, the vacuum of signifiers of political leadership and power is the immediate reason for the atrocities. Alldridge never changed his mind about the fact that what he had witnessed were violent upheavals. What changed was his way of visualizing, of narrating, and therefore of understanding the reasons for the violent outbreak. Alldridge was not a naïve colonial spectator. On the contrary, he had on various occasions been directed to mediate or exact punishment in the ensuing conflicts as an agent of the British colonial government. Yet in his first published book, Alldridge did not link this vacuum of political power to the human leopard attacks and the "Tongo player" incident in Bogo. A photograph accompanying Alldridge's reference to the "installation of

Fig. 40.—INSTALLATION OF THE SOKONG OF IMPERRI, SHOWING TASSO MEN, AND THE LAKA WITH HIS SHIELD, TO RIGHT OF THE PICTURE.

FIGURE 4. Installation of the sokong of Imperri. Photo by T. J. Alldridge. Alldridge [1901], facing page 132.

a chief" in his 1901 book portrays a large group of standing people, posing behind two seated figures—the new sokong and his speaker— and powerful leaders from neighboring territories with their retinues (fig. 4). The image's caption singles out for special mention "four Tassos," heads of the men's secret Poro society, who "took a prominent part in the ceremony" (Alldridge 1901, 131), and whose headdress was made up of "human skulls and the thigh-bones . . . of defunct Tassos" (132). Alldridge then discussed the Poro and other key officers in the society in detail, and after the following page inserted another photograph, a close-up of the four Tassos who had presided over the chiefly installation ceremony (fig. 5).

In his second book, published in 1910, subsequent to a return visit to Sierra Leone after his retirement in England, the Imperri episode received a more detailed and sustained treatment in a whole chapter dedicated to "The Making of . . . a Sokong of Imperri." Indeed, the dif-

Fig. 41.—THE PORO SECRET SOCIETY—GROUP OF TASSO MEN.
IMPERRI COUNTRY.   (Page 132.)

**FIGURE 5.** Four Tassos at the installation of the sokong of Imperri. Photo by T. J.
Alldridge. Alldridge [1901], facing page 134.

ference is mapped visually on the photographs that this amateur photographer placed in each of the two books, as I discuss below. The title
of Alldridge's second book, *A Transformed Colony,* points to his perception that the country that he had first encountered in 1871 was, by
his final visit, after the turn of the twentieth century, well on its way to
developing into a modern, "civilized" nation. Structured as a journey
into the interior on the newly built railway, Alldridge's second book has
much to say about the positive impact of roads and railroad in "opening up" the country and bringing produce to markets, about the progress
in tapping the country's "undeveloped wealth," and about the ways in
which the establishment of the British protectorate had freed the population of what he called the "shocking terrorism" of its prior existence
(Alldridge 1910, vii).

The chapter dedicated to the making of the sokong describes the
links between his selection and the Poro Society, in whose secret enclosure elders gathered for the chiefly election, and whose masquerade
appears in public to announce the event. Over several pages, Alldridge

THE INSTALLATION OF A GREAT CHIEF, THE LATE SOKONG OF IMPERRI

The Sokong is seated in the centre, distinguishd by a top hat, with his Speaker, or Lavari, on his right, wearing a bowler. The hat behind is the place of seclusion, where they were both confined for some time prior to the installation. The four men whose barbaric costume is surmounted by a skull are Tassos, whose fetish influence is very great.

FIGURE 6. Cropped image of the installation of the sokong of Imperri. Photo by T. J. Alldridge. Alldridge [1910], facing page 270.

goes into the sequence of rituals he observed and provides more general information derived from his other experiences with chiefly installations elsewhere. He also comments on his image of the event, which is a cropped version of figure 4 (see fig. 6). The picture's caption is entitled "The Installation of a Great Chief, the Late Sokong of Imperri"—a curious choice of adjectives given that this chief turned out to be, during the 1898 war, a perpetrator of the very sort of "shocking terrorism" that Alldridge was happy to leave behind. Further, his "lateness" was due to his execution at the hands of the British as a result of those actions. The caption also describes characters in the picture: "The Sokong, seated in the centre, distinguished by a top hat, with his Speaker, or Lavari, on his right, wearing a bowler. . . . The four men whose barbaric costume is surmounted by a skull are Tassos, whose fetish influence is very great." (Alldridge 1910, 270). Conspicuously erased from the commentary is the presence of the lone European in military uniform, who in this cropped version of the photograph becomes identifiable, whereas it is difficult to pick him out in the crowded long shot published in the 1901 book. All the signifiers of local and global violence are erased or held at a distance from Alldridge's textual interpretation of the image.

In the later book, Alldridge's text also engages more with the photograph of the sokong's investiture, providing information on the context in which the picture was taken and the background of various individuals portrayed in it. For instance, he writes, "This photograph is rendered of more than usual interest from the part which these three people took in the native rising in 1898" (Alldridge 1910, 271). Note that the rising had already occurred before the publication of his earlier book, and yet only twelve years later does Alldridge observe that, of the main chiefs portrayed in it, "not one of them is alive to-day; the Sokong and his Lavari having suffered the full penalty of the law," and an additional ruler having been deported to the Gold Coast for his role in the Hut Tax War (271). He then cheerfully states his "pleasure" that during his return trip, he met another chief, portrayed in the photograph, whose village he participated in destroying in a punitive expedition during the war.

Having devoted several pages to a general discussion of chiefly installations and to historical details in recent Imperri and Sherbro politics, Alldridge (1910, 274) writes,

> In 1890, when the Imperri country was under the control of the chiefs, a numerous but select body of natives associated themselves together under the title of the "Human Leopard Society," for the purpose of "keeping alive" a most drastic solid medicine called "Borfimor," which required to be anointed with human fat in order to be perfectly efficacious in its action. To obtain such an emollient the killing of human beings was necessary.

On the page opposite this text is a photograph of the Tongo players discussed earlier, whose brand of violent punishment Alldridge had an opportunity to investigate in Bogo. Alldridge then goes on to discuss in detail the workings of the Human Leopard Society and of the Tongo players, again making a specific reference, this time to the 1890 events and their aftermath, which included the ban and criminalization of the Tongo players by the British administration (Alldridge 1910, 275). Given the role their public detection practices had in making visible, as it were, the Leopard Society crimes, one might wonder whether the decline in attacks after the British suppression of the 1898 anticolonial insurrection was due at least in part to their ban on Tongo activities.

The difference between the two versions of the event is perhaps owing to Alldridge's position as an active member of the British colonial administration in Sierra Leone when he wrote his first book (in which under his name on the title page is written "District Commissioner, Sherbro, West Coast of Africa"), whereas he wrote the second book during his retirement in England. It also may have to do with the changes he observed upon returning to Sierra Leone after an absence of several years and the urge to revisit more fully a past that seemed to be receding rapidly as the country modernized. I would argue that the difference is a result of "belatedness," the reordering over time of memories of violent, traumatic events that could not be fully processed when they were first experienced. Alldridge, after all, had seen firsthand the violence of Leopard Society murders in Imperri, and had fought in the Hut Tax war only three years before the appearance of his first book. In the immediacy of the original, traumatic "seeing" and witnessing of the Imperri events, Alldridge's textual presentation of the event was fragmented and spread out in different parts of the first book, leaving it to that wide, long shot of the installation scene with the four Tassos to do the work of telling the story from afar, as it were (fig. 4). It is a case of disavowal: Alldridge's textual inscription denied the immediate connection between the violent murders, sacrificial killings, and the institutional powers of the chief, while his photos proved the contrary. Writing dismembered the event, suppressing any signifier of violence, whereas the image disclosed the gesture as an act of disavowal. But to be consistent with the theoretical position developed in these pages, the disavowal was itself an expression of the not-knowing that is associated with traumatic events. No wonder the later Alldridge speaks of the "fetishism of power" to underline the extent to which it will go to conceal itself behind apparently benign rituals. By contrast, with belatedness came the possibility of drawing closer into the image, and of textually linking disparate events, grouping them around signifiers of violence, a "knowing" that was articulated in reflexive statements about the circumstances in which the author took the pictures, and their after-stories.

I now want to turn to a different context of belatedness in my own fieldwork experience and recollections, which have uncanny echoes with Alldridge's witnessing of the installation of the sokong of Imperri and of the performance of the Tassos in the ceremonies that followed. I suggest that my own initial distancing from an event involving figures reminiscent of the Tasso in a Freetown performance I witnessed in 1985, and my writing about it here and now, parallels T. J. Alldridge's deferred linkages between writing and voice, testimony and disavowal—though with a difference—in the successive iterations of the horrific Imperri events in his two books, as well as in his earlier reports as a colonial functionary. In both cases, I shall argue, what is perceived as troubling and intractable in the present leads to an impossibility of speaking of and knowing the event without concealing its shockingly traumatic structure.

## HISTORICAL PALIMPSESTS: TRAUMA, FILM, AND REMEMBRANCE

In early January 1985, two days after my arrival in Sierra Leone (my first ever trip to Africa), I was caught up in a violent event whose role in shaping the focus of my research over the following two years, and beyond, I would not realize until much later, when other circumstances prompted its remembrance. I was in Freetown, the country's capital, acclimatizing and taking care of administrative formalities before going into the rural interior of the country to visit potential field sites, where I might settle for my research. In those days preceding the advent of personal computers and cell phones, I noted first impressions, experiences, and preliminary contacts in my diary, which I kept separately from fieldnotes. I thought of this as a private text, a "diary in the strict sense of the term," as Malinowski's widow chose to entitle some of his posthumously published writings (Malinowski 1967). Like the diaries of the anthropologist most closely identified with the discipline's modern, immersive fieldwork research, mine were a blend of prosaic chronicles—I went there, did that—with more introspective, more personal, and sometimes naïve observations about all the novelties around me.

But when I consulted my diary and fieldnotes several years later, to see what I had written about the event I narrate below, I found in the latter several blank pages between entries dated the day before and two days later, suggesting that I had originally planned to write about it in detail but in fact never returned to that day. My diary entry for that whole day consisted of only a few shorthand notes about the "soko incident," its time and place, the friends who had come to talk about it later, and my fears. Eventually I "forgot" that event—and certainly never wrote about it—only consciously remembering it in spring 2000, after the airing on CNN of *Cry Freetown*, a graphic documentary about the January 1999 rebel attack on Freetown, one of the bloodiest episodes of the civil war. The documentary was introduced by the anchor of CNN's Africa program, who warned viewers of the disturbing content and assured them that the network's senior staff had spent the better part of a year debating whether and how to show the footage captured by Sierra Leonean photoreporter Sorious Samura.

Concerned about accusations of voyeurism, CNN program directors had decided to send him back in December 1999 to provide context and follow-up to his earlier film footage—all this being stated in introductory remarks to the first showing of the film on the broadcast channel. The film begins with a close-up of a distressed youth, arguing, and Samura's voiceover says, "I am still haunted by this boy. My camera has saved lives, but not this time" (Samura 2000). As the camera pulls back, the viewer sees that the young man is pointing to his lower legs to explain some wounds that had been taken as evidence of his rebel affiliation. He addresses, in turn, the camera, looking straight at it, and a few Nigerian soldiers, who are closing in on him, to say his name several times in Krio—the national lingua franca—and explain how he came to be in that location. He points to a man behind him, outside the camera's frame, telling the soldiers, "that man knows me . . . ask him, don't kill me." But the machine gun–wielding soldiers push the youth, as Samura asks, "Could I have done more to save him?" A few seconds later, the soldier walking behind the youth and pushing him along, away from the camera, takes aim. A volley rings out, and the young man falls to the ground.

Thus is the viewer plunged into a film about the rebel attack on Freetown, which during two weeks in January 1999 was responsible for some six thousand casualties, and about the revenge executions of Nigerian forces, who suffered heavy casualties in their fight to take back the city. This was a time when a few scratches on the legs could count as criminal evidence and get a young man killed. Samura shares his own shocked response in an all-too-real way for this viewer, who was familiar with the places in which this and other dramas portrayed in the documentary took place. Samura frames the film with the question of the camera's role in witnessing the violence without attempting to stop it—"could I have done more to save him?"—reminding the viewer of the long modern tradition of "regarding the pain of others," in Susan Sontag's words, of coexistence between war and its representation in images, and particularly the forms of congruence between "the camera and the gun," between "'shooting' a subject and shooting a human being" (Sontag 2003, 66).

The implication of representing suffering as a spectacle is that it cannot be stopped, and the answer to Sorious Samura's question is that he had already made his choice when he stayed behind the camera. Later in the documentary, at the site of another impending slaughter of an innocent boy, Samura tells the viewer that a passerby, who happened to be a government minister, intervened to stop the execution. Was this an instance where the camera saved a life? Later in the film, in footage taken during the return December trip, the boy is found in a shelter for war-traumatized children. In these scenes viewers realize that he is severely mentally disabled, can barely talk, and cannot have been the dangerous sniper the Nigerian troops accused him of being, when they were about to execute him. One of the packaging moves shaped by CNN's editorial input, this thread in the film's narrative was perhaps intended to frame in a more hopeful light the brutalities filmed during the January 1999 attack on Freetown, thereby making the violence portrayed appear less pornographic, since the viewer sees the boy one year later, happy and cared for. Conversely, the move to frame the event this way may have been intended to leave the viewer with an even greater sense of shock at the horrors of war.

## EMBODIMENTS OF PAIN

Viewing these images of suffering against the backdrop of familiar sights and places in Freetown was an uncanny experience and produced a visceral response: vomit, flashbacks, anxiety, and sleepless nights, bringing home the fact that traumatic experiences are often lived first in embodied ways—somaticized in the loss of control over one's bodily responses or speech. Recall the reaction of Foday Y's grandson Abdu, mentioned in the introduction, when in 2002 he was reminded of his grandfather's abduction by the rebels, which he had witnessed while crossing the forest clearing where the event had taken place.[3] In a similar manner, my own visceral response to the *Cry Freetown* film brought back the memory of a different event that had produced a similar reaction of embodied fear, some fifteen years earlier, when I had just arrived in Sierra Leone. What follows is a reconstruction from memories of the friend who was with me that day and from my own. In a way, my "reconstruction" follows the same reflexive structure and paradoxical impossibilities outlined in Alldridge's text. In his case, the presence of a documentary image with the four Tassos was pivotal in shaping his alternative readings of the same event with regard to the signifiers of political power and the spectacle of violence. In my case, it was the CNN documentary and the interrogating voice of the cameraman, still traumatized and in shock after all these years, that led me to revisit an event I had inscribed in my diary. I had recorded the event without elaboration, but I had for a long time completely forgotten its significance. What is interesting is that even writing in a private journal may repeat the erasures and gaps that are visible in a published work, though for different reasons.

### HISTORICAL PALIMPSESTS II: THE SOKO INCIDENT

My host in Freetown, whom I shall call Kadiatu, was a nurse-midwife, a relative of a Sierra Leonean friend in the United States. She lived in Kissy, a densely populated and ethnically diverse neighborhood in the eastern end of the city, which at the time was the main point of entrance into and exit from the capital city. It was in a part of town opposite from the western, hilly areas overlooking the sea, where wealthier Sierra Leoneans and expatriates tended to live. Kadiatu had taken a few days off from work to show me around the city and introduce me to her family and friends. That early January day, we were returning home after a family visit. At various points in the city we came across masked dancers associated with hunting societies, the women's Sande Society, comic entertainment masks, and so on—the New Year's holidays had brought them out in numbers. Just before reaching the house, we walked by an enclosure made of reeds, which had not been there when we had left in the morning. It had been erected along the highway, where car and pedestrian traffic—both local and long distance—was dense around the clock.

A crowd had lined up at the entrance of the new enclosure, and a couple of men posted there slowly gave individuals access to its interior. Curious about the fact that the structure had materialized so suddenly, Kadiatu and I asked what it was and were told that a "cultural show" would be taking place inside. The man who collected admission fees at the entrance encouraged us to attend, and he also told Kadiatu that if I had a camera, I should bring it, since I would want to photograph the performance I was going to see. Though still unfamiliar with almost everything that made up this new environment, I noted that this enclosure was similar to others we had seen sprouting up around the city, which Kadiatu had told me were secret societies "bushes," erected to take advantage of the school holidays to initiate new, young members. This was the dry season, so harvests were in, the food for celebrations was plentiful, and travel to such events over the country's many unpaved roads was easier.

Kadiatu was told that the entertainment we were going to see had to do with *soko*—a term with which she was unfamiliar and which she

claimed was not from her native Mende area. In his discussion of institutions of the men's Poro Society on the Sherbro coast, Alldridge mentioned that the soko was "another head man of the Poro," who was
tasked with exacting fines and sanctioning any woman who may have
"become acquainted with some of the mysteries" of this secret society
(Alldridge 1901, 133). Principal among these sanctions was the forced
initiation of such a woman into Poro as a "Mabori," who "is then considered to be both man and woman" and is tasked with distinct ritual
roles and privileges with respect to male and female domains in everyday life (Alldridge 1901, 133; Ferme 2001b, 74–79). The language spoken around us that day in Freetown was Temne, which is historically
related to the coastal Sherbro and shares with it terms such as *soko* and
*Tasso* (Thomas 1916, 143–45). This was the same geographical area
where Alldridge had documented the events discussed above. Note that,
even though in preparing for research in Sierra Leone I had read
Alldridge, I had forgotten these terms and, more importantly, had no
recollection of the pictures that went with them. At some level, therefore, I was encountering them anew that day.

Kadiatu knew and trusted the man, her neighbor, at the entrance of
the enclosure. She also noted that women and children were entering
the enclosure, so she assumed that we would be all right and went home
to pick up my camera, even though I had reservations about bringing it
along. I was warned by diplomatic authorities that another recently
arrived graduate student like myself had been mugged by some youths,
who stole his camera and recording equipment while he was walking
alone on a popular beach on the west side of town. I also felt uncomfortable carrying a camera and tape recorder in those new surroundings, where they seemed to be objects of commentary and distraction,
rather than aids in my research, so I usually left them at home.

We entered the enclosure where the soko performance was to take
place, and the ticket seller guided Kadiatu and me to a bench in the
front row. Not yet used to the attention that my obvious foreign status
attracted, I tried several times to move toward the back, rather than
stay in such a visible location. But each time, friendly voices and bodies
pushed me toward the front, incredulous that anyone would give up the
privileged vantage point of front row seating. Surely, like the British
colonial officer in Alldridge's photo, I would want to be right up front,
where all the action was, to see and be seen? One of the reasons I
retreated toward the back rows was my discomfort at a performer, who
appeared in the center of the enclosure while the audience waited for

the main event. He was a frightening figure, whose behavior, alternately menacing and clownish, provoked the crowd surrounding me to laugh but also to recoil fearfully, when he occasionally lunged toward the audience. This mixture of induced fear and laughter was to become a common feature in the public ceremonies that accompanied initiations that I witnessed over the years in Sierra Leone.

Designed to engage members and nonmember audiences alike, public events associated with any "society business" often crossed the line between laughter and fear, or celebration and the reiteration of "the law" and its liminal boundaries—to paraphrase Clastres. Thus during public ceremonies associated with initiation into the men's Poro, the *Goboi* masquerade (fig. 7) could provoke fear and flight among noninitiates as it lunged toward them. During the soko performance I attended in Freetown, my own fear was aroused in part by the opening event: an almost naked man made the rounds of the clearing around which the audience was assembled before the beginning of the dance proper. He wore a loin cloth from which his penis protruded—his body decorated with paint, amulets, and animal teeth that gave him a sinister appearance. A stick, attached at the tip by bloodred wax, elongated the projecting penis, giving the impression, especially at a distance, of bloody self-mutilation. This display of sexual violence was at eye level for the first-row audience, where I was seated.[4] As this grotesque figure made the rounds of the clearing, extending a palm-sized platter composed of a mirror edged with cowry shells, he demanded money and did not hesitate to thrust his pelvis toward those who did not comply with his request. In his other hand, he held a knife, accentuating the sense of threat.

The man's exhibitionism, the bloody mutilation and modification of his sexual organ, his threatening gestures with the knife, and the ease with which he used his fetishized body to get members of the audience to hand him money as he held up a mirror to their fear and surprise, had something of the grotesque (Bakhtin 1968, 44–46). It was a demonstration of power in its corporeal form, within the context of an "aesthetics of vulgarity" that provoked both fear and laughter in a carnivalesque juxtaposition some have characterized as a distinctive feature of life in the African postcolony, with its spectacular displays of arbitrary power and disproportionate wealth alongside life-crushing misery (Mbembe 2001, 102–41). Laughter and carnival are very close to fear and can vanquish it as well as increase it (Bakhtin 1968, 39)—the very indeterminacy of the outcome produces a constant state of tension. In his displays, this performer flaunted himself through techniques of

FIGURE 7. *Goboi* masquerade. Wunde Chiefdom,
Bo District, 1986. Photo by author.

exaggeration, displaying a kind of persuasive power that was not lost
on his audience.

Eventually, he gave way to dancers and musicians, disappearing from
the clearing as they filled the space. Several dancers, clothed in grass
skirts, with large headdresses perched on their heads and their bodies
covered with white and red painted dots, began to move to the rhythm
of drums. Their headdresses consisted of a round horizontal plane, a sort
of tray, on top of which two braided reeds formed intertwined arcs.
Later, when I went back to T. J. Alldridge's published work, I found a
striking resemblance between their appearance and those of the four
Tassos pictured in his books (Alldridge 1901, 132–34, fig. 41; 1910,
270). In Alldridge's pictures, the flat tray part of the headdress carries

**FIGURE 8.** Tasso performer. Bo Coronation Field, Bo District, April 2011. Photo by Gary Schultze.

human skulls and bones, and these are still featured in contemporary Tasso performances that have been documented by others (fig. 8). I cannot remember whether there were bones or human skulls on the headdresses I saw in Freetown, but they had the same shapes and decorations, and the performers had similarly painted dots all over their bodies, grass skirts, amulets, and bells tied around their lower legs.

Kadiatu removed my camera from the bag on the bench between us and handed it to me, urging me to take pictures. I reached for the camera, intending to put it back in its bag, uneasy at the prospect of attracting further attention. But before I could touch it, I felt my head being jerked back by the hair, painfully, and found myself staring at the face of the man who had been making the rounds earlier. He was close enough for me to smell the alcohol on his breath and feel the sweat pouring off his skin. Appearing out of nowhere, he placed his knife at my throat and pulled my head back with his other hand, all the while breathing and shouting in my face. Kadiatu and several men near us in the audience seized him by the arms to pull him away while crying for help. Eventually, a group of men restrained him and made him release my hair, but he moved on to physically harass and threaten Kadiatu, grabbing my camera from her hands. The racket interrupted the dance, and the performers joined audience members in the effort to restrain our aggressor. Finally, a man who appeared to carry some authority intervened, calmed the man, and removed him. Kadiatu went to find the man selling tickets at the entrance of the enclosure, who had encouraged us earlier to take pictures, to recover my camera from our aggressor.

When Kadiatu returned empty handed, I asked to leave. I was terrified and did not want to stay for the rest of the performance. But the spectators around us intervened, saying that we should not leave, that we should stay until the end of the performance. They expressed sympathy, criticizing the behavior of our aggressor, and sought to reassure us. Ironically, I finally had achieved a little of the "invisibility" I had sought since I first entered the space, as our neighbors in the audience placed themselves between us and the performers dancing in the clearing. Hands placed firmly on my shoulders were protective, but they also held me in place, preventing me from leaving. I was encouraged to continue watching the performance, which in the interim had resumed. On many occasions over successive years, I saw adults similarly holding young, fearful children firmly in place, forcing them to watch masquerades that obviously terrified them and from which they wanted to turn away. Confronting the "devil" (as masquerades are aptly called in Krio) with a mixture of laughter and fear appeared to be a key pedagogical moment in the socialization of Sierra Leoneans and strangers alike, as was the imperative to see it and be seen by it. "A stranger is like a child," goes the Mende proverb.

The spectacle reached its peak toward dusk, when the group of dancers left the middle of the clearing to form a circle around something they were carrying, which was not clearly visible to the spectators. We saw what appeared, to those of us who could see only the backs of the dancers, to be violent jabs and punches, and we heard guttural, menacing cries emitted in unison, after which the circle of men opened slightly to reveal a stretcher.[5] On this stretcher was a human form covered with a white shroud. Only the face was visible, its darkness bisected by a white horizontal band painted across the two closed eyes. On the front of the shroud, fresh blood was splattered around the chest area. The advancing darkness and dust stirred up by the dance prevented the audience from seeing clearly whose bright red blood was spilled: was it a sacrificed animal or the human figure's own blood? Nor was it possible to know whether the man on the stretcher was dead or alive. In my state of mind at the time, I was convinced that the blood we saw had been shed by the human body lying immobile on the stretcher, and that Kadiatu and I had inadvertently stumbled upon a gruesome perform-ance of ritual human sacrifice. The stretcher was carried across the clearing and displayed to the public. In the commotion that followed, and under cover of darkness, I grabbed Kadiatu's hand and dragged her out of the enclosure to run home, followed by the pounding of drums that continued throughout the night.

The soko incident had terrified me: I was unable to sleep, had night-mares over the next few days, and took the first opportunity to leave Freetown, where I did not return for several months. However, I had to reflect, whenever I witnessed public exhibitions of masquerades in the following two years, on the staged quality of these aggressions in order to reassure myself. Clearly certain public amusements staged in connec-tion with Poro initiations were meant to get out of hand. Indeed, the eventuality is built into the performance of the *Goboi,* the chief masquerade that appears at coming-out ceremonies for Poro initiates today and is always surrounded by a retinue of attendants forming a cordon between *Goboi* and the audience, who move to contain or stop his charges toward the crowd. This element is present even when the masquerade is performed in entertainment contexts that are purport-edly unconnected with secret initiations. But an element of volatility is always present, in part because the performers consume alcohol and drugs to enhance their daring and to bring them to the altered state that informs the poetics of masking. Context also introduces unpredictabil-ity: at one particularly contested chiefly election some eighteen months later, an elder greeted the victory of his candidate by breaking out in the *Goboi* dance in the middle of a public meeting. He was wearing ordi-nary clothes, and was not concealed under paint, mask, or costume, but the moves were unmistakable, and the allusion was confirmed by the response of all the men present. They broke out in the chilling unison cry that accompanies the arrival of Poro to town and opened up a space for him to perform. The man's gesture was spontaneous and unscripted, and before other men could take up the role of containment assigned to the *Goboi*'s assistants, the unmasked dancer charged toward the house-holds of his political opponents, wreaking havoc, overturning pots cooking over fires, and causing distress as he went. Expecting the unex-pected does not necessarily make it acceptable, or harmless.

More ironies and palimpsests tied my own experience at the Free-town "cultural show" with earlier histories of European sightings (and cameras) of Tassos and sokos. On the one hand—Alldridge informs us—a woman could be punished and fined (by the soko) for transgressing into male ritual domains (the same was true for men doing the obverse), but on the other hand, women could also enjoy a high rank in the men's Poro Society, in the role of what he called "Mabori" (Alldridge 1901, 133), which I observed and wrote about later. In this role, a woman could enjoy a prominent role in the "royal processions" accompanying male initiations and celebrations, as well as in the other duties concealed from the noninitiates. Nearly a century later, it was a different form of transgression on my and Kadiatu's part that brought us into the presence of other sokos, though it is unclear whether this term meant the same men's secret society officials discussed by Alldridge. The dancing performers at the event where I was the victim of aggression certainly resembled them. The fact that my (scopic) transgression, preparing to shoot pictures with a camera, could have produced images similar to those Alldridge took of similarly costumed performers seems to suggest, in the very failure caused by the confiscation of the photographic equipment, a kind of troubling mimetic gesture in postcolonial Sierra Leone.

It is difficult to say whether Alldridge's subjects willingly posed for his photograph: given the photographic technology of his days, they certainly would have had to be still for some time, giving anyone who did not want to be portrayed plenty of time to move away. But the colonial presence and gaze were also more immobilizing, and techniques of governance were more rooted in place, as we shall see when changing forms of sovereignty are discussed in later chapters. By contrast, over the years my portable cameras, which initially produced only negatives and prints, then went digital, were of a different generation—more easily concealed and more mobile. Indeed, though the camera that was stolen at the entertainment was eventually returned to me two days later, through the efforts of Kadiatu, who was a well-known and respected midwife in the neighborhood, it was later stolen from the house of a paramount chief whom I was visiting in rural Sierra Leone. This was after I had taken some photographs, with his permission, of the public procession after a Poro Society initiation.

Was it stolen by someone who disagreed with the paramount chief's granting me permission to take pictures? Or was it stolen simply because the crowds that had assembled brought many outsiders in and out of the house, and someone may have even gained access to my locked room there? Impossible to say. What is certain is that in that case the camera was not returned, and the pictures of that particular Poro celebration are not available now, though many photographs of successive celebrations I witnessed are.[6]

## GETTING AWAY

Part of the reason I was able to be freed when my aggressor grasped my hair during the soko incident may have been because I wore my hair short, in a "masculine" cut. At least on a superficial level, my appearance seemed to place me in the role of the *mabole*—observed by Alldridge and, later, by myself in Mende rural settings—a woman given a place of honor at a performance associated with male rituals and entertainment. My being at once female and masculine in appearance also seemed to confirm the old stereotype according to which female anthropologists could be "at the same time man and woman" because of their privileged status as foreign observers in the host society. That day in Freetown, I was introduced to the unpredictable violence that can be generated by transgressing the liminal domains of gendered performances, and by moving from the excessive vision to its mediated (photo-graphic) representation. Freezing the image erased the kind of knowing about the scene I had just witnessed. In a way, I had been part of the event, not just a detached observer. The register of representation through which I invaded the scene intensified multiple levels of transgression that were not tolerated by some of the performers. I caught a glimpse of these dangerous intersections among vision, image, and performance and decided to turn my back: throughout my stay in Sierra Leone, I avoided getting too close to these dangerous liminal zones. For me, this meant everything that had to do with secrets and secret societies.

I left Sierra Leone at the end of 1986, only a few months after elections that had taken a violent and contentious turn locally and had poisoned relations among my neighbors and among entire communities in the chiefdom, and even beyond (Ferme 1999). An event that took place toward the end of my stay—and whose echoes continued for me well after my departure—demonstrated that the responses to the questions I asked were located at the very intersection that I had wanted to avoid since the start. This was the intersection of institutional secrecy and discourse, on the one hand, and recorded voice, on the other. The first of these events was a series of conversations that two elders of the Sande women's society engaged in with me, which were related to secret aspects of an initiation that had taken place two years before, just after my arrival. These elders insisted that I record my questions and their answers, which is why these secret conversations are among the rare audio tapes that I could bring back with me from Sierra Leone. It is interesting to note that the fact that these elders of the Sande society, who revealed secret affairs I had witnessed without understanding or knowing (another impossible paradox: the secret can be seen but not immediately "known"), were women describing the logic of secret initiations to another woman, though one who was foreign and prone to leak the information outside of the borders of the same society. In a way, they did not trespass the liminal spaces that divide Sande and Poro in Mende society.

They had given me permission to play the tapes only in the presence of those who could not understand them (thus obeying the prohibitive force of secrecy to be spread without being known as such) and to write about them in English. I did so, while changing their names so that they would not be recognizable, but I left the village's real name in place. In those days, this would have been protection enough of their wishes, since there wasn't even a primary school in the village or resident teachers, though educated, English-speaking relatives did come to visit occasionally. It was unlikely, however, that they would come across my elliptical academic writings, buried in an edited volume, which in any case did not reveal anything that was not already in the scholarly record about this region.

I later learned that my excessive concern over protecting the trust I had been granted was for naught, as the three women themselves, at a later date, used this event to work out their conflicts—I had become the anthropologist-as-pawn in local strategies, in which accusations of violating, or leaking, secrets can serve political purposes. After my departure, a German friend, who had visited the village to go hunting, sent a videotape of a meeting organized to convey greetings and messages to me in the United States. While the male leadership tried to keep the meeting formal and organized—and attracted the camera of my friend, who was also male, and, perhaps more importantly, could not understand Mende—a woman's voice off camera insistently addressed me by the Mende equivalent of my name, "Ma(ri)ama"! Off camera, she began telling me how one of the other Sande village elders had publicly "outed" her after our conversation for telling me their secrets. In a plaintive voice that made me feel very guilty as I listened, she went on to say that she had been fined and had left for a couple of years as a result of the accusation. But she was there, obviously back, and able to speak to me—albeit not visible—as I recognized her voice and the event about which she was talking. I was frustrated playing this tape, because I could not see my friend as she was talking. I was more interested in the soundtrack of this footage, but from a distance I had no control over the direction of the camera's lens.

When I returned for my next visit, I was worried about my role in my friend's misfortune and was prepared not to find her, and to have to address questions about my role in those conversations. Instead, I found her there, having done well in business during her absence as a food vendor for the artisanal miners in the diamond fields to the north. She had succeeded her elderly aunt as the head of the local women's Sande Society chapter. Perhaps her "outing" was part of the political succession struggle between her and one of my other interlocutors during that earlier trip. She had gone away, and gotten away from the hostility to which other Sande elders had subjected her at the same time, and eventually had returned to a prominent position. The VHS tape on which her appeal was made is now virtually an encrypted record, since the technology required to play it is almost obsolete. Unless they are transmitted by a different technology, her secrets are once again safe.

A few years later, I finally had the opportunity to participate in making a documentary about this village (*The Mende,* Granada TV, 1990). During the filming, my own familiarity, access, and linguistic competence, in time and space, produced tensions with the foreign, technically competent male director, who was mostly focused on the quality of visual images, sometimes in voyeuristic ways—particularly of scantily clad women but in general of all who were "different." Once again, voice and image were out of sync, though this was a documentary that was made precisely for a series known for its faithfulness in translating dialogue in particular filmed sequences. Though I gave a rough English translation of Mende dialogue that unfolded as the director was filming, I refused to translate into Mende requests he whispered in my ear to follow up on certain topics. I declined if I deemed them too intrusive or potentially dangerous for the subject being filmed—in this case a child, who had been accused playfully of being a witch and whom the director wanted to use as a serious subject for analyzing the topic. This pushed the director to openly discuss our disagreement in his voiceover for this part of the documentary.

For older individuals, whom I knew could extricate themselves from embarrassing or inappropriate questions, I did translate into Mende for the film subjects and received predictably elliptical responses, or awkward laughs. Here the Mende dialogue was in sync with the image but was not particularly revealing of secrets to a Mende audience—albeit it would perhaps be of interest culturally to an English-speaking one reading my subtitles. Among the subjects, whom I was made to ask uncomfortable (for me) questions about whether men knew about women's secrets, was Kema, a respected elder in the women's Sande Society.[7] She predictably turned serious in the midst of what had been a smiling, friendly exchange, and she gave a forceful but generic answer explaining that any man who tried to learn what women did in their secret bush would be cursed and die. After that, the conversation moved on.

Later, in editing this material, more disagreements with the director emerged over matters of cultural and linguistic translation, including which images and voices to include or exclude in order to produce a film that would not replicate colonial stereotypes of "savagery," such as those that emerge from accounts like Alldridge's. At the same time, it was important to be true to the ordinary, but complex, realities of a place where unpredictable violence could occur but where opportunities to "get away" also existed. The disagreements were in part about incidents concerning human sacrifices and events over the border in Liberia, which turned out to be anticipatory of the advent of the civil war in Sierra Leone. When the film made its way back to Sierra Leone, many of its subjects did not worry about the voyeurism and the reinscription of colonial stereotypes of "savagery," as I had anticipated they would. Instead, now that they were experiencing lives of displacement and upheaval in camps, or were living as squatters in the urban compounds of relatives and friends, they appreciated the film as a historical record and visual reminder of their lives before the war.

In the next section, I provide some context for these different encounters with vision and voice, and the temporal lags between them, and for the politics of secrecy. The reorganization of memories from the advantage of long-term engagements over time is also aided by traumatic "returns" of a different kind to sites of violence and war.

## RETURNING TO THE ORIGINAL EVENT

The phenomenon of repression is linked to traumatic experiences but is in tension with the work of memory—through the body and its visceral responses, or through language—to effect the return, a reliving, of what has been forgotten, though in a different form. That awakening of the experience is sometimes coincident with the first narration after a long period of time, as was the case of the soko incident, which had not been fully written down and had been forgotten but was then remembered after I viewed a graphic documentary film about the 1991–2002 civil war. In other cases, as in Alldridge's account, it involved a return to the same material for a different narration, contextualization, and representation. But it is a different kind of return I want to discuss here, to illustrate the specific ways in which mediated "truths" can turn out to be dangerous rumors and, therefore, anticipate harms or losses that do not materialize. This different kind of return also illustrates the ways in which these fears are amplified in wartime.

My first book was in production in 2000 as violence once again flared up in the decade-long civil war. It was dedicated in part to the memory of Kema, whose demise was narrated in a tape recording of recent news, prepared that year by her fellow villagers and sent to me by way of a visiting Sierra Leonean friend. I grieved for Kema, whom I had last seen in 1993, during a visit cut short by the news that the rebels were advancing from the neighboring chiefdom, attacking and burning villages, which sent us all fleeing elsewhere. Most went to internally displaced persons' camps, usually the large one in Gondama, outside Bo, which was poised to become the second largest "town" in Sierra Leone, after the capital city of Freetown.

After the war was declared over, and British special forces and UN peacekeepers had secured the country, I returned to Kpuawala to find Kema alive and well over the span of several visits (fig. 9). When everyone had scattered halfway through the war, she said, she had not followed them to the displaced persons' camps. She had headed south on her own, toward the Sherbro coast and had sought shelter in a rural village where nobody knew her. She had been separated from her relatives, who had not known that she was alive. This sort of uncertainty about the whereabouts (and, sometimes, the loyalties) of even the most intimate relatives was a constant refrain during the war. After all, this was a place where someone's father or spouse could arrange to have one killed for power medicine during ordinary times. During the conflict, this strategy had been adopted to recruit combatants and prevent them from returning to their communities. But it was also a war in which women could sometimes cross enemy lines, dissimulate their identities, and establish life-saving intimacies more easily than men.

Images, and the affect they exhibit, however, can be misleading. In the picture portraying me and Kema, for instance, smiling versus serious facial expressions can be multiply interpreted. While Kema's serious expression bespeaks the affect of other villagers of her generation posing

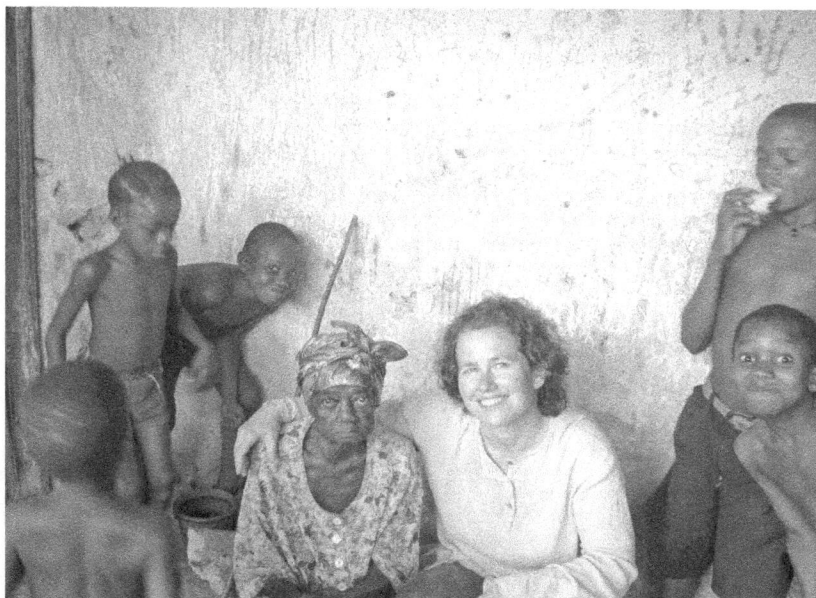

**FIGURE 9.** Portrait of the author with Mama Kema. Wunde Chiefdom, April 2008. Photographer unknown.

for portraits, my own smile belongs to conventions of a different place and generation. But the picture also tells of my pleasure in finding her alive to me once again, so many years after I received news of her death.[8] My smile also was linked to the anticipation of the joy this evidence would give others—friends near and far, Sierra Leonean and foreign, and my mother, who during a visit to me in the field had gotten to know Kema and enjoy her company. Perhaps the anticipatory joy was also at the thought of having to expose myself, at a different level, as having unwittingly participated in spreading the false rumors of her death.

In this chapter, I have suggested commonalities between my own experience of an early encounter with soko/Tassos and Alldridge's account of his experience with Tassos in his two publications. There are some differences though. Alldridge added more details to the description of the Tasso event as it became more distant in time, whereas I removed some of the details the second time around, to deal with my realization that I had been exposed directly to the violence of an attack during the performance. Alldridge did not seem affected by the performance he saw. He was not under attack. I was directly affected by the physical aggression that disrupted the performance, though it took a long time for me to come to terms with it. My initial reaction after the soko event was to leave a gap in my journal. Writing this book has entailed interrogating the gap in an effort to come to terms with the violence I testified to decades earlier, while at the same time understanding what is involved in the very act of witnessing an event.

# Chronotope 1

## Prefiguring Shifting Alliances—The *Sobel*

One neologism that materially captures popular tensions at a particular point in time during the civil war was that of the *sobel,* or "soldier-rebel," which was the subject of anxious rumors circulating in Sierra Leone when I returned in 1993. The neologism was accompanied by the saying "soldier by day, rebel by night," which addressed the increasing porousness of the identity lines separating fighting factions. In this case, stories of *sobels* were variable and multiple, applicable to different individuals and events. Nevertheless, the common thread among the stories was the unknown identity behind the appearance of soldiers: were they truly soldiers in the service of the government or impostors? The *sobel* cast doubt on whether a uniformed fighter was a member of the ruling military regime at the time or a rebel. Behind the neologism were indeed embodied memories of events where soldiers engaged in rebel-like activities and, conversely, of rebels who had donned the stolen uniforms of soldiers to mount stealth attacks on communities. Similar work on the duplicitous logic of the figure of the "impostor" has been done by Natalie Zemon Davies. Her analysis focused on several cases of imposture, among them that of an individual who had forged his identity and true age to be accepted at Princeton University with thousands of dollars in fellowship funds. The point Zemon Davis makes is that such stories of imposture owe their universal appeal to their being "quite specific to their time and place." Part of our interest, she says, "comes from this historical depth and embeddedness" (Zemon-Davies 1997,

7).[1] In other words, the logic of imposture is a powerful anchor for the collective imagination, because it is grounded in specific concerns, anxieties, and desires of the population at large. We are all fascinated by stories of young individuals who act a part in order to gain influence and power in a privileged society that is susceptible to corruption.

This particular concern in Sierra Leone condensed around the figure of the *sobel* in wartime and pointed to collective anxieties about the participation of particular fighters in opposing factions in the conflict, where individual identities and loyalties were always marked by uncertainty and a state of not-knowing. Identity claims in these circumstances could not be verified or proved to be false. Like the rumors concerning the "Rebel Cross," analyzed in the next chapter, this chronotope prefigured the double logic of events. It embodied a kind of anticipatory preview (see Simons 1995) of an imposture that became magnified later in time. This psychic pull between truth and lie embedded in the *sobel* chronotope in wartime was captured in an event that occurred during my wartime return to the village where I had been working since before the war. On that occasion, a uniformed man who wandered into the village and asked about a white woman residing there was given erroneous information about my whereabouts as I was spirited into hiding in the bush, because residents mistrusted his intent. The uniform was not capable of instantiating trust in the lawfulness of his request, because any rebel could have stolen it and concealed his true identity. Even as a soldier, he would not have inspired trust in the population because of their past encounters with the army, and with other fighting factions that had attacked the village on three separate occasions.

Evenings during this visit were spent anxiously listening to radio newscasts about rebel incursions into communities to the south of the chiefdom, which eventually led to our evacuation to safer locales to the north. This general mistrust in military figures slid across all levels of ordinary existence where individuals might come face to face with the law, from checkpoints to government offices. It was this specific connection between the time and place of a generalized mistrust that gave rise to the neologism of the *sobel*. The *sobel* belongs to the register of performative language, "a region of language with the potential to make us experience events, not simply by pointing to them as to something external, but rather by producing them in the very act of telling" (Das 2007, 108). In a way, then, telling the story of *sobels* introduces instability, indecision, and anxieties about the identities of these groups that determine lack of trust in either of them.

This figure embodies in some ways social anxieties about the true nature of the identities of fighters in a culture where dissimulation and secrecy could be the dominant domain of everyday speech, and in a region where secret societies still exercise considerable sway over the population. In ordinary life, the domain of the night was where local folklore places shape-shifting spirits and nighttime was the time when initiates into the world of secrecy are transformed into adults. Even during the day, boundaries between village and forest may conceal traps for the living. In the folklore surrounding *Ndogbosui,* this Mende spirit takes on a familiar human form to trick those he encounters in the forest into following him to his lair. Unless they can respond with absurd replies to his riddles, his victims remain entrapped in the forest (Harris and Sawyerr 1968).

The realm of culture prefigures a general situation where familiar appearances might conceal dangerous aggressors. The belief in the potential duplicity of events informs other domains as well, such as that of peoples' real intentions in the economic and political domains, in which both state agents and rebels sought aggressively to control material resources—not only the diamond fields and alluvial gold mines in the territories they occupied but the farms and ordinary livelihoods of civilians whom they conscripted as quasi-slaves into indentured labor.

Around the same time as the *sobel* figure emerged, I heard Mende-speaking Sierra Leoneans naming this a "war of theft" (*huma gɔ*), because of the propensity of all fighting factions, including the government army, to prey on civilians and loot their possessions. Regarding the figure of the *sobel* and the generalized climate of collusion between the different fighting factions in the civil war, some scholars later commented on the "cooperative" dimensions of a conflict that at one point was characterized as a "sell game" (Keen 2005, 107–31). Thus popular narratives centered around the true intentions behind a conflict in which waging war and prolonging insecurity were unmasked as tactics to gain control over these territorial enclaves in order to extract and sell their wealth.[2]

This was not only a rural phenomenon: urban dwellers too found themselves attacked and robbed by armed aggressors when leaving home during nighttime curfews, when only soldiers were supposed to be at large in town. In December 1994, rebels disguised as refugees staged an attack on Bo, the second largest urban center in the country, after changing into stolen army uniforms (Richards 1996, 15). Significantly, the *sobel* rumor pointed to an emergent phenomenon that later became a formal alliance, when in 1997 a group of rogue elements from the national army—the Armed Forces Revolutionary Council—formed an alliance with the organized rebel movement, the Revolutionary United Front (RUF), staging the coup that toppled the civilian government elected the previous year.

The media and communication technology used in spreading rumors, albeit sometimes unwittingly, and the confusion characterizing the earlier phases of this conflict, also require some comment here. When, in April 1991, the BBC Africa Service received a call by a Sierra Leonean claiming to be Foday Sankoh, and asserting that he was the leader of the RUF, this announcement was received with disbelief. Only a few years later, a combination of heavy media coverage and a series of major internationally brokered peace talks made Foday Sankoh's identity familiar worldwide, but it had not been early on during the war, when the only reliable way to communicate at will were satellite phones—a rare commodity. Sightings of Sankoh and of some of his more famous field commanders were the stuff of exotic tales. During the first four years of the war, news of rebel attacks was accompanied by rumors, the effect of which was to question the very existence of an organized rebel movement, not to mention the identity of its membership and leadership (Richards 1996, 5–7, 14). Only in 1994, with the appearance of their manifesto, and their practice of regularly contacting the international media, did the RUF and Foday Sankoh become widely acknowledged as enemies to be reckoned with.[3]

Even as the rebels became more adept at publicizing their identities and goals through the international media, the rumor-driven nature of the conflict was captured within Sierra Leone by the ambiguity of the *sobel,* particularly between 1993 and 1997. In 1994, after a campaign by the ruling military regime to expand its ranks, in order to face the mounting rebel challenge, the army more than doubled in size to between thirteen and fourteen thousand (Keen 2005, 97).[4] This rapid expansion brought poorly trained, equipped, paid, and disciplined recruits into the army ranks—a critical feature in the social diffusion of the figure of the *sobel,* as the background and characteristics of soldiers came to resemble those of recruits in the rebel ranks. The national media carried stories about individual *sobels* captured while looting, but 1994 also saw signs of mutiny on a larger scale, such as the defection of "up to 400 disgruntled troops from Teko Barracks, excluded from the rich pickings at the war front. . . . According to reports, they either built their own RUF-style camp as a base for raiding activities in the Kangari Hills forest reserve or were absorbed within the RUF" (Richards 1996, 13).[5]

Though, as mentioned above, in some cases what was at stake in the *sobel* rumor was dissimulation—of rebel identities behind military uniforms or of illegal preying on civilians by soldiers mandated to defend that very population and its property—the fear of fraternizing across enemy lines was also a crucial factor. For this element, there are parallels in other conflicts. In World War I, evidence of mutinies (for instance, of Russian troops after the 1917 Revolution), or of fraternization across enemy lines (of Flemish soldiers in the Belgian army with German troops), gave rise to rumors that considerably exaggerated their frequency (Loëz 2010, 233). One of the most common rumors circulating in World War I featured deserters from several armies—Italians, Austrians, Canadians, French, English, and so on—all living together in underground caves at the front. They were believed to emerge after battles to wander among the wounded and dead to rob them of their possessions (Fussell 1975, 123). That conflict too—a long war of attrition, during which there were constant exchanges between enemy troops in close proximity to each other, and to civilian life—placed loyalties in question. The resulting anxieties found their outlet in popular anxieties.

2

# Wartime Rumors

## Red Cross as Rebel Cross and Other Figures of the Collective Imagination

The circulation of wartime rumors frames the history and experiences of particular conflicts, as well as widely shared popular anxieties that mark turning points and critical events—transitions that define clear "befores" and "afters" in the memories of those who live through a conflict and characterize the distinctiveness of its successive phases (see Das 1995; Henry 2005; Simons 1995). In this sense, therefore, the different rumors that emerge at the forefront of the popular imagination as a conflict unfolds can serve as temporal markers in its history, documenting, through the neologisms and popular expressions to which they give rise, widely shared preoccupations and experiences.

Rumor is a discursive form that lends itself well to times of heightened insecurity: it operates as an alternative source of information about an unfolding conflict in the absence of reliable information from official media outlets. It also provides the cover of anonymity and is therefore politically useful: rumors communicate truths about events that cannot be verified, or are not covered in authorized—and authored—communications put forth by traditional media channels. In part, this is because rumors give shape to collective emotions—palpable fears about events that are taking shape and have not yet crystalized in precise historical outcomes. They offer a compass, a sense of direction when the present is still filled with the opacity of indecision. This is especially the case for conflicts, such as the 1991–2002 civil war in Sierra Leone, that unfolded before the advent of mobile phones and transmission towers. Conventional communication infrastructure had so deteriorated by the beginning of hostilities that the only reliable ways to communicate synchronically over long distances were radio sets or satellite phones. These expensive and sparingly used technologies, which were in the hands of very few, were not employed spontaneously when the need arose but according to preordained schedules.[1] As the cases examined in this chapter suggest, rumors do not just signal anxieties rooted in the collective imagination: they also may act as indexicals, that is, performative statements understood to be self-fulfilling prophecies that bring about what they ostensibly report. This is one reason for their ambivalent and troubling status in public opinion.

Popular anxiety about the power of rumors in Mende-speaking parts of Sierra Leone is manifested in the practice of referring to them as "noise" (sɔlɛ), a derogatory reference to forms of speech, akin to gossip, that signal the inability to exercise one's judgment and remain silent when required—valued traits in a society where secret initiation societies are an important aspect of cultural and political life, and are a key element of self-representation in this small, ethnically and linguistically heterogeneous nation (see Bledsoe 1984; Bledsoe and Robey 1986; Ferme 1994). However, unlike gossip, rumors can become dangerous to the extent that they embody sensations shared by large groups and have the ability to predict the course of events. The cultural discourse about rumors is also a gendered one, as making "noise" situates social actors who engage in this sort of speech within a liminal, feminine realm, regardless of their sex. This gendered quality is staged in the public performances of both male and female secret societies, whose initiations include public displays of the society's power to silence and regulate the speech of noninitiates (see Bellman 1981, 9).[2]

Speech degraded to the status of rumor can be disavowed, a feature underscored when people use the passive voice to discuss it. Rumors are referred to as something passively heard, or circumstantially understood (humɛi), rather than as something to engage a more active listening (wolo) stance—another signal of popular ambivalence toward them. In the state of passive listening, one captures impressions, sensations, volatile ideas that have not yet been fully spoken. This is why when one speaks about rumors, one is not exercising full judgment. On the contrary, one is using the senses to apprehend something that escapes the light of reasoned speech. In this chapter, I focus especially on one rumor, involving the Red Cross, that circulated among Sierra Leoneans in very different educational and socioeconomic circumstances, in rural and urban settings, and among expatriates. But whenever I pressed my Sierra Leonean interlocutors for more details about the formulaic, almost identical story I heard everywhere, they would preface their responses with "so we heard" or "so it was told to us"—stressing the auditory register that deemphasized their own roles in passing on the rumor, and moving them into a noncommittal judgment stance in relation to its contents. One hears a rumor and passes it on in a transitive and quasi-passive mode, without admitting to an active or authoring role in so doing. Yet the transmission constitutes a chain, a network of signifiers, a communication that hints at a possible meaning without quite being sure of its referent.

Rumors have a social life: they have beginnings, a spatiotemporal range of circulation, and an end, too—they operate like chronotopes by anchoring anxieties in a specific time and place, and they become exaggerated or die depending on their capacity to capture larger truths, in which social actors are able to recognize themselves. Though not exclusive to war, they flourish in this and other settings of insecurity, suspicion, and fear.[3] For example, Luise White (2000, 82–83) writes that variants of a widespread rumor in colonial eastern and southern Africa about vampires revealed

> genealogies of local concerns and historical fixations that would not otherwise be apparent. During the Great Fear of 1789 in France, some regions were said to fear a British invasion; others were fearing that Croatian troops were massing on their borders; and still others feared Poles or Moors. These were not hysterical accusations but concerns and interests grounded in local historical experience. They do not "explain" the rumor, but they explain how it was locally credible. . . . rumors can be a source for local history that reveals the passionate contradictions and anxieties of specific places with specific histories.

The "vampires" examined in the African rumors that were the subject of White's study (18–19) assumed the forms of firemen, surveyors, or medical personnel with syringes, who took the blood of their African subjects, but her study reproduced to some extent the circularity in the dynamic transmission of rumors. By contrast, my focus here is on the historical changes manifested in particular rumor regimes, on their geographic boundaries, and on other aspects of context—including their demise—that can shed light on the particular collective representations that facilitate their transmission, or put an end to it. This chapter, therefore, outlines the historical advent of a specific rumor, its specific discursive regime, while also drawing from other examples that illustrate the diversity of applications of this discursive genre.

## HISTORICAL OBSESSIONS AND A FLOATING SIGNIFIER

A rumor [*fausse nouvelle,* literally, "false news"] always
emerges from collective representations that precede its birth;
this is apparently only by chance or, more specifically, what
is fortuitous is the initial incident, which could be absolutely
anything that sets in motion the work of the imaginations.
But this setting in motion happens only because the imaginations are already prepared and quietly fermenting. An event,
for example, or a negative impression that does not tend
toward the direction in which everyone's sentiments are
already inclined, could at most be the origin of an individual
mistake but not of a popular and widely spread rumor.

—Bloch (1921, 31; McF's translation)

When I returned to Sierra Leone in spring 2002, after the end of the civil
war, I was struck by the fact that everywhere I went I heard the same
story concerning the ways in which the Red Cross had purportedly
demonstrated its collusion with the Revolutionary United Front (RUF),
one of the key actors in the conflict. Since RUF members were referred
to as "rebels," the Red Cross had become the "Rebel Cross"—an
expression I had never heard while visiting during the first half of the
1991–2002 civil war, and one which by 2005 no longer had much currency in public discourse. This rumor, then, can offer insights into popular sentiment, fears, and collective "obsessions," in Bloch's words, at
a particular time during the war and the postconflict transition: it
emerged in the aftermath of a wartime power shift that took place in
1998; it peaked in the aftermath of the January 1999 rebel attack on
Freetown, becoming especially pervasive in 2002, after the end of the
civil war; and it was no longer in circulation a few years later. It was
also remarkable because it singled out for slander a well-established and
known humanitarian organization at a time when Sierra Leone was seeing a massive increase in the number and type of aid groups. Some of
them had gotten embroiled in compromising situations that were potentially worse than the imputed transgressions committed by the Red
Cross, but they did not suffer consequences as serious as those that
eventually befell that organization in Sierra Leone. The transgressions
consisted of several instances in which personnel of the International
Committee of the Red Cross (ICRC) purportedly acted in partisan ways
that contradicted the neutrality at the heart of its humanitarian mission.
The narratives that invoked the Rebel Cross conveyed the deep mistrust

that developed at a certain point toward one of the key institutions that was supposed to protect people from illness and death. The Rebel Cross rumor crystallized general fears about the real interests animating the intervention of this organization.

I first heard the "Rebel Cross" story in 2002, at the table of the Irish Catholic nuns in Bo, a provincial town in Sierra Leone. They were friends whom I stopped to greet when I could on my way to or from the rural area where I carried out my research over the years. They were normally tolerant and cheerful, but their tone changed when another lunch guest brought up the subject of the Rebel Cross and reported as incontrovertible fact that the organization had colluded with the rebels. At the center of the rumor were multiple sightings of a white helicopter, purportedly carrying armed rebels of the RUF, bearing the Red Cross emblem, in violation of the organization's commitment not to take sides in conflicts. This group found the rumor credible because an Italian missionary priest based in the north had confirmed this sighting. This story did not do justice to the history of the ICRC in this conflict. The organization had sacrificed personnel and property, choosing to remain in the country even during times when other humanitarian organizations had withdrawn their personnel out of concern for the safety of their members.

Thinking I'd heard a bit of expatriate mythology, I asked about the origins of the story about the Rebel Cross once I arrived in the village where I was headed. There, too, the question elicited passionate responses, ranging from anger to sarcasm, and accusations that the organization had colluded with the rebels during the 1991–2002 civil war. Asked for evidence of this claim, my interlocutors told me the story of how, in the final years of the war, "they saw" a white helicopter bearing the ICRC emblem that was flying so low and slowly that people on the ground could easily see that it was carrying armed rebels. Its doors were open, and armed passengers could be seen through them. Furthermore, the helicopter landed in a forested area near one of the big rebel bases, only a few miles away from where we were located, and several of the people in the group around me said that they had seen it drop off supplies and weapons and pick up rebel leaders before flying away.

Note that before the war, the skies over much of this part of the Sierra Leonean interior were virtually empty of air traffic, as there were no regular domestic flights flying overhead, and the international ones arriving and departing from the Freetown airport—on the country's Atlantic coast—by-and-large followed coastal routes. The sound of an approaching airplane or helicopter was so unusual that most people stopped whatever they were doing to look up. During fieldwork in the mid-1980s, I heard and saw airplanes flying overhead twice over a period of two years while I was living in this part of rural southeastern Sierra Leone, and both times they were the object of considerable commentary among my neighbors. The civil war brought more air traffic, ranging from the Nigerian Air Force flights that dropped bombs on suspected rebel havens after the 1997 coup (of which more below) to the helicopter gunships used by South African "Executive Outcomes" mercenaries. But there were, too, the helicopters of humanitarian missions with visible brands or logos, particularly the UN peacekeepers and the ICRC. Thus though the war made the sound of air traffic more common, the experience of airborne threats among them made people on the ground even more attentive to—and fearful of—overhead aircraft.

When I asked who had actually seen this helicopter firsthand, only one man, who had been imprisoned behind rebel lines near the Liberian border for a time, came forth. Upon further investigation, it turned out that the ICRC flight he had witnessed as a captive carried only food and medicines, but he was quick to point out that, since these were being delivered to rebels, it was plausible that on another trip they could have carried RUF members or other cargo, like weapons. I pointed out that the only way to get aid to him—a prisoner—would have been to deliver it to his captors, and though he protested that none of it got to him, he eventually conceded the point. But he continued to insist that there was more evidence to support the Rebel Cross rumor.

In a similar vein, several professional Sierra Leoneans and some expatriates, who were familiar with the ICRC's mandate and had been present at other iterations of this story, commented that this helicopter sighting contradicted the widely advertised prohibition against carrying weapons in vehicles bearing the Red Cross emblem. ICRC employees sometimes took considerable risks to affirm this principle: in a 1992 incident, several staff of the Sierra Leone Red Cross Society (SLRCS) driving a marked vehicle were captured by the RUF in the Kono diamond-mining areas and were forced to give a ride to some of the rebels. The Red Cross personnel insisted that only they could drive, and nobody with weapons could ride inside. I was told by one of the captives that the armed rebels climbed on the roof or hung outside the vehicle, while the unarmed Red Cross captives drove the almost empty van to their captors' destination (O'Neill, personal communication, 2011).

Suspicion about the partisan motives of the ICRC were linked to the notion that aid in war inevitably has political effects—a common perception given the antagonistic context of all humanitarian interventions.[4] The ICRC, in particular, lends itself more than other humanitarian organizations to misinterpretation, in part because of the code of silence that sometimes has prevented it from providing exculpatory information that could put in context apparently problematic missions. Since its nineteenth-century foundation, the "corollary of the authorization for it to intervene in conflict situations was an implicit secrecy clause. To bring aid, the Red Cross had to remain silent" (Fassin 2011, 205). To make things worse, its organizational complexity and constituent components—the ICRC, the national Red Cross societies, and the International Federation of Red Cross and Red Crescent Societies (IFRC), which coordinate relations among these entities—can present confusing, sometimes contradictory messages, in light of their different mandates (more on this below). Finally, in Sierra Leone the mandate of the ICRC, in which its familiar, visible emblem of neutrality is often used for secretive, diplomatic operations, inscribed it—to its detriment— within locally familiar juxtapositions of publicity and secrecy maintained in the pursuit of political ends. Red crosses on white backgrounds on vehicles, on helicopters, and on the personnel's clothes were ubiquitous during the war—often in multiple, redundant iterations in convoys crossing the landscape during times of heightened insecurity. But when this visible presence accompanied diplomatic missions, it acted similarly to the masks used in performances during initiations into Sierra Leonean secret societies: they were the public signs of secret activities. Public appearances of masquerades during particular phases of secret society initiations signal the presence of a parallel universe, to which only initiates have access, and thus serve as reminders to onlookers of boundaries whose transgression carries considerable dangers. In a similar manner, onlookers presumed the recognizability of the red cross emblem concealed a multiplicity of relations and interests to which they had no access. In both cases there was a symbolic charge, a surplus of meaning.

The red cross emblem acted as a kind of "floating signifier," a "zero symbolic value" requiring "a supplementary symbolic content over and above that which the signified already contains" (Lévi-Strauss 1950, 64). Over time and in different contexts, a red cross against a white background has been "liable to take on any symbolic content whatever" (64), including opposite meanings, such as specific (Swiss) national and (Christian) religious associations, but also universalistic connotations of neutrality above partisan affiliations. Like all floating signifiers, the red cross signaled the ability of the symbolic to operate despite contradictions and, therefore, transcend the limits of other forms of discursive thought, including what Levi-Strauss characterized as "finite thought," like scientific knowledge.

Testimony collected after the war made clear that there had been instances of misuse of the organization's emblem by unauthorized personnel. Such events reinforced the fears of local actors that at least in a few instances the Red Cross had taken a side during the conflict. This problem, which has dogged the ICRC throughout its history (Benthall 1993, 142), increased as attacks on Red Cross property enabled fighting factions to acquire clothes, vehicles, and communication equipment bearing the organization's emblem (TRC 2004, 3B:77–79; SLRCS n.d., 20–21, 24). In addition, postwar investigations found compelling evidence that a "mystery helicopter" other than the one used for Red Cross missions, but using its emblem, flew into Sierra Leone from Liberia on one or more occasions during the "junta time"—a nine-month period beginning in May 1997, when a joint force of RUF rebels and rogue military under the banner of the Armed Forces Revolutionary Council (AFRC) overthrew the civilian government that had been elected the previous year. With the 1997 election of Charles Taylor to the presidency of Liberia, one of the main warlords in this conflict came into possession of the military apparatus and infrastructural resources of the state, which greatly aided his intervention in what, notwithstanding its characterization in Sierra Leone as a "civil war," had from its inception been a de facto regional conflict (Marchal, Ero, and Ferme 2002; Hoffman 2011b, 27). During Charles Taylor's trial at the Special Court for Sierra Leone, evidence emerged both of the regional nature of the conflict and of the fact that aircraft, including of helicopters fraudulently painted with the emblem of the red cross, had been used to ferry weapons at the time of his presidency of Liberia. Testimony pointed out that the former warlord and president "provided much needed road and air transportation [including flights departing Liberia's main airport] to the RUF of arms and ammunition into RUF territory," particularly during the international embargo to isolate the junta that took power in Sierra Leone from May 1997 to February 1998 (Charles Taylor Summary Judgment 2012, 19).

Furthermore, the label Rebel Cross may have gained currency thanks in part to volunteers for the SLRCS, the national chapter affiliated with the ICRC: in one documented instance, a former staff member joined a fighting faction after leaving the organization and led an attack on one of its offices (SLRCS n.d., 20–21). The secretive, diplomatic nature of some of the Red Cross's work made it impossible to counter accusations of malfeasance in some cases, even though whenever possible the organization did communicate its planned activities through the mass media. The Red Cross had carried out its own investigations and offered the evidence of its flight ledgers to clear its name with the Sierra Leone government. Despite these efforts, theft and misuse of the Red Cross emblem continued to be widespread. At various points during the conflict, ICRC and SLRCS property, vehicles, and staff were targeted by different fighting factions, including the government's troops and their allies. After the January 1999 rebel attack on Freetown, the capital city—two weeks during which up to six thousand people lost their lives—the ICRC was expelled from the country by the government. As I will mention below, this instance is linked to accusations that Red Cross personnel had used their communication equipment to reveal the location of government troops and their allies to the enemy.

As I noted earlier, rumors are often indices of historical anxieties that are specific and local. They are, as the historian Marc Bloch wrote in his own reflections on the rumors that spread among French soldiers during World War I, windows into collective representations and imaginaries that preexist their circulation and thus facilitate their "fermentation." If this were not the case, he argued, they would remain circumscribed to individual instances rather than proliferating among the population, since rumors often originate in mistakes or misunderstandings. One of the examples analyzed by Bloch involved cultural mistranslations of the sort that often occur in conflicts that pitch different societies and cultures against each other. Thus at one point during World War I, a rumor spread among German soldiers about their being targeted by "blood-crazy" Belgian sharpshooters, who were purportedly led by priests (Bloch 1921, 25). The rumor was especially shocking to German Catholics, who were struck by the notion that priests could be leading such treachery.

In his analysis of why this rumor spread without being contradicted, Bloch opined that it was partly owing to the fact that young German recruits were still adapting to the notion of being at war with the Belgians, who were unfamiliar enemies. Bloch's analysis of the effect of this story on German Catholic troops underscores the fact that rumors spread not in a homogeneous manner but in ways that reflect internal differences, which account for what makes them "locally credible" among particular social groups (White 2000, 81–83). The empirical evidence for this "false news," as rumors are known in French, was that Belgian houses had fissures in their exterior walls, which were presumed to be where sharpshooters were posted. But in reality, these gaps were built into the walls to install scaffolding for painters or window cleaners—an architectural detail unfamiliar to Germans, according to Bloch (1921, 27). This misunderstanding fed rumors about widespread Belgian atrocities perpetrated against the Germans, who in turn destroyed houses with fissures and their inhabitants. Thus, Bloch concluded, "an innocent architectural detail (was) taken for the anticipation of a knowingly planned crime," with real consequences: "from the instant in which the mistake caused blood to flow, it found itself permanently established. . . . One may assume that the majority of them would have recoiled in horror, had they recognized the profound absurdity of the panicked terrors that had pushed them to commit such ghastly acts" (28).[5]

In the case discussed by Bloch, the rumor was perpetuated in part by the reality it helped establish—purported cruelties on one side brought about retribution from the other. It also had a kind of material inscription, because its circulation was facilitated by particular interpretations of a foreign-built form in the imagination of an opposing army. But to be perpetuated, rather than dispelled by contrary evidence, rumors need the support of more than popular word of mouth. In the case discussed by Bloch (1921, 27), the rumor was lent authoritative weight by the Red Cross itself, which circulated pamphlets that suggested these fissures concealed Belgian sharpshooters in their campaigns to raise funds for war relief. In a similar manner, in 1994, the SLRCS was accused by elements in the Sierra Leonean army of "helping to spread . . . rumours through their sensitization messages" during a campaign to inform the population about international humanitarian laws, which also addressed growing concerns "that some soldiers were colluding with the rebels" (SLRCS n.d., 15). The campaign was supposed to limit itself to statements about the ethical treatment of prisoners and enemies in conflict, but the SLRCS used the opportunity to warn the population of potential attacks by members of the ruling military government, who were colluding with rebels.

Before returning to my analysis of these events, I want to stress that the Red Cross' structure has contributed to the problem. The Red Cross is made up of three types of organizations—a) the International Committee of the Red Cross (ICRC), b) the International Federation of Red Cross and Red Crescent Societies, and c) the 188 or so autonomous national chapters, of which the SLRCS is one. These entities all use the Red Cross emblem, even though they have different statuses and missions, which means that different meanings have been attached to the emblem and sometimes led to the perception that the Red Cross' claim to be a neutral organization is false. Compounding this is the popular practice of referring to all of the organizations as the "Red Cross." On the one hand is the ICRC, an intergovernmental organization funded by states that issues Swiss diplomatic passports to its delegates, who in turn have diplomatic duties and protections. On the other hand are nongovernmental, privately funded charities, such as the national chapters affiliated with the movement, all with local agendas and different levels of engagements.

The hybrid nature of the ICRC has to do with its "international legal personality," mixed with its status as a private organization subject to the Swiss civil code, which grants it "inviolability of premises and archives as well as immunity from legal process and execution" (Lindbloom 2005, 72). The rights of inviolability and immunity, first established under the Geneva Conventions, are consolidated in the developing body of customary international law. For instance, a ruling in the International Criminal Tribunal for Yugoslavia protected an ICRC employee from disclosing information to the court because of the "working principle of confidentiality" attached to the organization's mandate (Lindbloom, 72), thus further enshrining into law the secretive aspects of the organization's work. Even though it is a "private" institution, the ICRC's history, dating back to its nineteenth-century foundation as a humanitarian enterprise and its legal expression through the Geneva Conventions, gives it a distinctive role with respect to other nongovernmental institutions (Koenig 1991). And though it has a global reach, the ICRC has a "Swiss" history and culture too, which are visibly enshrined in its familiar emblem—the Swiss national flag with inverted colors.

Key events in the ICRC's history brought to the fore the contested history behind its ubiquitous emblem, the cross, with its religious and political connotations. Thus in 1876, the war between the Russian and Ottoman empires saw the formation of the Red Crescent Society and its emblem, in the face of the "offence to Muslim soldiers" brought by the society's identification with the red cross (Provost 2007, 617–18). More recently, the politico-theological overtones of both cross and crescent moved the organization to engage in semiotic debates to reach agreement on a more neutral, unified emblem. In 2005, this resulted in the adoption of a diamond-shaped "red crystal," "a widget, a thing without any specificity to which could be attached an objectionable quality," owing to "its apparent lack of cultural meaning" (615). To date,

**FIGURE 10.** Sierra Leone Red Cross Society director, Emmanuel H. Tommy, and Red Cross vehicle. Freetown, 13 May 2012. Photo by author.

however, this widget has been unsuccessful in replacing its ubiquitous predecessors, particularly the red cross, which remains the most potent and recognizable "brand" (fig. 10).

## BRANDED VERSUS GENERIC HUMANITARIANISM

The historical role of the ICRC in war interventions is a crucial feature in understanding how the Red Cross was the source of anxieties and popular rumors during the Sierra Leone civil war. The Red Cross intervened at a time, during the second half of the conflict itself, when both Sierra Leone and the global scene witnessed a proliferation of NGOs and of humanitarian interventions as a set of discursive and regulatory practices. This proliferation signaled the increasing privatization and fragmentation of aid interventions, and the shift within the purview of humanitarian organizations of governmental responsibilities, particularly in states undermined by conflicts. In other words, they established state-like modes of managing and controlling populations and even bureaucratic practices that implemented the "matrices of individualization" (Foucault 1994, 334) pivotal to integrating citizens in modern states—registering refugees and internally displaced persons; issuing them identification cards; providing services, health care, food, and security; and documenting their activities for the purposes of fund-raising and audits (Gupta 1995; Weber 1978, 222–51)—even as the countries in which they intervened could no longer do so. All of these organizations tried to provide the appearance of law in its absence, in the name of a depoliticized humanity. In camps, in particular, any appeal to the law remains within the framework of a generic identification with "bare" humanity writ large (Agamben 1998; Malkki 1994).

In Sierra Leone, the transition from a developmental regime with lingering ties to the theories and practices of modernization, with long-term planning and systematic, incremental interventions in the domains of health and education—of which the Red Cross, despite its contested history, was an example—to the short-term interventions of aid organizations focusing on "complex humanitarian emergencies" was marked by a bewildering proliferation of "NGO-*sisia*" (in Mende), the plural form of NGO. Until the civil war, humanitarian projects had been characterized by longer-term commitments such as the German government–supported GTZ investments, which included visible infrastructural projects and branded vehicles of the Bo-Pujehun Rural Development Project. These investments were the basis for broader, systemic changes in the landscape, including interventions in agriculture and other subsistence activities. By contrast, beginning with the conflict, emergency humanitarian interventions had more ad hoc interests and only dealt with the management of contingency.

Many of these wartime NGOs worked at cross-purposes with each other and were driven by narrow agendas, despite overarching organizing and coordinating efforts by entities such as the United Nations. During one wartime return to rural Wunde, I found ducks in several villages brought by one organization and sheep brought by others, which locals complained had arrived in such poor health that they had mostly died off, while the survivors were destroying—as some farmers complained—the incipient gardens that they had begun to reestablish. Villagers did not know which organization had brought what, but though they still had enough protein from consuming what they could fish and hunt, they complained of not having a well with clean drinking water. This had been a constant refrain during my earlier visits, and one of the top items on their collective "development" wish list.

The NGO Action against Hunger had come during the war and planned to dig a much-needed well for drinking water. They had left a letter indicating the date when this would happen but never returned. When, in 2002, on my way out of the country, I visited the organization's offices to find out what had happened, I was told that they could not keep that promise because of the 1997 junta coup and the increased insecurity in its wake. The particular program that covered this project had ended, so they had moved on to something else, in a different part of the country. In a gesture typical of the short-term nature of particular programs and commitments of the day, I was told that if I were willing to apply for a grant to cover the costs, they might be able to dig a well in six months, when the current program would finish. But by then, the French employee to whom I was speaking would have completed her two years in the country, and I would have to persuade her successor.

These short temporal horizons and disrupted actions are in part a product of the "crisis mode," the discourse of emergency brought forth by the contexts in which NGOs intervene in wartime, but they are also linked to an "experimental" ethos that is foundational to some organizations. Thus the history of Médecins Sans Frontières (Doctors without Borders), founded in 1971 by a group of French Red Cross doctors frustrated by the slowness with which their organization responded to the 1967–70 Biafran crisis in Nigeria, is linked precisely to emergency medicine in times and places of acute crisis and the deliberate avoidance, for the most part, of longer-term, "development"-style commitments (Redfield 2013, 27, 53–78). Indeed, Médecins Sans Frontières has developed a reputation for its logistical "global kit," which enables it to deploy within forty-eight hours of a humanitarian emergency (Redfield, 78).

The Rebel Cross rumor spread in Sierra Leone precisely when earlier experiences with established, recognizable humanitarian "brands" with a global reach, but also long-term investments in particular locales, gave way to the multiplication and saturation of less identifiable NGOs, once the civil war earned the country the label of "complex humanitarian emergency." In a way, the very practice of the ICRC of operating in conjunction with national Red Cross societies, many of which had been founded during the colonial era as charitable arms of the "civilizing mission," was also a legacy of the 1980s, when World Bank and IMF policies in Africa dictated economic and fiscal conditions that undermined nation-states. The collapse of the Cold War order during that decade and the forces of globalization and privatization shaped new forms of intervention aimed at "managing and controlling populations" rather than at partnering with governments on large-scale and more durable infrastructural projects.

During the second half of the Sierra Leone civil war, which began with the transition to civilian elections in 1996, a combination of shorter and accelerated temporal commitments, on the one hand, and security concerns, on the other hand, dictated a much lighter footprint among many humanitarian organizations. Some of them also eschewed identifying emblems on their offices and vehicles, which were leased rather than owned to minimize losses in case of attacks.[6] They also accounted for a bewildering proliferation of acronyms, which increased confusion among the subjects of their interventions—hence *these NGOs* was their collective term of reference, to avoid singling out individual targets that could become the subject of accusations like the ones aimed at the Red Cross. At the same time as they were multiplying in numbers and decreasing their investment in durable infrastructures like vehicles or permanent offices, however, many NGOs made special efforts to publicize their activities in war zones through the media. In contrast, the ICRC fell victim to the gap between the ubiquitous and loaded visibility of its widely recognized emblem, on the one hand, and the secrecy of its practices of diplomatic mediations, on the other, particularly during missions to facilitate peace talks. However, even the ICRC resorted to using public media when working to reunite families separated by war.

The ICRC also fell victim to the "impossible problem of neutrality," a concept that for much of its history was not concerned with the denial of self-interest or a kind of depoliticized stepping aside that has become dominant in twenty-first-century humanitarian invocations. Instead, in past centuries neutrality was seen as a political strategy with political effects in dealings with sovereign nation-states at war with each other— "its very claim suggests a potential limit to the sovereignty of another." But its enduring commitment to an impossible neutrality undermines the organization's effectiveness in contexts of civil and ethnic conflicts. Wherever the ICRC is, it is seen as taking a particular side in the conflict (Redfield 2011, 56).

This was especially the case with the SLRCS, which at one point warned about sporadic collusions between soldiers and rebels (*sobel* rumors). The Sierra Leonean Army has often been, and continues to be, an important partner in the activities of the SLRCS. In 1994, however, the army took a confrontational position toward the organization when the National Provisional Ruling Council, or NPRC—the military regime then ruling the country—accused the Red Cross of colluding in spreading rumors about *sobels*. An event in 1992 helped set the stage for the military government's hostility toward the Red Cross, when a fire destroyed one of the organization's storage facilities in the Kono diamond-mining region, which contained more than thirty tons of food for war-affected populations. The SLRCS investigation, which was leaked to the media, found that the fire had probably been set to conceal the fact that the food had been stolen and suggested that this could have happened only with the collusion of soldiers who were guarding the facility. This leaked document led to one of the first open accusations by members of the Sierra Leone government of collusion between Red Cross staff and the rebels[7]—an episode all but forgotten in popular memories by the time the Rebel Cross rumors emerged, much later in the war.

## SIGNIFIERS OF SOVEREIGNTY AND NEUTRALITY

The general state of not-knowing that is pervasive during the beginnings of wars—the impossibility of gathering reliable information in the midst of great insecurity and the deliberate misinformation that fighting factions and state institutions deploy to fuel enmity—conspires to make rumors powerful tactical weapons. They are especially destabilizing among the civilian population, wreaking havoc well beyond the reach of armed combat. The Rebel Cross rumor points, too, to the quandaries in which an organization could find itself when engaged in forms of intelligence gathering—for instance, to "maintain family ties" and, where possible, to reunite families separated by war, which were longstanding mandates of the ICRC (Mercier 1995, 81). In this process, the ICRC and SLRCS publicized some of their activities through the national media, but they also engaged in behind-the-scenes diplomatic work that was less transparent.

The work of gathering and verifying information could itself be seen as a way of dealing with potentially dangerous rumors, and engaging in these practices puts the Red Cross at risk of becoming caught up in the circulation of half-truths that make up the rumor mills. This effect is sometimes exaggerated by the juxtaposition of behind-the-scenes work to gather information with the ubiquitous and visible presence of the Red Cross's emblem—which figured prominently in all versions of the helicopter story. In this respect, note that the Red Cross's 1994 "sensitization campaign" mentioned above sparked accusations by members of the army of collusions between the SLRCS and the rebels. This campaign sought to educate the public about international humanitarian law and the Geneva Conventions, central to which is the distinction between civilians and combatants, among other things. Doing so at the time in which *sobels* were undermining that very distinction, and thus fomenting popular anxieties about the true identities of combatants, including soldiers, could have been interpreted as a direct attack against the military regime then in power, and therefore have provoked a government response. Indeed, whenever rumors about the Red Cross emerged during the war, state or government actors were sometimes key to amplifying their circulation through the media.

And here the SLRCS—the national Red Cross Society—had an ambiguous position, because of its history of entanglements with colonial and postcolonial government institutions. The SLRCS was established in 1918, under British colonial rule, as a branch of the British Red Cross Society, to deal with the influenza epidemic (SLRCS n.d., 1). This charitable extension of the colonial mission was followed, after independence, by a 1962 Act of Parliament that recognized the SLRCS as an "auxiliary to the central government" (SLRCS, 4), but since the 1991–2002 civil war it has been treated as an NGO (SLRCS, 2). Thus over its history, the national Red Cross Society moved from being the humanitarian arm of the colonial and postcolonial state, to an NGO— albeit one with a special relationship with government.

In addition to exacerbating the tensions embedded in its multiple components and legal identities, the interplay between visibility and secret practices in the history and culture of the Red Cross found a familiar terrain in Sierra Leone, thus facilitating the "fermentation" of mistrust in the popular imagination, to which Marc Bloch alluded in the World War I case discussed earlier. In January 1999, the government of Sierra Leone expelled the ICRC from the country, and even after the organization was allowed to return in May, its presence was not tolerated for several years in Kailahun, a major town near the Liberian border, which had suffered some of the worst rebel attacks and was the theater of some of the SLRCS's earliest wartime relief efforts (SLRCS n.d., 13). After the 1994 accusations of Red Cross collusions in spreading *sobel* rumors, suspicion about the organization emerged on three different occasions: around the 1996 elections, during the 1997–98 junta time (the AFRC-RUF junta—effectively a *sobel* regime), and during the January 1999 "*sobel* attack" on Freetown.

In 1996, under pressure from international donors, the military NPRC government that had been in power in Sierra Leone since 1992 agreed to hold multiparty elections. Because of the threats to security posed by the prospect of campaigning in war zones, the United Nations and other international humanitarian organizations offered support in carrying out what was to be the first multiparty election in a quarter of a century. The Red Cross did its part by transporting politicians from different parties by helicopter, at a time when roads were extremely dangerous (M. C., personal communication, 2002). After the election, the new civilian government set as its priority seeking a dialogue with rebels. In light of this goal, the Red Cross, acting, in its own words, "as a neutral intermediary, provided transport for representatives of the Revolutionary United Front (RUF) from areas under their control to Abidjan," in Ivory Coast. They did this to participate "in the first bilateral meeting with representatives of the government of Sierra Leone" (*ICRC News* 1996a). The press release giving an account of this event stated, "A helicopter bearing the Red Cross emblem went to two locations in the Sierra Leonean jungle to collect the members of the delegation and take them to Kissidougou in the Republic of Guinea. From there an aircraft . . . [flew] the RUF representatives to Abidjan. When the negotiations are over, ICRC delegates will supervise the return of both the governmental and the RUF delegations." The statement went on to say that "the operation was organized by the ICRC at the request of the government of Sierra Leone and the RUF." The following month saw the repetition of this movement of rebel leaders to Côte d'Ivoire for peace negotiations, in a Red Cross helicopter (*ICRC News* 1996b). The press release announcing this also stated that Red Cross helicopters would deliver food to Kailahun, in the eastern border region, because roads to the area were impassable owing to rebel activities.

## SOVEREIGNTY: VEHICLES AND OTHER MATERIAL
## "FRAGMENTS OF SWITZERLAND"

These official accounts were not inconsistent with the stories I heard throughout the countryside, which lingered on the image of a low-flying helicopter landing in rebel territory. And as the press releases quoted above make clear, at the time the ICRC and SLRCS had publicized the reasons for their missions, which had government consent. But the key difference was the question of whether the people being carried in the helicopter were bearing arms—the Red Cross communiqués did not mention them, but popular rumors, circulated by others in the media, said otherwise. In a way, it did not much matter, since one of the surpluses of the "zero symbolic value" represented by the red cross emblem was the familiar notion in the Sierra Leonean landscape that publicity and visibility were presumed to mask concealed agendas.[8]

The ICRC's insistence on the inviolability of its property and vehicles, and the exclusion of arms-bearing combatants from them, also made it stand out in the humanitarian landscape. The extension of Swiss neutrality to the organization's property and delegates is enshrined in law, where, as mentioned earlier, it is granted "the inviolability of premises and archives" (Lindbloom 2005). This is not just an abstract principle—it is reiterated in framed statements on the walls of the Freetown SLRCS office, in press releases, and in conversations, and it appears to animate the practices of Red Cross employees at all levels. For instance, in talking about the end of his captivity in RUF territory in 1992, M.O.N.—the only expatriate among the captured SLRCS employees—described how, at the news of his arrival in Kenema, the Eastern Provincial headquarters town, an ICRC delegate based there drove up to him in a Red Cross vehicle, urged him to jump in, and shut the door as the crowds gathered outside at the news of the end of this highly publicized kidnapping. At this point in his account, M.O.N. said "I was in Geneva, nobody could touch me" (personal communication, 2011).

Indeed, it had been the delegate's intention to pluck the former captive, who had managed to escape out of his Sierra Leonean surroundings, and take him to a small area of Swiss sovereign territory—his Red Cross vehicle—where nobody could threaten or interrogate him. Hoping to learn what he had experienced during a month-long captivity that was the object of intense rumors and media coverage, a crowd gathered outside as news spread in Kenema that the last of the captive Red Cross staff was now free. Recall that little was known about the RUF at this early stage of the civil war. Another SLRCS employee, who had been in the vehicle with M.O.N. at the time of the kidnapping, had gotten away because as a Sierra Leonean he could blend in better with the local population. He described how when the RUF captured the town where they were investigating the food disappearance and burned storage facility, they "decided to turn the compound into a Red Cross neutral zone" by painting a red cross on the wall surrounding the building where they were staying (M.L., personal communication, 2012). This delayed the entrance of armed rebels into the compound, and even after entering and commandeering the Red Cross vehicle, the RUF leaders abided by the SLRCS staff's refusal to carry anyone bearing weapons inside it, suggesting that the expectation of "inviolability," however limited, was broadly shared. Whether opposing meanings and contradictory goals will attach to floating signifiers such as the red cross, and the figures of humanitarian neutrality to which they attach, is unpredictable. Nevertheless, the evocative image of a hurried painting of a red cross on a white wall, or of an SLRCS vehicle carrying its captive staff while its armed captor hitches a ride by hanging onto its exterior, points to a shared belief in the legally binding power of the neutral status of this "piece of Switzerland." It was a neutral space, where even in the face of violence and captivity, a claim to the protection of the international community could be advanced (Redfield 2011).

## COMMUNICATION AND MOBILITY

This effort to protect the quasi-sacred inviolability of Red Cross vehicles and premises as spaces of international law contrasts sharply with the difficulty of managing the transmission and communication of information. The ICRC and SLRCS issued their staff shortwave radio handsets for communication and investigative purposes. One SLRCS employee said an event contributing to the Rebel Cross label involved "walkie-talkies" and first emerged when the handset belonging to a SLRCS employee began transmitting while he was sharing a taxi in Freetown during the 1997–98 junta rule. The nature of the communication raised the suspicion of a fellow traveler, who stopped the taxi at a military checkpoint to accuse the SLRCS employee of passing on confidential information. This was a time when covert information was used to single out supporters of the deposed civilian regime of president Kabbah for persecution. In addition, an international embargo heightened the tensions between the few humanitarian organizations that chose to remain in Sierra Leone and the AFRC-RUF junta, which routinely tried to commandeer their resources. For his part, ousted president Kabbah waged a media war of sorts from his exile in neighboring Guinea, through a "prodemocracy" radio station that went on air in December 1997, jamming the programs of the Sierra Leone Broadcasting Corporation.

After the ousted President Kabbah returned to power, with the support of international allies, the three international humanitarian organizations that had remained in the country under the AFRC-RUF regime were dubbed "junta NGOs" and were suspected of collusion with the coup plotters. The Red Cross was among them, and later that year the minister of information, Julius Spencer, stated in a radio interview "that the government was investigating allegations that the ICRC helicopter had been delivering materials to the RUF" (TRC 2004, 3B:78). The reinstated Kabbah government also significantly curtailed freedom of the press—condemning as treasonable wartime media coverage that was critical of the government. The following month, five journalists were found guilty of treason and sentenced to death, though the sentences were not carried out. This led to the formation of an Internet-based group of journalists, the National Independent Neutral Journalists Association, or NINJA, which posted news about the war under cover of anonymity (more on this later).

In the midst of this increasing control on information and communications, the *sobel* junta retreated to the north but continued to engage in skirmishes with government troops and allies, controlling most of the diamond-mining areas that enabled them to arm and provision themselves. In a typical move of government propaganda in wartimes, the government's Ministry of Information often concealed the true extent of AFRC-RUF *sobel* resistance, and its control of the country outside the capital city. Thus communication and miscommunication abounded during the months leading up to "Operation No Living Thing," as the January 1999 attack on Freetown was dubbed. This was the single bloodiest event of the war and was purported to have produced at least six thousand casualties over a two-week period.[9] Because it happened in one of the few places with media coverage, it was also better documented than other war theaters.

**MEDIATIC RUMORS**

During Operation No Living Thing, most international humanitarian organizations once again left Sierra Leone. The ICRC and IFRC reduced their staff to five delegates but continued to maintain a presence in Freetown, remaining the only international humanitarian organization there at the height of the fighting (SLRCS n.d., 24). Members of the SLRCS who had become trapped behind rebel lines during the attack on Freetown used their handsets to communicate with their colleagues in unoccupied parts of the city on the security and humanitarian situation (M. C., personal communication, 2002). This was happening at a time when Julius Spencer, the country's minister of information, was announcing on the national broadcasting system that, apart from minor violent incidents, the city was under government control—with dire consequences for citizens who ventured out thinking themselves safe. In this case, then, the Red Cross' networks created an informal information circuit parallel to the government's public pronouncements, which at best were uninformed about what was actually happening on the ground and at worst were waging a deliberate disinformation campaign that put citizens' lives in danger. But as the rebels advanced and captured SLRCS employees, along with their communication handsets, they gained access to this circuit as well. The Nigerian-led West African peacekeeping forces of ECOMOG[10] eventually pushed the invading rebels out of the city and purportedly found Red Cross communication handsets on some of the captives taken during this operation. During this same January 1999 attack on Freetown, Red Cross vehicles were also taken and driven around town by armed combatants, so other equipment and personnel came under rebel control (SLRCS n.d., 22).

On 13 January 1999, "armed soldiers . . . visited the ICRC Delega-tion several times, in a bellicose mood, accusing the ICRC of 'helping the rebels.' They . . . alleged that the ICRC staff (local and foreign) had in some way facilitated the entry of the rebels into Freetown on 6 Janu-ary. The soldiers took away ICRC communication equipment," so the military defending the city also became complicit in the (mis)appropria-tion of communication equipment (SLRCS n.d., 22). ICRC delegates were attacked, harassed, and expelled from the country. The govern-ment also officially expelled the organization, and the IFRC soon there-after. In the months after this event, the UN's special representative in Freetown negotiated conditions for the return of these two organiza-tions with the Sierra Leonean government, which demanded "restrictive regulations . . . concerning, *inter alia,* the use of communications equip-ment and compulsory monitoring of the movements of humanitarian players" (ICRC 1999).

By May of that year, the ICRC and the IFRC had returned to Sierra Leone, but even then it took the organizations some time before they were able to resume the use of communication and transportation equipment with confidence. Before the ICRC began operating an air-craft in February 2001 "to speed up the reunification of unaccompanied Sierra Leonean children in Guinea and Liberia with their families," it announced that it had been granted authorization to begin resuming flights by all the relevant authorities, including the Civil Aviation Authority, the Ministry of Foreign Affairs, the Ministry of Defense and the armed forces, and that the plane was "clearly marked with the ICRC emblem" (*ICRC News* 2001).

## CONCLUSION

Four factors conspired to bring about the transformation of the Red Cross into the Rebel Cross toward the end of the 1991–2002 civil war, the proliferation of rumors that gave rise to this moniker, and the ICRC's expulsion from Sierra Leone. The first was the slippage between the different institutional identities of the ICRC, IFRC, and national societies, with their divergent histories, cultures, and mandates, which sometimes led to contradictions. The second, which is similarly linked to the history of these organizations—and the ICRC in particular—was the tension between a familiar, visible emblem with a long presence in Sierra Leone and its distinctively "Swiss" culture of diplomatic secrecy, which was connected to the organization's politics of neutrality. In other words, the Red Cross got caught in its own erasures and silences within the economy of rumors and anxious media exchanges, which characterize conflicts in general but in Sierra Leone took on more freighted meanings. There, this dynamic dovetailed with local understandings of secrecy and dissimulation, in which ubiquitous, visible emblems sometimes masked concealed practices, such as those associated with the secret societies found throughout the region.

The third factor points to the critical roles government agents and media played in both fermenting the rumor mill and suppressing information. A cloak of suspicion was cast over the Red Cross for the role Sierra Leone's national chapter performed in communicating principles of humanitarian law concerning, and warning of, *sobel* actions. The motives of a mission to investigate the possible collusions of a previous government in the disappearance of food aid was said in certain branches of the media to be owing to a covert diamond-mining or spying expedition. Journalists who tried to disseminate opposing views of the war were arrested. The proliferation of rumors was in part the responsibility of people who were in positions of authority and who had privileged access to the media, even though they were mobilized by partial truths like the one concerning the defection and betrayal of a SLRCS employee, who joined one of the fighting factions.

Finally, the Red Cross story ultimately shows the fragility of collective memories for reconstructing the meaning of events that remain hidden from the public record (e.g., some of the circumstances surrounding the 1992 kidnapping of SLRCS employees in the Kono diamond-mining area then held by the RUF rebels). Because they cannot be verified in any form for a long time during the conflict, a different collective historical archive is needed to create the legacy of crises in times of war. Earlier events (palpable sensations, rumors, uncorroborated communications) are often difficult to reconstruct after the fact, as more recent events and memories layer themselves over a conflict's earlier history. By the time the Rebel Cross rumors emerged toward the end of the war, a lot more was known about the specific identities and responsibilities of the various fighting factions, and evidence collected later did support the notion that a "fake" Red Cross helicopter may have flown into Sierra Leone carrying armed personnel.

But the 1992 kidnapping of Red Cross personnel, and the rumors surrounding that event, had disappeared from public discourse, although at the time it had been covered in the national media. The ease with which this event disappeared from the collective popular memory as the war progressed underscores that, even in a time in which conflicts are recorded and reported, their remembrance and inclusion in historical accounts cannot be taken for granted.

# Chronotope 2

## Numbers, Examples, and Exceptions

Many accounts of war given by engaged scholars, humanitarian actors, and the media use exemplary cases or events to visualize data and facts about the war—aggregate figures of casualties, displacements, and destruction. Dynamic events are frozen on visualization tables to become storytelling. Often, this kind of narrative rises to the status of "exemplary case," which empties the singularity of any specific event in order to make a claim that can be attributed to the whole. Thus, no event can be perceived as an outlier, since for it to be understood, it is made into an *example of* the generalized phenomenon. Numericality increasingly informs evidence-based governmental, humanitarian, and human rights discourse, advancing claims to objectivity and transparency through aggregations, averages, and statistical samples (see Merry 2016). Numbers aggregated in the form of estimates of casualties, or to convey the scale of a catastrophic event, are the companion aspect of exemplary cases.

The use of these numbers introduces common indicators intended to produce commensurability across different, heterogeneous states with enormously divergent levels of development, wealth, and government transparency. They are used to mask the political project behind the production of purportedly technical indicators of violence, rule of law, and health. In other words, they serve the purposes of transnational bodies of governance and aid their aim to "shame" national governments that do not reach minimum levels of compliance, as, for example, the global community responded with horror to the violence in places like Sierra Leone, Kosovo, and Rwanda during the 1990s, or Syria and Afghanistan today.

I address here the possibility of putting forth alternative forms of bearing witness that do not rely solely on statistical samples and numericality to make a truth claim about the long-term effects of war. The numbers of war casualties and atrocities rely heavily on witnesses' accounts and body counts to prioritize the visualization of extreme forms of physical brutality over the less visible forms of violence. In the giving and recording of others' accounts of atrocities, testimony clashes with the demand for objective truth, which translates what is experienced as a singularity into the generality of an exemplary account. The testimony of a singularity is suspended and subsumed into something that is quite foreign to it. The horrific and spectacular instances of harm take precedence over other kinds of harms inflicted on the population, because they are more accessible to, and commensurable with, the international community.

There is a corresponding temporality for this modality of testimony: it is the temporality of emergency, of crisis experienced in the haste and fog of the present instant, which filled with the visible signs of destruction. What is forgotten by the temporality of the emergency is the slowness of the event, what happens over time, and the less visible forms of violence that are distorted when viewed through the prism of the spectacle. During the Sierra Leone civil war, the temporality of the emergency was the preferred mode of accounting of the war's casualties. The humanitarian apparatus focused its own accounts on the most disturbing figures of the war: the body counts of amputation, decapitation and violation of men, women, and children, in order to elicit sympathy and interventions from the international community. The report of the Truth and Reconciliation Commission went into the smallest details, giving account of individual limbs or body parts affected by the war. The force of numericality traversed the number of severed arms, legs, lips, heads to make its truth claim before the international community. There is something profoundly disturbing, for me, in this modality of testimony, which points to the antinomy at the heart of what is called the humanitarian project of democratic accountability. The desire to produce public "outrage" is supported by the seriality of numbers, which assigns value only to the enumeration of similar harms in other conflicts.

## THE "RAGE OF NUMBERS" IN HUMANITARIAN NARRATIVES

The accounts demanded by the temporal urgency of humanitarian crises and the interventions carried out to stop them follow predictable scripts. In the short spatiotemporal span demanded by executive summaries and policy recommendations that preface reports running in the dozens of pages, or in two-minute TV news items and eye-catching titles in the print media banner headings, the focus on the catastrophe of the Sierra Leone civil war was condensed on the figure of mutilated, decapitated, and violated bodies in both image and writing. The writing that stood out in the news reports on the media and in policy pages was of a particular kind. It often began with shocking images and descriptions of the wounded body, particularly of amputees as the canonical image of incommensurable suffering. At the heart of this project to make perpetrators of violence accountable was a kind of "rage" for counting and accounting for those amputated and violated bodies. Numbers of amputees were counted in the range of three hundred in Freetown, the capital city, and "several thousands" nationwide, broken down into the most detailed classifications.[1] By contrast, war casualties overall were estimated by the same organizations to be between fifty and seventy-five thousand.[2] The horror of the civil war was communicated through the exegesis of numerical scales that disarmed the shocked audience of Western spectators, to produce immediate compassionate interventions on their part.

Sierra Leone, a small country ("half the size of Illinois," the media told their American audience) with a relatively small population (at the time, estimates ranged between 4.5 and 5.2 million), had ranked near the bottom of the United Nation's "Human Development Index" since before the war (at one point, it was 174th out of 174 countries), because of a combination of high infant and maternal mortality rates and low life expectancy more generally.[3]

The numerical indicators of casualties from war violence in Sierra Leone were meant to shock the international community, with their purpose summed up by the following: if humanitarian interventions don't work here, in this relatively small country with a relatively small population, where else (in Africa but also globally) can they work? Notwithstanding the fact that since then peacekeeping missions—including ones larger than the those deployed in Sierra Leone—have become common, Sierra Leone set a precedent in the deployment of UN peacekeepers.

In this case, the rhetoric of what I will call "scalar dissonance" was deployed within the UN Security Council to double the already-large deployment of peacekeeping troops in the UN Mission in Sierra Leone (UNAMSIL).[4] A force that in early May 2000 stood at 8,700 (and was already the "largest UN mission in Africa") more than doubled very rapidly thereafter.[5] By April 2002, with an annual budget of US$717.6 million, UNAMSIL counted more than 18,000 military personnel, military observers, police, and civilian support staff, which was the largest deployment anywhere in the world.[6] Sierra Leone became an example within a larger project of humanitarian expansion that took place without those responsible having much concern for the sometimes unreliable statistics that were marshaled to support the increase in peacekeeping deployments.

In a similar vein, when the Special Court for Sierra Leone was established—at the time among the first in a generation of "hybrid" courts in the expanding international war crimes system[7]—numbers, statistics, and comparisons among victims of the neighboring and distant wars underscored the bureaucratization of scalar dissonance. At a cost of a mere sixty million dollars over three years, or a "fraction" of the cost of the international tribunals for Yugoslavia and Rwanda,[8] this Special Court was supposed to set a precedent for the transnational rights of victims, imposing justice, and holding perpetrators accountable "on a shoe string." The reasoning was that its being located in the country where the war crimes occurred, and its prosecution of only those in the highest leadership positions among the several factions, would expedite the resolution of the harms produced by war.

The use of contrastive scales in the Sierra Leone case (small country, small population, low population density, very high mortality rates, very low life expectancy, very large UN troop deployment as a ratio of number of inhabitants, and so on) calls for attention. Indeed, in the context provided by the other figures (numbers, statistics, comparisons) of brutalized bodies, what is one to make of the "raging" estimates given by the humanitarian agencies of surviving amputees? These ranged from one thousand to "several thousands," even though during the whole month of January 1999—a time that saw one of the bloodiest events of the war, a week-long rebel attack on Freetown said to have produced five-to-six thousand casualties—"Freetown's three main hospitals treated [only] ninety-seven victims of amputations."[9] Surely one must assume that many amputees did not make it to a hospital, and that many others did not make it to Freetown, as the reports of the Truth and Reconciliation Commission also admitted in the face of numbers that seemed to clash with body counts in hospitals, shelters, and refugee camps. But one needs to question the numbers as well.

The point is not to minimize the harm of amputations, which were a horrific form of violence, but to note that the enumeration of amputees does not tell the whole story of the war's casualties. Indeed, most of the shocking testimonies of amputees circulated and consumed by the international media were obtained in a single camp located in Murray Town, on the west side of Freetown, a short distance from the major international hotels. Between 220 and 239 amputees lived in this camp during the period when the international media took to photographing mutilated bodies.[10]

Didier Fassin made a critical parallel argument regarding violence in the "new" South Africa. There, the public imaginary was fixated on spectacular reports of violence against children, which was attributed to "monstrous," exceptional pedophiles. This occluded the fact that this form of harm was statistically insignificant compared with the number of women of all ages who were victims of routinized intimate sexual assaults linked to male domination in South African society (Fassin 2011, 171). In a similar manner, the general fixation on mutilation in the Sierra Leone civil war inflated the number of amputations and occluded the presence of more routinized forms of violence.

If the order of numericality is to remain a central feature of quickly written humanitarian accounts of crisis, this must be critically discussed and analyzed, rather than taken for granted, especially when estimates can range from two-to-four digit figures, as do those of amputations in Sierra Leone. The magnitude of this range is such that it not only raises questions about the political use of numbers, statistical samples, and comparisons but also asks those who take humanitarianism seriously— if not for its underlying conceptual apparatus and premises, then as a strategic political engagement—to always question which figures are selected. This means both in the sense of numbers and in the sense of victims chosen as visible icons of unspeakable suffering, for "any serious attention to statistics requires us to deal closely with individuals and their experiences in a way that is not done in the simple confrontation between alternative totals" (Cribb 2001, 83). Revisiting numbers forces us to reconstruct carefully the history of a conflict as it unfolds over time and space—a process that recognizes not only harms but also the "grey zone" of mutual accommodations among purported enemies that characterize some long, drawn-out conflicts.[11]

In Sierra Leone, the evidence published since the January 2002 formal declaration of an end to the civil war shows that the correction of the historical record and the serious attention to statistics point to downward revisions in the number of casualties, mutilations, and displaced people published in 1996–2002, when the "humanitarian international" came on the scene. Consider for example the following: on 18 April 2001, the Amnesty International website stated that "More than 2 million people—roughly half the population of Sierra Leone—have been forced to flee their homes by an armed conflict that began a decade ago." By 2003, however, a review of peacekeeping operations estimated that a more accurate count of those displaced, both internally *and* beyond national boundaries, was about half that number.[12] Although the numbers are still large, both in absolute and proportional terms, the hyperbolic statistics put forth in humanitarian discourse in the heat of a crisis, which may later turn out to be exaggerated, produce in the immediate present a numbing effect of speechlessness. But in creating this condition, humanitarian discourse ironically touches a realm of truth that is also not limited to the domain of numerical exegesis, because the sense of uncertainty and stupor conveyed by shocking figures is also the product of the extent of trauma (including that experienced by members of the humanitarian apparatus itself as a result of constant exposure to the sites, scenes, and reminders of violence).[13]

For the notion of accountability goes beyond the representationalism and sensationalism of humanitarian reports: it also undergirds the accounts of those who try to adopt alternative postures in moral witnessing. The demands of the victim or of survivors, in other words, are often "to be counted" in the face of powerful political institutions that have the means to suppress or mask knowledge about the very occurrence of violent events, let alone the casualties they produce (see Das 1985, 4; van der Veer 1997, 189; Simons 1995). If, as Agamben (1998b) suggests, the core of the democratic ideals underpinning the humanitarian legacy is the linkage between the democratic and the demographic—where the rule of the people ("kratos" of the "demos") is first and foremost the inscription of that people ("graphia" of the "demos") in a bio-national body—it is important to understand that this orientation runs into problems when it becomes too obsessed with the despotism of numericality. This numericality pretends to saturate the domain of commensurable being and in the process forgets that a degree of incommensurability (truth lies outside the specific horizon of numbers) is necessary in any project that is also committed to democratic ideas of justice-as-fairness. Justice-as-fairness is a complex notion—one that exceeds the confines of law and formal rights. It refuses equality's logic of seriality and circularity—the notion that each right-bearing person is equal to and thus possibly interchangeable with any other person. It is a notion of justice in which lack—the "digital zero"—has a constitutive role.[14] For this reason, it demands a relationship to its "truth" that humanitarianism should aim to share, perhaps using a methodological naïveté that never assumes knowledge, and therefore always seeks to witness rather than represent:

> What counts is not that the event took place, but that it was felt. It is not the fact in itself that constitutes the proof, but the trace it leaves in the psyche or the mark it makes in the telling. In the testimony that is brought to the world's awareness, affect is present both as that which bears witness (people's suffering) and as that which is produced by the testimony (the compassion of the public). (Fassin 2011, 208)

My argument is that the methodological impasse I just mentioned partly derives from humanitarian accounts still being problematically linked to the governmental practices of the technical apparatus (Badiou 2008, 2)—or of the state as an actual apparatus of capture (as Deleuze and Guattari have argued). Like the rooted and tendentially *static* state apparatus criticized by Deleuze and Guattari, therefore, humanitarian discourse anchors itself in the order of numericality in the form of comparable statistics given the status of transparent, synthetic statements about facts, events, and body counts. In so doing, numerical exegesis reduces witnessing to a limited set of violence indicators, where no incommensurability exists.

But the representations of humanitarianism are also linked to intimate narratives of actors on the ground, so that today it is not uncommon in Sierra Leone for people who themselves were physically and psychically damaged in atrocities that left less visible scars to turn to the sight of an amputee and say, "Look over there, this is what the war did to us." This act of indexical pointing to an amputee, of naming war trauma as belonging to the register of embodiment, of visibility, is essentially mediatic. It displaces traumatic affects on the visibly mutilated body of another and in so doing occludes other signs of violence, including those suffered by the very person who is pointing the finger. By contrast, the kind of moral witnessing I advocate here is one that foregrounds a politically inflected understanding of the experience of violence and war, one that while attentive to physical brutality also considers its relationship to other less visible forms of violence. I advocate paying attention also to the relationship between visibility and other registers of intractable experiences, including the ways in which they are organized into a narrative of historical accounts.

Examples of the mediatic reproduction of the extreme figures of the victim's mutilated body are poignantly conveyed by the child amputee. For example, five-year-old Maimouna Mansaray became an emblem of the peace process, when she was held up for all to see by Sierra Leone president Ahmed Tejan Kabbah, at the 7 July 1999 ceremonial signing of a peace accord with rebels held in Lome, Togo.[15] Three years earlier, pictures of Maimouna's two-year old body, with one arm amputated just below the shoulder, were transmitted across the world, accompanied by stories about the ways in which the senseless mutilation was damaging not just the present generation but also the country's very future. It was an image that defied all efforts to produce a "reasoned" analysis of the rebels' mutilation campaigns, begun in 1996 around that year's election, which systematically focused on adults whose hands were cut at the wrist. In the rebel's manifesto, the mutilated hands were associated with the act of voting ("one hand, one vote," as the slogans went) and contrasted with the peasants' hands, which performed the manual labor of farming to eke out a subsistence living.[16] A two-year-old child whose right arm was amputated just under the shoulder defied that "logic," for her dependency from the mother, to whose body she was still attached as a nursing infant, defied the RUF's rationalization for its mutilation campaign. Maimouna's mutilated body bespoke, among other things, what President Kabbah said in holding her up for public viewing: may this girl, who for the rest of her life will not have the use of her hand, remind all of us of the atrocities of war. Maimouna is a living memorial, warning, and witness to what befalls society when it slips into the posture of responding to strength with strength, to violence with violence.

These visibly harmed bodies proliferated in visual footage distributed in a "citational circuit," magnifying the effect of numericality. For those people who did not have direct access to amputees, the humanitarian agencies and their mediatic circuits projected onto a visual plane what they performed in their texts, namely, they used a small, known statistical set of sampling data to attain a disturbing "reality" effect. But these mutilated bodies, on whose behalf and about whom much was narrated visually, seldom spoke for themselves. When they did, their individualization in humanitarian accounts was limited to the narration of their stories of disability, the telling of their names (like Maimouna's) and ages, and the showing of their faces.

My point here is not to dismiss the mediatic role of humanitarians who portray dramatic disasters, magnifying casualties, catastrophes, and critical events in order to elicit sympathy and trigger military and medical intervention.[17] Instead, I want to contrast the sense of the incommensurable gap that belongs to the register of testimony with the closure of signification that is inscribed in humanitarian accounts of brutalized bodies. In a way, the humanitarian project is a biopolitical enterprise that makes use of bare life to tell its story of critical engagement. By contrast, I want to give a different account of the war, one in which the singularization of the victim's own "biography"—its incarnate subjectivity—contrasts with the numerical sampling of statistically stable victims, who become faceless, generic "body-objects" of political science through the visualization of data. Why? Because an excessive emphasis on the "barbaric" nature of this war that offers a mediated representation of the mutilated and violated body and the body's dismemberment eclipses the whole spectrum of the truth of trauma. This includes casualties and deadly events that are locally attributed to the war, even though they appear to be more prosaic because they were purportedly produced by the renunciation of life, by a "spoiled heart"— by an affect. What I want to speak to is the register of the experience of witnessing through a broader range of traumatic war wounds.[18]

## DEATH AND UNEXPECTED INTIMACIES

When I returned to Sierra Leone in 2002, after the war was officially declared over, narratives of those who survived were replete with lists of relatives I had known, who had died during the years since my last—wartime—visit. But when I asked about the modalities of their deaths, I learned only a fraction were casualties of physical brutality; most of the alleged war-related casualties were from apparently "natural" causes. The accounts accompanying the names also revealed the relative intimacy among enemies during phases of the war that were sometimes longer, if less noticed, than the few violent conflicts that punctuated it. But the aggregate number meant the deaths from "natural causes" resisted being categorized as "normal," a fact underscored by Sierra Leone's then ranking at the bottom of the so-called Human Development Index. Here the less singularly named, aggregate notion of "life expectancy" does important work, too: life expectancy for Sierra Leoneans dropped at least ten years, to age thirty-eight, during the civil war, and I present here singular instances of the form this mortality took.

Among the casualties was Foday, one of my neighbors during several long stays in a particular village, who was said to have died in rebel hands. I braced for the details, falling into the trap set by the mediatized representations of the conflict. I expected to hear a story of atrocities of the sort I heard about Braima the hunter, another friend and neighbor. In those stories, Braima died like a warrior, surrounded by rebels who first disarmed him and then cut his throat. This death was consistent in my mind with prevailing narratives of this war. In 1994 or so, when stories began to circulate in the international media about the mobilization of hunter militias, I imagined that Braima might be a prime candidate for a leadership role in such militias. This meant that when a rebel-military junta took power in Sierra Leone over a nine-month period in 1997–98, and began settling scores with those in leadership roles among the hunters who were their enemies, he would have been singled out. In other words, Braima died the death I had expected him to die, assuming he didn't survive.

By contrast, Foday's death in rebel hands appeared less tragic, the result of an illness an elderly man might have contracted even in peacetime—though it may have been brought on by the hardships of imprisonment, as it often was for the "drowned" in Primo Levi's account of Auschwitz. Those inmates in Nazi camps who could not survive through linguistic skills or other kinds of expertise entered the "grey zone" of compromises made to secure enough food for survival or to be assigned to marginally easier forms of labor. More importantly, though, the story of Foday's life and death in rebel hands revealed the complicities and intimacies that often characterize the grey zone of victim-perpetrator relations in conflict, especially long-lasting ones like this civil war. As in other cases, a particular place triggered a different version of Foday's death that changed for me the image of how he became a war casualty.

Once again, this happened on the way to somewhere else, when I came with my companions to a clearing not far from the village where we had been neighbors, where his family had long come to process palm oil. I had often visited them there in prewar days. As my companions told it, Foday heard voices while walking on the same path and came into the clearing to investigate, only to find himself face to face with a band of rebels. They took him to the large camp the rebels had set up across a river in the neighboring chiefdom, leaving behind other family members who had witnessed the scene. While he was in rebel hands, Foday and his family communicated through messages relayed by intermediaries traveling across enemy lines. Often these were women, who were allowed to move more freely than men. Eventually, the family received word that he was ill, and later that he had died and had received a proper burial. This attention to the small gesture of civility—keeping a family informed, giving a body burial—testifies to the fact that social relations could be maintained across enemy lines, especially when people on either side of that divide had conflicted loyalties toward their own sides and intimate knowledge of the "enemy." This fact complicates the picture of the *sobel* conveyed in the previous chronotope.

Foday's story emerged as an individual, particular case from the aggregate list of cumulative "war casualties" described to me. No difference was made among different causes of death when people responded ritually to the timeless question, "*gbe va nya woma?*" (what happened behind my back [while I was away]?), always asked by a returning friend or family member. I had posed the question before the war, and the first response was always a list of the deceased. This way, the circumstances of the death could be revisited, and any questions or information could be brought into the open in a kind of final reckoning for the returning person. This account also provided an opportunity for the person to perform a retroactive act of presence, through a token but tangible contribution (usually money). This gift has affective (in Mende, literally "crying," *ngoo wie*) and material (the shroud, *kasange*) components in the event of death. Thus the whole interval of one's absence was rehearsed in a collective narrative, in which members of the community chipped in to fill the memory gaps of an individual teller, punctuated by deaths but also filled with information about the living. When I returned, after the war and an unusually long absence, the list was extensive, but the retellings were punctuated by statements such as "this war took away this person," which suggested a more univocal attribution of all wartime deaths to the conflict itself. And, too, this time the narrative had more young people on the list. To provide context for why people attributed wartime deaths to what appeared to be unrelated illnesses, I turn now to my wartime visit to this particular village.

### DYING OF A "SPOILED HEART" *(NDI NYANI)*

It was a feeling in the air. When I returned in 1993, three different groups of combatants, some French speakers and others who spoke English with Liberian accents, had just passed through. And yet I experienced only relative calm during my visit, as people tried to return to their ordinary farming activities. I say "tried" advisedly: evening conversations were peppered with references to the several days and nights the villagers spent sleeping in the bush, where the entire village had hidden during these raids. Days were regularly interrupted by someone's death, and the funeral arrangements that followed, and were constantly remarked on, occurred with a frequency unknown before the war.

What was uncanny at this time was the fragility of the sense of normalcy, the way insignificant events unmasked a generalized, thinly disguised tension. It was enough for a man in uniform to walk alone into the village one day, asking about "a white woman," for people to grab me and hide me in a house, or for a new face to appear among a group of visitors for us all to become suspicious. Note that this was the period (1993) when the neologism *so-bel* gained currency, which by joining together *soldier* and *rebel* underscored the fragility of the distinction between opposing factions—or at the very least that these factions were in practice virtually indistinguishable for the civilian population on whom they equally preyed. Amid this uncertainty, people were dying, and those who mourned them understood their deaths to be caused by "a spoiled heart."

Small communities like this one (200–300 people), where before the war a year would go by with no more than one or two deaths among its senior elders, were losing them at much higher rates. On one particular day, we were gathered to celebrate the seven-day sacrifice for the death of a household head, who also happened to be a very skilled blacksmith—an especially serious loss—when a man ran into the gathering to announce that the chief's speaker had just died in another village compound. He was ill, but coming one day after the death of a third senior member of the community, this announcement was greeted with a sense of shock, of the uncanny, of ordinary life torn asunder. Hyperbolic representations of violence and its casualties, like the mediatic representations discussed earlier, which are expressed in the active voice, occlude the fact that one of the most terrifying aspects of the death and fear wrought by war unfolds in the passive voice, in the cessation of a life that is not immediately and recognizably linked directly to physical brutality but is instead attributed to a renunciation of the will to live. The rapid acceleration of "ordinary" deaths meant that the living were also war fatalities. They were left with "spoiled hearts" in a different sense, caused by grief and loss. In rural areas of Sierra Leone, therefore, "letting oneself die" was by far more common, and was in some ways equally brutal from the perspective of the witnesses, than the spectacularized and horrific killings represented in the humanitarian reports. It was an experience that cut across cultural and ethnic factions, disclosing the tragedy of the civil war in the common idiom of letting go.

# 3

# Hunters, Warriors, and Their Technologies

What has returned with war, or remains of it, has nothing obviously to do with military technologies. For these technologies have never stopped being used during the course of all quasi-wars, guerrilla wars of liberation and their repression, or in all the political, economic, or judicial police operations. What is achieved primarily by the technologies regarded as properly military can be just as well, if not better, achieved by the use of so-called civil technologies put to military purposes. In fact, it is almost impossible to distinguish between these two.
—Jean-Luc Nancy, "War, Right, Sovereignty—Techne"

In the National Museum of Sierra Leone, a display case contains a strip-woven, brown cotton tunic with amulets and cowry shells sewn onto its external and internal surfaces. It is flanked by a cap in the same material, also laden with amulets and a medicinal fat-filled animal horn, and other objects associated with the *Kamajor* militias active during the civil war. The accompanying text explains that, while the civil war had "disrupted many cultural traditions," others, "paradoxically," had been revived: "These 'war vests' speak to how local militias revived traditional hunting lore as a weapon in modern conflict," the text continues, to defend communities in the absence of protection from the national army. Later the text refers to vests as *ronko*s, protective garments for hunters facing the dangers of nighttime hunting in the forest. During the war, these vests became a "kind of magical flak jacket" and "almost a uniform" for the hunter militia that emerged as one of the war's factions (fig. 11).

The cultural referents in the text and iconic display of the museum speak not so much of a revival but rather of a hybrid bricolage of terms

**FIGURE 11.** Kamajor outfit on display at an exhibit dedicated to Kamajor lore at the National Museum of Sierra Leone. Freetown, 28 April 2012. Photo by author.

and traditions from disparate cultural areas in the country. Thus the colonial-era spelling of the Mende word for "hunter" (*kamajor*), the majority language in southeastern Sierra Leone, is juxtaposed with the word for tunic in Limba, *ronko*, an ethnic group and language from the country's north. The linguistic mix also points to the juxtaposition of different hunting traditions and idioms in the areas historically linked to the thirteenth- to seventeenth-century Mali Empire and its Manden cultural assemblage. The hilly savannah of northern Sierra Leone and beyond, which is inhabited by the Limba, is contrasted with the coastal areas and forested hinterlands of the southern half of Sierra Leone, which are more closely related to Atlantic Africa—where the Mende are mostly based.[1] This bricolage of different hunting idioms (variously named *Tamaboro, Gbethi,* and *Kamajɔ* in the country's multiple languages) was the product of the redeployment and reorganization of hunters as war militias during the 1991–2002 civil war, which were overseen by local actors as much as by national politicians and the international media. Bricolage was conveyed visually by the juxtaposition of protective amulets with weapons of modern warfare.

The text in the museum exhibit also points to the reinvention of hunting traditions in the service of warfare and locates its roots in the region's history, but this is in fact an artifact of the 1991–2002 conflict itself. Thus the rise of hunter militias during the civil war offers us a glimpse of how, in times of crisis, history offers a rich landscape from which familiar institutions, idioms, and practices can be creatively transformed, and in the process become something different, under the legitimizing guise of tradition. But it also offers an example of the ways in which a superficial resemblance to earlier phenomena can mask a different logic of violence—the cynegetic versus warfare. One of the key transformations of hunters, halfway through the civil war, was the consolidation of a heterogeneous array of locally organized groups into a national paramilitary force aligned with the civilian government elected in 1996, after which the state began to issue them identity cards. In 2002, a demobilized rural hunter brought out several IDs he had been given at different times since 1996, each marking a change in his status. "At first—he said in Mende—we were just ordinary hunters (*honta gbama gbama*). But then we became *kamajɔsia* (*mu wotea a kamajɔsia*) . . . when Hinga Norman became minister, and they gave us these IDs."[2]

During the earlier phase of the conflict, when, under the authority of paramount chiefs, local hunters organized in an ad hoc fashion, and according to diverse ethnic, linguistic, and historical logics, to protect rural civilians from the incursions of various armed factions, the man used a vernacularized form of the English word, hunter (*honta*). This was remarkable given that, as a Mende speaker, he had always used the word *kamajɔ* for hunter in the years leading up to the civil war. By contrast, at the end of the conflict, he used the Mende word, *kamajɔsia* (the plural for hunter), to refer to the time, during the second half of the decade, when the heterogeneous local hunting groups that had organized around the country became integrated under the national umbrella of the Civil Defense Force (or CDF, of which more below).

Thus when they were closer to their home communities and to their historical mission as explorers of the forest and stewards of their resources, these groups did not figure prominently as "hunters" (*kamajɔsia*) in the representations of the war that came to shape postfacto histories of the conflict. At that time, when they did go into combat alongside the Sierra Leonean military, the South African private contractors of the "Executive Outcomes" firm—who had been hired by the National Provisional Ruling Council government in 1995 (see Howe 1998, 313–15)—or the Nigerian contingent of the Economic Community of West African States Monitoring Group (ECOMOG), they served primarily as guides and trackers. Their names reflected their heterogeneous and local histories: *tamaboro* in Kuranko and Mandingo-speaking parts of the north, *gbethi* in Temne, and *kamajɔ* in Mende. Part of what made them "just" hunters, according to my friend, was that they had not yet undergone the process of bureaucratic recognition, state regulation, and induction in a national force for which the Mende name *kamajɔ* came to stand. So in saying that he was "not yet a *kamajɔ*," he was acknowledging that the term *kamajɔ* had become unmoored from its earlier Mende culture and history. The term and the militias to which it applied had now been captured by elements of the state apparatus, a process completed with the unification of the disparate hunter militias under the umbrella of the national CDF. Among the multiple signs of homogenization of disparate paramilitary groups within a single entity was the use of the term *kamajɔ* for all of them—a semantic process retroactively sanctioned in its enshrinement in the National Museum exhibit as a national phenomenon connected with the 1991–2002 civil war.

In my friend's telling, he became a *kamajɔ* when he was issued an identification card that had his name and portrait on the front and the *kamajɔ* box checked on the back. The state's legal documentation, in other words, made my friend a *kamajɔ*, not his earlier life as a skilled and successful hunter. The assigning of a legal document, correlated with the ritual induction into the new army, redeployed hunters within a regulatory entity that launched them on the national scene, under the leadership of renown initiators and the deputy minister of defense, Samuel Hinga Norman, who was also a Mende regent chief. In a parallel move, the figure of the hunter wore his storied, strip-woven, brown kola-dyed tunic, with each additional appendage to the shirt chronicling specific protections, experiences, and hunts, which those left behind incorporated into their evening storytelling sessions. These tunics became visible through media representations only when prewar double-barreled hunting guns, which were often artisanally made, were replaced by semiautomatic rifles or rocket-propelled grenade launchers and other weapons of modern combat.

In what follows, I trace the layered history and multiple genealogies of the figure of the hunter that emerged from the 1991–2002 civil war, and its eventual hyphenation with the warrior, in spite of epistemological, technological, and political differences in their genealogies. I begin by analyzing how the prewar *kamajɔ*, who often hunted alone in the area where I worked and acquired his skills through individual apprenticeship with an experienced practitioner, gave way to the hunter as member of an esoteric association that required initiation and enforced codes of conduct, body discipline, and so on, during the conflict. I suggest that this is in part because of hybrid conflations and borrowings among different hunting traditions elsewhere, made possible in part by increased mobility and a growing awareness of regional hunting traditions, both elsewhere in Sierra Leone and beyond. These hunters were celebrated by governments as examples of local folklore heroism and by global environmental NGOs as potential stewards and conservers of a forest environment at risk. During the 1990s, with violence encroaching upon several West African states, many of which had poorly trained and supported militaries, some countries, including Sierra Leone, turned to organized hunting groups for protection. I now turn to an analysis of the technologies and awareness of alternative, nonrural genealogies of hunting traditions.

## THE ASSOCIATIONAL LIFE OF WEST AFRICAN HUNTERS

Hunting associations have a long and storied past in the Mande-speaking forest and savanna belts of West Africa within the confines of the Mali empire (see Cashion 1982; Cissé 1964, 1994; McNaughton 1982). However, as I mentioned above, Sierra Leone sits at the southern periphery of this historical, linguistic, and cultural area. The Sierra Leonean hunter militias that emerged during the civil war were not straightforwardly linked with earlier hunting practices in this region, nor for that matter were they always forest based or rural. Nonetheless, they appealed to the evocative power of tradition, adopted clothes modeled on historical hunting dress, and even performed in public spectacles in the years leading up to the war.

During the war, the militias amplified and made public any prewar esoteric initiation rituals to lend legitimacy to their modern combat techniques and roles in the civil war. They put a "civil technology" to military purposes—in the words of Jean-Luc Nancy, cited in this chapter's epigraph—because in some ways the assemblage of skills, expertise, and materials required in hunting departs from those used in violent warfare in the Mende world, even though these two worlds intersected in some instances.

Initially formed under the leadership of local chiefs to address the failure of the army to protect civilians caught up in the ongoing conflict, the incorporation of *kamajɔ*s into a national defense apparatus closely allied with the government of President Ahmed Tejan Kabbah, who was first elected in 1996, and appeared to be a classic illustration of what Deleuze and Guattari wrote about the state's ability "to appropriate this war machine that is foreign to it and make it a piece in its apparatus, in the form of a stable military institution" (Deleuze and Guattari 1987, 230).[3] On the other hand, the hunting militias were not merely passive bystanders controlled by state power. In the service of combat, they used new forms of esotericism introduced under the aegis of tradition during the second half of the civil war. Institutionally, this process, which even Deleuze and Guattari recognized to be unstable and easily reversed, was instantiated by the appointment of the CDF leader, Samuel Hinga Norman, as deputy minister of defense in Kabbah's government.

The hyphen linking hunters to warriors—the overlap between their roles in West African history—is tenuous at best, though it is perhaps made compelling by the firearms they alone shared in rural Sierra Leonean history. The skills, expertise, and technologies that shape the use of guns to hunt animals are different from the requirements of continuous violence in combat, as are the philosophical, technical, and sociocultural roles of hunter and warrior. As Deleuze and Guattari (1987, 395–96; emphasis in original) suggested in *Mille Plateaux,*

> The war machine releases a vector of speed so specific to it that it needs a special name; it is not only the power of destruction, but "dromocracy" (= *nomos*). Among other advantages, this idea articulates a new mode of distinction between the hunt and war. For it is certain not only that war does not derive from the hunt, but also that the hunt does not promote weapons: either war evolved in the sphere of indistinction and convertibility between weapons and tools, or it used to its own advantage weapons already

distinguished, already constituted. As Virilio says, war in no way appears when man applies to man the relation of the *hunter* to the animal, but on the contrary when he captures the force of the *hunted* animal and enters an entirely new relation to man, that of war (enemy, no longer prey).

The fundamental difference between the violence of hunting and that of combat is that in the latter it becomes durable—even unlimited. In Sierra Leone, the guerrilla warfare practiced by the *kamajɔs* came very close to the type of war described in Deleuze and Guattari's text. Under the guise of esoteric techniques of concealment in hunting, the *kamajɔs* carried out a modern form of combat, with sometimes carnivalesque overtones in their choice of disguises. Furthermore, superficial technical similarities, such as the presence of guns, or "magical flack jackets," should not be mistaken for technological similarities. Nancy's opening quote to this chapter is drawn from reflections prompted by the first Gulf War, in Iraq. This was one of the first wars to deploy now-familiar language about the precision of remote "surgical bombings," in a conflict that initially envisioned virtually no American and allied "boots on the ground." Nancy (2000) wrote that discourses that focused on the new technologies "had nothing to do with thinking through [the question of] technology; instead, they espoused all the established prejudices, problems, or aporias of the war itself" (115), in which "war-with-missiles is neither better or worse than war-with-catapults; it is still a question of war" (116). Sierra Leonean expressions of the relationship between hunting and warfare embodied in the mythopoetic figure of the *kamajɔ* required knowledge of the potentially duplicitous nature of behavior. Though some of the hunters recruited to these militias did embody this historical knowledge and earlier techniques of violence, there was a generational gap between this group and the young recruits brought in by the civil war, who did not have the same experiences and long apprenticeships. For a time, the civil war in Sierra Leone brought them together under the pressing demand for a technique of combat, yet they deployed fundamentally different technologies of war.

## TRANSLOCALITY AND THE MULTISCALAR: WEST AFRICAN HUNTERS

The Sierra Leone hunter organizations were part of a broader phenomenon that spread across West Africa during the 1990s (for instance, the *dozos* in Côte d'Ivoire and Burkina Faso; see Hellweg 2011; Hagberg

2004). During that decade, hunting associations gained prominence across West Africa, aided in part by transnational phenomena, such as the rise of environmentalism on a global scale and of nongovernmental organizations that helped national groups forge connections across state lines to protect endangered animal species and forest habitats, where hunters made their living. At the same time, in several countries in the region, and because of the state's redeployment away from the provision of services and infrastructure in its historical welfarist conception, hunters gained access to NGO arenas such as environmental protection (see Leach 2000), the mediation of disputes between cattle herders and farmers arising from demographic pressures on rural lands, and the provision of security (e.g., Hellweg 2011; Hagberg 2004; Traoré 2004)—both public and private. In Sierra Leone, too, hunters became a cultural phenomenon that could be "securitized" and politicized. The revitalization of hunting associations and their repurposing for new roles were a fit for a particular moment in the historical rearticulation of states in the aftermath of the structural adjustment programs of the 1980s.

The northern half of Sierra Leone shares with the Mande world a history of hunters organized in associations, but the southeastern part of the country—where Mende is spoken—is outside this zone. The closeness of the words *Mande* and *Mende* notwithstanding, major differences were introduced between these two worlds over several centuries by the insertion between them of Atlantic languages and people. This separation was further accentuated, beginning in the sixteenth century, by the seaward turn of coastal peoples toward the European economic and political presence in the trading entrepots of the Atlantic shores and their hinterlands.[4] The cleavage between the Mande world of the centralized Saharan and Sahelian Muslim states, whose economies depended on revenues from trans-Saharan trade and the exploitation of slavery, on the one hand, and the smaller, heterogeneous, and more decentralized polities of the coastal forest belt, on the other, also gave rise to myriad sociocultural, economic, and political articulations between these zones. Muslim clerics and traders from the north moved into the forest belt, bringing along indigo, cattle, and technologies ranging from weaving to firearms, while commodities prized in the desert regions, like kola nuts, moved northward from the south.

Techniques of governance overlapped with these exchanges. When Sofa warriors under the command of the Malinke Samori Ture moved south into Sierra Leone in the 1880s, they brought with them the hybrid politico-military practices that had enabled their leader to parlay his military services as a war chief into political rule in newly formed states to the north (Tymowski 1981, 432–33). Descendants of this Malinke (Mandingo) migration are still part of the political and economic land-scape of Sierra Leone at multiple levels, ranging from "stranger" (foreign) ruling families in rural chiefdoms to Alhaji Ahmed Tejan Kabbah, who was the country's two-term president from 1996 onward. As discussed in chapter 4, among these nineteenth-century implants was the clan of the paramount chiefs who ruled Wunde chiefdom from the 1930s for some six decades, and who, even as they settled and intermarried with the local Mende population, continued to maintain ties with their homeland in Guinea. Some married Mandingo women, and the language (prevalent in Guinea) was spoken in their compound. They also hosted Guinean Qur'anic teachers. Thus their Sierra Leonean compounds could become linguistic enclaves within their Mende-speaking surroundings, with fam-ily members switching to Malinke whenever they wanted to communi-cate without being generally understood. This history, however, also made this rural area remarkably multilingual and cosmopolitan.

I shall return to this history below, but first I want to discuss the "regionalization" and translocality of the associational life of West Afri-can hunters. The 1990s saw an expansion of the roles of hunting associa-tions in countries ranging from Guinea to Côte d'Ivoire, Mali, and Burkina Faso. In Côte d'Ivoire, for example, hunters were increasingly hired as urban and rural security guards across the country, to stem a ris-ing tide of crime that the state's national army could not control. But beginning in the middle of the decade, the Ivoirian government began to regulate hunting associations for fear of the veritable "social movement" the expanding role of hunters helped set in motion, and of their potential alliance with the political opposition (Hellweg 2011). It did so by restrict-ing hunting associations and their activities to their "geographical zone of origin, which is the North," where they were "part of ancestral traditions" (Bassett 2004, 41; see also Hellweg 2011, chs. 6, 7). In other words, once the genie was out of the bottle, the government appealed to history and tradition to "localize" hunters in areas far from the capital and urban areas to which they had moved, depriving them of any brokerage power within national political alliances. This would seem to prove Deleuze and Guattari's point that the state by means of its appara-tus of capture (its assemblage) has enormous power in coopting and neu-tralizing the revolutionary power of potentially critical social movements. Variously understood as social movements, as symptoms of decentralization or of the privatization of state functions—in particular, the provision of security and the management of natural resources (see Leach 2000; Hellweg 2004, 2011; Hagberg 2004)—the expansion of hunting associations and their public visibility also appealed to collective representations of cultural heritage in rapidly urbanizing countries (Traoré 2004). As the Ivoirian case underscores, hunting associations were in many cases part of the state apparatus from the outset, providing sometimes more responsive, better-disciplined security than the police did at the time. In other Ivoirian locales and times, however, hunters themselves took the initiative in capturing elements of the state apparatus.

Among the political strategies available to hunting associations once they became coopted by the state was a "scaling up" of their activities from local-ethnic to national, and even transnational, stages, as happened over the course of the civil war in Sierra Leone. As their roles underwent a radical transformation, so too did their way of relating to space: from the local and ethnically marked context of influence of the hunters preying on animals to more far-reaching forms of securitization in both rural and urban areas as they transformed into a paramilitary force. Conversely, as the Ivoirian case also illustrates, a state presented with the increasing strength and organization of hunting associations could contain them by "scaling down" their range from the national arena to a particular region (in this case, the north), by bringing into play identity politics, tradition, and folklore and by representing them as ethnically based groups (Bassett 2004). As we shall see, this move was also attempted in Sierra Leone, to counter the increasing power of hunter militias once they became an integrated force within the Sierra Leone People's Party government.

The rituals and exotic appearance of hunters, attired in clothes covered with amulets and protective medicines, made them visible bearers of ethnicized "culture" for locals as well as foreigners. In Sierra Leone, in addition to their exotic appearance, these visual markers of "culture" included food taboos, the avoidance of sex before going into battle, and the invocation of songs that reiterated the rules imparted during initiations, which became large public events that were unprecedented in pre–civil war times. At the same time, the authority of well-known initiators, such as Mama Munda in the town of Bo, and Alieu Kondewa in the Bonthe District was reinforced through these public performances. While some initiates fell under the psychological spell of these powerful initiators, who claimed supernatural powers, others were cynical about these claims. But even they feared transgressing some of these prohibitions amid the rumors of sacrificial killings and the spectacular mutilations and murders that characterized this civil war.

These initiators only acquired this prominent status on the national scene during the second half of the civil war. By contrast, during the earlier phases of the civil war, the hunter militias derived their legitimacy mostly from their embeddedness within local patronage networks. The international media, humanitarian actors, and scholars brought to the scene in this earlier phase of this regional conflict focused on the role of these militias as grassroots, local responses to abuses perpetrated against civilians in wartime, or in the midst of rampant criminality. As I mentioned above, the role of hunters as protectors of the land is what captured the imagination, but under the leadership of Sam Hinga Norman, and especially after the elections of 1996, it was their institutionalization as a paramilitary force that launched them on the national scene and brought them in closer association with a Mende identity. This reliance of the government on a paramilitary force produced tensions within the Sierra Leone Army, whose resources, food, and salary allocations had to be shared with the Civil Defense Force. The discontent to which this led was one of the key factors in the 25 May 1997 coup that overthrew the government of President Kabbah, who had been elected the previous year (see Riley 1997, 290; Zack-Williams 1997). This coup, orchestrated jointly by rogue elements of the army and the rebels of the Revolutionary United Front (RUF), led to "the junta time," a chronotope of sorts, for many Sierra Leoneans experienced and later remembered this as one of the most brutal phases of the civil war.

In addition to taking up prominent roles in the cultural politics *and* politicized cultures of their individual countries, hunting associations developed transnational networks, and international meetings served to share ideas, skills, and technologies. Thus a former Ivoirian civil servant was inspired to found an environmentalist hunting association in his hometown using lessons learned at a meeting of hunting associations in Mali (Hellweg 2011, 140). As a result of these exchanges, even hunters in remote rural areas became aware of their membership in transnational networks, making it difficult to reduce hunting associations to a local phenomenon, even though in many instances their links to particular communities and traditions were key to their legitimacy. But their increased popularity cannot be understood without attending to the ways in which these associations played into the demands within states for private services once provided as public goods and the demands of international donors for certain forms of decentralization. These trends, in turn, were often an aspect of global dynamics—such as those exerted by environmentalists, global governance reformers, and the NGOs animated by their values. In all these instances, treating West African hunting associations as "traditional," local, and overwhelmingly cultural phenomena misses key elements of their modern—and changing—character. More importantly, it overlooks the fact that there is a mutually constitutive relationship between state power and local politics, which informs not only the ethnicity and traditionalism of some hunter groups but also their transcendence of local attachments in some instances.

The Sierra Leonean case underscores the salience of the hunters' local attachments, not only for their quest for legitimacy, but also for their ability to transcend particular ethnic affiliations as they became a national phenomenon—a phenomenon flagged by the linguistic bricolage in the museum display of "Kamajor War Vests" (fig. 11). In 1992, when hunters first became involved in combat in the Sierra Leone civil war, these militias were quite heterogeneous. In some areas they were organized under the leadership of the Poro secret society for men, in others, they were under the protection of paramount chiefs, and in others yet they mobilized to protect refugee camps established near the major towns in the country's interior (see Muana 1997, 85–96). From the beginning, groups also formed at the level of districts and provinces. Among the first civil defense militias were those formed in the eastern region, near the Liberian border—whence came the fighters and resources that sparked the conflict in Sierra Leone. This area also encompassed the diamond-rich parts of the country, which the RUF rebels had occupied on several occasions in 1992–94. Among the early forms of mobilization were, in 1992, the Eastern Region Defense Committee and the Kailahun District War Effort Committee, both located in the country's eastern region (see Henry 2000, 46).

A number of these local and loosely organized defense committees were made up of hunters, but some were not. In rural areas, hunters knowledgeable of the local terrain were used first as guides for regular troops, and especially for the foreign mercenaries hired by the government, whose army was increasingly no match for the growing ranks of the RUF rebels (Rubin 1997, 47). Experienced hunters do have an exceptional knowledge of the forest and of animal behavior, and are also thought to be capable of securing spiritual protections against dangerous forest beings. Hunters' ability to move in and out of hidden trails in the forest shaped their epistemology and local politics. Their knowledge of the land and esoteric technologies enabled them to translate relations of knowing (a move on the ground) into relations of power (political decisions). As they scaled up to the national stage, the forms of ritualization became more publicly staged. The claims of *kamajɔ* initiators increased, to include the esoteric power to make fighters impervious to bullets, for which combatants consulted them in large numbers.[5]

But it is also important to note that, despite the representations dominating the international media during the war, the association of hunters with the forest could be misleading, as increasingly the *kamajɔsia* were recruited among not just farmers but drivers, "casual or seasonal labourers or craftsmen," and other urban under- or unemployed youth (Muana 1997, 88). So while the leadership of these groups in rural villages might well have included expert hunters familiar with the surrounding forest and connected to the local political elites, the recruits brought in when the demands of security called for their expansion were not.

After 1996, representations of the Sierra Leone civil war in both media and scholarship produced increasingly systematic and "Mende-fied" accounts of the hunter militias. In other words, they were identified mostly with Mende ethnic areas in the southeast, in part because of their alliance with the Mende-controlled party in power, and their organization was integrated nationally within the CDF framework. These representations reflected changes within these groups, especially after 1995, but these were political, not ethnic, changes. They were similar to the events that led the southern- and Christian-controlled government in Côte d'Ivoire to contain the hunting associations by portraying them as a northern ethnic and Muslim movement and requiring them to operate only within their "traditional territory" in that region (Bassett 2004).

In the context of the Sierra Leone civil war, iconographic images and writings appeared—reproduced, for instance, by Lueders (1999) and McKenzie (1998)—which represented men wearing exotic clothes and protective amulets but also holding modern combat weapons. The narratives accompanying these images portrayed hunters as reservoirs of moral legitimacy, capable of mobilizing supernatural powers, and as key players in the region's history. The "scaling up" of the hunter militias as a Sierra Leonean national phenomenon, then, coincided with their reduction—at least at the level of representation—to a narrowly Mende ethnic identification. This became especially pronounced after the 1996 victory of the Sierra Leone People's Party, whose political stronghold had historically been the Mende-speaking southeast. In particular, the return to power of the Kabbah government in 1998, nine months after it had been ousted in the RUF-AFRC coup of 25 May 1997, was owing in part to the support of the hunter militias, who kept on operating within the country even as their leadership was in exile in Guinea.

As mentioned above, one of the signs of the "Mendefication" of a much more heterogeneous and hybrid movement was the increasing use of the term *kamajɔ* to designate these heterogeneous militias. Among the early hunting mobilizations were the *tamaboro,* organized in the Kuranko-speaking areas in the north of the country. One of these groups was led by an elderly female healer named Mariamma Keita, whose magical protective amulets were considered especially powerful (Tostevin 1993).[6] In 1993, *tamaboro* militias, who played a key role in an offensive against the RUF there, were deployed outside their region of origin, in the Mende-speaking area of Kailahun, on the Liberian border (Muana 1997, 81). Even while operating in areas far removed from their own home base—as in this case—these forces were still described as "local" militias by the international media (Tostevin 1993, 26).

The northern context of the early mobilization of hunting societies in the civil war served as a model for their expansion into the south. In some parts of southern Sierra Leone, armed hunters practiced their craft individually, though they also gathered in groups for specific occasions, like infringements against hunting etiquette (see Leach 1994, 168) or for the funeral of one of their own—as happened in the village where I was based in 1993, during the civil war. When they mobilized as a protective force during the civil war, hunters were seen initially as popular heroes, disciplined protectors of rural civilians at the mercy of various armed factions, but by the middle of the 1990s, attitudes toward them became more ambivalent, as like the other fighting factions they often became caught up in acts of criminal violence. All along, however, they were already more heterogeneous in their composition than their (Mende) ethnic label would suggest—theirs was an "invented tradition" (Hobsbawm and Ranger 1983). And this tradition was already in formation during the two decades preceding the civil war, through a powerful alliance with the dominant political forces in the country. But this politicization of hunting traditions was also a departure from the historical role of hunters in this region, because the social, economic, and ritual roles of hunters tended to weaken their engagement with the realm of organized, formal politics. The more fitting historical antecedents of the warlord and other figures of warriors who reemerged during the civil war were what in Mende were called *kɔ mahɛi* (war chief), or *kugbei* (warrior)—leaders in armed combat who used violence not so much to provide food for both ordinary and ritual meals, as the hunter did, but for political ends, for example, by conquering and annexing territory.

### THE HUNTER-BLACKSMITH-GUN ASSEMBLAGE

As mentioned above, in contemporary rural Sierra Leone, hunters emerged as potential fighters because, among other things, they were the only members of the civilian population entitled to own and regularly use guns. They also had the local knowledge and technology required for moving in invisible ways and engaging in combat in the bush. Throughout the war, hunters acted as guides for government troops and their allies, an activity for which there were precedents in the region's history (Malcolm 1939, 47–52). In the regional folklore, hunters were also perceived as experts in unmasking and controlling certain kinds of transformations. For example, they had to be able to distinguish between ordinary animals and witches, who could take animal form in order to approach and fight their targets. Their survival at nighttime in the forest depended on this ability, lest they be attacked and killed by the prey they stalked.

The seriousness of the risk hunters run while stalking prey was brought home in 2008, when a young hunter disappeared from a rural community and was found dead the next day on the edge of the forest. He was a "hunter," but of a different kind—he had gone out to check on animal traps he had set in the secondary forest growth interspersed with the village farms. Setting traps in such areas was a common strategy to protect crops and capture game at the same time. His body— I was told—was found amid trampled grass and hoofprints. From the scene and evidence, the villagers who found him concluded the young man had been attacked by water buffaloes, which are considered among the most dangerous animals in rural Sierra Leone. They are especially feared for their large size and unpredictable, aggressive behavior, and their increasing rarity makes the possibility of encountering them the subject of fearsome tales, so it was unclear whether this was indeed the cause of the young man's death.

His past history of depression and a night panic attack or seizure I had witnessed years earlier left open the possibility that he may deliberately have put himself in danger—another instance of the traumatized, "spoiled heart" deaths discussed in the previous chronotope. But as I pointed out there, intentions are difficult to discern after the fact. What is sure is that his family's heart was spoiled by his loss.

Hunters need to be able to tell the difference between animals, on the one hand, and witches transmogrified into animal form, on the other hand: this ability is critical to their survival, while their own mimetic skills are critical to success in pursuit of prey. The hunter's success, in other words, is determined only in part by his ability to detect the presence and behavior of his prey through a highly developed interpretive sense of sight to find tracks, of smell, and of awareness of almost imperceptible traces, such as changes in the texture of forest growth, where the passage of an animal might have snapped a low branch. He also needs to camouflage his *own* presence by putting on masks and special clothing to avoid others (animals, humans, witches) recognizing him. In this respect, hunters inscribe themselves within an established and widespread tradition of trickster figures in West African folklore. Among the best and longest known of these tricksters was Sundiata, the mythical founder of the powerful thirteenth-century Mali Empire, from which the Mande cultural and linguistic expansion that shaped the northern reaches of this forest region emanated. In Mande folklore, Sundiata was a trickster *and* a hunter-warrior, who dissimulated his extraordinary powers in an apparently weak, disabled body, which in most surviving oral traditions is represented as hunchbacked (see Innes 1974).

During the civil war, the trickster figure took on a new shape in the figure of the *sobel*, the so(ldier-re)bel discussed in chronotope 1. In a way, the *sobel*, "Soldier by day, rebel by night," shared with the hunter the use of the matrix of the night to process the (self-) transformations required to elude dangers. In towns, the rise of civil defense forces such as the *kamajɔsia* was a response precisely to the nighttime looting of houses by unknown armed attackers, particularly in 1994, when urban areas and nearby refugee camps saw the arrival of large numbers of displaced people from the countryside (see Keen 2005, 134, on one town; Richards 1996, on an attack in another instance). Thus the rise of the *kamajɔsia* as a militia, and their subsequent integration as a unified CDF phenomenon on the national scene, must be seen relative to this conflict. The lines distinguishing opposing factions and loyalties were porous.

In addition to its association with hunters with shape-shifting skills and with trickster figures, the Mande world on which periphery modern

Sierra Leone sits has shaped a close relationship between this occupation and that of blacksmiths, who carry out dangerous work with fire to forge objects out of metal, including guns. Indeed, blacksmiths are also often accomplished hunters in the broader region (McNaughton 1993). Since the seventeenth century, the relationship between hunting and gunmaking in Sierra Leone has underscored the fact that technical experimentation was also an aspect of the hunter-blacksmith complex. As I have pointed out elsewhere (Ferme 2001a), this was true for a number of reasons, including the need to make do during the economic hardships of the decade leading up to the civil war. In order to procure guns and ammunition, and repair their weapons, hunters and blacksmiths have always been among the most outward-looking members of their societies, the most experimental, the bricoleurs. Indeed, they are the most "modern," and nowhere more so than in the search for materials and the know-how to make guns. It is not a coincidence that in Marcel Griaule's exploration of Dogon life and thought ([1948] 1965), he was instructed to talk with Ogotemmêli—the elderly hunter made blind by the malfunction of his artisanal gun—who became the anthropologist's key informant. Griaule was told the hunter was chosen as his interlocutor because of his hermeneutic expertise in Dogon myths and traditions, but I would argue Ogotemmêli was also selected because of his ability to craft relations with outsiders, and his openness to novelty.

## BRICOLAGE, PATRONAGE, AND MOBILITY

The bricolage element of the hunter's craft, his need to make do with the materials at hand, especially in situations of scarcity, often came to the fore during the 1980s, when the economic hardships imposed by structural adjustment programs regularly caused acute shortages of the cartridges and smelting materials required for gun repairs and hunting—among other things—in rural Sierra Leone. Because a gun was often the most valuable item in a hunter's possession, it was used as loan collateral in times of crisis. Skilled hunters sometimes had to borrow guns to hunt and use any "bush meat" they caught to pay off creditors and retrieve their own weapons. Cartridges were expensive in the 1980s, and could only be found in town stores, so the rural hunter-blacksmiths I knew were sometimes enlisted to reconstitute viable cartridges from spent ones. Alternatively, they sought wealthy patrons—such as chiefs or businessmen—who could front the cost of cartridges against part of their catch. Often these patrons were the traders from whom they bought cartridges.

During the civil war, such personal and business partnerships often developed into protection agreements that led to the expansion of the hunters' roles in providing security (for instance, to the businesses and shops of patrons or benefactors or creditors). Thus the hunters' skills as bricoleurs extended to social relationships, which began as business partnerships and expanded into providing security and other services. But the extension and direction of their networks of bush meat distribution are of interest here, for during the war some local hunters, who had already strengthened exchange links in particular directions, also joined fighting forces there.

One of the local skilled hunters I knew, whom I will call Musa,[7] specialized in killing monkeys, which were in demand in Liberia and were plentiful in the chiefdom, for among other reasons because pious Muslims would not eat them. Sometimes, after the rice harvest was in, several months would go by before one would see him back in the village, even though his wife and son lived there. He once left with a hamperful of smoked monkeys for Liberia and did not return for six months. During the war, anxiety about his whereabouts set his wife in motion too. She took her son and went toward the border region of Kailahun, where her father lived, and for much of the war the (remarried) mother she left behind was unable to see her daughter and grandson, or receive reliable news about them. About her son-in-law, it was rumored that Musa had joined fighting forces in Liberia. By contrast, another local hunter, Braima, whose family connections took him between Wunde and the neighboring Jaiama-Bongor chiefdom, joined the *kamajɔ* militias there. As mentioned in the previous chronotope, Braima had been attacked, tortured, and killed by rebels during the war, while Musa had disappeared. But both were remembered for their powers of narration, based—like those of Ogotemmêli—on their solitary hunting travels in the nighttime bush.

## NIGHT AND DAY . . . HUNTERS AND STORYTELLING FRAGMENTS

Only upon a later return to the Dogon of Mali (a people he characterized as "warrior-farmers") was the French anthropologist Marcel Griaule taken under the stewardship of the blind hunter Ogotemmêli, who told him the stories that make up *Dieu d'Eau: Entretiens avec Ogotemmêli* (1946). The English translation omits the poetic "water God," a reference to the cosmology that preoccupied them during most of their encounters, and elides the ambiguity of "entretiens," which can mean conversations but also interviews. Griaule was on a fact-checking mission of sorts during this return visit, to ensure that his earlier data were correct—a journalistic gesture (the ambiguity of *entretiens*) but also the move of careful scholarship in a durable engagement over time.

Ogottemmêli comes through as a great storyteller—about the past and its traditions, about the behaviors of animals, about the uses of the bush, or about adventurous encounters during the solitary quest for prey. In Sierra Leonean villages, storytelling, like hunting, unfolds during the transitional time between day and night—a time when the epistemic boundaries between truth and "lies" are challenged by this genre. And though hunters, dependent "strangers" in rural areas, and other mobile groups can engage in the occasional evening storytelling to this day, evening entertainment in rural Sierra Leone and itinerant storytellers were a more common sight in prewar rural areas. In Mende, there is no higher praise of itinerant storytellers, who during the dry season travel from village to village to provide evening entertainment, than to say that "he is good at telling lies" (*ngi bɛɛngɔ a ndɛ gula!*), and good performances are punctuated by amused exclamations of "that's a lie!" (*ndɛ mia!*) by members of the audience. Among the Kuranko of the North, writes Michael Jackson (1982, 56),

> There is an exact analogy between storytelling and hunting. It's an analogy recognized by the Kuranko themselves. Keti Ferenke attributes the origins of storytelling to a hunter-*griot,* Fa Braima Yanka, who accompanied the ancestor of Mande hunters, Fabori, and celebrated his heroic deeds. The connection between storytelling and hunting is in the fact that both these activities unfold on the margins. Hunting always happens at night, and hunters move from the village into the deepest forest. . . . Similarly to initiation and hunting, stories are separated from ordinary time and space.

The close relationship between storytelling and hunting is crafted in the liminal space of the nocturnal, the margin, the dark edge of towns, as well as in the dark areas of signification. By pushing language toward the figural, away from the letter, storytelling communicates a world of suspended possibilities for the audience. The initiatic nature of hunting technique is also strengthened by the use of figurative language, in the sense that the best hunters tend to conceal in enigmatic expressions the secrets of their craft, which is often presented as riddles to uninitiated audiences in storytelling sessions (see Ferme 2001b, 27–30). Thus among the technical competences of hunters are hermeneutic skills tied to their aforementioned ability to track down and make the prey's presence visible through the decoding of their traces, their passages in the bush, while concealing themselves. In the telling of narratives, this skill manifests itself in the ability to dissimulate specialized knowledge of hunting techniques in cryptic, apparently meaningless words, whose utterance reveals who in the audience are the expert hunters—those who know how to decode them—and who are the nonhunters. This constitutes a reversal of the order of skills required of the prey to escape the hunter, which are primarily speed and anticipation, rather than decoding signs of an earlier presence, patient waiting, and concealment. The hunter's repertory of expertise is mostly based on methodical, descriptive analysis of the past behaviors of his preys, which amount to an epistemology of the trace and which can offer only predictive clues to the future whereabouts of hunted game.

In Mende, as mentioned earlier, the roles are distinguished at the level of language: the warrior is a *kugbei,* a war chief who also holds political power is a *kɔ mahɛi,* and a hunter is a *kamajɔ.* The game procured by hunters, and bush meat distribution along the patronage networks they formed in the course of their activities, made them socially astute and valued, but this seldom translated into outright political power in rural Mende areas. The very mobility of hunters like Braima, who was often on the move alone, cultivating relations with patrons, procuring cartridges, and finding new hunting grounds and markets for his meat, got in the way of him becoming politically rooted in any given place. Doing so would have required a deep understanding of, and involvement with, local power interests, in order to become an effective political leader. Instead, he was often quite literally out of the loop, returning to the village after several months' absence to find unfolding dynamic social situations, in which he had not been a party from the beginning, which made finding his place difficult.

He was admired and sought after, for instance, as a hunter and killer of pests that consumed the rice crops of farmers, and he maintained a foothold in the social worlds of each of the communities he inhabited through wives and relatives based there. His deep knowledge of the forest, and the fearlessness with which he ventured into it alone at night, made him both valuable and potentially dangerous—during the civil war, he was one of the first casualties in the community, tortured and executed during a rebel attack. Moving freely at night evoked associations with the esoteric realms of witches and sorcerers, hence charging the figure of the hunter with mythical and esoteric meanings and powers. When in the village, Braima used to live in the same compound as two other hunters, who embodied an even stronger link between *kamajɔsia* and metal working, since they were also blacksmiths. These two brothers, who maintained the only forge in the village, had a heavy workload—repairing farming tools, buckets, transforming metal from wrecked vehicles into cutlass blades, hoes, and so on—which limited their movements. For them, therefore, hunting was an occasional activity.

The older among the two, Momoh, was also a well known gunmaker and gun-repairer, so when he worked the forge, other hunters—and men, more generally—gathered to chat while waiting for their tools and weapons to be repaired. Though most villages of more than 250 or so inhabitants tended to have at least one blacksmith in residence, very few of them were able to make guns. This was recognized as a special talent even among blacksmiths, and Momoh was known and sought after from far away for this work. Many of his clients came from outside the chiefdom, and he was the villager who most assiduously asked me—in advance of my trips to town—to buy smelting materials, chemicals, and other materials useful to his work. On one occasion, when a European friend who was a keen hunter came to see me in the village, Momoh began talking with him about technical aspects of gunmaking, and the two established a long-lasting relationship, with my friend supplying Momoh with new materials for gunmaking and smithing experiments and Momoh taking him hunting in the local forest. Despite all this, Momoh did not appear to engage in the kinds of coordinated, ritualized activities described in connection with Mande hunting societies further north in Sierra Leone and elsewhere in West Africa (see Cissé 1964, 1994).

In this region, the only occasion when hunters appeared in public as a group was when Momoh himself died of an illness in 1993, during the civil war. His brother and other hunters from nearby villages took charge of Momoh's body, washing it and preparing it for a Muslim burial, for which important, wealthy mourners came all the way from Freetown, the capital.[8] But generally hunters in this chiefdom did not have a group identity that distinguished them, such as membership in the men's secret Poro Society or in other esoteric healing societies, like the Humoi Society, might have. However, the situation was different in the neighboring chiefdom of Jaiama-Bongor, which was part of the same political constituency, for reasons we will see below. After 1994–95, when rebel incursions in the region destroyed several villages, hunters gathered in the Jaiama Bongor chiefdom, along with their apprentices, to join the *kamajɔ* militias and receive training.[9]

But the technical and sociopolitical skills of hunters were different from those of a nineteenth-century warrior like Samori. Operating in the interstices of the expanding French colonial occupation in the Guinean interior, the disruption of the slave trade, and the new forms of polities emerging in the face of these changes, Samori and his advent to power marked a time when war leaders of organized armies acquired *political* power in the region. During the 1860s and 1870s, Samori, who adopted the title of "war chief," and was never especially known for his hunting skills, became a force in the dynamics of state formation, in part by raising armies loyal to him, which constituted "a new and separate social group unknown to societies pre-dating the formation of the state" (Tymowski 1981, 433). He used existing social institutions like age grades to raise his army, offering guaranteed food, clothing, and training, as well as a share of war spoils, in exchange for service. Furthermore, Samori parlayed his military strength into political power by forging alliances with town chiefs and councils from his own and allied Dyula clans, and, through the security, administrative, and regulatory arrangements he set in place (including taxation), he was a critical force in the emergence of states in this region.

Samori's army was a mercenary force, and among the novel technical advantages in the assemblage mobilized by this remarkable war chief were the horse and the gun, with which his Sofa warriors were equipped. The shock of their horse-mounted attacks in the northern parts of Sierra Leone, where warfare was conducted on foot and using guerrilla tactics under the cover of forest, still informed oral histories collected a century later, in the 1980s. T. J. Alldridge (1910, 291), the British colonial district commissioner discussed earlier, wrote about "the mysterious power that controlled" the Sofas and helped expand "the empire of the mighty Samory . . . Commander of the Faithful." His book includes a photograph of a mounted Sofa warrior he encountered while traveling in northern Sierra Leone (292–93). The religious passion of Samori's empire building notwithstanding—historians often refer to his campaign of military conquests as a jihad, or Muslim holy war (see Person 1968–75)—it also adroitly exploited the competing British and French interests in the region. In the local historical imagination, then, Samori blended political and military skills—he was both a war and a land chief, in Mende parlance, or, rather, he managed to convert military conquests into political sovereignty and administrative control.

The final element accounting for the mythopoeticization of the hunter-blacksmith-gun assemblage, in Sierra Leone in particular, is that in many parts of the country, hunters are linked in oral histories and folktales to settlements founded where a large beast, like an elephant, was killed.[10] Having killed such a large and dangerous beast, a hunter must settle at the site and invite others to join him to consume the animal, lest it go to waste (see, for instance, Hill 1984; Little [1951] 1967, 26–28). Thus, while moving alone in the forest to make his kill, the hunter also enabled human settlement there, through the sociability of food-sharing—elegantly symbolizing the relationship between this region's subsistence on settled, though shifting, agrarian production, and its supplementing by the mobile appropriation of forest resources. The present-day landscape in southeastern Sierra Leone is a mosaic, where settlements are surrounded by farmed tracts, seasonal and permanent waterways, and secondary forest regrowth on fallow land from previous farming seasons, interspersed with stands of mature forest. Very little of this landscape could be accurately described as a *jungle*—a term much used in wartime accounts of Sierra Leone. But this landscape also does not bear much resemblance to the vast continuous tracts of mature forest that up to two centuries ago made up much of this region—a world in which hunting and gathering were key subsistence activities, rather than the supplementary ones they are today.

## THE HUMAN-DOG-NET ASSEMBLAGE

As suggested in the previous section, the differences between hunting and warfare entail disparate human-animal-tool and mobility relations. Even though in conjunction with his horse he could move at great speed—indeed, the horse-rider unit became a fast projectile, an additional tool of warfare—the mounted warriors such as the Sofas of early colonial days were immobile, seated, and elevated above those standing on the ground. By contrast, the hunter moved on foot and close to the ground, blending into his surroundings, while his mobility was circumscribed and purposeful—from point to point—in pursuit of preys whose location he divined from their smell, spoor, tracks, and other traces.

Hunters who used firearms stalked prey at night in the forest, and in silence, but there were collective, daytime hunting expeditions of a different kind, in which the *kamajɔ* did not figure, and for which a different human-animal-tool relation shaped the action. These were the hunting expeditions with nets, beaters, and dogs, referred to as *kp(gb)e*. These contrasted with the *kamajɔ*'s craft, and his solitary wandering, as well as with the technological assemblage required. Not guns but locally made palm rafia nets were used for these daytime hunts. They required the collective participation of a more diverse group of community members of all ages and abilities (including women) and a carefully timed alternation of silence and noisemaking. Here detective and interpretive skills were required only of the beater or "land person" (*ndɔɔ mui*), who first scouted alone a secondary forest tract, where animal traces had been reported. He was then joined by the "dog person" (*ngila mui*)—a human-dog assemblage—and would return to a prey's likely hiding place with him, followed by "net people" (*mboma bla*) carrying ten or more coiled, long nets about four feet wide. Finally, the "noise people" (*sɔlɛ bla*) brought up the back of the expedition. Everyone quietly walked in single file behind the beater and the dog handler, following their hand signals to form a circle around a tract of forest. Male net people would form a semicircle with their nets, pinning them to the ground and propping them up on sticks. Their distance from each other was such that they could provide full coverage with their cutlasses to the section of net they guarded, and as soon as rustling and moving vegetation alerted them that an animal was in flight toward them, they would jump on it and kill it. The open part of the circle, across from the net people, was entered in silence by the beater, the dog handler, and his animals and quickly closed by the noise people. At this point the stealthy, quiet preparations gave way to a cacophony of sound: barking by the unleashed dogs, human shouting, and various other noises made by implements and instruments aimed at scaring the prey out of its lair and into the nets of their silent guardians, which were lying in wait across from them.[11] This was a noisy, exciting moment of the hunt, when everyone's senses were on the alert, people were shouting information about the prey's line of flight, and others were anticipating its entrapment in their nets.

While some of the same interpretive competence of the *kamajɔ* is required in a good beater, the detective quality and experience of the dogs also matters, as the animals ultimately detect the prey's presence and help scare it out of hiding. Beaters borrow each others' dogs if they are especially good in the hunt. Experienced net people were also crucial to the hunt's success, as smaller forest animals could easily escape under the nets if the men closest to their flight path did not see them and react quickly. But the whole tenor of the daytime net hunt made this a collective, sociable affair, in which men and women of all ages could participate as noise people, even though the detection and killing of the prey were reserved to agile, adult men armed with cutlasses—their main farming implements—rather than a specialized weapon. These hunts were called for community-wide events, such as requests by chiefs for food contributions to host visitors at village initiation rituals or by the paramount chief in advance of the annual district officer's visit. They were not for the solitary, nighttime pursuit of prey by a gun-toting *kamajɔ*. The collaborative nature of this kind of hunt, for which women, men, and animals all have specific roles, is mirrored in the consumption of its captured prey in collective ritual or political functions that involve a village, section, or chiefdom community as a whole.[12] Every social category, from chiefs to religious leaders, from women to men's working groups, was entitled to a specific portion of the prey, unless whole animals were designated for a collective village offering to chiefdom events.

The social nature of this form of hunting was also manifested in the sanctions applied if somebody ignored the call to participate. On one occasion in 1990, when a village hunt was called for a chiefdom occasion, a small group of disgruntled young men complained that these random calls, which interrupted their farming activities, were really troublesome, and that the fishpond that one of the villagers had just completed would be a better alternative to provide meat than "town hunts." Nonetheless, they went along, in part because they all knew that ignoring the call to collective town labor could result in hefty fines and punitive labor. So when the leader of this group saw another young man tagging along without his cutlass, he told him that he would sue him, for clearly he was not coming along to hunt. He explained, "We and the animals (*fuhainsia*— living things) have to engage in this fight, and yet he didn't bring a cutlass— clearly he is not here for that reason, for the hunt."

The young man was eventually fined and was made to clear the grass encroaching upon the main access road to the village—an activity often at the center of calls for collective town labor. It was a form of humiliation, since clearing brush on the roadsides was one of the most resented forms of collective labor, and this was the most mundane use of a cutlass that could be required of this man for his failure to use it as a weapon. I was surprised by the gravity of the sanctions for what appeared to be an accidental oversight, even though I had hardly ever seen a man leave a rural village without a cutlass in hand. Mende proverbs and folk expressions underscore the metonymic relationship between cutlasses and their male owners, who keep them carefully sharpened and spend hours at the smithy discussing the finer attributes of new or repaired blades for these tools. They are used for a range of purposes, from farming to self defense against animal and human aggressors.

Just as the *kamajɔ*-blacksmith-gun assemblage was at the heart of the night hunt, the beater-dog-net assemblage characterized the occasional collective hunts called by village and chiefdom authorities. And while in the latter assemblage, a human-animal unit used a specialized net, this was only a modified form of the nets used for fishing and of the hammocks used by men to sit and rest. Furthermore, the main killing implement in this form of hunt, the cutlass, also underscored its continuities with the ordinary implement of daily life, as opposed, as I mentioned above, to a specialized weapon like the *kamajɔ*'s gun. Finally, while—as I suggested earlier—the *kamajɔ* hardly has the attributes of a warrior, and is seldom a skilled political actor, the collective hunt is predicated on social and political cooperation. It can even be imposed on resentful, unwilling participants, and failure to participate can be punished and become the occasion for further rifts in a community. This is the case precisely because the events that call for collective hunts tend to be political from the outset.

## FROM "CULTURAL" HUNTERS TO CIVIL DEFENSE MILITIAMEN

During the decade preceding the civil war, the only context in which hunters appeared publicly as a group in the rural Wunde chiefdom was in staged performances organized by paramount chief B. A. Foday-Kai, in the neighboring chiefdom of Jaiama-Bongor. These staged performances are critical for understanding the dramatic rise in visibility and power of *kamajɔ* militias in this very chiefdom during the 1991–2002 civil war, and their eventual transformation into the CDF. (Samuel Hinga Norman was in part responsible for this transformation and became the CDF's leader, as well as the country's deputy minister of defense after 1996. He became regent chief in Jaiama-Bongor after Foday-Kai' death.) "B. A.," as he was known everywhere in Sierra Leone, was a prominent Mende man, as well as an educated and cosmopolitan former civil servant. In 1977, he represented Sierra Leone at FESTAC, the second World Black and African Festival of Arts and Culture, held in Nigeria, and this spectacle of cultural politics, in which high modernism, contested perspectives on Pan-Africanism, and Nigerian nation-building were on display, left an indelible impression on Foday-Kai.[13] It helped that the shared history of Nigeria and Sierra Leone—whose Krio population and language originated among the Yoruba-speaking freed slaves, settled in the region surrounding Freetown from the 1820s onward—was the object of special note at FESTAC. As Nunley observes, a Sierra Leonean performing group "won the hearts of many FESTAC fans for their fanciful and traditional masquerades," making a big splash in the regional press. In response to this success, the government liberalized its regulation of public masquerades and other cultural entertainment at home as well (Nunley 1982, 42). Masked performances could trigger unpredictable, violent outcomes, particularly during times of heightened political tension. The mask had the power to evoke both fear and laughter, and depending on the entertainment context, this could have dangerous consequences. During public spectacles, a performer was equipped with a range of objects used in ordinary life. But in the ritual context of the performance, these very tools could be directed aggressively toward members of the audience. The divertissement of the public spectacle could dramatically shift register and take on the potentially dangerous outcomes of ritual performance. The shift from one register to the other was undecidable and unpredictable, and it loaded the performance with multiple meanings and expectations.

Foday-Kai often remarked that FESTAC was for him a turning point, when he realized the importance of cultural heritage. On his return, he became a patron of traditional Sierra Leonean arts and crafts, for which he became well known thereafter in his own country. B. A. was often invited to write and give lectures about "Mende culture" for the Freetown diplomatic community and for Peace Corps training sessions, and he traveled to Europe and the United States for the same purpose.

During the 1980s, Foday-Kai's chiefdom headquarter, in Telu, was the site of workshops to preserve or revive older Mende traditional crafts and performances, such as the costumes, which were modeled on colonial era photographs, and had long since disappeared elsewhere in the country (e.g., Alldridge 1901, 138, fig. 45), with which he equipped dancers for girls' initiations into the women's Sande society. B. A. also sponsored the training in his compound of several young weavers in the complicated and largely abandoned techniques of weaving the *kpɔkpɔ wa*, a cotton cloth made from broader and more ornate strips than the striped cloths still used as blankets, chiefly robes, and prestige gifts. B. A. insisted on the use of locally grown and spun cotton, and of older, natural dyeing techniques, even though most weavers elsewhere routinely incorporated imported threads and chemical dyes in their work. Foday-Kai considered his promotion of historical heritage to be an aspect of his educated, development-oriented outlook, and not of his traditional rural upbringing. He never wore "traditional" chiefly garb except for the cultural performances he sponsored, preferring instead T-shirts, jeans, and a cowboy hat sent to him by his son, who lived in Texas. It was through this work as a patron of traditional crafts that Foday-Kai became known as a cultural broker, both among his Mende subjects and among foreign visitors. Having learned, through FESTAC, that iconography, cultural objects, and displays could be an entry ticket to the global stage, and provide political capital as well, he became a cosmopolitan promoter of Mende traditions.

During several visits with B.A., I witnessed what he referred to as "cultural dances," among them one involving "warriors," or *kugbeisia.* These were occasions ranging from national political events like party congresses, to the sendoff celebration for my own departure at the end of my first fieldwork stint in Sierra Leone. Foday-Kai participated in person, with a group of older men from his Jaiama-Bongor Chiefdom. The dancers were all dressed in locally woven, strip-cotton shirts, dyed brown with kola nuts and decorated with duiker and other animal horns filled with medicinal substances, bundles, cowrie shells, and other decorations typical of Mande hunter ceremonial attire (see McNaughton 1982, 54–58). These shirts also served as models for the *"Kamajor* war vests," made famous again during the 1991–2002 civil war and displayed thereafter in the National Museum. The performances consisted of choreographed, slow dance movements in a circle, in which the warriors brandished swords in mock battle, while spinning around for the audience. Thus in the years preceding the civil war, a certain slippage was at work between the figure of the warrior and the historical attire of Mande hunters in these hybrid cultural performances devised for entertainment purposes. The revival of these masked dance performances was certainly part of the renewed visibility of the hunter's role in the Mende social imaginary. It legitimated the uses of secret power and symbols for the realization of political hegemony.

The popular discourse had prefigured, in the form of the *sobel,* the soldier-rebel alliance that in 1997 came to power in the country in the guise of the AFRC-RUF junta. Similarly, the collective imaginary terrain for the rise of hunters as a fighting faction in the civil war was prepared, well in advance of that conflict, by the cultural bricolage of expert politician-entertainers such as Foday-Kai. In this it was aided by transnational events such as FESTAC, where cultural heritage was theatrically staged, and the "hunter congresses" described by Hellweg and others for hunting associations in Francophone West Africa.

Chief Foday-Kai died in 1989, several months before the war broke out in Liberia, and more than one year before it moved into Sierra Leone. In Telu, chiefly succession would have been complicated at best, given the fact that alluvial diamond mining in the chiefdom could bring considerable wealth to any successor paramount chief whose role would be crucial in securing mining rights. In the event, it also became inextricably tied up with the arrival of the civil war in the region. The chiefship remained vacant until Sam Hinga Norman, who had been a career military man and was not even originally from this chiefdom, was installed as regent chief.

Chiefdom elders were eager participants in the cultural exhibitions—including those involving hunter-warriors—staged by Foday-Kai during his chiefship, in part because of the social and political visibility they acquired through them. These performances played out well in Jaiama-Bongor politics as well, since being asked to join them was understood as showing public support for the paramount chief—something not insignificant in a chiefdom rich in alluvial diamonds. Recall that it was the diamond economy that brought hunters from neighboring chiefdoms here in search of wealthy patrons, who could furnish them with cartridges and other materials they required. And the chiefdom's diamonds were also an element in the links established on the global scene between the paramount chief and economic actors, such as the Lebanese businessmen and others who came to Foday-Kai seeking support in exercising mining rights.[14]

These were the kinds of networks and social connections that later on put Hinga Norman in a position to organize and arm his hunter militias (see Muana 1997) as a defense force. Thus Foday-Kai had managed to convert the economic and cultural capital accumulated from his chiefdom base into a powerful political position on both local and national levels. More remarkable yet, he had managed to do this in part through an idiosyncratic mythopoesis of hunting lore and public exhibitions, loosely based on West African Mande traditions, which informed his exhibitions at political and recreational events. Also at the state level, he was a consumed politician, who throughout his career had covered a number of roles in civil service, party politics, and parliament. As a paramount chief (a "land chief" in Mende), he managed to capture the hunters' dispositions and aesthetic for display at state spectacles—the installation of a new member of parliament and the entertainment of official dignitaries—well before the outbreak of the 1991–2002 civil war.

During the war, the *kamajɔsia* initially constituted a better disciplined, more accountable security alternative to the government military—a fact that shaped the tense relations between these two bodies and was a factor in pushing some army elements into an alliance with the RUF rebels, who overturned the Kabbah government in a 1997 coup. By then, however, the *kamajɔ* militias had already become the CDF, and their leader Sam Hinga Norman the deputy minister of defense. This chief—like Foday-Kai before him—demonstrated an ability to bridge local and national political arenas, and to use mythopoetic history in the service of his military and political ambitions, in part through the evocation of the powerful idioms of the hunter's past. They both did so from the same chiefdom, which was part of the same political constituency that encompassed the chiefdom where I carried out the bulk of my research.

One indication of his creative adaptation of historical and cultural heritage was the increasing elaboration of initiatic, esoteric aspects of hunter recruitment, which proceeded apace with the spatial unmooring of these groups from their rural bases. *Kamajɔ* initiations became massive affairs, in which large numbers of recruits participated in public rituals, that were orchestrated by "superstar" initiators with national reputations. These initiators competed with each other to attract recruits, and they charged very high initiation fees, which were determined on the basis of the reputation of the symbolic and material power of their protective medicines.[15] By 1999, the fees exacted by these initiators had become so high that Hinga Norman himself spoke out publicly, demanding an immediate end "to the extortionary rates charged for the initiation of able-bodied men into the *kamajor* militias" (Momodu 1999).

## URBAN HUNTERS AND THE INSTITUTIONALIZATION OF A MOVEMENT

Hinga Norman consolidated the CDF from his *urban* base in Bo, after escaping rebel-occupied Telu in 1994 by adopting a classic hunter's ruse: the villagers who were captured with him told me he camouflaged his appearance, took advantage of the fact that his captors did not know his identity, and slipped away from the village undetected. Dissimulation tactics are also standard in guerrilla warfare—the more likely source of inspiration for this Sandhurst-trained military man. Sierra Leonean scholars pointed out early on in the conflict that "the Kamajoisia are neither peasants nor village dwelling hunters as most uninformed media sources suggest" (Muana 1997, 88), but such statements were seldom treated seriously by humanitarian actors, the international media, and scholars, who took the exotic appearance of *kamajors* as evidence of their immersion in rural- and forest-based cultural worlds. Instead, they occupied a distinctive modern political and urban space, which was shaped by their skillful reinvention of the hunting tradition, patronage, and ability to form into paramilitary groups. The *urbanization of the hunter figure* was very different from that evoked by the Mande traditions, which were mimicked by Foday-Kai's "traditional" dancers. And even in that urban world, hunters had long been associated with entertainment, political spectacles, and even violent outbreaks.

Urban hunting societies have existed in Sierra Leone since the beginning of the nineteenth century among the Krio, descendants of freed slaves, who settled in the region encompassing today's Freetown. Their activities combined entertainment, politics, hunting, and other more or less licit practices (see Nunley 1987). These societies developed initially among the Yoruba-descended Krio inhabitants of the Freetown peninsula, particularly in the capital city, but by the second half of the twentieth century, they were also well established among the heterogeneous, creolized populations of major towns of the interior, such as Bo and Kenema.

The urban *ode-lay* hunting societies of Sierra Leone blend Yoruba idioms and religious symbols (such as the cult of Ogun, the *orisha* patron of blacksmiths, hunting, and iron) in syncretic practices that underscore in particular how important the historical and cultural ties with Nigeria were in the formation of Freetown society (Nunley 1987, 27). This shared history came to the fore during the civil war, when Nigerian-led troops sent in by the regional intervention force, or the Economic Community of West African States Monitoring Group (ECO-MOG), fought alongside the Sierra Leone government. The iconography of *ode-lay* masquerades recalls forest animals (fig. 12), even though they appear in urban festivals, thus underscoring for their audiences that the hunters who make up the society's membership move easily between urban and forest worlds.

Like other such groups, these urban hunting societies are secretive about some of their activities even if—as I mentioned above—they appear publicly on celebratory occasions such as the 27 April Independence lantern parade. In Freetown, for instance, different neighborhoods formed hunting societies, whose members supported political parties. In 1977, during the months that preceded the referendum on the single-party state, a new masquerade, associated with *ode-lay,* appeared at the Kenema agricultural fair, decorated with photographs of president Siaka Stevens and of his vice-president (Nunley 1987, 205, 211). These masquerades played an active role in eliciting anxieties and solidarity from potential enemies, as well as from the constituency of Siaka Stevens. They evoked the ambiguous power of political iconography to destabilize the political domain. During the same year, many political activists, particularly university students, who were members of these

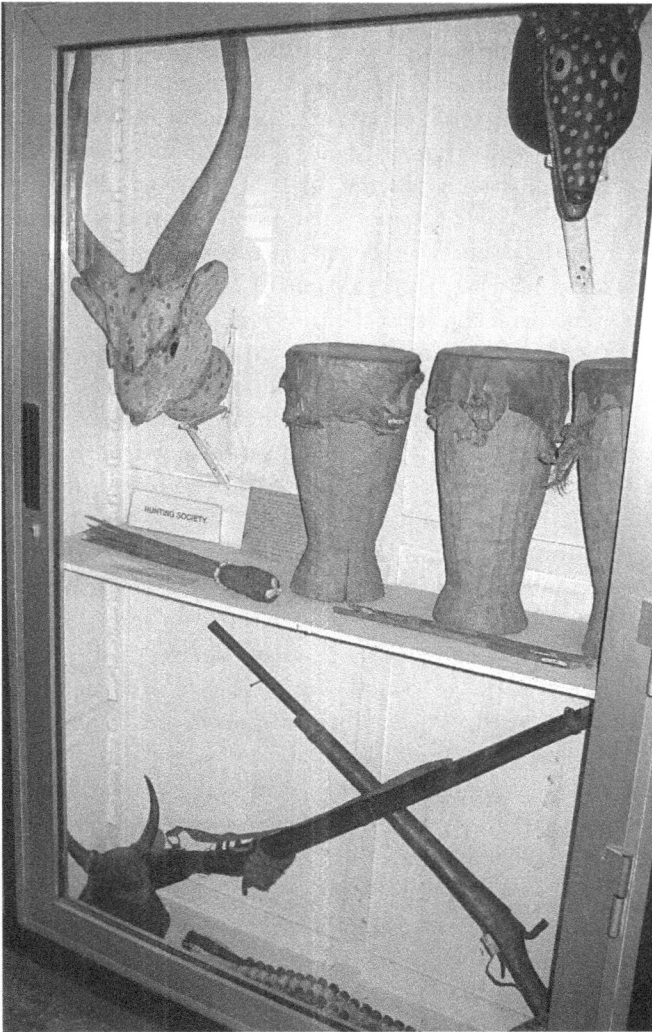

**FIGURE 12.** Urban hunting society display case with mask and guns. Freetown, 28 April 2012. Photo by author.

societies, were dealt with harshly by government forces (Rashid 1997, 28n15). Thus, right up to the years leading to the civil war, the All People's Congress recruited young thugs from these urban hunting societies to serve the single-party regime. It is this genealogy of using young thugs, street fighters (urban as well as rural), as violent foot soldiers for political struggle, on the national level, rather than a presumed traditional role of hunters, that best sets the context for understanding the ways in which the hunter militias were mobilized, particularly during the second half of the civil war.[16] Here, too, however, the boundary between violence and entertainment could be porous, as in all situations—rural and urban—involving large crowds. Once the bans on large parades were lifted in towns during the war, and since then, public festivities like the annual celebration of the country's independence anniversary brought out not just floats with party logos but also other floats portraying "chronotopes" of the moment: the speed boat ferrying passengers between Freetown and the airport, for instance. And the large concentration of sometimes inebriated youth could turn into a melee.

Despite the mobility and speed hunting require, the hunter-warriors of the civil war were closely associated with the sedentary, fixing practices of the state, and were invested in protecting it from its enemies (Deleuze and Guattari 1987, 380). By contrast, the *kamajɔ* who roams the forest spends his time, often in isolation from other human beings, exploring the natural and animal world. The hunter's ability to circumvent and kill animals does not directly translate into similar skills in violent combat with humans. The assemblage formed by the hunter-blacksmith-gun in West Africa is a specific figure of modern technology and environmental expertise, which in the present can be activated—and has been—in the context of global insecurity and resource management. But the rural hunter's nomadic wanderings in search of prey, and the skills he needs to manage the dangerous spaces of the forest, are akin to those of the nomad, whose "life is the intermezzo," a constantly mobilized trajectory that keeps him moving from point to point without ever fixing any sequence into a stable path: "every point is a relay, and exists only in a relay" (Deleuze and Guattari 1987, 380).

During the civil war, the fusion of the previously separate roles of hunter and warrior was visibly conveyed by the juxtaposition of an exotic, culturally marked body with weapons bought off the global arms markets, and furnished with rounds of ammunition too numerous to count, rather than the sponsor-bought, carefully husbanded individual cartridges of stalkers of forest prey. And the training of these fighters resembled more that of a modern guerrilla, or soldier, than the apprenticeship through which rural hunting and gunmaking skills were passed on from one generation to the next.

In addition to witnessing the institutional and technological layers added to the "bare hunter" in his transformation into a *kamajɔ*, the second half of the war also saw the addition of protective layers bestowed by large-scale initiations, as I mentioned above. Thus in my friend's narrative about this transition, 1997—during the (AFRC/RUF) junta time—was the date he joined the *kamajɔ hale*, the hunting "medicine," or secret society. It was the year in which he underwent his initiation as a *kamajɔ*. In the prewar years, this man had been a skilled marksman, successful hunter, and a powerful healer in his own right. His account of the initiation did not dwell on the mystical and mythical protections offered by the food taboos, medicinal formulas, and songs that were part of the initiation process, and which received a great deal of attention in the scholarly and media studies of these militias, particularly because of the trial against the "high priest" and initiator Alieu Kondewa in the Special Court for Sierra Leone.[17] Instead, he dwelled on the burdensome cost of the initiation, fifty-thousand leones, which at the time corresponded to about sixty-five US dollars, an enormous burden for a rural subsistence farmer, in wartime, and during the food scarcity connected with the international embargo against the AFRC/RUF junta then in power.[18]

## THE MODERN GENEALOGY OF HUNTER MILITIAS

The first of several consolidated trials at the Special Court for Sierra Leone began in 2004 and featured key CDF leaders accused of war crimes. The court's adversarial proceedings produced a more complex picture of the CDF and its practices, and of the role of its "chief initiator," Alieu Kondewa, as it changed over time. This trial—more than others held at the Special Court—brought to the fore the difficulties of dealing with the complex relationship among cultural practices, religious beliefs, and criminal acts in institutions of international humanitarian law (see Kelsall 2009, 105–40; Provost 2012, 195–97). During the trial's closing arguments, the prevailing views dwelled on the occult powers of initiators who kept the rank and file in the thrall of mystical beliefs and the fear of supernatural retribution, and which purportedly accounted for the particularly "savage" forms of violence (Anders 2011). This was the case even though some witnesses characterized the *kamajɔ* militias as a militarized form of patronage networks, which had long shaped the political economy of modern Sierra Leone and had turned criminal once they came unmoored from the closer controls of chiefdom and neighborhood authorities (e.g., Hoffman 2011b). The *kamajɔs* had transformed themselves from locally and ethnically organized groups to mystical and mythical militias on the national stage.

Their exotic representation, fetishized by the press, was the result of the exorbitant exhibitionism initiated by a series of leaders, who aimed to rise quickly in the hierarchy of political power through the process of reinvention of tradition.

What began as an example of successful grassroots mobilization of *kamajɔ*s for the protection of civilians, who were being victimized by all parties involved in the civil war, grew in size and moved farther afield from the home bases that held them accountable and disciplined, becoming just another violent faction in this decade-long conflict. As the composition of the *kamajɔ* militias became more heterogeneous, they became more and more "Mendefied" in ways that aligned them with the party politics of the Sierra Leone People's Party, and those of Kabbah's government, in ways that fueled tensions with the national army and eventually led to the mutiny that resulted in the 1997–98 coup (Henry 2000; Khan 1996; Riley 1997; Zack-Williams 1997).

But as I have shown in this chapter, the civil war *kamajɔsia,* particularly since the 1970s, have had a more nuanced genealogy linked to the modern, often urban political history of Sierra Leone. It was in those years the secretive, creole, urban *ode-lay* societies, along with other youth organizations, became instruments of thuggery in the competitive party politics of postcolonial Sierra Leone. The hyphenated linkage between hunting associations and violence (between hunter and warrior) was a product of this period, or at any rate, of the hybrid associational forms that emerged out of colonial society. In the precolonial landscape of this region, dominated by warlords in fortified towns, surrounded by tributary farming villages populated by enslaved war captives, assemblages of technologies, know-hows, and mobilities deployed historically by hunters contrasted with those of warriors, as did the relationship of each of these figures with the realm of the political. The hunters were adept at detecting the identities of shape-shifting forest beings, at negotiating relations between human and animal worlds, and were perhaps founders of settlements, but their lives on the move, in search of prey and sponsors, were fundamentally at odds with the warriors, who were more deeply engaged with settled politics. By contrast, the collective, daytime hunt with nets was the quintessentially sociable and political event.

Finally, my argument here has been that hunters, even in their "traditional" acception, in the brownshirted, amulet-laden personae that haunted the forests of West Africa in the nineteenth and early twentieth centuries—and were commemorated in the Sierra Leone national museum and elsewhere in West Africa—should be thought of as outwardly oriented figures of modern technological experimentation. Their mobility, necessitated by their reliance on game, and on the patronage strategies that secured them guns, ammunition, and other materials, made them something quite different from the rooted protectors of settlements on the edge of the forest, as they had been represented during the war and as they had become once they allied themselves with state institutions.

## CODA: CULTURE AND HUNTERS AT THE SPECIAL COURT FOR SIERRA LEONE

In May 2008, during closing arguments in the trial of Alieu Kondewa, which I witnessed at the Special Court for Sierra Leone, in Freetown, the Sierra Leonean chief justice gave an impassioned speech lasting over an hour. In it, he dissented from the majority opinion, which had just increased the prison term of the defendant to twenty years. Kondewa had taken on the role of "chief initiator" of the CDF "hunters," and in this position he had been credited with bestowing the power to see at night and protect naked bodies from enemy bullets. Justice King objected that it was a mistake to accuse him of crimes he could not possibly have committed, because no rational, civilized person could believe in such powers. The transcript of this dissenting opinion runs to thirty-seven pages, and in it the presiding justice, George Gelaga King, disputes the notion that Alieu Kondewa could be called a "high priest," a plank in the prosecution's argument that he was a superior in a chain of command that put him in a position of responsibility with respect to crimes committed by his subordinates.[19]

> A Priest—wrote Justice King—in the non-metaphorical sense, is an ordained minister or a person who performs religious ceremonies and duties in a non-Christian religion. Kondewa was none of these. He was, in fact, a "juju man" or "medicine man" . . . he was a "masked dancer" or in local parlance "deble dancer", a "gorboi" dancer.[20] It is ludicrous to say that Kondewa's so-called High Priest appellation is analogous to "Chaplain" in an army.

The dissent was not on the clash of meaning between high priest and medicine man. Instead, Justice King implied that Kondewa's distance from the battlefield meant he could not have had a psychological hold over his followers. The ruling, on the other hand, suggested that Kondewa's role was not similar to that of a Christian priest (true), but that did not mean that he did not, from a distance, have a hold on his followers, just as any other leader in a religious tradition, including

Christianity, might have. Justice King's refusal to be drawn into emic, internal understandings of Kondewa's reputed magical powers over his followers was grounded in his position among "right-thinking persons in civilized society"—in this he was a man of logic, albeit with a Christian bias—manifested in his refusal to countenance a word like *priest* to describe the defendant's role. Not only was a Sierra Leonean judge the one to raise this objection, in an attempt to demystify "magic" from a rational perspective, but he took to task anthropologist Danny Hoffman, who had testified at the court, for his "mind-boggling" naïveté in falling prey to such mystifications. The problem was that other testimony at the court also unfolded in such a way that it reinforced over-mystical readings of the roles of Kondewa and his ilk in the transformation of heterogeneous bands of hunters into the paramilitary CDF, thus swaying the majority of the non-Sierra Leonean judges.

Meantime, in the observation gallery at the court, Mende-speaking observers next to me chuckled and whispered to each other that Justice King himself must have taken this position because he was afraid of Kondewa's magical powers. While he was standing up for logic and organized religion, the members of the audience whispering near me thought he was prey to superstitious beliefs. Meantime, Kondewa's attractive, well-dressed, and well-fed wives smiled and waved to the defendant from the front row of the observation gallery. If he was an "ignorant" farmer, as the justice said at one point in his oral arguments, Kondewa certainly was not an impoverished one—the number and appearance of his wives being in themselves testimonies to the wealth he had accumulated through his wartime work as an initiator. Kondewa's sentence was upheld, but he did not have to spend it in the then-dilapidated Sierra Leonean main prison in Freetown. After leaving the jail at the court, where he was served regular meals and housed in humane, clean facilities, he was remanded to imprisonment in Rwanda—a fate that at the time the sentence was handed down was preferable to serving his sentence in the local Freetown prison of Pademba Road, not too far away.

# 4

# Sitting on the Land

## The Political and Symbolic Economy
## of the Chieftaincy

In Africa, where in some countries the traditional chieftaincy has been revitalized in recent years, the degree to which the performativity of chiefs' roles has coincided with the actual staging of political "space" for social events, public spectacles, and economic mediation varies. What scholars have seen as distinctive of Sierra Leonean paramount chiefs has been the ways in which they served as agents of modernization of state politics during the postcolonial transition, in the sense that they were agents of social inequality, while at the same time they had more significant roles in "modern," state-level politics than chiefs had elsewhere (Bayart 1993, 126). Paramount chiefs were variously seen as conservative, autocratic local representatives of the central state or as potential innovators, who used their network of kinship and social alliances to politicians on the national scene (Kilson 1966)—and played a critical role in delivering votes at election time—to ensure a measure of accountability to local constituencies. What was certain in the postconflict moment in Sierra Leone was that they were the lynchpins of a series of projects inspired by the neoliberal vision of reforming rural lands and their use. In Mende-speaking parts of the country (roughly half the national territory), the title of paramount chief is *ndɔ(l)ɔ mahɛi* (s/he who sits on the land/ground), and among the chieftaincy's key roles is stewardship of chiefdom lands and their resources. In rural areas, these lands can hold valuable resources, such as diamonds, gold, rutile, and rare woods, for global markets. They also have ideal conditions for farming crops for food or fuel on a large scale.

In what follows, I analyze efforts to reform the chiefship within broader campaigns to redefine the national political space in the name of decentralization, and to imagine new forms of governance in the aftermath of war. Early postconflict reform attempts drew clearer distinctions between the office and the officeholder in order to make the institution more accountable. Additionally, the high turnover in officeholders at this time also ushered in a new generation of chiefs best described as "delocalized" and more unmoored from the lands that historically were the basis of chiefly rule, hence evoking the fiction of precolonial nomadic chiefs. Finally, the reintroduction of elected district councils was aimed at establishing institutions that might set limits to this hereditary, or lifelong political office in relations with the central state and with citizens, by expanding responsibility for the provision of services, the collection of revenues, the undertaking of development activities, and other aspects of governance. Ironically, this reintroduction of district councils initially displayed some of the same weaknesses of their earlier iteration in the aftermath of World War II, when they advised the British colonial government in development matters (Kilson 1966, 203–5), in that they had the effect of reinscribing chiefly powers in even stronger ways.

But even as reformers (the local elites, international donors like the World Bank, the Chiefdom Governance Reform Programme) attempted to curb the political power of the chieftaincy and render the institution more "transparent," chiefly jurisdiction over land resources gained in importance in some chiefdoms, where resources were valued on the international markets. At the same time, the state renewed the legacy of colonial signifiers of chiefly office by redeploying symbols of office (new chiefly staffs, insignia, medallions) as visible expressions of power. These new symbols, introduced at significant national political occasions, reinscribed the role of chieftaincies as mediators between local and national, and even transnational, economic politics.

## CHIEFS AND THEIR STAFFS

On 26 April 2012, the Special Court for Sierra Leone handed down the judgment in its final trial against Charles Taylor—former president of neighboring Liberia—for war crimes and crimes against humanity committed in the 1991–2002 civil war. In Freetown, the judgment was streamed live to giant screens set up in the court's two chambers, since the trial had been held since 2008 in The Hague, and among the notables attending the event were many of the country's 149 paramount chiefs

**FIGURE 13.** Paramount chiefs at the Special Court for Sierra Leone. Freetown, 26 April 2012. Photo by author.

(fig. 13). They wore new insignia of office, medals hanging off ribbons sporting the colors of the Sierra Leonean flag, which had been given to them the previous year by the country's president, along with new staffs of office. In a speech after the judgment, the chiefs were told by the Special Court's registrar that their support was critical to the court's work. They had assisted the Special Court in reconstructing the conflict's history, tracking down potential witnesses, and in outreach efforts, but they also had a more complex relationship with the 1991–2002 civil war.

By 2012, ten years after the end of the civil war, paramount chiefs had become, among other things, partners in a number of entrepreneurial initiatives involving the state and private business, in efforts to generate revenues from natural and mineral resources in their chiefdoms. The Sierra Leone Investment and Export Promotion Agency (SLIEPA), established in 2008 with World Bank support, produced documentation for potential land investors, in which they were instructed to directly approach paramount chiefs—whose signatures, among others, were required on the template contracts provided—to arrange for long-term land leases. The cultural rhetoric relating to chiefs' roles in brokering economic deals in rural areas was suggestive of what some have called the "retribalization" of modern politics and identities in many parts of Africa, a significant feature of the neoliberal turn since the beginning of the millennium (see Comaroff and Comaroff 2009; Ntsebeza 2008; Obarrio 2010; Oomen 2008). The forms of this "retribalization" were not univocal in Sierra Leone because chieftaincies had multiple genealogies in different parts of the country. In parts of the Temne north, for instance, the institution was said to be surrounded by supernatural prohibitions linked to secret societies in some areas, or to be linked to Muslim rituals elsewhere (Dorjahn 1960, 110), whereas it has always been more secular in the Mende southeast. Over time, however, the chieftaincy as a whole underwent a process of delocalization as well.

The chieftaincy in Sierra Leone began to recover its relevance and importance with the advent of economic ventures. These made knowledge of rural lands and control over their allocation—particularly for mining rights and large-scale agribusiness projects—a lynchpin of neoliberal reforms for the Sierra Leone government. So, too, did its ceremonial, performative value as a visible display of power, in important public events such as the Special Court occasion mentioned above. In this regard, another postwar novelty of this office was the proliferation of ceremonial chieftaincies bestowed upon foreigners, who were thought to be potential patrons and enablers for local development initiatives. This phenomenon had a longer history in other West African countries (e.g., Barnes 1996, 22–23; Nyamnjoh 2003, 234–35), but it was relatively new in Sierra Leone. It gained ground during the war as a form of recognition to members of the British government in particular, for their intervention in support of the country in various phases of the civil war.

Among the earliest honorary paramount chiefs was Peter Penfold, who as British high commissioner in Sierra Leone gained folk hero status in the country for his role in managing the crises precipitated by the 1997 coup, in which rogue elements of the national army (which formed the Armed Forces Revolutionary Council, or AFRC) formed an alliance with rebels of the Revolutionary United Front to overthrow the civilian government elected the previous year. Penfold had circumvented a UN arms embargo to help arm and reinstate ousted President Kabbah, leading to the so-called Sandline Affair, which publicly embarrassed then-foreign minister Robin Cook.[1] Others similarly invested with an honorary chieftaincy for their roles in supporting the country included Tony Blair—whose premiership in Great Britain overlapped with critical phases of the

FIGURE 14. Tony Blair as honorary paramount chief.
Mahera Chiefdom, 30 May 2007. Photo PA Images.

war and the postconflict transition (fig. 14)—and Keith Biddle, who between 1999 and 2004 served as inspector general of the Sierra Leone Police Force and led efforts to train and reform this institution.

The fact that the chiefdom in which former British prime minister Tony Blair was invested with the chieftaincy in 2007 includes the country's international airport, at Lungi, is perhaps indicative of the extraterritorial orientation of some of these honorary investitures. The investiture of former members of the British government with a "traditional" office that the British colonial administration had historically played a key role in shaping in its modern form, and their use of this honor in the pursuit of business opportunities, partially reproduced colonial logics of power. In Tony Blair's case, his signature on ventures ranging from

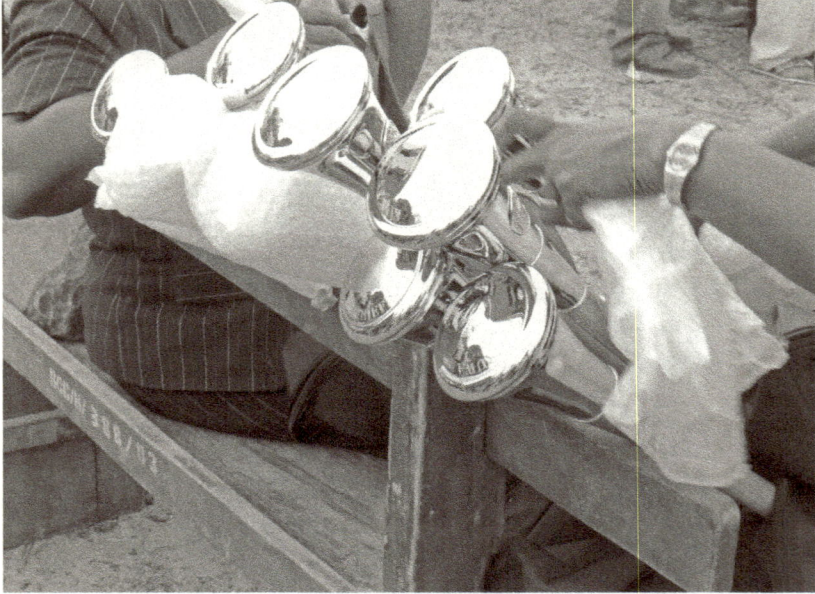

**FIGURE 15.** New paramount chiefs' staffs of office. Distributed in Bo Town, 2011. Photo by Gary Schulze.

business initiatives to religious and educational institutions suggested new configurations of aid and philanthropy.[2] His intentions may, too, have been tinged with Freudian echoes, as he often told Sierra Leonean audiences that his father had taught law there in the 1960s and Sierra Leone loomed large in his childhood memories (e.g., Blair 2007).

Thus the chieftaincy in Sierra Leone appears to be moving "the politics of ethnicity into the marketplace," in a way that is similar to the mobilizations of the institution elsewhere (Comaroff and Comaroff 2009, 7–8), by de-localizing the control over land that is inscribed in its genealogies, title, and historical mandate. However, in some chiefdoms the office was becoming increasingly instantiated in transnational politics and less grounded in local realities at the chiefdom level, and was thus more oriented toward development and business ventures with international donors and companies.

During a national conference of paramount chiefs held in Bo, Sierra Leone, on 19–22 April 2011, only days before the fiftieth anniversary of the country's independence from Great Britain, President Ernest Bai-Koroma—dressed for the occasion in the flowing robes of chiefs, rather than in his customary suit—ceremonially replaced the staffs of office that had been the emblem of chieftaincy since colonial times (fig. 15).

A Sierra Leonean observer wrote of the event as follows:

> The National Conference of Paramount Chiefs . . . was symbolically and politically important. The conference was well-timed to coincide with Sierra Leone's 50th Independence Anniversary celebrations. It was preceded by a Durbar of Paramount Chiefs at the Bo Coronation Field and it was the first time since the visit of the British Monarch (Queen Elizabeth II) to Sierra Leone (and to Bo) in November–December 1961 that all the Paramount Chiefs had again congregated in Bo for such an event.
>
> The Durbar showcased the cultural regalia connected with the institution of chieftaincy in the various regions of the country. *Another highlight of the event was the replacement of the old staff (which represented the symbol of authority of the Paramount Chiefs but which still bore the vestiges of colonial rule) with a new one that truly portrayed the sovereign state of Sierra Leone.* (Bangura 2011, 2; emphasis added)[3]

The paramount chiefs in attendance received light-colored wooden staffs with shiny steel tops engraved with the country's coat of arms. While the new staffs, along with the medals on display at the Charles Taylor Judgment, may have replaced colonial symbols, they also featured a cheaper metal and lighter construction in place of ornate brass tops weathered with the patina of age, which had been featured on the old staffs of office. There were also new emblems, such as the medals hanging off lanyards with the colors of the national flag in figure 14. In some ways, the chieftaincy itself could have appeared to increase some of its cultural value in a superficial way—to have become shinier in appearance—while politically lighter. But that was not the case.

The journalist's characterization of the staff of office as bearing "vestiges of colonial" rule also occluded the fact that it had a significant history in the times preceding the formalization of colonial rule, when the older staffs that were now being replaced were handed out. In 1879, a British observer noted that the ruler of a powerful Mende confederacy was accompanied by "a stout walking stick with heavy brass mounting borne by a messenger . . . [which] was the symbol of authority" (quoted in Abraham 1978, 36). This early observation points to an enduring use of the staff of office as a symbol of authority that was separate from the actual person of the paramount chief, in this case carried by a member of his or her retinue. Though the event discussed belongs to the colonial period, today the paramount chief can also extend his or her reach through his or her human advisors, dependents, deputies, and employees—his *human* staff—and they still do so while investing them with his authority through the symbols of office. In particular, so ubiq-uitous, historically, was the identification of paramount chiefs with their staff—the object—that it was sufficient, as I once observed during my earliest stint of research in this rural Sierra Leone chiefdom, for a chief who was unable to attend an event to send it with a representative, who would then be entitled to speak on the chief's behalf.[4] The meto-nymic relationship between the chieftaincy and the staff of office is rec-ognized even in the Sierra Leone Chieftaincy Act of 2009, the main postconflict legislation covering this institution, which in Article 30(1) states that, "No later than one month after the death or removal of a Paramount Chief, the Provincial Secretary or an officer deputed by him in that behalf, shall retrieve the Staff of Office from the family of the Paramount Chief or from him, as the case may be" (Sierra Leone Chief-taincy Act 2009, 14). But as I discuss below, even though chiefly powers were established before colonialism, they are imprinted with its legacy. The investiture of chiefly powers through state control over subjects and symbols of rule in many cases may become performances that dis-simulate the ways in which the office is becoming unmoored from the administrative territories that for most of the past century were the foundation of its legitimacy. Being away from the chiefdom does not subtract from the legitimacy of paramount chiefs, as long as they can trace back to its territory their ties to land and people

During the 1991–2002 civil war, the relationship between paramount chiefs and the land was called into question by the death or displacement of some 60, or 40 percent, of their overall numbers (149). Some were targeted during the conflict, and others died of natural causes during the decade-long war. In addition, the proliferation of regencies; the election of members of ruling houses returning from the diaspora (referred to popularly as "American chiefs"); and the increasing absenteeism of chiefs who came to power in this period and often chose to reside outside their chiefdoms, usually in towns, further weakened the ties of some chiefs to their lands. Local knowledge of the land, its boundaries, his-torical splits and amalgamations of chiefdom territories, and the control over natural and mineral resources continue to be both sources of legiti-mation and contestation for particular chiefs and their councils.

## TERRITORIAL RULE AND STRATEGIES OF DECENTRALIZATION

A number of colonial and postcolonial policies account for the close ties between the paramount chieftaincy and national politics in Sierra Leone, and for its role as a potential driver of "social inequality," as noted by Bayart, particularly in relationship to fiscal and political domains. Legislation enacted in 1954 exempted chiefs from taxation, and by ending the criminal liability for embezzling taxes, apparently gave them a free hand to prey on their subjects. In 1959–60, a new round of reforms led to stronger chiefly control over local courts (where, among other things, they took to prosecuting their political opponents) and to the establishment of a new chiefdom police force, which was under their control (Kilson 1966, 205, 280). While elsewhere in Africa, nationalist and anticolonial political struggles often reversed the British colonial policies that gave chiefs such powers, and made their roles in national politics mostly advisory ones (e.g., for Ghana, see Rathbone 2000, 66), in Sierra Leone this was not the case. Twenty-six of forty-two seats in the Protectorate Assembly, established in 1945–46, were set aside for chiefs (Kilson 1966, 155). Since the establishment of a House of Representatives in 1954, each of the country's twelve districts has elected a paramount chief, who has full voting rights in the House. Paramount chiefs often held ministerial posts in postcolonial Sierra Leone, and they continued to do so in the postconflict setting. Thus the close proximity between local and national politics in Sierra Leone was facilitated by the fact that paramount chiefs themselves are involved in politics on different scales. On the one hand, they could hold national office themselves, while on the other hand, they could leverage their kinship ties with national political elites.

In an analysis of electoral politics in the 1950s and 60s, Martin Kilson (1966, 232, 233) noted that "some 35 percent" of national officers in the ruling party "were either sons, grandsons, or nephews of Chiefs, . . . as was the overwhelming majority of . . . ministers" and that in the local government elections of 1959, in one district 54 percent of the ruling party's candidates "were sons of Chiefs or were educated persons holding traditional office." For an example of the ways, even during the civil war and its aftermath, chiefly families in Sierra Leone could use kinship and marriage ties to span different political scales, consider the Dabos of Wunde Chiefdom.

In the decade before the civil war, the brother of paramount chief M. K. Dabo II had been a member of parliament (MP) for the political constituency that encompassed Wunde and the neighboring chiefdom of Jaiama-Bongor. As an Oxford graduate and a European-trained physician based in Freetown, the MP represented well Kilson's portrait of modern Sierra Leonean elites tied to traditional rural ones. However, he had lost his seat to the brother of a local section chief in the 1986 national election (see Ferme 1999), a political contest that profoundly divided chiefdom subjects, many of whom rebelled against the paramount chief's authority.

The chief's staying power in those turbulent prewar years was tied in part to some of the many marriages he contracted over his long chieftaincy. Like other paramount chiefs at the time, Chief Dabo claimed to have some thirty wives, an unusually large number compared with his rural subjects, most of whom—if they practiced polygamy at all—felt that having more than two wives was possible only for the powerful. Among the chief's wives was the female paramount chief of a neighboring chiefdom, which encompassed Blama, a large market town on one of the country's main highways.

Between his own political networks and those of his extended family, Chief Dabo managed to resist calls for his replacement from a growing number of his subjects in the years leading up and into the civil war. Among his siblings, children, and nephews were officers in the national army; the police; high-ranking functionaries in ministries, as well as opposition politicians; civil servants; and prominent professionals. These extensive networks enabled him to secure shelter, protection, and patronage for himself and for some of his subjects, who had been displaced by rebel attacks on the chiefdom. This brought him back into favor with them.

Though the paramount chieftaincy is a lifelong position, it is not a hereditary one in the narrow sense of the word: a number of ruling houses can present a candidate to fill a vacant office, and chiefdom electors (one for every twenty taxpayers) meet to consult and vote for a successor. In the aftermath of the 1991–2002 civil war, when, as mentioned above, about half of the chieftaincies—including Wunde, after Chief Dabo's death in 1998 from an illness—were vacant, these were the elections that most Sierra Leoneans with local connections were concerned with, even though national political elections also loomed on the horizon. In Wunde the process for selecting a successor chief took a few months (fig. 16). Elsewhere it took longer since over the course of the postconflict decade electoral lists were contested, voting results were challenged, and in some cases elected chiefs were denounced as impostors.

In July 2011, Sierra Leonean members of the *Leonenet* listserv were debating the political virtues of potential opposition candidates who might challenge the incumbent in the following year's presidential elections. But many devoted as much attention to the contested paramount chief elections in Njaluahun chiefdom. Sierra Leoneans at home and in

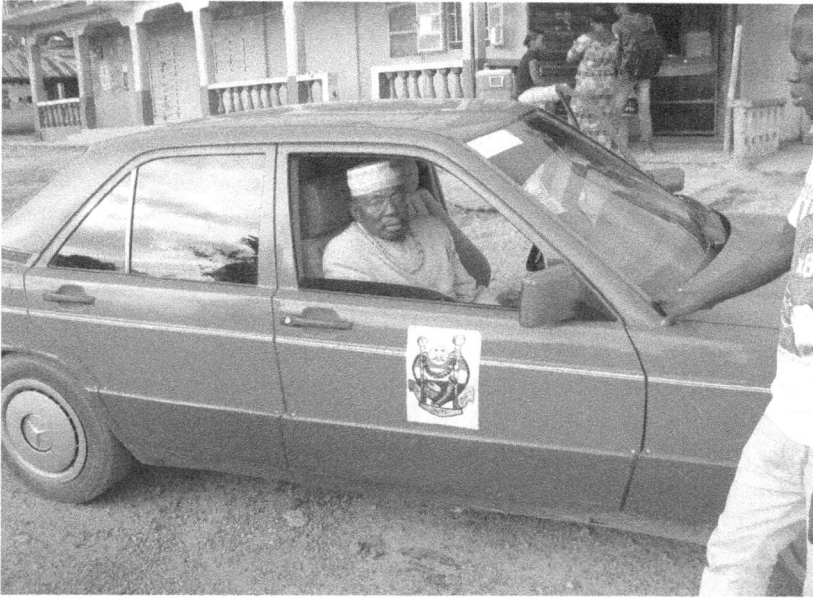

**FIGURE 16.** Paramount chief Mohamed Tshombei Kargoi II in car with official emblem. Bo town, 21 October 2015. Photo by author.

the diaspora were contributing almost as much vigor to debating political matters in this chiefdom near the Sierra Leone-Liberia border as they were to national elections. Far from being incommensurable in scale, these two domains were linked in the minds of some participants in the online exchanges—their positions regarding chiefly elections in Njaluahun being aligned with their support of, or opposition to, the ruling All People's Congress government.

At issue was whether Njaluahun was an "amalgamated" chiefdom, meaning one formed by joining two previously territorially separate, sovereign chiefdoms. The Sierra Leone Chieftaincy Act of 2009 specified that chiefs be elected "on a rotational basis" from "recognized ruling houses" in each of the chiefdoms composing an amalgamated chiefdom (Sierra Leone Chieftaincy Act 2009, 5). An effort to reform and render more democratic the procedures for electing paramount chiefs, the act instead enshrined in law some of the contradictions of this institution as it was shaped during the British colonial period. In particular, it solidified the chief's problematic relationship to territory, law, and taxation.

Njaluahun Chiefdom has twelve sections, each with its own section chief and speaker, which in turn encompass villages with their chiefs and speakers. The chiefdom as a whole is ruled by a paramount chief, assisted by a chiefdom speaker, and this nesting order of chiefs and speakers, from village to chiefdom levels, is typical of the country at large, except for the capital city. Since the December 2009 election of paramount chief James Sheriff Coker-Jajua, two of the chiefdom's twelve sections—those making up the Old Jahn Chiefdom before the amalgamation with the Old Njaluahun Chiefdom—had refused to recognize his authority and declared their secession (Barrie 2010). By rights, they argued with the support of state authorities, it had been their turn to present candidates for the chieftaincy. The Jahn people—a numerical minority—availed themselves of the rotational provision in the new law to present one of their candidates and thus break some 110 years of continuous rule by the Njaluahun majority.

The Njaluahun people protested to the minister of state for their region, who declared that "the two chiefdoms were not amalgamated but that Jahn with only two sections were (*sic*) added to Njaluahun" (Barrie 2010). Thus, the fraught linkages between territory, demography, and chiefly rule were played out in the discursive interstices between "amalgamation," which recognized the formerly sovereign, autonomous status of the constitutive chiefdoms, and hence the right of ruling houses from each to take turns contesting the chieftaincy, and "addition" (of subordinate sections to an existing chiefdom). At stake in the Njaluahun dispute was the fact that the chiefdom possessed mineral and other valuable resources and encompassed the large town of Segbwema—with its markets and commercial enterprises—which provided a considerable tax base for the paramount chief's coffers.

Such contestations over amalgamations and splits, and the redrawing of boundaries, can have lasting political consequences. In 1931, district boundaries were redrawn for the third time since the British had established administrative districts in the protectorate in 1896, and as a result of a territorial dispute, the majority of Wunde Chiefdom shifted from Kenema District—where it had been since this district came into existence in 1920—to the newly formed Bo District (J. Clarke 1969, 30–31). It was under the leadership of Ibrahim ("Braima") Dabo, who until then had been a section chief. Chief Dabo, in other words, succeeded in doing what the old Jahn ruling house had not managed after the 2009 Njaluahun elections: he parlayed his leadership of a subordinate territorial unit into a paramount chieftaincy. The family's control over the office lasted for some six decades, until the 1998 death of the original chief's son and successor. From Dabola Faranah, in neighboring Guinea, the Dabos were originally Islamic scholars and cattle traders, who settled in Wunde in the early decades of the protectorate.[5] Ironically, it was the Dabos, a family with no direct claim to the land and its people, that came to signify the postcolonial resurgence of the chieftaincy's relationship to territoriality in the constitution of power.

The emphasis on territorial sovereignty, on the demographic basis for chiefdom aggregations and splits, on the legitimacy of "ruling houses," and on the symbols of office—primarily the staffs of office mentioned above, and thrones introduced by the colonial administration—all date from the consolidation of the office within the British colonial state and in postindependence Sierra Leone. Key to that historical transition phase were processes of territorialization of the chieftaincy, by which I mean both the ways in which the state works as an apparatus of capture that "is capable of internalizing, of appropriating locally," and, in so doing, is capable of becoming a stable entity that reproduces itself (see Deleuze and Guattari 1987, 360). This is done through practices of rooting the chieftaincy in space, of immobilizing it, which are characteristic of that broader process. One marker of this process was that the British administration tended to privilege those precolonial institutions of political authority, and the variable linkages they had to territorial rule on different scales, which stabilized and standardized the administration of land, law, and taxation. Thus a variety of precolonial forms of rule became standardized, ranging from relatively stable territorial states (land chiefs) to the domains of charismatic war chiefs, who controlled large fortified towns with satellite agrarian villages populated mostly by slaves, to rulers of confederacies. As elsewhere in British Africa, chiefdoms were established, led by "paramount chiefs," whose main tasks included holding land in stewardship for their subjects, administering and providing services on behalf of the colonial state, and collecting taxes for these purposes. In Sierra Leone, this process began later than in other parts of British African territories, as the system of "native administration" was not introduced there until 1937 (Barrows 1976, 100). This may account in part for the different role of chiefs in modern Sierra Leonean politics, in contrast with elsewhere in Anglophone Africa.

The very term *paramount chief* was used only occasionally during the nineteenth century by British administrators dealing with overlords in the Sierra Leone hinterland. More commonly, they used titles such as "king" and "queen" to refer to the people in authority from whom they sought permission for trading, support in legal matters, and eventually collaboration in signing territorial cession and peace treaties—further corroboration of the tendency to project titles associated with their own experience of rule in the metropole. However, the practice was also associated with early British officials' perception of the nature of sovereignty and of chiefly rule. For instance, T.J. Alldridge (1910, 193), the first traveling—and later district—commissioner on behalf of the British Crown, had this to write about changes he had observed in the chieftaincy during his time in Sierra Leone: "The old patriarchal chief as I remember to have seen him in other days, walking about among his people with his large retinue of wives and followers, was an absolute ruler of autocratic power, whose word was law and whose authority was never questioned. Life and death were in his hands, and his people knew it. But he has gone;. . . . the present paramount chief is responsible to the British government." Note that control over large numbers of "wives and followers," more than outward symbols of office, was a key marker of visible power in precolonial chieftaincy.

This sovereign relied on a rather mobile, and changing assemblage of chiefly attributes and powers, which were more difficult to stabilize: human subjects to autocratic rule have legs and can pick up and move to a neighboring territory if they are not happy with their chief. They do so today in Sierra Leone (Mokuwa, Voors, Bulte, and Richards 2011), as they did in precolonial and colonial days. Precolonial chiefs could be powerful nomadic forces, violent warriors who eschewed particular territorial locations in favor of "personal-amorphous" polities mobilized in an ad hoc manner, depending on needs (Abraham 1978, 33–37): for instance, to raise mercenary armies in the service of different rulers, rather than in the conquest and settlement of land. They could act, in other words, as forces for deterritorialization, that is, "the movement by which something escapes or departs from a given territory" (Deleuze and Guattari 1987, 508). The hold these rulers had on their subchiefs and subjects could be very powerful but also fragile, and it was therefore dependent on continuously enlisting the support of their followers.

By contrast, during the same period (1800–80), there were at least five territorial states in the region that makes up today's Sierra Leone, coexisting with the more fluid polities described above. Some of these territorial states were confederacies of smaller entities, and they were mostly located along the Atlantic coast and its immediate interior, where control over land and its resources was key to linking the expanding coastal European trade with the areas of agricultural production

(Abraham 1978, 37, 89). These contrasting processes of territorialization and deterritorialization were at work, then, throughout the history of chieftaincy, though they were more pronounced in times of conflict, as was once again in evidence after the 1991–2002 civil war in ways that seemed to mimic precolonial models of chiefly sovereignty.

During the series of colonial reforms that consolidated the chieftaincy, subjects rebelled against them at various times, particularly in the late 1940s, when the impact of policy changes began to be felt (Barrows 1976, 102–3), and again in the mid-1950s, in protest against oppressive taxation (Kilson 1966, 60). In several instances, these rebellions led to the deposition of the paramount chief. More often, they could lead to the evacuation of his or her authority, and to the establishment of an informal parallel, or shadow administration, a strategy for undermining unpopular chiefs that is still common. For instance, in the part of the Wunde chiefdom where I lived—right between the hometowns of the two main contestants for office—there was discontent among the supporters of the opposing faction about the paramount chief's role in advancing his brother's candidacy for a seat in parliament in the 1986 national elections. His brother was the incumbent MP, which meant that their combined interests could considerably advance their political agendas against any challengers. Nonetheless, the opponent pulled off an upset victory at the ballot. At that point, political opponents of the paramount chief stopped settling land disputes in his court, turning instead for counsel to the section chief. This strategy was similar to that deployed by those unhappy with the outcome of the 2009 paramount chief elections in Njaluahun, discussed above.

The large number of vacant chieftaincies in Sierra Leone, and the controversial use of the office in the service of undemocratic practices in the country's postcolonial history, led to serious debates about eliminating the institution altogether in the post–civil war transitional moment. Those opposing this view, however, saw the institution as potentially balancing the corruption of the central government. This debate took place internally, among elements of the Sierra Leonean population (primarily women and youth) who tended to be disadvantaged by the hierarchical structure of chieftaincy, and in scholarly and policy circles, where solutions were being sought to end chiefly abuses of power that had fueled grievances during the 1991–2002 civil war (e.g., Broadbent 2012; Chauveau and Richards 2008, 155–67; Fanthorpe 2004, 2006; P. Jackson 2005, 53–55; Mokuwa, Voors, Bulte, and Richards 2011). At the end of the war, the country was dealing with the power vacuum left by the displacement and death of many paramount chiefs and other local authorities. In the eleven years since the war's inception in 1991, most vacant offices had been filled only with regencies. So by May 2002, when national elections were held for the first time since the end of the civil war, about 60 of the country's 149 chieftaincies were vacant.

This would have been a propitious moment, some argued, to do away with the institution entirely, especially in light of the evidence that some of the war's grievances were linked to the excessive prewar demands by paramount chiefs for labor, taxes, and fines from their subjects.[6] Instead, two years earlier, the Sierra Leonean government had launched a Paramount Chief Restoration Project, later renamed the Chiefdom Governance Reform Programme, with support from the United Kingdom's Department for International Development and other international donors and NGOs. British policy advisors planned to go beyond restoring chiefs or electing new ones, to reform the chieftaincy within a broader reorganization of local governance that included the revival of elected district councils, but in practice the most visible outcome of the project for the affected, mostly rural, population was a program to rebuild chiefdom houses (see Fanthorpe 2004).

These new chiefdom houses were intended to have a standardized footprint and appearance and replace the variety of residences of different shapes, sizes, ages, and materials (many of wattle and daub with thatched roofs) that had housed paramount chiefs before the war. In some cases, this rebuilding effort provided an opportunity to move the seat of the chieftaincy to a place considered more central to a particular chief's jurisdiction. The hope was that in this way the chiefdom house would be identified with the territory's people, rather than with the paramount chiefs and their extended families, as had been the case previously, and would be used for chiefdom matters, rather than being a site of personalized power. The program was plagued by controversy, lack of participation by chiefdom "stakeholders"—in the parlance of project staff—and expense overruns. Among the controversial aspects of the program was the call for resident "volunteers" to work on behalf of the chieftaincy, when the extraction of *corvée* labor had been one of the most resented chiefly prerogatives and in some areas was still at the root of conflicts between paramount chiefs and their subjects (see Mokuwa, Voors, Bulte, and Richards 2011). By 2002, the program's budget had been depleted, in part because of the need to employ paid labor, and only fifty new chiefdom houses had been built. Many chiefs had refused to move into the houses because they found them too small in comparison with the expansive compounds most of them associated with their office, and required to accommodate their large families and numerous dependents—the "staffs" in the social sense of the term, as discussed earlier.[7]

Whatever the numbers of the chiefdom houses, or their eventual use, as residences for paramount chiefs, as guesthouses, or as shared community spaces, the fact that contestations were a reason why some chiefdoms did not see one built applied in Wunde. The new structure was proposed for Fanima, a village closer to the geographic center of the chiefdom, in part because local factions wanting to put an end to the six-decades-long hold on the chieftaincy of one ruling house wanted to move it away from the chiefdom headquarter town of Gboyama that had become so closely associated with it (Wunde Consultation 2000). In the event, Wunde Chiefdom did not get a new chiefdom house, because the parties could not reach consensus, and this was a prerequisite for the donors. This lack of consensus was to be expected, given that the family of the incumbent also presented its own candidate, and the opposing ruling houses united behind the eventual winner.

What was clear when I visited the chiefdom on several occasions after the election of the new paramount chief, was that the new paramount chief was not residing in the official headquarter town, or for that matter in any permanent way at his own base, a weekly market town on a main road.[8] Ironically, then, postcivil war efforts at governance reform seemed to be working at cross-purposes with each other: staying rooted in place versus mobilizing new, alternative political and administrative institutions.[9]

## HISTORICAL PALIMPSESTS AND COLONIAL REVENANTS

The immediate postwar tendency to focus on physical structures and the chieftaincy's emplacement—on building new chiefdom houses, reconsidering their locations—appeared to be a palimpsest of the territorializing tendencies of the colonial state, an impression strengthened by the fact that the main supporter of this strategy was the British government's development agency, and this connection had neocolonial overtones. During my 2002 visit to Wunde Chiefdom, one of the late paramount chief's younger brothers told me in a disbelieving tone, but while laughing, that "the British masters" were back, offering as evidence the fact that "DC" (district commissioner) Ronald Fennell, who had known him as a child and was well remembered by adult members of the local rural population, had visited the chiefdom. He had done so, however, not as a young member of a colonial regime in its final days, as he had been when he was a district commissioner, but as a mature consultant for the British government who had spent the better part of his career working for the World Bank, mostly in Asia.

Since 2000, British special forces, who had intervened militarily after the capture by rebels of UN peacekeepers and English military advisors, had also maintained a presence in the country and could be seen conducting physical training and other exercises in the streets of Freetown. Many in Sierra Leone were grateful for the British commitment to help return the country to peace, a gratitude manifested, as mentioned above, with the investiture of some UK officials with honorary chieftaincies,[10] but few had envisioned this presence to include the very same personnel who had been part of the colonial administration.

After the global financial crisis of 2008, revenants and newcomers began to take on a more decisively neoliberal and imperialist approach, as they partnered with the Sierra Leone government to implement laws and regulations aimed at aggressively promoting business ventures and public-private partnerships. The 2004 Local Government Act sought "to provide for the decentralization and devolution" of central government functions by establishing elected local councils, whose members were supposed to stand for office in general elections every four years. Over the decade since the act, difficulties in implementing its provisions echoed those encountered under the British administration after it introduced district and local councils in the 1950s, mostly having to do with the raising of revenues to finance the councils, which in the present as well as under colonial rule was left to paramount chiefs.

The 2004 act provided that local councils set taxes and benefit from a significant share of rents collected from mining, agribusiness, and other private business operations dependent on the land, but it was left to paramount chiefs and counselors in the affected chiefdoms to ensure the collection of these revenues, of which they were to receive a share as well (Art. 59, 3; see also Sawyer 2008, 402).[11] Additionally, one or two paramount chiefs in each town, or two to three in each rural district, were to join respectively the town, or the district council (First Schedule, part 2). These measures, particularly those covering revenue collection for district councils encompassing mostly rural areas, made the effectiveness and the very survival of these new administrative entities to a large extent dependent on paramount chiefs, as had been the case when these councils were first introduced during the colonial period.

Colonial councils were never able to collect sufficient revenues to fund services ranging from road maintenance to education, in part because paramount chiefs underreported collections to keep a sufficient share for their own operating costs, in an environment of underfunding. After their inauguration in their postconflict iteration, district councils appeared to be headed the same way, leading some participants in the postcivil war deliberations on decentralization to argue that "post-war re-bureaucratization should have started at chiefdom rather than the district level (especially in respect to revenue collection)" (Fanthorpe 2006, 44–45)—in the form of paying paramount chiefs much higher salaries, increasing their accountability to their subjects, and auditing their business and fiscal practices (Jackson 2005). Higher salaries—it was hoped—would put an end to the arbitrary exploitation of rural subjects that was in part driven by the need to support chiefly patronage networks, staffs, and so on (Archibald and Richards 2002; Mokuwa, Voors, Bulte, and Richards 2011).

Other postwar reforms were linked not so much to the colonial past but to the "millennial capitalist" climate, in which "the politics of consumerism, human rights, and entitlement have been shown to coincide with puzzling new patterns of exclusion" (Comaroff and Comaroff 2001, 2) and have been part of a more general tendency in Africa of extending to "the local elite" the purported benefits of market liberalization (Berry 2004). In rural areas, "agricultural business units" had been introduced in 2004 with the support of the United Nations and other donors, to help farmers scale up their production and work cooperatively. In some ways, these resembled the cooperatives and farmers' associations established by the government during the 1970s, which offered some of the same services. But there were crucial differences: the earlier schemes did not involve entrepreneurial, or even private and global partnerships, as the agricultural business units did in the postconflict scenario: they relied more heavily on the central government.

## CHIEFDOM POWER AND NEOLIBERAL BUSINESS VENTURES ON THE LAND

I now turn to some concrete examples of the new articulations of chiefly land management oversight of business ventures. Though drawn up in the name of public-private partnerships, these ventures often look like practices of extraversion by unpopular chiefs, who use economic alliances with external actors to remain in power, rather than relying on internal political legitimacy (Bayart 2000). My 2012 visit to neighboring villages on the main road connecting the two provincial headquarter towns of Bo and Pujehun unfolded against the almost uninterrupted background noise of power chainsaws at work in the nearby bush throughout the daytime hours. Loggers from outside the chiefdom were at work turning trees into wooden boards. They claimed to have the permission of the paramount chief and were taking advantage of the convenient location of the village along a main road that was regularly plied by transport vehicles. Fueled by a construction boom that also increased exponentially the demand for sand, gravel, and water, these artisanal logging ventures were only one of the many extractive activities going on in Pujehun, a district that at the time had 60.48 percent of its total area and 81.64 percent of its arable land under contract with major agribusiness companies. One main project already under development in a neighboring chiefdom was an oil palm plantation. But what was notable about the local logging was that it directly contravened an official, nationwide moratorium on the practice, implemented because this practice was rapidly leading to environmental degradation and soil erosion (Samura 2011).

In 2011, the government granted Socfin Agricultural Company, the subsidiary of a European multinational, a lease for an oil palm plantation in the neighboring chiefdom (Sahn Malen). The lease was for 6,500 hectares, with the possibility of expanding it to 30,000 hectares (Oakland Institute 2012, 23; see also Baxter 2013; Oakland Institute 2011). Considering that in this area, as elsewhere in Sierra Leone, most smallholder farmers' plots were between 0.5 and 2.5 hectares, the "scalar dissonance" of the project was bound to produce strong responses, even though the core of the project was on the site of an already-preexisting oil palm plantation. Later that year, a labor protest by local farmers employed in the new plantation scheme over low wages and compensation for their land sparked a violent response from the police, and a number of villagers were imprisoned. Among their complaints (Oakland Institute 2012) was that about half of the annual rents paid under the terms of the contract went toward fees and taxes for the paramount chief and the district council. They accused the former of having been "bribed" with a new vehicle to facilitate the deal.

Charges and countercharges followed among the affected parties, and many were still pending when I visited the area in 2015 and 2016. But the fact that the paramount chief, and the chiefdom counselors remained central figures in these complaints suggests the extent to which the postwar, government-supported reconfigurations of the landscape entailed by the large-scale land deals can potentially serve as premises for major conflicts over territory. For reasons suggested earlier, it is unlikely that this will lead to the demise of paramount chiefs, if only because their roles as guarantors and protectors of chiefdom lands are becoming increasingly valuable.

Farmers opposing the scheme in Malen noted that the massive clearing operation to prepare for the new plantation had eliminated all the natural features that marked the boundaries separating each patrilineage's ancestral lands. Since the promised survey had not yet taken place, therefore, nobody would remember who had rights to which plots once the leases expired some fifty or more years in the future (Oakland Institute 2012). Their fears may have been anticipatory and misplaced, as it was hard to tell whether the contracted annual rents and the employment offered to members of some of the displaced landowning families, as well as other business ventures tied to the commercial project, would compensate for a loss of land considered permanent.

At any rate, it is unlikely that even surveys would have permanently settled the question of boundaries in some cases, particularly those involving projects on such a large scale, given the numbers of interested parties. History—of particular territories and of the ways in which the allocation of resources has been politicized—has also had a role to play, even beyond the appearance of conflicting interests.

## REGENTS, ABSENTEES, AND "AMERICAN" CHIEFS

The spatiotemporal unmooring of the chieftaincy from the land was especially in evidence in Wunde at the end of the civil war and in its aftermath. Before the election of a new paramount chief in 2003, people in Wunde Chiefdom recognized two different men as regent chiefs. But to complicate matters further, three different district and provincial authorities had each appointed a separate regent at various times, and each of these individuals claimed to be the legitimate one.[12] For most daily administrative and bureaucratic needs requiring permits, payments, and receipts, many people ignored all of the regents, going instead to the old Chiefdom Headquarters. For minor court cases, they dealt with the deceased paramount chief's brother Umaru (who as the chief's informal speaker had attended to these matters even during the his lifetime) and the former paramount chief's administrative apparatus (clerks, court messengers, chiefdom police force, etc.). The practice of continuing to consult the administration of a deceased chief during a regency is linked to the fact that regents often are not from the chiefdom to which they are appointed and do not live there (two of the three competing regents in Wunde resided elsewhere). Therefore, they lack the local knowledge required to, for instance, navigate complex land disputes or court cases among locals. As we shall see, the practice of circumventing titular chiefs extended in some cases to paramount chiefs themselves.

After a year-long campaign, during which electors' lists were proposed, challenged, and revised with animosity and under the threat of a return to violence, Siddiq Dabo—a younger relative of the late paramount chief—was presented as the family's candidate. However, the winner was Mohamed Tshombe Kargoi, a member of a competing ruling house, and the Dabos accepted the outcome. But even when paramount chief elections were settled, as eventually occurred in Wunde, the contours of chiefly powers and the modes of exercising them departed significantly from those of preconflict chiefs. Many candidates who stood for paramount chief elections in the years after the war were more cosmopolitan and better educated than their predecessors, and for this new generation, the chieftaincy was not a main occupation. For example, the new Wunde chief was a lecturer at Njala University, who divided his time among his house in Bo, the campus—some hundred kilometers away from the chiefdom, on the way to Freetown—and his house in a small settlement on the Bo-Pujehun highway, which provided easy access to transportation and good roads. He did not occupy a chiefdom house, whether he was in the center of Wunde territory or elsewhere.[13] Instead, he could be seen as perpetuating the tendency of chiefs to turn their family compounds into seats of power—personalizing his political office—or as an example of the unmooring of chiefs from their territories brought about by the 1991–2002 civil war, when many had left their chiefdoms and even the country because of the heightened insecurity.

Among the new paramount chiefs elected after the war were several from the diaspora. Some, like Alie Marah, a relatively young man elected in the northern Sengbe Chiefdom, had spent their formative years in the United States (see M. Jackson 2004). Others stood for office upon returning to Sierra Leone for their retirement. Like the honorary British chiefs—Tony Blair, Peter Penfold, and Keith Biddle—the ties of these chiefs to the chiefdoms where they were elected were tenuous at best, even though they belonged to local ruling houses. In a way, even though their titles were permanent, their roles were similar to those of a regent—a ruler without a strong attachment to or knowledge of the chiefdom. In some quarters, this was an asset for different reasons. On the one hand, I was told in Wunde that "American" chiefs should not dwell in the chiefdom and immerse themselves in local affairs but should instead stay in the urban centers from where development and humanitarian aid flowed, using their connections to secure aid for their constituencies. On the other hand, an absentee chief made it possible for local intrigue to proceed without interference, as some commented in relation to the deceased Chief Dabo's relatives continuing to run chiefdom business from their base in Gboyama, even though the authorities had appointed a regent elsewhere.

## CONCLUSION

The paramount chieftaincy continues to exercise a strong hold on the political imaginary of modern Sierra Leoneans everywhere. During the 1991–2002 civil war, many chiefs were credited for taking great risks to protect their subjects; as a consequence, some were targeted by rebel militias. Thus the effort of some donors and NGOs to move away from this life appointment to more democratic forms of local governance, like the local councils, was not successful, even though the degree of involvement by chiefs in their chiefdom affairs varied.

In the aftermath of the war, the chieftaincy held greater promise of accountability for rural Sierra Leoneans than voting for national candidates—one of the reasons for the greater interest in chieftaincy elections. In addition, chiefs had proven records for delivering resources by drawing on their connections with the national political and socioeconomic elites, whereas the local councils they had to deal with still lacked the enforcement authority and budgets to provide autonomous alternatives to this "traditional" office. Members of the diaspora, who lived continents away and communicated on social media and Internet chat groups, were as interested in whether an adopted son could legitimately claim membership in a ruling house in order to contest a paramount chieftaincy, as they were in national and international political events. The symbols of chieftaincy—the staffs, medals, and thrones—continue to be metonymies for the office, if only to attract potentially beneficial investments from those in whom it is invested as an honorific title.

Despite the novelty of phenomena such as honorary, absentee, or part-time chiefs, roots in a particular territory, descent from ruling houses, and ownership of the emblems of chieftaincy are still important foundations for legitimate claims to power. However, postwar chiefs with weaker ties to residency in the chiefdoms they represent also evoke, paradoxically, more nomadic, alternative models of chieftaincy from the days of precolonial warfare. At the same time, formerly diasporic chiefs and chiefs who reside outside of the land, who are selected in the hope that they will bring more development and resources from outside to the chiefdom, are sometimes left out of its realpolitiks. The expectation is that they may make better deals because they are more mediated than their predecessors: they don't need to be physically present in the chiefdom to address land disputes, for instance, which are among a paramount chief's most serious tasks. This is because these disputes are resolved on the ground and through the identification of locally known landmarks that distinguish ownership from usufruct rights. The local knowledge necessary to wield this particular kind of competence can be grounded, to be sure, in the colonial archive that established the names and numbers of legitimate ruling houses. But this archive is also embodied at the local level by the elders, who carry within them the historical memories linked to dwelling on the landscape, its features, and the ways in which they came into existence.

Elicited by a chief surrounded by his elders—his human "staffs"—and validated by them as a collectivity, though not without vigorous debate, this form of local competence continues to carry great weight in chiefdom mediations over contested land. As chiefs become disengaged from their local chiefdoms, they will find it difficult to reinforce their connections to the land and to their people, and to acquire the competence necessary to establish legitimacy and power in the territories they rule. It is those who hold this knowledge, and who remain connected to the land, who are actually in charge.

# Refugees and Diasporic Publics

## The Territorial State Reconfigured

In chapter 4, I analyzed the relationship between politics and territoriality by focusing on the effects of the civil war on the paramount chiefs and their chiefdoms, that is, the unmooring that left almost half the posts vacant by the end of the conflict, or filled by temporary regents. The vacant chiefships were eventually filled, albeit sometimes after contested and drawn-out electoral consultations. Many of the new chiefs were educated professionals, and several had spent decades abroad and had returned to Sierra Leone only to contest the election. Of the newly installed paramount chiefs, even those who were longtime residents of the country tended to have occupations and residences that kept them elsewhere—mostly in the country's towns or even the capital city. These include the current office holder in Wunde Chiefdom, who as a lecturer at Njala University commuted between his home in Bo and the university's campus, until his retirement almost a decade later. This younger generation of paramount chiefs often operated as "remote chiefs," with weaker ties to the land and the people they governed.

In this chapter, then, I approach the issue of politics and territoriality from an inverted perspective. I look at the social and political commitments and alternative visions of diasporic citizens in shaping the political futures of their home countries. The power of states to shape the social collective imaginary and the practices of even those who live beyond their territorial boundaries is, after all, a key dimension of their existence: "The State is sovereignty," wrote Deleuze and Guattari

(1987, 360), "but sovereignty only reigns over what it is capable of internalizing, of appropriating locally." To understand fully how the state and its institutions have exercised sovereignty in Sierra Leone, then, it is necessary to look at the modes of existence that have been appropriated by its agents and overcoded in language. In this chapter I focus on some of the strategies in which the Sierra Leonean state (and states more generally) exercises its sovereignty-operating processes of reterritorialization, which aim at the redefinition and occupation of ever-expanding territories by attempting to assume control of diasporic populations through processes of internalization and appropriation. States generally do so by colonizing the social imaginary and appropriating the existence of citizens, although they differ in their capacity to do so. At the same time, I show how these colonizing tendencies are always partial at best, given the multiple political horizons opened up in diasporic settings. In particular, I examine ways in which the emergence of new forms of digital communication and communities have shaped the expansion of the Sierra Leonean and other diasporas during the 1990s. It was an expansion of a particular kind, since this was before Facebook, Twitter, Instagram, and the smartphone revolution. Scholarship on diasporas in the digital age has stressed that cyberspace enables the emergence of a transnational public sphere in which "identities are deterritorialized" (Bernal 2005, 660) and strangers can communicate with each other outside of traditional boundaries. But, as the cases examined below suggest, cyberspace also offers a context through which diasporic communities can undergo processes of reterritorialization and rerouting to the homeland: the bond with the homeland is not loosened in digital space. On the contrary, it is tightened and lives by means of new channels of transmission of desire (identity, roots, culture). These processes can be invaded and locally appropriated by the state and other entities as well.

States always have an uneven interest in, and control over, territory and populations, so it is not necessary to go beyond geographical borders to find instances in which groups are weakly "internalized" by their naturalizing of property, money and possessions. As Philip Goodchild (1996, 96) has argued, paraphrasing Deleuze and Guattari,

> The State is not so much a real social formation, therefore, as an ideal origin of society which attempts to realize itself by overcoding the existing social formations, it is a social abstraction. It is an abstraction that can be realized as internalized abstraction; it only attains concrete existence when it serves other interests such as those of the dominant classes . . . This abstract State

may be internalized in a field of decoded social forces such as private property, commodity production, and class relations. It may also be spiritualized in a metaphysical or religious system which overcodes everything.

Among the ways in which the state manages to shape and appropriate the biopolitical life of citizens, even those in the diaspora, are practices of documentality and bureaucratic administration that can shift the legal status of citizens, preventing or facilitating their ability to obtain passports, visas, permission to work, property deeds, and so on. Nevertheless, diasporic populations, which overall tend to be wealthier than those left behind, have become an additional resource available for strategies of extraversion in African state politics, insofar as such strategies help keep the powerful in place through the mobilization of "resources derived from their (possibly unequal) relationship with the external environment" (Bayart 2000, 218). In the case of Sierra Leone, a combination of the spike in emigration during the 1991–2002 civil war and its relatively small size and population increased the diaspora's relative weight in the country's internal politics in the decade after the conflict.

My focus here is on the set of practices, conditions, and modes of existence that situate individuals and communities in interstitial spaces between home and host countries, where the state is "localized," or "integrated," into the life of its remote citizens. These are the processes of documentality, classification and identification that constantly remind expatriates of their roots, which the state uses to appropriate segments of lives that have moved out of spatial reach. In this sense, the state is not intended to be static, or to be conceived of in spatial terms, but as a site of practices and aspirations that operate on the register of the imaginary and desire and govern the horizon in which concrete political, economic, and social actions take place, even at a distance. Crucial to the practices of the social and political imaginary in the 1990s—the period under consideration—are the new media and digital technologies, which have multiplied the ways a sense of belonging is experienced, displayed and performed, especially in the diaspora. Digital space enables heterotopic scenarios, aesthetic ways of living in alternative worlds of belonging without the vertical control of institutions.

Among the experiences shaped by the state's tendency to reterritorialize itself in unlikely places are those pertaining to the legal and political predicaments for refugees in camps or for those otherwise in exile. Unlike the diasporic condition, which can entail a measure of choice, war refugees are forced to leave their homeland. Indeed, in their initial dislocations from their home territories, refugees are often "exiles not yet recognized under an institutional category (neither refugees nor immigrants, nor asylum seekers, nor even 'undocumented'), i.e. literally stateless" (Agier 2011, 41). Depending on whether their livelihoods and modes of being are predicated on mobility between cross-border points—as was the case in this regional conflict whose frontlines moved among Liberia, Sierra Leone, and Guinea—or whether they settle permanently abroad after being officially registered and recognized by humanitarian governance bodies such as the UN High Commission for Refugees, refugees navigate fields of existential, legal, and political tensions. The camp is at once a space of extraterritorial rule—a space of exception—and one in which nonstate organizations rule, administer, and control on behalf of "humanity." But as Arendt (1951), Agamben (1998), and others have pointed out, the absence of political protections linked to the nation-state can produce its own forms of social alienation.

Refugees live in the legal limbo between a home country that no longer protects their rights of citizenship—since they have fled it—and a host country that has not yet recognized them as subjects worthy of their own political protection. In this limbo, refugees are held, identified, documented, "relocalized" with reference to their countries of origin. This point addresses the most dispossessed of the war refugees. Wealthier Sierra Leoneans with families or connections abroad were able to escape the "camp" experience altogether, while still facing some obstacles in resettling abroad during the war. Finally, the vicissitudes of members of Sierra Leonean governments in neighboring countries in West Africa present another dimension of life in exile, a political form of "refugeeness" after two coups that took place during the decade-long civil war. The experiences of exiles in neighboring West African countries underscore the mutually constitutive relationship between localization and spatial proximity.

The ways in which geographic proximity and political projects of return intersect with diachronic distance from the homeland are underscored in the following sections, which are devoted to analyzing the diasporas that have acquired visibility in the digital space of Internet chat groups and online publications (particularly, as mentioned above, before the advent of social media, smartphones, and the social communities they make possible). Despite the celebratory discourse about the democratic potential of social mediation and online liveliness of digital communities in the wake of the Iranian "Green Revolution" of 2009–

2010, and of the "Arab Spring" of 2011, the cases analyzed here show that the political outcomes of these mobilizations depend on a number of factors that vary from case to case, and with the technologically mediated social platforms that become available. Though in some cases these digital communities act as extensions of critical public spheres—bridging class differences and spatial distance to shape opinions around shared interests and desires, independently of the direct influence of state political agents and institutions—in others they seem to operate in a spatiotemporal gap, or anachronistically, with respect to the very political causes they purport to champion. In yet others, they operate as little more than extended gossip circuits.

## REFUGEES AS AGENTS OF TERRITORIALIZATION

According to Deleuze and Guattari (1987, 385), "It is a vital concern of every State not only to vanquish nomadism but to control migrations and, more generally, to establish a zone of rights over an entire 'exterior', over all of the flows traversing the *oecumenon.*" The state works as an apparatus of capture and integration by controlling flows of peoples and goods, and policing its boundaries, particularly urban ones (*polis,* the Greek word for city, is also at the root of the political and of policing, they point out). A locality, they argue, is not a given. On the contrary, it consists in the emergence of a particular social configuration that has been extracted from a diversity of features the stratification of the social world. What is visible as "local" is the result of a process of filtering that eliminates any feature that is not perceived as stable within a multiplicity of features. The identification of locality takes place at the level of discourse and of the social imaginary of desire as well, for instance, in the ways in which urban citizens or rural villagers might frame their understanding of the state and its agents through daily discussions about corruption (Gupta 1995; Smith 2007). States also engage in legal, administrative, and governing practices that localize citizens in the sense of linking them to particular places, some of which have as their objects those who live beyond their territorial borders. Among the ways in which the state manages to shape the daily lives of citizens, even those in the diaspora, are practices of documentation and administration that can determine the suspension of the legal status of citizens, preventing or facilitating their ability to obtain passports, visas, permission to work and study, and so on. Requiring emigrated citizens to obtain documents from local administrative offices, where their births were first registered, and deposit there all subsequent documents, such as marriage or death certificates—regardless of where they later reside—or delaying documents necessary to their residence and work abroad are some of the ways in which the state exercises its reterritorializing pull well beyond its borders. By contrast, processes of de-territorialization—the unmooring of culture and affect from place, or their freeing from particular locations and redeployment elsewhere in novel ways—are common features of modernity that are neither especially associated with diasporic life nor always in operation at the level of the state.

Refugees are one population through which processes of de- and reterritorialization are highlighted, not only in relation to their country of origin, but to the host country as well. They are, too, the quintessential dispersed population, and though this is not necessarily synonymous with diaspora, the cases analyzed here do trouble this distinction. During the civil war of 1991–2002, the dramatic increase in the number of Sierra Leoneans who became international refugees opened up new avenues for mobility and, therefore, for a diasporic existence on a more permanent basis. Tens of thousands sought shelter over the border in Guinea or in nearby West African countries, and for many of these refugees new forms of life (suspended between inclusion and exclusion from political and legal rights of citizenship) were shaped by the experience of a specific kind of territorial enclave, the refugee camp. Additionally, a little-studied aspect of the impact of wars involves the ways in which even diasporic populations residing at a distance from conflict can be turned into refugees if their legal status is unsettled. Many of the Sierra Leoneans I met in Cairo in 1993 had arrived there initially as students, without legal working permits, and when their meagre scholarships ended, they joined the submerged economy of undocumented workers in Egypt, or of seasonal labor migrants to Gulf states. Some had been residing there in precarious conditions for decades, well before the outbreak of the civil war. They saw new opportunities for moving to wealthier countries like the United States and the United Kingdom, as a result of their classification as "refugees" and the easing of immigration restrictions that this reclassification entailed (Ferme 2004). Thus a relatively unstable, diasporic life in one host country could lead to renewed mobility under the rubric of refugee programs, even at a distance from conflicts in the homeland—a paradoxical dimension, perhaps, of the capacity of humanitarian resettlement programs to shape the desire of diasporic subjects for new places to inhabit.[1]

By contrast, for refugees immediately affected by war, residence in camps subject to the ministrations of humanitarian aid organizations is an increasingly common experience. Refugee camps, usually established as spaces under the sovereignty of international humanitarian bodies such as the United Nations, but located within the territory of host states that temporarily cede certain forms of administration and service provision to these entities, have become spaces of "dislocating localization,"[2] where the very condition of dwelling is that of being dislocated from one's homeland. And they are also increasingly normalized sites for dealing with "undesirables" of all kinds, whose management is the purview of specialized sectors of the humanitarian apparatus (Agier 2011; Fassin 2011, 83–108). In addition to the United Nations, these specialized agencies include nongovernmental organizations (such as Médecins Sans Frontières and religious organizations) and representatives of host states, which create clinical, administrative, and military spaces inside the camps (Fassin 2011, x). Different regimes of legality and jurisdiction can produce tensions in these sites.

Working with Burundian Hutu refugees in Tanzania, Liisa Malkki analyzed the complex ripple effects on forms of belonging and citizenship—among citizens and refugees alike—of the fact that refugee camps often are located in places of marginal interest to the host state. So while the Tanzanian government sought to use Burundian refugees in the Mishamo camp to settle an inhospitable and isolated frontier region, the camp's success in becoming self-sufficient through the agricultural ventures of its residents, who even generated surpluses for sale, made them, paradoxically, models to be emulated by the more territorially rooted citizens (Malkki 1995, 43–44). In an interesting way, then, refugee camps can serve as sites of territorialization not only for the refugees' countries of origin—evoked in narratives of national desire and longing—but for the host state, which in this case regulated the camp's life through quasi-military logics and hierarchies. In this case, Burundian refugees settled an "out-of-the-way place," making it a productive frontier and therefore a place for reimagining the Tanzanian state.[3]

In a similar manner, Guékuédou—a "poor and rundown" border town in Guinea—became a boomtown in the second half of the 1990s with the influx of up to four hundred thousand refugees from the Liberian and Sierra Leonean conflicts in UN High Commission for Refugees camps, only to experience an economic collapse after they and the humanitarian infrastructure that accompanied them left the country at the end of the war (Moorehead 2005, 208).[4] The alternation between the neglect of this region by the Guinean state, the intensification of settlement and the presence of humanitarian entities during the refugee crisis, and then the area's recession into the backwater it had been before the war exemplifies the spatiotemporal elasticity of processes of territorialization. It highlights the unevenness of a sovereign state's interests in its borderlands.

Refugee camps bear witness to the suspension of certain aspects of host state sovereignty, which are ceded to supranational bodies such as the United Nations. But other kinds of places see similar withdrawals or intensifications of the state's presence and of its services. For example, state-like powers are sometimes ceded to private businesses in resource-rich territorial enclaves, where they might provide security; improve infrastructures, health, and educational services; and even leverage to renegotiate the terms of loans from international donors (Reno 2002). In 1954, the British colonial administration in Sierra Leone drafted an agreement, whereby the Sierra Leone Selection Trust would pay an annual fee to the state for local development in exchange for diamond mining rights in the Kono region. But the company "began making unauthorized direct payments to chiefs as private citizens . . . [and] also provided electricity to chiefdom compounds and extended 'loans' for the purchase of cars or building materials" (Reno 1995, 65). Indeed, since the 1950s this region—the heart of Sierra Leone's diamond fields—has seen an alternation between times when the central state tried to tighten controls and periods in which it relinquished them to private entities. At various times during the decades preceding the civil war, the state issued special passes to control the movements of the male population employed in Kono, while at others it ceded administrative controls over these areas to companies involved in diamond production. Notably, this occurred during the civil war, when the state agreed to make mining concessions to the private South African security firm Executive Outcomes and its subsidiary businesses. In exchange the firm agreed to provide security, make infrastructural improvements, and take on some administrative roles (Reno 2002, 209ff; 1997, 180–83). The presence of such enclaves—refugee camps partially subject to the sovereign rule of global humanitarianism, or extraction sites like diamond-mining fields, where multinational private investors exercise state-like functions—suggests that even within the territorial boundaries of a state, the nature and contours of sovereign rule remain undetermined.

The camps in Tanzania and Guinea mentioned above exemplify the paradox that, though refugees are among the poorest human beings, having had to abandon everything as they flee disasters, they often bring relative wealth in their wake—ranging from improved healthcare and educational and vocational training opportunities to the development of infrastructure and employment in NGOs.[5] In these cases, refugees in camps run by international institutions like the United Nations High Commission for Refugees may end up living in better conditions than the host population in their immediate surroundings. This relative care for refugees, and protection of their rights, in areas of host countries where citizens live at subsistence levels and have few protections from the abuses of the powerful, complicate the relationship between political citizenship in liminal spaces and transnational forms of belonging at multiple levels, for both refugee and host populations. Increasingly, in Africa, these tensions produce invidious comparisons between autochthonous populations and "strangers," which can lead to violence, as was the case during the civil war in Côte d'Ivoire (Dozon 2000, 45–58; Hellweg 2011), and elsewhere (e.g., Geschiere 2009). This form of experience shapes the senses of political subjectivity and the social imaginary, not only for refugees, but also for the host populations among whom they are located. It can become one of permanent diasporic life, as for the Palestinian refugees created after the state of Israel. They have been living in neighboring countries for decades, making their plight an intergenerational condition (see Gabiam 2012).

The refugee experience can transform the scale of political belonging and action, as these "citizens of humanity" envision themselves to be members of a global community of nations (Malkki 1994), whose humanitarian governance is more tangible than that of their own states, which have ceded the provision of social welfare to these entities. Refugees, as Malkki discusses, may also turn to the transnational community for a sense of belonging if their own nations are unable to peacefully accommodate diversity, as was the case for the Hutu refugees within the Burundian state. However, the Burundian case also highlights the fact that the imagined lives and desires of exiles can turn back on national communities of belonging in ways that make identities and alliances more fixed than fluid in the exchange and flow of social interactions. In situations of conflict, the stakes become even higher, and identities and differences are reproduced even in diasporic settings well away from actual violence. Malkki (1994, 4) analyzes this phenomenon by contrasting the ways in which Burundian refugees reterritorialized their sense of belonging to their homeland through nationalist imaginings in the isolation of the Mishamo camp, while Burundians who were integrated with local Tanzanians in the border town of Kigoma "dissolved national categories in the course of everyday life and produced more cosmopolitan forms of identity instead."

Diasporic communities can be reinvested with a kind of ethnic sentiment that fetishizes the territorial markers of the homeland regardless of their distance in time from an original place. In a study of the global mobilization of ethnic Chinese in the wake of the 1998 anti-Chinese riots in Indonesia, Aihwa Ong (2003, 88) pointed out that too often "diaspora becomes the framing device for contemporary forms of mass customization of global ethnic identities." A Huaren (global Chinese) website was set up to mobilize the millions-strong global Chinese diaspora in support of Indonesian Chinese, to inform the media and public opinion about the violence perpetrated against them, to host discussion fora, and to organize protests in front of Indonesian embassies around the world. The intervention was motivated by the assumption of a shared identity with the victims of violence in Indonesia, but Ong (2003, 92) showed that this assumption obscured the fact that the subjects of these representations in fact saw themselves first and foremost as Indonesians, who over generations of living in Southeast Asia had become assimilated linguistically and culturally, so that for them "diaspora sentiments . . . implie[d] disloyalty and lack of patriotism to the country of settlement." Ong demonstrated how a relatively rigid conception of shared ethnicity by the diasporic Chinese, who had set up this activist cyber-community, in some instances worked against the practical interests of the Indonesian Chinese on whose behalf they were intervening. For instance, as they were mobilizing global public opinion against the Indonesian state, Huaren organizers overlooked the fact that there had already been significant action: the Indonesian state responded to the 1998 violence with policy measures aimed at safeguarding against the future marginalization and scapegoating of all ethnic minorities in the country, including the Chinese.

As the case discussed by Ong suggests, online fora and social media can expand the global reach of transnational Chinese belonging, as well as of class, gender, and other forms of identification.[6] As Malkki observed for Burundian refugees in the Mishamo camp in Tanzania, they also can expand communities of "primordial" identification, for example, ethnic ones formed on the basis of birth, at the expense of elective affinities developed through shared aspirations and political projects. As a consequence, they do not necessarily deliver the promise of a deliberative public sphere that critically engages with state institutions in order to achieve democratic political ideals (Tettey 2001).[7] Among the factors that must make one cautious about subscribing to digital diasporas as sites for expanding the critical potential of the public sphere is the spatiotemporal distortion that can shape these debates. When these unfold mostly across different diasporic locations, they can become anachronistically unmoored from the concerns of those who continue to reside in the (newer) homelands. Nonetheless, as I point out below, even citizens in the diaspora who are not engaged politically on the Internet figure prominently in the economic calculus of the state, for within the logic of extraversion, the resources they can offer have political uses.

## THE SIERRA LEONE CYBER-DIASPORA: SPATIAL PUBLIC SPHERE VERSUS RELATIONAL NEIGHBORHOOD

The production of locality, according to Arjun Appadurai (1996, 191), occurs through the imaginary construction of particular kinds of neighborhoods "as instances and exemplars of a generalized mode of belonging to a wider territorial imaginary"—the nation-state. Refugee camps, in his view, are a key site where "the nation-state localizes by *fiat*, by decree, and sometimes by the overt use of force" (191). This tension between context-driven and context-generated notions of neighborhood is enhanced by a conception of the public sphere as both spatial and virtual (178–79). In examining the diasporic communities that emerged during the civil war in Sierra Leone and in its aftermath, a more parochial kind of neighborhood was sometimes in evidence (a locality apparently stripped of any relevant social features other than those that circulate in the realm of rumors and gossip), one that highlighted the inadequacy of using neighborhood as a trope for the political mobilization of diasporic actors, or as one of the sites manifesting a public sphere.

The Sierra Leonean civil war saw an escalation of migration from the country as refugees sought asylum abroad, but it also coincided with the technological revolution that brought computers into private ownership; reduced their size, weight, and cost; made fax machines and cell phones affordable and ubiquitous; and made travel relatively cheap. All these changes shaped the forms of political participation but not always in straightforward and predictable ways. Internet access in Africa—and in Sierra Leone in particular—remains an elite phenomenon, although here, too, access has expanded in the postwar decade. It was estimated that in 2010 there were 14,900 Internet users in a population of just over

5 million in Sierra Leone, representing a 0.6% penetration rate, up from only 5,000 or so in the year 2000. For a comparative perspective, consider that Nigeria, which with an overall population of about 155 million is the most populous African nation, had two hundred thousand Internet users in 2000 and an estimated forty-four million by 2010, or a 28.3 percent penetration rate (Arisenigeria.org 2018).[8] But in the diaspora, access to the Internet increases in proportion to usage by the overall population in the host country. The refugee crisis brought about by the civil war increased Sierra Leonean emigration, and this in turn created more opportunities for enlarging the virtual, technologically linked diaspora.

World Bank and UN figures suggest that during the first half of the Sierra Leone civil war, the country saw a net emigration of 450,000, or about 10 percent of the country's population overall, with about 380,000 seeking asylum as refugees in 1995 (World Bank 2011, 386).[9] By contrast, in 2005–10, after the end of the war, the country saw a net immigration of 60,000 people. The regional nature of the conflict, which, though ignited in Liberia, at various points was linked to violence in Guinea and even Côte d'Ivoire, meant that the same country could be sending and receiving refugees, depending on where hostilities flared up. And while many Sierra Leonean refugees sought asylum in the United States and Great Britain—the country's former colonial occupier—which were the destinations of, respectively, about 23 percent and 18 percent of the emigrating population, sizable numbers moved to other countries as well. To put Sierra Leone in regional perspective within West Africa, between 1995 and 2000, Sierra Leone, with a 7.8 percent net rate of migration, had the highest rate of emigration among West African Economic and Monetary Union and Economic Community of West Africa member states (Ammassari 2006, 9).[10]

The 2010 US census lists just under 1,600,000 people of African birth in the country (Gambino, Trevelyan, and Fitzgerald 2014, 3). Statistics for the year 2000 list about 20,830 people of Sierra Leonean descent in the country, of whom 14,535 were not citizens. Of these Sierra Leonean immigrants, two thirds had entered the country during the 1990s, compared with only 1,963 immigrants during the decade preceding the outbreak of civil war (Gibson and Jung 2006, table 3). The increase in the influx of refugees during the civil war of 1991–2001 was also tied to the fact that destination countries set in place various measures to lift normal limitations on immigration. In 1997, the US Department of Justice (since then reorganized under the Department of Homeland Security) granted Sierra Leoneans temporary protected status, an emergency provision explicitly targeting people who are in the United States "in nonimmigrant and unlawful status," offering them the right to regularize their positions and work legally until it was deemed safe for them to return to their countries of origin (US Department of Justice 1997). During the seven years in which Sierra Leone was included in the Temporary Protected Status Program, annual reviews of the program changed the quotas of eligible individuals from about 4,000 during the first year of its operation to about 2,209 in 2002 (National Immigration Law Center 2002, 6). This program supplemented normal immigration policies, allowing for a greater influx of immigrants from Sierra Leone than previously had been possible.

Among the Sierra Leoneans fleeing to neighboring West African countries, many were temporary refugees, but a proportion of these did not return to Sierra Leone after the end of the civil war (Maconachie, Binns, Tengbe, and Johnson 2006, 226). Among the key destinations for emigrants in West Africa were Liberia (18%), where many Sierra Leoneans have longstanding historical, cultural, and linguistic ties, and Ghana (5%), which was the site of a key UN refugee camp for people displaced from this regional conflict (Barajas, Chami, Fullenkamp, and Garg 2010, 18). However, the circumstances under which Sierra Leoneans moved to neighboring West African countries during the war shed light on the variable political profiles of different diasporic communities, depending on their spatial location.

In 1984, several key leaders of student protests, who had shut down the Fourah Bay College campus of the University of Sierra Leone, were expelled and went into exile in Ghana, where they initially enrolled in the University of Ghana at Legon to complete their studies. Some of these young political activists had first coalesced in Sierra Leone around "Green Book" study groups focused on the political agenda laid out in the book of that title by the Libyan leader Colonel Muammar Gaddafi. From their exile in Ghana, several traveled to camps in Libya where they were trained in revolutionary ideology and combat (P. Muana, personal communication, 20 July 2011).[11] It was from this core opposition group of the diaspora that the original leadership of the Revolutionary United Front (RUF) emerged, setting off the civil war with material support from Ghaddafi and Charles Taylor, the warlord who was leading his own attack on the ruling regime in neighboring Liberia and became that country's elected president in 1997. These dynamics illustrate the ways in which diasporic populations are key to political mobilizations in situations where opposition is banned, as was the case in

Sierra Leone during the years leading up to the civil war, when the country was under the single-party rule of the All People's Congress (APC).[12]

The potential role of students as organic intellectuals who trained in leadership roles abroad, only to return home to enact radical programs for change, has a long history in Africa. Diasporic student groups, through organizations such as the West African Student Union (WASU) for expatriates originating from British colonies, were key to the anticolonial and nationalist struggles of many African countries. Kwame Nkrumah, Herbert Bankole-Bright, J.E. Casely Hayford, and others who went on to lead nationalist and anti-imperialist struggles in their home countries honed their skills as political leaders in the diaspora.

But diasporas do not harbor only exiled opposition figures or intellectual elites-in-training. They also may harbor, in unstable times, entire government cabinets. When a military coup put an end to APC single-party rule in 1992, the ousted president, J.S. Momoh, sought refuge in neighboring Guinea with other key members of his regime. Five years later, another ousted Sierra Leonean president, Ahmed Tejan Kabbah, took refuge in Guinea with his entire cabinet and top military brass. The presence of a critical mass of Sierra Leonean exiles in Guinea allowed Kabbah to plan his return to power and, from Guinea, seek political, military, and logistical support from other governments and international institutions. After some nine months in exile in Guinea, Kabbah was able to return to Sierra Leone following the military defeat of the rebel-military junta that, in 1997, had overturned his democratically elected government.

Arjun Appadurai (1996, 188) suggests that "the production of neighborhoods increasingly occurs under conditions where the system of nation-states is the normative hinge for the production of both local and translocal activities," and that the latter, in particular, are key to the power relations that produce locality. In other words, the nation-state enables—and, we might add, is in part produced by—activities that link particular "local" places, even when these apparently by-pass the centralizing tendency of state institutions. Consider, for instance, Janet Roitman's (2004) study, which showed the ways in which the road bandits, smugglers, currency speculators, and rogue customs officers crisscross the Cameroonian border region near Nigeria and Chad. Their translocal activities are predicated on the existence of those borders—how, otherwise, could one speculate on the prices of commodities in different currencies and markets? And these forms of mobility among places generate the wealth that enable those who engage in them to support families in particular localities, even if they do not reside there for extensive stretches of time.

The staging of overturned Sierra Leonean regimes in Guinea, with the border-crossing this engendered, were another form of "translocal" activity, one with political, as well as wealth-producing, goals. During the 1997–98 exile of the Kabbah government, for instance, loyalist factions—particularly of the Civil Defense Force—remained in Sierra Leone to fight against the Armed Forces Revolutionary Council-RUF junta, while receiving orders and supplies from a leadership that was in part across the border. Thus the spatial location of particular diasporic populations matters in relation to actual political, let alone military, projects. Spatial distance is usually minimized in the scholarship on cyber-diasporas, however, which generally points to the equalizing effect digital connections have on distance. As recent Sierra Leonean history suggests, a government in exile in neighboring Guinea, or an opposition in Ghana, was more invested in political events in the homeland—and more likely to return within the country's territorial borders—than émigrés residing farther afield.

From the mid-1990s, the main forum linking Sierra Leoneans in the diaspora—particularly those based in the United States and Europe—has been the "Leonenet" listserv, which after being hosted at MIT at its inception moved to the University of Maryland-Baltimore County (UMBC). A study of Leonenet conducted in 2007 mentioned a membership of between 350 and 400 members, of whom, however, only 40 or 50 were active at any given point in time (Tynes 2007, 503). However, in 2004, a group of members split off in disagreement with what they perceived as the heavy-handed intervention of the UMBC webmaster, and started a competing "Leonenet" list hosted at Texas A&M university (TAMU), where one of the dissidents was a faculty member. This list is now said to number about 810 members (interview with P. M. 2011), but my own monitoring of postings in the summer of 2011, and sporadically since then, showed about 60 unique email addresses, with only about 20 contributing to debates on a regular basis. Additionally, a member of the original subgroup of the Sierra Leonean cyber-community calling itself "the Sulima group" has created a web archive of "select email exchanges on Leonenet during wartime" (www.sulima .com/leonenet/lindex.html), of which he appears to be the sole manager.

Apart from this last, mostly archival site, the UMBC and TAMU Leonenet lists present their members with a high volume of postings.

186 |   Refugees and Diasporic Publics

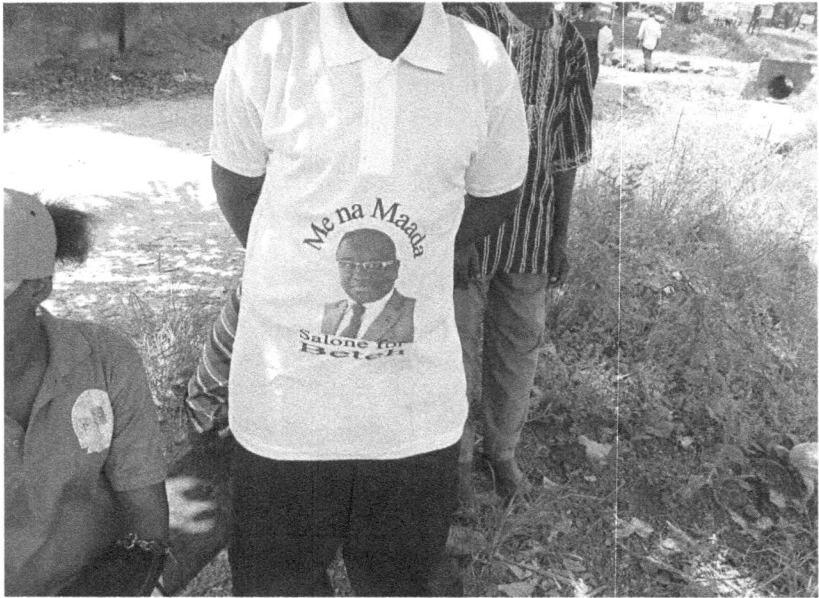

**FIGURE 17.** T-shirt of Julius Maada Bio supporter. Bo town, 24 October 2015. The expression *me na maada* plays on a visual and linguistic pun. The portrait is of the politician named Maada Bio, but the expression *me na maada* also means "I am a chief/grandfather." Photo by author.

During a month beginning in mid-July 2011, 3,574 messages, or an average of 126 messages per day, were posted to the TAMU Leonenet list. During the 29 July—1 Aug national convention of the opposition Sierra Leone People's Party in Sierra Leone, when a field of some nineteen candidates to the position of party "flag bearer" for the national elections of November 2012 was pared down to one, 259 messages were posted to Leonenet (TAMU). Over an equal number of days, immediately after the selection of Julius Maada Bio to challenge the ruling party (and the country's presidency) as the Sierra Leone People's Party candidate in the 2012 elections, about 100 more, or 357 messages, were posted, most of which discussed the controversial choice of this candidate (see fig. 17). Maada Bio had been second in command to Captain Valentine Strasser in the National Provisional Ruling Council military junta that ruled the country in 1992–96, during the first half of the civil war, and postings that criticized his selection referred to that regime's failed promises to clean up the corrupt politics of the APC single-party rule it had overthrown when it came to power. Nonetheless, even this high volume of postings did not reach the daily average of the month, perhaps because these messages were longer and more thoughtful than the many short, superficial ones that seemed to prevail at other times.[13]

Doing research for substantial amounts of time on this cyber-community is challenging because of the large volume of messages one receives as a subscriber—as the numbers above suggest—but also by their topical range from broad collective concerns and the public good to personal, even intimate matters. My sporadic monitoring of the list since I first joined it in 1994 suggests that often the bulk of the messages were about social gossip, rather than about the critical, rational discourse Habermas envisioned when theorizing the public sphere as a space where private individuals deliberated matters of common interest and intervened in political affairs (Habermas 1991). In his own reflections on the "virtual neighborhoods" formed by Internet communities, Arjun Appadurai sees them as sites where a "transnational intelligentsia" can form a critical public sphere (Appadurai 1996, 195). The volley of thirty-eight messages that followed one Leonenet member's July 2011 posting of an image of a woman dressed in form-fitting clothes, however, evoked a different image of neighborhood, one of licentious, mostly male locker-room gossip, rather than one of rational exchanges among cosmopolitan citizens. Indeed, the same 2007 published study found that 37.5 percent of Leonenet postings fell into this "personal" category of exchange, another 3.5 percent had to do with information and news, and only about 24.5 percent touched on politics (Tynes 2007, 507, table 3).

However, a focus on the nature of active participation in this virtual associational life—on Leonenet or any other digital platform—should not occlude the variable importance of passive monitoring of its activities. Thus active participants in Leonenet discussions point out that members of the Sierra Leone government, or of the opposition, or prominent sympathizers regularly "lurk" on their lists—they read, but do not post messages—to keep in touch with concerns in the diaspora.[14] Perspectives that focus on communicative participation in the public sphere have not fully accounted for the variety of ways in which silent presence in certain domains may translate into more active forms of engagement in others, or that secrecy may offer opportunities for deliberation when undemocratic regimes make open critique dangerous (see Ferme 1999, 160–64).

Other forms of online and paper publications by diaspora groups were more politically focused, so much so that their authors became recognized parties in transactions at the national or international level—for instance, as formally organized expatriate branches of political parties, or as parties to peace talks during the 1991–2002 civil war. These were often extensions of welfare groups focused on development projects at home, which though often organized according to relatively narrow, subnational criteria, such as geography (e.g., the Sewa River Descendants' Association or the Pujehun District Development Association) or education (the alumni associations of the country's prestigious educational institutions), also displayed the features of associational life typical of a vibrant civil society. These diasporic groups sometimes operated as local welfare associations, while at other times they mobilized for political projects. Furthermore, the focus of these groups on development projects at home (and on fundraising for them) underscores at a different level how their desire for the home country may be "intercepted" by the state machine in the sense of their having to provide welfare services that were formerly offered by the state. Indeed, these local NGOs are often a neglected component of the global humanitarian enterprise (in which emphasis is usually on the large international organizations like Médécins sans Frontières, or the International Committee of the Red Cross), an aspect that is key to understanding the granular ways in which diasporic practices and imaginaries are translocally deployed in home countries.

This is a remarkable oversight in light of the enormous amount of time and material resources invested by the more active core in these diasporic communities. Each week, Sierra Leoneans I know in the London area and in a wide range of metropolitan areas in the United States, including Washington, DC, Dallas, Texas, and San Jose, California, are involved in, among other things, organizing celebrations for naming ceremonies, weddings, funerals, or fundraisers to upgrade the facilities at the schools they attended in their youths in Sierra Leone. Local and regional meetings among diasporic communities in contiguous US states of Sierra Leonean political party branches are conspicuously advertised and documented on websites, and people travel considerable distances to attend these events, spending large sums of money in the process. For some, this "participation," which is indexed by monetary contributions, even in the physical absence of the contributor, can become a financial burden, leading the less fortunate to withdraw from active participation in activities they otherwise would feel obliged to attend. But even when an individual is absent from the activities of the multiple Sierra Leone–centered associations to which she or he might belong—a religious community, geographic community of shared descent, alumni association, political party—the intimacy of everyday life of even a Sierra Leonean who has lived abroad for decades is often redolent of the homeland. Images of iconic sights in the country's landscape, or of its historical and contemporary political personalities, are hung on the walls. Ceremonial occasions are marked by the wearing of fabrics and tailored clothes "from home," and even the most ordinary of daily meals tend to be typical Sierra Leonean fare—rice with a variety of palm oil–based relishes. People go to great lengths to procure the ingredients from the source, rather than substitute locally available alternatives. Thus the sensorial surroundings—the sights, tastes, and smells—of daily life for many members of the Sierra Leonean diaspora are saturated with these material traces, which act as a potent element in their imagined connectedness to the homeland (see also D'Alisera 2004, 37–57).

## WAR, CIVIL SOCIETY, AND THE SIERRA LEONE MEDIA

At the end of 1994, after vicious rebel attacks on his hometown of Serabu, and a Christmastime attack on the provincial town of Bo by rebels masquerading as soldiers, London-based attorney Ambrose Ganda, the brother of Catholic archbishop of Sierra Leone, Joseph Ganda, launched *Focus on Sierra Leone.* This was a desktop-published (and later online) subscription newsletter that offered frank political criticism, thoughts on avenues to peace, and often alternative or suppressed news items about the ongoing civil war.[15] Through the newsletter and other avenues, Ganda became actively involved in peacemaking efforts, eventually traveling to Abidjan with another UK-based Sierra Leonean expatriate, Omrie Gollie, in the months leading up to the 1996 accords signed there. Ganda had been critical in the pages of *Focus on Sierra Leone* of the National Provisional Ruling Council military regime then in power in Freetown, but at the same time he sought dialogue with all parties to the war. This sparked a smear campaign against him on the Internet—and Leonenet in particular—by regime sympathizers, in which he was accused of being a mouthpiece for the RUF rebels (*Focus on Sierra Leone* 2, no. 6 [July 1996]). Though Ganda distanced himself from the RUF after the collapse of the 1996 peace accords and the beginning of rebel mutilation campaigns, Gollie went the opposite way—he became the RUF's official spokesman. By the beginning of

2006, Gollie was imprisoned for treason for purportedly plotting an attempt on the life of former vice president Solomon Berewa.[16] As for *Focus on Sierra Leone,* its main impetus having been to put an end to the civil war, it was discontinued around 2001, once peace was on the horizon.

Another attempt to expand public dialogue and political engagement in Sierra Leone—partly from the diaspora, or with support and outlets there—was carried out by the NINJAS, the National Independent Neutral Journalist's Association (of Sierra Leone). The underground but ubiquitous group was founded by a handful of Sierra Leonean journalists in response to curtailment of press freedoms by President Kabbah's government in 1998 and 1999. These journalists refused to accept the notion, put forth in public pronouncements by Minister of Information Julius Spencer and others, that freedom of the press in wartime could be treasonable, and began posting their news and opinion pieces anonymously on the Internet. They sought interviews with leaders of all fighting factions—including RUF rebels—and often reported evidence that countered government propaganda on the unfolding conflict. The government went to some length to identify, detain, and prosecute the NINJAS, and in June 1999 arrested two journalists for allegedly passing on information to them that was "prejudicial to the state of Sierra Leone."

Like the community of readers and writers of *Focus on Sierra Leone,* the NINJAS sought to maintain an impartial stance and access to all parties in the civil war—including enemies of the state—because, as Ambrose Ganda wrote in one of his editorials, "you don't have to make peace with your friends." Their best interventions fulfilled precisely the call for a persuasive, rational, and critical debate that Habermas saw as a crucial element of the liberal public sphere. The content of their communications, even when these involved personal attacks on public figures, tended not to veer toward the gossip that regularly emerged on Leonenet, even at the height of the civil war. Nonetheless, it is difficult to gauge their impact and the scale of the phenomenon they represented, and whether they were critical to bringing opposing parties together to broker a peace deal.

The different trajectories of Ganda and Gollie also underscore the potentials and pitfalls of political engagements, often animated by idealism, with, and in, the homeland by diasporic citizens. During the negotiations leading to the November 1996 Abidjan peace accords, both men traveled there several times, at their own expense, as members of diasporic Sierra Leonean organizations. In an effort to cleanse Sierra

Leonean politics of the taint of the APC single-party regime that dominated the decades preceding civil war, and which was blamed for the squandering of the country's human and material resources, many called on the diaspora to offer their best and brightest in the run-up to the 1996, and successive, elections. Thus James Jonah, a career UN civil servant from Sierra Leone, who rose to the rank of undersecretary general for political affairs, left in 1994 to serve as interim chair of the National Electoral Commission, and later became a minister in President Kabbah's elected government. President Ahmed Tejan Kabbah himself was a career UN civil servant (in the UN Development Programme), who returned to Sierra Leone after a 20-year absence to run in the 1996 internationally brokered elections. Indeed, the 1996 elections saw a marked shift in the scope of Sierra Leonean electoral politics beyond state boundaries, with candidates canvassing for votes and fundraising among diasporic communities, especially in Europe and the United States, both through personal visits and through Internet websites. The pattern was repeated and expanded for the elections of 2002, 2007, and 2012.

As mentioned above the expansion of the canvassing territory for Sierra Leone elections beyond national boundaries, among members of the diaspora, is not in itself a new phenomenon. Historically, the best and brightest among colonial subjects traveled abroad for their educations, and these residencies in the diaspora—usually in the metropolitan centers of the colonial powers that ruled their homelands—were often formative periods in the political careers of many early African leaders. Several postindependence leaders were recruited in the diaspora for their political careers at home. However, these diasporic experiences in pursuit of education were usually understood to be temporary, whereas today study abroad is often undertaken as a springboard to permanent relocation. And with a larger citizenry abroad, where even the less-educated members of the working class have high incomes compared with Sierra Leoneans at home, the scale and character of the state's effort to pull the diaspora back to its own roots has changed as well.

In a study of the Eritrean diaspora, Victoria Bernal (2006, 165) underscored that "Despite their lack of wealth, the diaspora has contributed millions of dollars to Eritrea, not only in the form of remittances to family members, but also through taxes paid to the Eritrean state, donations contributed for various projects and, most significantly, to fund the 1998–2000 border conflict with Ethiopia." The Eritrean case is perhaps an extreme example of a state that was already in existence as a fiscal and regulatory entity (e.g., was levying taxes), even before it gained sovereign independence in 1991. Its legitimacy as a state was in part predicated on the ability to incorporate its diaspora into its sovereign grasp. As we have seen above, the Sierra Leonean diaspora also played a role in supporting the 1991–2002 war, as well as the peace efforts that periodically sought to put an end to the conflict.

## THE POLITICAL ECONOMY OF DIASPORIC NETWORKS

Diasporas and their extraterritorial spaces are increasingly factored into the domestic politics of states, particularly those in the Global South, like the Eritrean diaspora mentioned above, that have large and engaged populations abroad. In some cases, like the island nations of Cape Verde in Africa or Tonga in the Pacific, the diasporic population outnumbers residents in the homeland, so demographic factors amplify the economic and political weight of émigrés (Bourdet and Falck 2006; Besnier 2012). For Sierra Leonean and other African governments this is in part because of the rising importance of remittances, which saw a dramatic increase when the conflicts of the 1990s produced waves of refugees that joined established diasporas abroad, as factors in their economies.[17] Emmanuel Akyeampong analyzed the case of Ghana, which had a large and very successful diaspora, not only in Europe and North America, but also in Nigeria, after the 1970s oil boom made this an attractive nearby destination, at a time when Ghana itself was going through a slump owing in part to the fall in value of its export commodities on the global markets. Akyeampong noted that every year between 1983 and 1990, private individual remittances from Ghanaians abroad outstripped foreign business investments in the country, and the government began to send representatives on regular missions to the United States to discuss investments and the economy with the diaspora (Akyeampong 2000, 211). Broader comparative studies show that even when direct foreign investments in a developing country exceed remittances, which is usually the case, those investments are themselves often as a result of the influence of members of the diaspora (Newland and Patrick 2004). For Sierra Leone, remittances coming into the country were estimated in 1995 to be twenty-four million US dollars. This figure had almost doubled to forty-seven million US dollars by 2009 (World Bank 2011, 386). Since the 1990s, no major candidate for election, either in person, or through proxies, websites, and emails directed to the diaspora, has neglected to fundraise and campaign among Sierra Leoneans abroad. The country's president has set up an Office for Diaspora Affairs, and there is a link to this office on the government's website.

The perception that the diaspora has a "value added" effect on the political and public sphere at home is evident in Sierra Leonean electoral politics. Prominent members of the US and UK diasporas were not only asked to run for national political office, or to attend and support fundraisers, as I mentioned above.[18] In the postcivil war decade, several of the vacant chieftaincies were filled with candidates from the diaspora. In some cases, the officeholders, after having spent most of their lives abroad,[19] returned from the diaspora for the purpose of canvassing for electoral office, and their "foreignness" was seen as an asset in harnessing development and economic opportunities for their chiefdoms.

Additionally, some of their constituents—and governance reform advocates—felt that bringing back diasporic Sierra Leoneans, whose livelihoods did not depend on their political office, made them less corruptible. Better to choose paramount chiefs who could count on savings and secure pensions built over lifetimes of employment abroad—the argument went—because they would be less prone to extract excessive fines and tributes from their subjects. In this regard, it is worth noting that strategies of extraversion can be deployed toward democratic outcomes as well, for the dependence on foreign pensions, businesses, and investments was seen as minimizing inducements to using the chiefship to accumulate personal wealth. Finally, the exposure of these more cosmopolitan diasporic chiefs to the wider world beyond Sierra Leone was thought to provide some protection from their becoming too embroiled in shortsighted and local factionalism.

Thus the increasing participation of diasporic Sierra Leoneans in the electoral politics of their home country, through campaign fundraising, returning to stand for office, fostering vigorous debates in the media, maintaining Internet lists, and other means, has reshaped the idiom and vision of national politics over the past decade. But as the political debates surrounding chiefly elections examined in an earlier chapter suggest, the impact of these changes is especially notable in local politics, for which the choice of diasporic candidates who lack familiarity with the intricacies of chiefdom micropolitics is potentially more momentous. Reasons why political factions at the chiefdom level often form over time include historical land disputes, enmities that shape or break marriage alliances, kinship loyalties, intergenerational bonds of dependency, and so on. In this scenario, a "foreign" chief is at a distinct disadvantage, and often becomes a figurehead with little influence in a chiefdom's realpolitik, which instead is in the hands of established and longtime resident power brokers.

As a result, many of the new chiefs elected in the aftermath of the 1991–2002 civil war, including some who had returned from the diaspora to stand for office, were de facto absentee chiefs. Indeed, some were elected precisely so they could be in the capital city or large towns, where aid agencies, NGOs, and government offices were based, so that they might better advocate on behalf of their constituencies and harness the resources such entities could channel their way. In other words, a chief's ability to tap into networks that offered opportunities for extraversion was in the calculus of his or her election from the beginning.

**CONCLUSION**

If sovereign rule is in part shaped by the ways in which states incorporate their citizens and institutions, even well beyond their physical boundaries, what critical roles do diasporas and refugees play in this process? The broader point I have sought to make in this chapter is that, in the first instance, one must identify empirically where and how states produce and reproduce localities at particular moments in time, in order to understand the nature of the relation to the physical, imaginary, and moral landscape of those among their subjects who are involved in transnational migrations, or who live in established diasporas abroad. States extend their influence well beyond their territorial borders, for instance, through practices of registration and documentality like issuing or withdrawing passports and other identification documents or engaging in the rhetorical and economic practices that link governments to diasporic populations through discourse, flows of remittances, and so on. These forms and levels of extraterritorial state integration are, I argue, increasingly important for considering the relationship between democracy and security, in Sierra Leone in particular, as well as in Africa and other parts of the developing world. This point has been missed because scholarship on African weak or failed states since the 1990s has mainly focused on state institutions and services. Furthermore, focusing on the mobilization of diaspora as location and concept moves us away from normative notions of state sovereign rule, which tie it too closely to the static notion of territory, and privileges instead the practices through which it is made present, and effective.

In the aftermath of a violent civil war like the one that unfolded during the 1990s in Sierra Leone, as well as in other African countries, several factors led to the increasing importance of diasporic involvement in homeland politics: a) the size of diasporic populations increased as refugees from the wars of that decade permanently settled abroad, in part thanks to developments in the political and economic protections offered as humanitarian justice and its institutions gained traction globally; b) economies of scale and competition made long-distance travel more accessible to increasing numbers of people; and c) advances in digital technologies gave ordinary consumers access to computers, cheap fax machines, mobile phones, and the Internet. But saying that the diaspora has greater weight in a country's internal politics says nothing of future prospects for forms of democratic participation that lead to security and social justice. Indeed, linking democratic futures to practices of "free and fair elections," which often led to the opposite outcome in places like Sierra Leone—at least during the prewar decades—sometimes conceals more substantive prospects of emancipation.

Citizens in the diaspora are increasingly included in political and economic matters of concern to the state—both internally, as partners in development and business projects, health care initiatives, and so on, and externally, for instance, as participants in internationally brokered peace talks, as was the case for the publisher of *Focus on Sierra Leone* and for others during the 1991–2002 civil war. Furthermore, the analyses and debates they fostered shaped the shared political imaginary in significant ways. But the nature of these political engagements needs to be examined empirically in different settings, as their outcomes are not always democratic. Instead, they sometimes represent the interests of elites at the expense of the broader public.

The legal jurisprudence of the refugee changes the contours of diasporic populations and reactivates transnational flows of a people in sometimes unexpected ways. Thus in my work with Sierra Leonean and other sub-Saharan African populations in Cairo, I noted the ways in which programs set in place by international aid groups and host countries to ensure safe havens for refugees during the civil war also enabled migrants who had left Sierra Leone in earlier times to move on to more attractive destinations in Europe and the United States (Ferme 2004). But with the end of the civil war, and of those programs, many are now turning to human traffickers and taking more circuitous routes in order to move to new, nontraditional destinations for Sierra Leoneans, such as Turkey (an entry point to Europe) and Australia. At the same time, the war refugee crisis as both a demographic and a moral phenomenon has pushed political participation of the better-educated, wealthier members of the diaspora in national politics to a sort of "tipping point," with both sides of that relationship—diasporic communities and national governments—increasing the pace of exchanges.

Another, related point has to do with the kinds of publics and political communities produced by new digital technologies, especially mobile phones and the Internet. While sometimes online fora might seem to simply extend the reach of a neighborhood or gossip, Sierra Leone's example shows how Internet communities like those created by the contributors to and readers of the *Focus on Sierra Leone* and the NINJAS have allowed Sierra Leoneans within and outside the country to engage critically with political actors and institutions in Sierra Leone and neighboring countries. They have also enabled appeals to international and global institutions that were intervening in the civil war.

Finally, over time, diasporic populations change, as do their relationships with the home country. Many of the children of Sierra Leoneans in the United States, for instance, are American citizens, and though many parents want their offspring to visit the homeland and family there, this mobility may create a more cosmopolitan future in which national belongings are more muted. But the social and political mobilizations made possible by social media in Iran and in North Africa, or at the various global leadership summits held since the 1999 World Trade Organization ministerial meeting in Seattle, suggest otherwise. The efforts of *Focus on Sierra Leone* and other social forums of Sierra Leoneans abroad suggest that they, too, will continue to participate through the latest available technologies in the political life of their countries of origin, and on a global scale. But as is the case elsewhere, we cannot forecast that such efforts will have a democratizing effect—they may be co-opted for conservative, or even authoritarian, purposes.

In all this, the figures of the refugee in the camp and the diasporic citizen are increasingly important nodes for producing or shaping the linkages between national forms of political and social imaginaries. The former occupy a liminal space as displaced people outside their countries of origin in a "national order of things" (Malkki 1996). This is underscored by the strict humanitarian nomenclature that distinguishes them from "internally displaced people" within national borders. At the same time, their relationships with the host country are mediated by the humanitarian agencies running and funding the camps where they reside, making them actors in multiple, nesting political arenas, minimally their home and host countries, and in the broader philanthropic communities upon which their livelihoods depend.

Diasporic subjects—and the diverse communities they evoke—paint a more complex picture, one not necessarily identified with the abject dispossession of the refugee described so far, but, if anything, one more invested by means of both imaginary and political practices in the project of fostering connections with the homeland. As I suggested above, their cultivation of the public sphere accessible to them in the form of alumni associations, geographic origin groups, and even extended families enables them to mobilize for political causes—local and national elections, funding for infrastructural projects, the performance of cultural spectacles that accompany such meetings, and so on. This sphere serves to anchor and create a sense of virtual community within an increasingly cosmopolitan and diversified Sierra Leonean population, for which life in the transnational diaspora can sometimes be a liminal stage they occupy before retiring "back home," or returning to invest in new businesses or political opportunities. In addition, these transnational actors are increasingly the focus of interest of the Sierra Leonean state, as it seeks to harness the intellectual, financial, and material capital generated in the diaspora

# Child Soldiers and
# the Contested Imaginary
# of Community after War

In the aftermath of war, it is not just specific individuals but entire communities, and the sense of belonging to them, that require restoration. Indeed, conflicts can challenge the ways in which collectivities are conceived, as families, neighborhoods, villages, and so on may be the very sites where the seeds of injustice and violence were sown. In what follows, I question the implication of benignity and safety that is often embedded in understandings of "community" in postconflict and transitional justice institutions and practices. When spatially conceived, the concept of community tends to privilege static principles of residence and (or) nativity (the natural fact of being born in a place), rather than other forms of belonging. And in postconflict transitions, humanitarian actors often assume there is therapeutic value in resettling populations displaced by war in their communities of origin. But rural Africans usually have multiple options in such situations, as the combination of extensive marriage, kinship, and patronage networks, on the one hand, and of flexible, easily changed living arrangements, on the other, means that many people make their homes in a series of heterotopic places over the course of their lives. The challenge is to identify which of these possible permutations of community, with their different scales, affective resonances, and localizations, can have therapeutic roles, and under what circumstances.

Though the Sierra Leone civil war initially unfolded in urban as well as rural areas—and for long stretches of time in terrain, such as the semi-industrial rural wastelands produced by intensive mining of alluvial diamonds, rutile, and other minerals, that could not properly be called either—its disruption of agrarian landscapes and societies was more visible. This was in part because economic inequality and social insecurity set rural farmers in motion toward the towns and nearby refugee camps, where security and humanitarian aid were concentrated. Thus the war in part reconfigured the social and livelihood options, especially for members of rural communities, such as youth and young women or members of dependent, nonlandowning lineages, who were at the margins of their power structures.

These members of rural communities greeted with some ambivalence the prospect of being "reunited" with the families from whom they were separated—reunions promoted by a number of humanitarian agencies. These programs assumed that the family structure and community offered the most appropriate "psychosocial" environment for rehabilitating, and thus healing, conflict-affected youth, in particular—a position often expressed rhetorically to naturalize the meaning of "local," especially in rural areas. When paired with community, as in "local community," rural locality appeared to offer the promise of stability, reintegration, and reconciliation so as to promote therapeutic healing. Even justice-seeking processes were relocated at the community level, for instance, in the *gaçaça* courts of Rwanda, which in 2004 were tasked with prosecuting perpetrators of the 1994 genocide. These were proposed as alternatives to the expensive and lengthy trials of the International Criminal Tribunal for Rwanda. Panels of nine judges, or "persons of integrity," were assembled in rural communities to sit in judgment over proceedings, at which accused perpetrators were expected to confess, witnesses were brought forward to corroborate the evidence, and victims were expected to forgive the contrite *génocidaires*.

But ethnographic studies of the *gaçaça* courts have shown that justice-seeking institutions characterized as local and traditional, and therefore as having greater legitimacy and restorative value in rural communities, can be by-products of top-down, state-mandated policies that are not especially responsive to the needs of those directly involved. Thus the state-mandated *gaçaça* courts sometimes reproduced the scapegoating mechanisms of fear, paranoia, and mutual mistrust at the origins of the genocide by using formal and informal surveillance to pressure community members to undertake the scripted role of witnessing audience (see Thomson 2011). Such collective mechanisms for justice-seeking and reconciliation, often undertaken in the name of national unity, put the interests of collectivities above those of grieving individuals, for whom processing grief and achieving closure—if even possible—may take different forms and lengths of time. Studies of the Truth and Reconciliation Commission (TRC) in South Africa similarly pointed to the temporal disjuncture between the needs of the grieving relatives and survivors of the terrors of apartheid, and the postapartheid state's project of "national reconciliation," which called for a relatively expeditious and complete closure to particular investigations (e.g., Hamber and Wilson 2002).

In what follows, I examine some of the problematic assumptions about rural Sierra Leonean life and "customs" that emerged in the context of postconflict transitional justice institutions, especially the Special Court for Sierra Leone (SCSL). In particular, I focus on assumptions about agency and kinship in the legislation of and courtroom discourse at the SCSL. The SCSL, the first war crimes tribunal to successfully prosecute individuals for the forced conscription of child soldiers, also distinguished itself for its vigorous prosecution of gender crimes. Though I focus in part on the discrepancies between perspectives at the SCSL and among my Sierra Leonean interlocutors on the rights and agency of children, I do so—to paraphrase Sally Merry on the topic of human rights more generally—not to fall back on anthropological arguments in favor of cultural relativism and against the universalizing discourse of rights, or to adjudicate whether these tribunals are "a good idea," but to analyze instead "what difference they make" (Merry 2006, 39; see also Wilson and Mitchell 2003, 1–2). In other words, while I aim to be attentive to the relationship between transitional justice mechanisms and "local" understandings of events and experiences, I want to avoid cultural moves that sometimes result from rather depoliticized, overly homogeneous and static views of culture, tradition, and locality, on the one hand, and from a humanitarian discourse that is also fraught with contested and contradictory aspects, on the other.

My insistence on the political dimension of humanitarian discourse owes much to Hannah Arendt's (1951, 299) observations on the links between the rise of broad allegiances to the "inborn and inalienable rights of man" and of totalitarianism in the twentieth century: "The conception of human rights based upon the assumed existence of a human being as such broke down at the very moment when those who professed to believe in it were for the first time confronted with people who had indeed lost all other qualities and specific relationships—except that they were still human. The world found nothing sacred in the abstract nakedness of being human." For Arendt, there was no way of transcending the realm of the political—and of the robust protections offered by the political rights of citizenship—in the name of a universal fiction of humanitarian law that protected bare life. As I discuss in the final section of this chapter, Arendt's understanding of rights as essentially political—and democratic, in particular—resonated with debates among some of the marginalized groups in Sierra Leone, whose grievances had fueled the conflict. In the war's aftermath, these groups embraced in novel ways the discourse of rights, for instance, to advance the interests of individuals against those of collectivities like patrilineages and extended households, which tended to favor the older, powerful, and wealthy in these communities. In the process, they also insisted on anchoring these rights in political institutions and practices.

Reworking the discourse of rights to extend beyond the sphere of humanitarian law and war crimes courts appears to parallel the push in these latter settings to focus on rights-bearing individuals to the detriment of rights-bearing collectivities, even though it does so in different ways. But in the court setting, the focus on individual perpetrators of crimes is problematic, since violence and abuses in war are often experienced as collective phenomena, which in some cases profoundly erode normal mechanisms of social reproduction, trust, and accountability. The developing body of international humanitarian law has moved, in its thinking about "personal responsibility," toward narrower definitions of individual accountability. This means those higher up in the chains of command are now being targeted for prosecution rather than the actual perpetrators of brutalities. Thus the indictment of "those most responsible" for particular war crimes accounted for dozens of indictments in the Yugoslavian and Rwandan tribunals, but by the time the second generation of "hybrid" war crimes courts (i.e., those covering war crimes in Sierra Leone, East Timor, and Cambodia) got under way, after 2000, prosecution had shifted to "those bearing *the greatest* responsibility"—a narrower designation that yielded fewer indictments and speedier trials.

The practice of humanitarian discourse is contested and contradictory, then: on the one hand, communities have been seen as key to accountability, reconciliation, and the rebuilding of national unity in the aftermath of violence, as in the cases of the South African TRC and of the *gaçaça* courts in Rwanda. These cases show that to some extent the healing of national communities comes at the expense of the grieving processes required by individual victims, or other communities, on a smaller scale. On the other hand, at the International Criminal Tribunal for Rwanda, for instance, the focus on individual responsibility for crime flew in the face of the collective forms of violence, with state collusion, which resulted in the Rwandan genocide—a violence that undermined the very possibility of community.

**AMBIVALENT RETURNS**

In this section, I explore the ways in which family reunification programs in the aftermath of war highlighted some of the aporias embedded in efforts to reconstitute the wholeness of prewar families and communities. The cases I examine here underscore the contested nature of practices aimed at healing individuals and communities traumatized by war displacement. Both cases involve young men who had been children or young teenagers at the outbreak of this decade-long war, and highlight the uneasy fit between the therapeutic needs of individuals and those of collectivities in the aftermath of extreme violence. Youth were also at the center of the proceedings in the SCSL where prosecutors issued indictments for the relatively new crime of forced conscription of child soldiers, and in the next section I analyze the contradictions in the developing humanitarian discourse about war-affected youth that is the foundation of these prosecutions.

In spring 2002, I was present in the rural Sierra Leonean chiefdom where I had carried out research since 1984, when a young man was brought back by an organization devoted to disarmament, demobilization, and reintegration (DDR), and to the reunification of families separated by war. Since the peace declaration in January 2002, efforts to repatriate refugees and reunite families separated by war were stepped up as the country prepared to hold its first postconflict elections in May. A van pulled up to the home of the chiefdom's section chief[1] and dropped off a young man, who looked vaguely familiar and was accompanied by an NGO employee charged with repatriating war-affected youth. The people who had accompanied me from the village where we were staying exclaimed with surprise that this was "Kaikulo"—a nickname I am making up for him that means "squirrel" in Mende—a child who had lived next door to me some seventeen years earlier, and who had often come by to play with other children in the compound or to offer to do chores in exchange for food.

Somewhat shell-shocked, Kaikulo circumspectly answered questions from people crowding around him, including myself. I assumed that, like all other people in the village who had known me since they were children, Kaikulo would remember me as the only Caucasian stranger in the village of some 260 people, especially since we had been neighbors. He said he did not remember me, nor any of the other villagers.

Kaikulo's father had died when he was young, and his mother had remarried and had other children, joining her new husband in his village, at the other end of the chiefdom. Her efforts to include Kaikulo in her new family had failed, so she had sent him to live with her widowed father, who occupied the house next to mine. This situation was not uncommon. Children were raised by foster parents for many reasons, including the death of a caretaking parent, a father preferring particular wives and children over others, incompatibilities between a parent and child, and the prospect of a better future with wealthier relatives. But Kaikulo and his grandfather were an unusual pair, since as a widower his grandfather would have been expected to live with a younger sibling or one of his adult children, in order to have his daily domestic needs met by a woman in the house. Instead, Kaikulo and his grandfather—one too young, the other too old and ill to farm—had lived alone in a half-collapsed mud house, with no female relatives to cook for them and often dependent on the kindness of neighbors for their subsistence. On one occasion when Kaikulo's grandfather was seen preparing a meal in his dilapidated house, other villagers commented on the shameful, pathetic sight of a Mende man cooking for himself, suggesting that this was the epitome of social isolation and poverty. Some blamed the daughter— Kaikulo's mother—for dereliction of her filial and maternal duties. After the death of his grandfather in 1986, Kaikulo was sent to live with relatives near the Liberian border and had never returned (till that day).

Kaikulo could not have been much younger than seven at the time he left—more likely, he was older. He certainly was already of an age when developing children form lasting memories. Perhaps his failure to remember his earlier life was linked to traumatic experiences in the intervening time, or to his concern that acknowledging any memories at all might lead to troubling questions about the more recent past. The section chief sent for Kaikulo's mother, in a village a few miles away, and while we waited for her arrival people began asking him about his life. Kaikulo said that he had been living near the country's eastern border with relatives when the civil war broke out, and had almost immediately been captured and taken over the border to Liberia. People fell silent at this news: everyone knew that the war had "come to the country" in 1991 from Liberia, and that Liberian training, armaments, and shelter were key to the formation of the Revolutionary United Front (RUF), whose "rebels" had been the conflict's instigators. It was not unusual for civilians on the Sierra Leonean side of the border to seek refuge from the rebels in Liberia when the conflict heated up in eastern Sierra Leone, but Kaikulo's admission that he had been captured by them immediately raised suspicions that he might have been enlisted into their ranks.

One bystander voiced this suspicion, asking Kaikulo what he had done during the war and prefacing his question with a comment about how "we" had heard that many horrible things were done in some of the places where Kaikulo had lived. He added that "we" wanted to make sure that nobody came here to stir up trouble. The man spoke in the first person plural to convey his sense that the community as a whole shared his sentiment—as the exchange of nods and looks all around seemed to imply. Before Kaikulo could answer, however, the section chief intervened, telling the man not to question him and challenging the notion that he was speaking for all. Turning to Kaikulo, the chief told him that he would not ask him what he had done during the war, but wanted him to know that if he wanted to live in the chiefdom, he had to follow the rules and stay out of trouble.

In silencing questions about Kaikulo's wartime experiences and discouraging Kaikulo from talking about them, all the while juxtaposing the interrogator's "we" (the collective) with his own use of "I" (the individual), the chief was doing the opposite of what many postconflict transition experts consider an essential element of reconciliation—publicly acknowledging one's actions in wartime, in the name of accountability and justice. At that very time, a group of South African advisors was in the country, offering advice as Sierra Leone's own TRC was beginning its work. To the TRC, which collected the bulk of its testimonies in 2003, "the need to know" was paramount in order to "heal communities," effect reconciliation, and move beyond the conflict. But to this chief. and to others I witnessed in similar situations, setting aside the war and its memories offered the best chance for moving on. And while the man who had asked Kaikulo what he had done and where he had been during the war did not share this attitude, it was by far the prevailing one I witnessed during this immediate postconflict phase.

The ambivalence toward public communications of intimate war experiences became evident from the reception given another village youth. He had been a young recruit among the "hunter"—*kamajɔ*—militias, which had formed initially under the patronage of paramount chiefs but by 1996 had developed into a national, progovernment civil defense force, whose leader acquired the rank of deputy minister of defense. Because most villages voluntarily "gave" some of their young men to the civil defense force for their own protection—especially during the early years of the war—they tended to enjoy the support of their communities, unlike other fighters kidnapped or forcibly conscripted by warring factions. But this young man could not find a sympathetic ear for his story of a wartime traumatic wound. He wandered in search of new interlocutors to whom he might show a wartime photo of himself in armed "hunter" attire and a bullet, which he carried with him. He would lift his shirt to show the scar left by the bullet and speak in a monotone about his illness.

Locals who had heard the story many times before moved away as he approached, while others asked him to let go of his complaints, reminding him that they had suffered too. The implication was that, in his pursuit of individual attention for his story, he was undermining their hope to move collectively beyond their suffering. This response was consistent with the skepticism noted by scholars and humanitarian NGOs toward the TRC process in Sierra Leone and the notion that "vent[ing] thoughts and feelings" was a precondition for transitioning to a stable peace. Thus Rosalind Shaw (2007, 184, 206) has noted the "friction" between "the concept of redemptive remembering," espoused by promoters of the TRC process and conveyed in the rhetoric of its proceedings, and the "local techniques of forgetting" that were preferred by many Sierra Leoneans, in part because they feared hearing testimonies about wartime experiences would "reopen old wounds" and bring about more violence (ICG 2003, 12). This resulted in lower-than-anticipated attendance at the TRC's open sessions throughout the country, a phenomenon anticipated by the scene surrounding Kaikulo's return in the year leading up to those proceedings and confirmed by the experience of the other young man who could not find sympathetic listeners in his home village. The young hunter felt an obligation to communicate the "shock of the Real" in such an obsessive way that the rest of the community perceived it as a threat. The local mechanism for dealing with wartime atrocities was to keep silent about them if they had occurred at a distance, where the context of violence was not fully known. In contrast, known perpetrators of atrocities would not have been allowed back at all.

When Kaikulo's mother arrived, there was an awkward reunion between the estranged pair, and nobody was surprised when, given a choice, he opted not to follow her but instead to return to the village from which he had left so many years earlier—where his grandfather's surviving brothers still lived. As Kaikulo and I walked around the village, he seemed ill at ease as I reintroduced him to people and places. He had been born there, but he had been left behind by his mother, had suffered cold and hunger through his grandfather's terminal illness—when even other children spurned him—and eventually had been sent away to live with distant relatives. He had been taken to a foreign country in the midst of a violent war, and now through the intervention of a project that facilitated family reunions had decided to return to this particular "local community," an expression the NGO staff member who had accompanied him kept repeating.

The contrast between the chief's avoidance of questions, on the one hand, and his interrupting of those who aggressively interrogated Kaikulo, on the other, suggests that whether it was preferable to disclose wartime deeds or move beyond them was not a settled question in this part of rural Sierra Leone, as was true at the national level as well. This may in part have been because, whatever Kaikulo did during the war—and regardless of whether he had been a victim, a perpetrator of violence, or both—he did while he was far away in Liberia. Since nobody could verify whether he had committed crimes elsewhere, he was left alone in his liminal status as a potentially suspect returnee.

I left a few days after Kaikulo's arrival, and when I next visited a couple of years later, he had departed for one of Sierra Leone's larger provincial towns. Set in motion by the war, and exposed to life in large, peri-urban refugee camps and towns, he apparently no longer considered the rural village where he had been born to be his community of reference. Instead, it was where he had spent only a perhaps insignificant fraction of his life—and not a very happy one at that. By 2012, however, Kaikulo was back, and when conversations turned to the conflict that had ended ten years earlier, people casually mentioned his having been "taken to Liberia" during the war without expressing suspicion. Kaikulo had been reunited with his mother: they lived and farmed together, now that the husband who had not wanted him in his house had died, leaving her a widow. An easy familiarity had developed between them, and with the broader village community. Kaikulo finally seemed at home. He had taken a long detour on his journey to resettle in his community of origin and had faced suspicion, rumors of war, and other forms of gossip. Kaikulo had to re-create his "natural" community by going away and coming back once again, to let time heal the intergenerational trauma of the war. In a place where the logic of dis-simulation was pervasive, he knew that a bond with his community could not be predicated on the regime of transparent truth. On the contrary, any process of truth-telling had to maintain the very structure of ambiguity and dissimulation and had to be revealed in the routinized organization of the everyday. For Kaikulo, this meant reorganizing his "home" (once the psychic and social space of the "father" remained void) and filling home with the truth of lived family and social action.

But what of situations in which known perpetrators of violence were reunited with the communities that suffered at their hands? Rwanda posed some of the most extreme scenarios of cohabitation between victims and perpetrators of war crimes. It also raised the issue of justice-seeking mechanisms at the local level in the aftermath of war, in the form of the *gaçaça* courts mentioned in the previous section. In a 2008 visit to a Rwandan village where a *génocidaire* lived, having served a prison term for the crimes he had committed and to which he had testified in the local *gaçaça* court, Philip Gourevitch found a climate of mistrust and ambivalence on all sides. The perpetrator had asked for forgiveness from his victim's relatives, but the survivors felt "forced" by the government to cohabit with the neighbor who had turned on them during the genocide. He had set up a checkpoint in front of his house, where he himself purportedly killed almost a dozen people. The man had not confessed to all of these murders, and for this and other reasons survivors did not entirely trust that he would not turn violent again, under the right circumstances. In turn, the perpetrator was now living and farming in greater poverty than most of those living around him, keeping to himself and to his family. Fear of retribution had made him a virtual prisoner in his house (Gourevitch 2009).

What was striking about many Rwandan cases was the intimacy of the violence, and the contradictory feelings generated in its aftermath. Among the victims of the Hutu *génocidaire* portrayed in Gourevitch's article were relatives of the man's Tutsi wife. She continued to live with him and wavered between defending him against his accusers and admitting that she feared him, while her surviving relatives openly expressed their hostility and disbelief that she could even consider remaining married to him. The "community" portrayed on this particular Rwandan hill in the aftermath of *gaçaça* did not seem a place of therapeutic healing and reconciliation. To the contrary, it was a place where outright terror had been replaced by a veneer of formal civility, and where surveillance and mistrust, along with the fear that violence could break out again at any time, were widespread.

In Kaikulo's Sierra Leonean village, memories of his past presence there remained among those left behind, but the violence of war had erased or made incommunicable his own memories of this place when he first returned in 2002. He barely spoke of his grandfather, from whom he had been inseparable as a child. At the same time, the crisis produced by war—the "tear," or break, in the original etymology of the word—opened up the possibility of creating different networks of belonging and perhaps of therapeutic forgetting. For Kaikulo, whose "community" had not been able to protect him even from the structural violence of social inequality, poverty, and maternal abandonment before the war, let alone from war atrocities, the silence surrounding his wartime activities in time made it possible for him to return.[2]

As mentioned earlier, the focus (for example, in the discourse of the TRC and of NGOs working on refugee repatriation) on communities as sites of reintegration and posttraumatic healing was in part justified by the youth of many perpetrators and victims of the Sierra Leone civil war. But the cases of Kaikulo and of the young wounded hunter underscore the ambivalence as to whether reintegration should include "coming clean" with the truths about a subject's wartime past, or whether instead these memories should be silenced and forgotten, at least in public. Indeed, while Kaikulo had eventually managed a measure of reintegration into the ordinary rural life he had known before the war, the wounded young hunter had become increasingly alienated over time. After being healed physically by humanitarian agencies, which along with the TRC offered him opportunities to relate his "victim's tale," which found no sympathetic listeners in his own community, he left the village.[3]

But the other realm in which these issues were debated was the SCSL—the alternative, judicial arena where war criminals were prosecuted—where contested memories of the war were elicited in the pursuit of justice and accountability. Indeed, in the opinion of David Crane, the first chief prosecutor of the court, this link between war crimes tribunals and TRC processes was to become a cornerstone of the new generation of hybrid national and international tribunals, of which the SCSL was one example (Crane 2006, 1684).

## CHILD SOLDIERS AND INDIVIDUAL RESPONSIBILITY

From the outset, the forced conscription of child soldiers challenged the boundaries between perpetrators and victims, civilians and combatants—and the very meaning of "responsibility"—for mechanisms of justice that depended on precisely this distinction. But it also challenged other boundaries. Graça Machel's influential 1996 report, *The Impact of Armed Conflict on Children,* commissioned by the UN secretary general, begins as follows: "Millions of children are caught in conflicts in which they are not merely bystanders, but targets." The normal expectation that children would be "caught" up in war and not actively participate went hand in hand with the notion that they should at most be incidental witnesses to violence, not its targets. Machel (1996) goes on to characterize this attack as a sign of "the desolate moral vacuum" into which the world was falling, and to identify the blurring of boundaries between combatant and civilian as one of its key symptoms. Even though, in her discussion of the ways in which child soldiers are recruited, Machel mentions that "youth also present themselves for service" (12), she hastens to write that this should not be construed as "voluntary" enlistment, since economic or other pressures often play a role in such decisions. The picture of vulnerability and limited agency tends to simplify the category "youth," but it also assumes much about the choices of adults, who might be "caught" in war in ways they cannot control.

In 2000, when UN secretary-general Kofi Annan presented to the Security Council the document establishing the SCSL and its statutes, he took a different position with respect to young perpetrators of violence. He wrote, under the heading of "personal responsibility,"

> Within the meaning attributed to it in the present Statute, the term "most responsible" would not necessarily exclude children between 15 and 18 years of age. While it is inconceivable that children could be in a political or military leadership position (although in Sierra Leone the rank of "Brigadier" was often granted to children as young as 11 years), the gravity and seriousness of the crimes they have allegedly committed would allow for their inclusion within the jurisdiction of the Court. (Annan 2000)

He goes on in the next section to discuss both the "moral dilemma" posed by the prospect of children being prosecuted for crimes against humanity and the debates pitting representatives of the government of Sierra Leone (who insisted that juveniles responsible for crimes against humanity be brought to justice) against representatives of international agencies and NGOs, who worried that such a move might jeopardize the youth rehabilitation programs set up during the postconflict transition. In the event, the recommendations were to shift responsibility for collecting the testimony of perpetrators who were fifteen-to-eighteen years old at the time the crimes were committed to the Truth and

Reconciliation Commission (which was yet to be established); to hire personnel with specific expertise in dealing with juvenile offenders at the court; to treat witnesses of that age "with dignity and with a sense of worth"; and to subject them, when necessary, to "alternative options of correctional or educational nature" (Annan 2000, 8).

In contrast with the Machel report, Kofi Annan's document balanced an approach to children as at once victims, who might have joined the fight because they were plied with drugs or subjected to psychological violence, and perpetrators, who had committed atrocities and should be brought to account, according to demands in Sierra Leone. His recommendation for the SCSL was that it should prosecute those "most responsible" for war crimes—the same mandate under which the International Criminal Tribunal for Yugoslavia and International Criminal Tribunal for Rwanda had issued dozens of indictments—rather than only those "bearing the greatest responsibility," as ended up being the case. Annan also invokes morality, but not in the sense of the "moral vacuum" created when a world no longer respects the sanctity of children, who are assumed to be innocent and "unarmed." Instead, the dilemma is that these very populations might be agents of violence, rather than its passive victims. The overlooked fact in this tendency to think of civilians as unarmed is that it is often championed by policy and legal experts from countries such as the United States and Canada, which rank first and third in world tables of civilian gun ownership, with, respectively, 42 percent and 26 percent of their citizens reporting they have guns in their homes![4]

In the event, Kofi Annan's more nuanced approach to the question of youth participation in armed conflict, and to the grey zone separating their moral responsibility for committing atrocities from their status as victims of violence, was overtaken in the SCSL by the agenda of inscribing the very act of recruiting them into the roster of crimes against humanities. The focus on the individual moral responsibility of the child combatant gave way to the individual moral responsibility of those who recruited children to fight. In the process, the child soldier became a de facto victim in a permanent, timeless way, even though the war lasted more than ten years, during which time a young person would have passed through different stages of moral reasoning, responsibility, and culpability—with respect to both the sociocultural institutions in which his or her life unfolded and international humanitarian legal mechanisms.

Though these subjects remained forever young in the language of legal debates and in the overly solicitous rhetoric of judges, who addressed them as vulnerable victims, even as they testified as full adults, the court transcripts sometimes reveal more complex profiles. Witness DBK-113, who testified for the defense in the Armed Forces Revolutionary Council (AFRC) trial, was the son of a military man who had grown up in Freetown army barracks. His father aligned himself with the rogue group of midranking military officers who in May 1997 formed an alliance with the Revolutionary United Front (RUF) to overthrow the civilian government elected the previous year. The man, born in 1974, testified about events that occurred when he was twenty-three or older, during the nine months in 1997–98, when the AFRC/RUF junta held power, and during the period after the March 1998 reinstatement of the Kabbah government ousted by the junta. The return of Kabbah was marked by efforts to weed out junta supporters among the civilian population, and atrocities were committed on the government side as well as by the retreating AFRC-RUF forces.

During a line of questioning aimed to clarify what the witness meant by the expression "soldier's affiliates" to describe some of the young men with whom he retreated toward the junta-held parts of the north in the face of advances by government militias, the witness explained, "When soldiers had been pulling out from Freetown . . ., because of harassment which they had been receiving, and they had been burning soldiers, some were afraid to leave their children or their nephews, and nieces, so they went with them. So those kinds of people were in that group."[5] Affiliates, then, were youth who joined fighting factions because these were the safest places for them to be in situations of generalized chaos, such as Sierra Leone was in May 1998. For these young dependents, remaining behind in the communities they inhabited was the dangerous option, not the safe one, and, paradoxically, joining fighting factions was the only way to remain protected *as civilians*. Later in his testimony, the witness spoke about the leader of a new group of soldiers who arrived in a village where he was staying. As his testimony unfolded, lawyers consistently distinguished civilians and combatants in their questions, and gradually so did he, for instance, when he described the officer as incorporating "his own civilians that he came with, who were the relatives of soldiers, children—soldier's children, who came from Freetown. They incorporated them into our own civilian group."[6]

The nature of such "incorporation" interested the defense lawyers, who asked their witness whether among these civilians there were any who had been abducted, but the witness was unable to say. Not only, then, was the line separating combatants from civilians difficult to draw in his own testimony and experience, so, too, was that separating abduction from forms of affiliation that, over time, transformed civilians either into camp followers, who supported the combatants by transporting loot or providing a range of services, or into soldiers. Even considering the partisan nature of the witness's testimony, which was elicited to defend an AFRC leader against accusations of forced conscription of child soldiers and forced marriage, his words echoed a point made by others who have studied the everyday unfolding of this and other conflicts—namely, that contemporary and historical evidence suggests that under situations of extreme social disruption, "armed children may actually be safer than unarmed civilians" (Rosen 2007, 299). Thus some youth—including this witness—joined the fighting factions to secure the protection of a group whose hierarchical structure blurred the distinction between their members' young "relatives" and other "affiliates."

In the indictments and judgments of the SCSL, nuances respecting an individual's degree of involvement, and hence of responsibility—and the attending moral dilemmas—were mostly overlooked. Even when testimony exposed different degrees and forms of involvement in the conflict, as in the passage quoted above, these were often left unexamined by the judges. By contrast, in this particular instance, lawyers for the defense echoed in their line of questioning the writings of anthropologists, who noted the parallels between the living and support arrangements put in place by military officers for youth who ended up in their care during the conflict and the expansion of extended family supervision in ordinary rural settings that provided a safety net for orphaned and abandoned youth in prewar times (see Richards 1996, 81–82).

Despite the defense's efforts to familiarize the court with the various forms of affiliation young followers had with fighting forces, by assimilating them with ordinary, peacetime social networks, the figure of the child soldier as "a generic archetype of humanitarian discourse" emerged in most of the testimony elicited by the prosecution. The determining factor for the prosecution was that moral agency—and hence responsibility for war crimes—had to do with the age at which young combatants had been recruited. During the proceedings, clarifications about the exact age of a witness or victim testifying before the court at the time of the events being discussed resonated with the language of international conventions aimed at establishing the thresholds of particular forms of agency and responsibility in growing children. For example, should the age of prohibition against child recruitment be eighteen or fifteen? There was little support for the lower age threshold from states that routinely conscripted men younger than eighteen in their armies. Here, even though "protectionist concerns about children have been central to major legal efforts to restrict the involvement of children in war," the "politics of age that underlies the development of the law . . . has engendered conflicts over the age of recruitment, privileged state over nonstate actors, and undermined local solutions to the problem of the culpability of children" (Rosen 2007, 300). It also has had the effect of depoliticizing "the uses of children as moral subjects" in international humanitarian thinking about peace and war (Malkki 2010, 60).

This outcome belies the highly politicized nature of the international discussions that led to treaties governing the use of young combatants in war. While early drafts of the protocols added to the Geneva Conventions in the 1970s, on the question of child soldiers, contained "anemic language" that encouraged signatory states to take "all necessary measures" to prevent the recruitment of child soldiers and the "voluntary enrollment" of children under fifteen, the final document was altogether silent on the latter, a fact that reflects the contested nature of much international norm-setting (Rosen 2007). Thus there are tensions in how the discourse on international human rights has framed the issue of child soldiers, ranging from exhortations to exclude children from armed conflict without any enforcement mechanism to making their recruitment a crime against humanity, as was done in the SCSL.

But while historical change is patently at work in the development of this jurisprudence, timelessness has characterized the representation of "child soldiers." And this in the context of conflicts, such as the Sierra Leone civil war and the broader regional conflict within which it was situated, that lasted for ten years and longer—a timespan that brings dramatic changes in the moral, physical, and psychological development of any child. Defendants and witnesses testifying in front of the SCSL were adults, but lawyers and judges tended to address the latter as though they were still the children involved in the past events they were discussing. On more than one occasion, court judges intervened to reprimand a lawyer for not treating a witness with a gentleness consistent with their vulnerable status. Perhaps this behavior was informed by the scholarship on trauma and memory. In the temporalities of trauma, a subject is shielded by mechanisms of erasure from the full, conscious knowledge of a "wound" in the moment in which he or she suffers it, only to experience the event consciously later, when a different trauma brings it back (see Caruth 1996).

But if this were the concern of the court, paradoxically its practices did more to fix in time such witnesses as "traumatized children," rather than to recognize—as Kofi Annan advocated in his more nuanced recommendations—the ways childhood, in particular, is characterized by differences and rapid developmental changes. That these changes had implications for moral responsibility was underlined by the ambivalence with which the villagers present at Kaikulo's return addressed the possibility of his speaking out about his wartime experiences. His story, too, makes one consider that war in its very destructiveness can offer people better choices by unmooring them from communities that sometimes are sites of social inequality, structural violence, and suffering.

## CONCLUSION

Ultimately, a more lasting legacy of the SCSL and of "justice sector reform" NGOs that tried to spread awareness of humanitarian law in the country is to be found elsewhere than in the domain of the courts. In the aftermath of the 2002 declaration of peace, I was struck by the appearance of the neologism *raiti* (rights), a vernacularized version of the English word, in Mende-speaking communities in Sierra Leone's rural hinterlands. When I spoke to some men I knew about the upcoming national elections, for example, one said the following, in Mende:

> We have democracy now, we didn't before, because now we have rights (*raiti*). Right now, here, I have rights, that man too—he said, pointing to the friend walking alongside him—has rights. . . . All of us, every single one of us has rights. Things were not this way during the APC time [the All Peoples' Congress single-party government, which had been in power in 1991, when the war began, and had dominated politics during most of the previous two decades]. (Ferme and Hoffman 2004, 84).

The stress on his separateness from his friend, on the fact that "every single one of us has rights" went beyond rhetoric: it informed new ways of thinking about the political relationship between individuals and the various collectivities to which they belonged. Thus when humanitarian organizations brought food or other resources to entire village communities after war, how the aid would be distributed was discussed, whereas before the war this would have followed a predictable pattern. In a village with ten extended households, for example, each of the male elders at the head of each household's core patrilineage would have been allocated an equal share of rice, tools, seed, domestic animals, or whatever, to share among his dependents. The latter, their rights, and their representations were subsumed under the collective, familial ethos of the extended household and its hierarchical organization.

Now this extended familial "community," this collective entity, was called into question, and those who had the most to lose in its unequal internal allocation of power and resources used rights discourse to assert their entitlement as moral individuals. In one instance I witnessed, in which ten fifty-kilogram bags of rice were brought for distribution, young men in the village refused to allocate one per each of the ten households, instead emptying their contents to form a large mound in the center of the village meeting place, so that each adult could be called by name, to receive his or her share, "no matter how small"—as the group overseeing the distribution kept on repeating.

Deployment of new words like *raiti,* and the politics of individual recognition they informed, was a deliberate strategy to undermine how collectivities such as the extended household masked the unequal distribution of power and resources within. The association with rights made by the man cited above was not accidental: in response to the elders' invocation of the familial and affective values of the extended household, these dissenting voices insisted on its inherently political nature. And in turn, they invoked particular political and economic rights, rather than appealing to more general values.

But we should not assume that the subject of these rights was a "sovereign" one, who having challenged one set of hierarchies was now in a position to make autonomous choices. Though women, for instance, also insisted on their individual shares of rice, within the discursive practices of marriage that defined their adult lives they continued to figure as passive recipients, rather than as subjects, in their roles as wives. As members of patrilineages, however, women, too, could become wife-"owning" subjects, on behalf of their brothers and sons, and of the collectivity—the lineage—for which their menfolk stood in metonymical relation. Thus, different subjects, endowed with different kinds of agency and rights, emerged at the intersection of two different kinds of collectivity—the patrilineage and its core kin on the one hand, and the extended household with its heterogeneous composition of kin and in-marrying affines, including "strangers," or outsiders to the community of both sexes, on the other.

The relationship between the two types of subjects examined in this chapter and the next one—and their rights—articulates with the collectivities they reference in particular contexts, and these too are conceived as rights-bearing entities. But their interests tend to be formulated in more overtly political, and therefore contested, ways, which contrast with the "antipolitics" of some kinds of human rights discourse, especially when it presents itself as "a pure defense of the individual against . . . instantiations of collective power. . . . as a moral discourse centered on pain and suffering rather than political discourse of comprehensive justice" (Brown 2004, 453). Thinking in novel terms about the political future—one in which resources can be distributed in a more equitable manner—rather than locating human compassion in the affective realm of "pain and suffering," may shed light on the lack of response to the young hunter's tale of suffering by his fellow villagers, discussed above. Though he was denied an opportunity to articulate his "victim's tale," Kaikulo was also spared the dangers of telling a different story, in which he may have figured as a perpetrator of violence. The register of collective war trauma exposed by the SCSL and the TRC did not generate empathy and compassion for liminal groups of people, who were always perceived as potentially "dangerous." But it did translate the legal demand for accountability into a vernacular of social and economic rights that circulated widely in the country.

Thus instead of thinking of postconflict transitions as a series of recursive events (with a linear feedback loop of remembrance, reconstruction, reconciliation, reintegration, family reunification, and so on), imagining a different political future required more radical acts of departure: experimenting with new forms of political subjectivation, equitable sociality, and communities of belonging. The neologisms that emerged during the war and in its aftermath, in rural villages as much as at the SCSL, and from *raiti* to "bush/junta wives" (discussed in the next chapter), speak to critical efforts, in different domains and on different scales, to harness the creativity that resides in even the most destructive forms of violence—the other side of the destruction it wreaks. The court and the jurisprudence it sought to advance are part of a global humanitarian trend that increasingly is moving toward a totalizing and timeless discourse about archetypal "subjects of human rights." This includes recognizing the totality of a woman's experience of victimization in war by identifying additional crimes like forced marriage at the SCSL, or linking particular ages to degrees of moral responsibility in the child-soldier debates. And while witnesses at the court, who described themselves and their experiences in the court's terms, appeared to be docile subjects—deprived of political accountability—as the concepts became unmoored from this setting, they took on a life of their own, challenging in unexpected ways the balance of interests between individuals and collectivities, and between the political and economic hierarchies of prewar times. In the aftermath of their testimonies, the witnesses could also begin to make the transition to a future life, through—and in spite of—the supports offered them by the court structures.

# 7

# Forced Marriage and
# Sexual Enslavement

Debating Consent, Custom, and the Law
at the Special Court for Sierra Leone

This chapter analyzes the legal, conceptual framework and evidence for criminalizing forced marriage advanced at the Special Court for Sierra Leone (SCSL) against the backdrop of marriage practices and attitudes toward sex crimes outside that institution and its discourses: before, during, and in the aftermath of the civil war of 1991–2002. The material elaborated here moves across interdisciplinary spaces and methodologies, including ethnographic research, interviews with staff and witnesses, and scholarly engagement with the literature on "forced marriage," at the SCSL. Also examined are antecedent cases at the International Criminal Tribunals for Rwanda and the former Yugoslavia during the same decade.

Legal differences between forced and customary marriages were critical to court arguments about the former's criminalization. My analysis here highlights tensions between notions of individual and collective consent (to accepting forced marriage), which in some instances mimetically reproduced dimensions of gender bias that were already present in customary law. I argue that the criminalization of forced marriage at the SCSL had paradoxical consequences for women's rights at the time, because it appeared to be predicated on establishing notions of infringement on consent and agency as crimes against humanity in some exemplary cases while accepting others as "customary." Witness testimony and ethnographic evidence offer a more complex understanding of women's experiences of marriage in Sierra Leone. My aim is in part to explore the messy terrain between ideas of agency and consent in marriage that emerged in international jurisprudence, humanitarian denunciations of forced marriage, and among ordinary Sierra Leoneans.[1] I do not seek to resolve the tension that inevitably exists between these different and to some extent incommensurable arenas; rather, I want to examine the configurations of power and knowledge that tension produces, particularly around the figure of the "bush wife," which emerged in court testimony. Understanding the historical legacy of enslavement and the politics of negotiations behind the figure of the bush wife allows us to grasp more fully the complex role played by different institutions, communities, and individuals in cases of customary versus forced marriage.

Forced marriage was added to the roster of crimes against humanity at the SCSL, first as precedent in the appeals phase of the Armed Forces Revolutionary Council (AFRC) trial and then as a successful article of indictment in the Revolutionary United Front (RUF) consolidated trial. Scholars writing or testifying in court in favor of establishing this new crime drew on anthropological scholarship on normative forms of customary marriage, as well as on wartime ethnographic evidence, to highlight the sui generis and harmful nature of forced marriage in war.[2] The juxtaposition was prompted by the way the crime of forced marriage mimicked arranged marriages in peacetime, insofar as in both, women lacked the power of consent. Additional evidence offered here, particularly on Sierra Leonean marriage practices and on the treatment of marital and sexual breaches in customary courts, provides a richer context for debates surrounding forced marriage in Sierra Leone and elsewhere.

The focus at the SCSL on a more robust prosecution of sex-related war crimes was predicated on varying degrees of erasure of peacetime violations of women's human rights in marriage, since these risked undermining the case in favor of criminalizing forced marriage. Furthermore, the "forced marriage" terminology euphemistically aligned a sex crime with ordinary conjugality, which did not have the stigmatizing resonance of "sexual enslavement." This was particularly the case in the collective imaginary of an older generation in postconflict, rural Sierra Leone, where marriage terminology memorialized the social humiliation of domestic slavery within recent historical memory. Ambivalent attitudes toward the forced marriage terminology even at the court gained the upper hand during the Charles Taylor trial—the final case heard at the SCSL—in which, despite the absence of indictments on this count, the judges held that forced marriage should "be considered a conjugal form of enslavement" (Oosterveld 2012, 15).[3]

## ADVANCING JURISPRUDENCE AND
## UNDERSTANDING VICTIMS' EXPERIENCES

Debates around the criminalization of forced marriage illustrate the process of "enriching the jurisprudence" in international humanitarian law, which is among the key goals of war crimes courts and is an aspect of their knowledge-production work (Toy-Cronin 2010, 576).[4] According to the court's first chief prosecutor, the American David Crane, the SCSL's notable achievement was making "gender crimes the cornerstone" of its indictments and contributing to the criminalization of forced marriage in particular.[5] Both women in the three-judge chamber at the AFRC trial discussed at length instances of sexual enslavement and rape prosecuted in the International Criminal Tribunal for Rwanda (ICTR) and the International Criminal Tribunal for the Former Yugoslavia (ICTY), together with the applicability of those precedents to the Sierra Leonean case. In the end, perhaps through their own efforts, sufficient novel thinking was introduced in the AFRC trial to set precedents and secure convictions for the new crime of forced marriage against the RUF.[6]

Court arguments about forced marriage at the SCSL also suggest, however, that the process of enriching the jurisprudence does not follow a linear progression; it is characterized instead by sometimes discordant developments. For instance, only in the RUF trial was evidence of sexual violence perpetrated against men and boys discussed at any length, even though conceptually the move to put "gender crimes" at the center of the court's agenda—Prosecutor David Crane's opening manifesto—would have called for including from the beginning a critical stance toward the automatic "feminization" of their victims (Oosterveld 2012, 14). This move also made visible the ways in which the complementary masculinization of aggressors had masked abuses committed by female combatants (Human Rights Watch 2003, 41).

Feminist legal activists and scholars greeted with enthusiasm Crane's plans to vigorously prosecute crimes against women at the SCSL (Nowrojee 2005a, 100–101). But in practice, the court got off to a rocky start in the area of gender crimes: during the first consolidated trial, involving three leaders of the CDF, evidence about sexual violence was excluded from the trial on procedural grounds (Staggs Kelsall and Stepakoff 2007, 362). In this placing "expediency and efficiency before the prosecution of crimes of sexual violence," critics saw an instance of the court's excessive emphasis on the rights of the accused at the expense of those of the victim-witness—a problem also noted in the war crimes tribunals of the 1990s, particularly the ICTR.[7]

Aware of the fact that the trials were unfolding in a country where "technically" customary marriages took place without the consent of the bride-to-be, SCSL staff sought to highlight differences between the practices they aimed to criminalize and those accepted as normal by the surrounding population. In one instance, the office of the prosecutor instructed an expert preparing a briefing paper "to create a clear distinction between the custom of arranged marriage and the crime of forced marriage. Without this distinction, the court might also declare arranged marriage a war crime, and that is something the prosecutor did not want" (Toy-Cronin 2010, 572). Though forced marriage as a war crime encompassed rape, forced pregnancy, torture, and sexual enslavement, debates at the SCSL about its specificity as a crime also tried to capture a broader range of harms, including the "distinctive status" conferred by being considered a "rebel" or "bush" wife. Attention was also given to the lasting stigma derived from having borne "rebel babies," who would live on as reminders of the violence of forced sex in which they were conceived.

A key expert witness for the prosecution in the AFRC trial, Zainab Bangura, testified in 2005 about her encounters with bush, or "junta," wives, who had been abducted and forced into marriages that, though *mimicking* (in the words of a judge summarizing her testimony) "peacetime situations in which forced marriage and expectation of free female labour are common practice," carried with them a stigma that permanently ostracized from their communities the women and any offspring conceived during the relationship.[8] In various ways, therefore, the court came to accept "common practices," even when they were harmful to particular individuals, because of the legitimating and supportive roles played by collectivities—in this case, the extended families contracting a marriage.[9] Thus, perhaps to further the goals of advancing the rights of individuals and protecting them from harm, the SCSL in this instance chose as a legal strategy to privilege collectivities over individuals. This position appeared to contradict arguments for the criminalization of forced marriage, in which the absence of an individual's consent was of central importance. Elsewhere, I have argued that this naturalization of what is, in effect, a logical contradiction has to do in part with implicit assumptions in some transitional justice thinking about the benign nature of familial, residential, and other "communities" (such as the extended family that consented on behalf of a woman to her marriage), which were problematic in the context of a civil war that highlighted deep divisions precisely within such collectivities (see Ferme 2013).

During the AFRC consolidated trial, the prosecution's indictment initially called for forced marriage to be considered under the rubric of "sexual slavery," established as a crime against humanity at the International Court for Crimes, with the first, precedent-setting prosecutions taking place at the ICTY in the *Kunarac* case.[10] But as the cases unfolded, arguments were advanced for making forced marriage a distinct crime under "other inhumane acts," to shift the focus away from sexual elements to the totality of the experience of submission to violence. The prosecution was unsuccessful in making this argument and failed to secure convictions in the AFRC trial.

The presiding judge, Julia Sebutinde, reprised Zainab Bangura's observation of the similarities between the violation of women's rights in arranged marriages in peacetime and forced marriage in wartime. In her opinion, she wrote that though the former were surely violations "under international human rights instruments," such as the 1979 UN Convention on the Elimination of All Forms of Discrimination against Women, they were not recognized as crimes in international humanitarian law. By contrast, she wrote, forced marriage in wartime "is clearly criminal in nature and is liable to attract prosecution"—even as she found that the prosecution had been unsuccessful in proving its case in this particular trial.[11] Judge Sebutinde favored classifying forced marriage as a form of sexual slavery, but in her partly dissenting opinion, Judge Teresa Doherty argued for distinguishing them because the former posed greater obstacles to the ability of victims "to reintegrate to society . . . thereby prolonging their mental trauma."[12] In the end, her argument won the day: the appeals chamber found that the trial judges had "erred in law" and that forced marriage should be considered "not predominantly sexual," "distinct from the crime of sexual slavery . . . [and] amount[ing] to other inhumane acts under Article 2(1) of the Statute."[13]

Thus, from the beginning there were concerns about the apparent mimicry between (the social logic of) forced marriages in wartime and in peacetime. The rights of the individual seemed to be subordinated to the social rights of family, residents and communities. And the logic of incorporation into an extended family was separated from the logic of individual agency and choice. Yet arguments proposing criminalization of *forced marriage* insisted on its value as an umbrella term that encompassed multiple harms. One article of legal scholarship that circulated widely among the lawyers working at the SCSL in 2008, and whose language was echoed in arguments at the court, asserted,

> None of the other crimes against humanity that comprise forced marriage describe the *totality* of the perpetrator's conduct or the victim's experience. Enslavement describes the loss of personal freedom, but obscures the sexual violence inherent in the crime. Sexual slavery describes the loss of personal freedom and the sexual violence, but does not speak to the forced domestic labor, childbearing, childrearing, and degradation of the institution of marriage. Torture, rape, and forced pregnancy do not address the victim's loss of personal liberty and individually may not be present in all cases of forced marriage. (Scharf and Mattler 2005, 17; italics in the original).

The authors went on to argue that forced marriage was "a profound deprivation of individual autonomy" and "the denigration of an important and protected social and spiritual institution." But the very fact that forced marriage could capture the totality of a complex experience for some was seen by others as a troubling lack of specificity and redundant in the face of prior charges of sexual slavery—an already established crime against humanity (Oosterveld 2011, 131).[14]

Judge Doherty added the element of time in her arguments in favor of using a distinct indictment for the crime of forced marriage. The conferral of this status on a captive, she argued, resulted in trauma well into the future of a victim's life, in part because "the label 'wife' may stigmatize the victims and lead to their rejection by their families and community, negatively impacting their ability to reintegrate into society and thereby prolonging their mental trauma," in part owing to the lasting and equally stigmatizing legacy represented by any children conceived in violence.[15] Here and in earlier arguments, the ICTY and ICTR precedents informed the concern for future harms. Furthermore, the marriage-like practice, it was argued, also enabled a perpetrator to continue abusing his victim over time. In other words, temporality—in the form of duration (of violent abuses) and of a future orientation in considering social stigma and traumatic consequences—was another key element in the conceptual apparatus supporting the criminalization of forced marriage.

Although the SCSL "entered the first-ever international criminal convictions for the crime against humanity of sexual slavery" in the RUF trial and "solidified" its definition in international humanitarian law, the jurisprudence on forced marriage ultimately had more ambivalent outcomes (Oosterveld 2012, 15). On the one hand, the precedent established in the appeals phase of the AFRC trial set the stage for its criminalization and led to calls for prosecuting instances of sexual enslavement and forced marriage elsewhere. On the other hand, some legal practitioners and scholars argued that the conceptual foundations for establishing forced marriage as a crime were shaky at best, since nothing resembling a "marriage" could be said to have taken place in cases examined at the SCSL Thus, already at the Charles Taylor trial, it was proposed that "conjugal slavery" better described what elsewhere had been labeled "forced marriage" (Oosterveld 2012, 20).

Contestations over terminology were in part centered on its euphemistic and nonspecific nature: "The difficulty with labeling what is otherwise sexual slavery, rape, enslavement, and torture as 'marriage' is that it distorts and conceals the nature of the victim's experience" (Toy-Cronin 2010, 577). Put another way, for those criticizing the introduction of forced marriage as an article of indictment, the very terminology that for its proponents captured the totality of harms suffered by victims ended up masking them. In the arguments presented at the International Court for Crimes for adding sexual slavery to the roster of crimes against humanity (and their subsequent deployment at the ICTY), many critics saw more solid legal foundations for prosecuting gender crimes committed in Sierra Leone. Already, they pointed out, the debates and jurisprudence around the criminalization of sexual slavery had moved away from the moralizing tone of earlier legislation against "enforced prostitution" in war, in which offenses against "human dignity" loomed large. Instead, at the International Court for Crimes and ICTY, the central concepts in debates over sexual slavery were consent, personal freedom, and the exercise of elements of ownership by perpetrators over victims (Oosterveld 2004, 650–51). Below I offer cultural reasons, in part owing to the ambiguous meanings of the word *wife* among speakers of the Mende language in Sierra Leone, why we should object to the euphemistic use of the idiom of marriage to describe the totality of this complex of crimes (torture, rape, forced pregnancy, childbearing, childrearing, forced domestic labor).

## ARRANGED AND FORCED MARRIAGES
## AND THE QUESTION OF CONSENT

One reason for the discursive weakness of the term *forced marriage* in the setting of twenty-first-century international humanitarian legislation is that, for most of its history, forced marriage was not clearly distinguished from arranged marriage. This historical slippage perhaps contributes to the mimicry observed by legal experts and practitioners in the SCSL setting, who nonetheless note that, even though a wife's consent is not necessary in customary marriages, sometimes "the parties consent to the parents' choice" (Bélair 2006, 565; see also 568–69). The matter of consent may rest with the extended family, even though it would ideally involve the wife's *assent*—a more appropriate term (normally associated with the limited consent of jural minors) because most women have no legal standing in customary courts and male relatives must "speak for them." But since the wife's assent is optional, its desirability hardly constitutes a robust distinction from a marriage to which contracting parties have not consented at all—in the views of more constrained legal institutions. This also seems to suggest that practices violating individual but not familial rights are somehow less harmful to the person affected than those that violate both.

The issue of consent and agency emerges from the testimony in court of victims of forced marriages, in the strategic setting of litigation, rather than of scholarship. A witness identified as TF1–016, who testified in the RUF trial, insisted on the illegal nature of her being "given to a man" because she was already married.[16] Other witnesses also used the objectifying, passive language of "being given" to combatants but described more complex experiences; one such witness, TF1–023, at the AFRC trial was only sixteen when she was "handed over" to a rebel combatant and forced to have sex with him. However, she refused to perform other domestic duties, such as cooking, and she could demand services from her captor's subordinates and their female captives.[17] In most women's testimony, the terms in which they referred to themselves as being passively acted on (given or handed over) mirrored those attending marriage transactions in peacetime, when members of the groom's patrilineage would beg the family of a prospective bride to "give" her to them. Thus, part of what emerged from court testimony was that the subjection and submission of women in forced marriage was consistent with that conveyed in customary marriage negotiations. This representation of women as passively accepting their subordinate and submissive role is a fiction of customary law. This feisty witness turned out, in person, to have weathered well some of the fears—including of public exposure—connected with her testimony. When I met her some ten years after the end of her testimony, she was a nursing student and appeared confident and hopeful about her future.

A distinctive feature of the expansion of humanitarian jurisprudence and international criminal institutions since the 1990s is the increasing focus on rights-bearing individuals, often to the detriment of rights-bearing collectivities. The SCSL's position with respect to the consent of families and other forms of "community" appears to contradict this move (Clarke 2009). Concurrently, there also has been a tendency to individualize responsibility for war crimes, even when this contradicted situations where violence and abuses in war were experienced as collective phenomena. One of the consequences of this focus on "personal responsibility" and war crimes tribunals' narrower definitions of individual accountability for those higher up the chains of command was that those targeted for prosecution were less likely to be the actual perpetrators of brutalities, which was one of the things that mattered most to those who had been victimized by violence. Part of the reason for this was that—unlike the international tribunals of the 1990s—the "hybrid" tribunals encompassing the SCSL were supposed to have a complementary relationship with national courts, where perpetrators further down the chains of command could be prosecuted. This by-and-large was not happening in Sierra Leone during the unfolding SCSL trials.

Feminist activists and legal scholars had great hopes for the SCSL, feeling that its unique, hybrid structure "and its location in-country could have potentially huge implications for the rights of Sierra Leonean women" (Shana 2004, 917). This was because crimes against women, such as domestic violence and rape, were sometimes weakly prosecuted in local and national Sierra Leonean courts, and the exemplary staging of their prosecution in a tribunal that was supported by international structures such as the United Nations was seen as a possible model for reforming national courts in this area. The SCSL largely continued the tendency in international criminal courts to "normalize" gender crimes—meaning, to bring greater attention to them—as an aspect of the broader process of holding accountable those with the greatest responsibility for war violence. However, though accusations of rape, sexual enslavement, and eventually forced marriage were listed as articles of indictments, these rarely resulted in convictions.[18]

## LOST IN TRANSLATION: THE VARIETIES OF MARRIAGE

Testimony at the SCSL and other reports on violence against civilians confirmed that women of all ages were subjected to brutal rapes, forced conscription as fighters, and forms of enslavement—particularly between 1997 and 1999. This period coincided with the May 1997 coup carried out by the RUF rebels, allied with rogue members of the military making up the AFRC, which brought them to power until their defeat some nine months later. Though pushed back at that time from the capital city, the AFRC-RUF junta remained in control of other parts of the country, and it attacked Freetown in January 1999. During this time, there were reports of women being taken as "wives" by combatants or allocated by them to their subordinates (Human Rights Watch 2003, 26). In one instance, witness TF1–016 testified that she was "given" by a RUF commander to his local palm wine tapper, who kept her and raped her for fifteen months; this suggests that noncombatants also took advantage of the war to perpetrate sex crimes and points to the generalized insecurity of wartime, especially for women.[19]

These forced unions with nonconsenting women were sometimes referred to as "bush marriages," and "bush wife" is commonly used in the reports of expert witnesses to the SCSL, in proceedings of the Truth and Reconciliation Commission (TRC), and in other documents to refer to the women trapped in forced marriages.[20] Yet the expression was not used nearly as much among the population in Sierra Leone as it was in postconflict transitional institutions and English-speaking circles. Witness DBK-113 testified at the Special Court that he had never heard the expression "bush wife" during his time as an AFRC captive, and the prosecution's key expert witness in this trial admitted that only in 1999 did she become aware that combatants abducting women and taking them as so-called wives was "common practice."[21]

In Sierra Leone, the bush is secondary forest growth, as distinct from a human settlement, cultivated farm, or mature forest. The bush is for humans an interstitial, liminal place that is crossed when one travels between village and farm or is visited in order to hunt animals or harvest wild foods (e.g., areas where smallholder rice farming prevails). Even in the daytime, activities in the boundaries between bush and town were governed by social norms that tended to keep them separate, and these norms could be enforced through levying fines on those who trespassed against them (see Ferme 2001, 72). Activities considered central to human sociality were proscribed in the bush, and among these were sexual relations carried out during the daytime. The combination of location and temporality—the bush, which offered more privacy than the village, and the daytime, when people were supposed to be engaging in productive farm labor rather than dallying in sexual liaisons, presumably extramarital ones—made this one of the circumstances in which customary law could intervene and punish (see Joko-Smart 1983, 127). In the cases of which I was aware, however, it was mostly in the deflowering of young, uninitiated girls that such punishment actually was enforced.

Before the civil war, in ordinary rural Mende parlance referring to something as being "bush"—for instance, clothing or the solution to a problem—meant that it was makeshift and temporary, lacking the resources one might have in the village. In this sense, then, securing a bush wife or husband was similarly temporary, in a time when all social norms were disrupted by war. In the case of wartime marriages, this meant that the fulfilment of proper marriage rituals and payments would be completed when families could secure the material means for carrying out these transactions.

Some witnesses at the SCSL testified to having been taken as what male combatants translated as *wives,* and the fact that female victims themselves used this terminology was key to arguments for criminalizing forced marriage (Bélair 2006, 565–69). However, for witnesses testifying in Mende, the translation of the term *wife* carries even more ambiguous connotations than bush. In Mende, *nyaha* means "woman" as well as "wife." It also signals the fact that a person has been initiated into the women's Sande (or Bundu) Society and is thus a social adult—ready for marriage and childbearing. Thus, using the Mende terms for *bush* and *wife* in the same sentence indicated an act of transgression of all the social norms that regulated the rites of passage into womanhood. It was not only an act against the individual but also against the collectivity.

Children in Sierra Leone become adults through initiation into the Sande Society, for women, and the Poro Society, for men. Both are secretive (kept from the opposite sex and the uninitiated) and hierarchical institutions that cut across familial and other social groupings. Sande rituals transform girls into marriageable, fertile, and adult members of the society, and the women responsible for this transformation gain lifelong control over the marriage prospects of their initiates; historically, they have turned their position to political advantage (see Hoffer 1974). In discussions at the SCSL, the legitimacy of arranged marriages was linked to family participation, but in fact other institutions, such as secret societies, were equally important. Consequently, when one breaks down the ill-defined concept of "community," whose legitimacy and consent were invoked by the court, one finds its components include powerful, hierarchically organized religious institutions with political and economic interests that crosscut those of secular institutions and of the family. These competing demands on members of collectivities are exercised in a context in which the young and unmarried of either sex are most fully embraced when they are "for" some-body, meaning that they are tied by relations of dependence to a "big" person, who, among other things, speaks for his or her dependents in customary courts. Fortunately, in many parts of Sierra Leone those "big persons" can be women, though for most ordinary rural women, the ideal is still to be married and dependent on a man (see Ferme 2001b, 81–111, 171–76; Ferme 1998, 571–73).

Historically, slavery was a key element in this system of interdepend-ence, and marriage mediated relations between the free and the enslaved. Though domestic slavery was outlawed in Sierra Leone in 1927, the discourse of domestic and debt enslavement still haunted and poten-tially stigmatized contemporary social relations in rural parts of the country before the war, as well as relations of dependence between rural- and urban-based relatives. In particular, it was implicated in mar-riages that were supposed to "ransom" individuals from certain forms of bondage and indebtedness, of which more below. These conversa-tions underscored the transactional and political character of marriage as an institution that mediated relations of social inequality, as well as potentially emancipating one from them. This is in part why I hold that the crime of sexual slavery "translates" much better than forced mar-riage in the broader Sierra Leonean context and thus offers the prospect of fulfilling the intent of transitional justice institutions to increase awareness of and access to women's rights.

Ultimately, the context in which gender and intergenerational rela-tions in Sierra Leone must be understood is one that values the (unequal) interdependence of members of familial, social, and political collectivi-ties—and even the powerful are beholden to those who depend on them. Individuals who seek autonomy from networks of mutual obligations usually do so in favor of alternative ones, though this is especially chal-lenging for dependents who are "strangers," or unrelated, relative new-comers, to an area. In marriage, this means that family authorities tend to want some indication that their female relative is interested in a poten-tial match before finalizing arrangements and accepting bridewealth, for if she dislikes her prospective husband, she might in future seek a divorce with the support of alternative patronage. This, in turn, would force the wife's family to return marriage payments at a time when financial cir-cumstances might make that a hardship. Though the collectivity is val-ued, then, and the language of hierarchical familial bonds is paramount in social and political rhetoric, the group's hold on any individual is, in some ways, quite fragile if there is not a measure of explicit compliance.

Individual agency is not eclipsed by familial interests: it hovers on the margins and is continually enlisted. In general, prewar conjugal arrangements tended to increase the possible range of unions that went under the rubric of "marriage," rather than drawing sharp distinctions between individual types, and this is also true for the postwar period. And the range of familial relationships women or men could draw upon to legitimate the preference of certain affective bonds and residential patterns over others is rather expansive, making it possible to offer alternatives to individuals who find themselves trapped in unhappy affinal, kin, or other relations.

The question of consent and violence in some of the unions formed during the war is similarly ambiguous. In one instance, a young woman I knew, whom I will call Moinyaha, was taken during a rebel incursion in her home village, where I had been based before the war. I was told that she was approached by a rebel who "liked her" and had not been seen since. The ambiguity of the language used did not exclude the possibility that Moinyaha had some voice in the matter. Though she was married when the war broke out, her husband had never been around much, and she was a relatively junior wife struggling to support an infant. Then her child died, so by the time the rebel leader who "liked her" arrived in the village, Moinyaha was alone in a context that in prewar days would have been potentially socially destabilizing for an unmarried woman. I was never able to follow up on her story in person during my return visits in the postconflict period, but on a recent visit to a neighboring district, I met up with another former war abductee, whom I had known well since before the war. She shared her memories of suffering hunger, experiencing the trauma of witnessing the killing of an accused spy, and grief over a brother who was killed while trying to escape RUF captivity. I knew that this abductee had been captured with her nursing infant and that both had survived (I had seen them after the war), but I had heard her story only indirectly, from family members. When I sat down and talked to her, I realized that my assumptions about the exact causes of the "harm" she had suffered in war were mistaken. She had formed a consensual union with one of the rebels who had captured her after three months of captivity, during which he had continuously told her that he liked her and wanted to be with her. Finally won over by his everyday gestures of kindness, she had agreed. She had not conceived a child with him—thus perhaps minimizing the chances that she would suffer from lasting stigma. The child with whom she had been captured grew up mentally impaired, but she left ambiguous the question of whether this had been the consequence of war trauma he had suffered during their five-month captivity. Once it became clear that "hunter" militias were advancing on the positions held by her captors, and would kill both RUF combatants and their captives in the uncertainty of their allegiances, she was taken over the border to Liberia and allowed to go free. Her "bush" husband gave her some money and went into hiding in Liberia, fearful of the consequences of an eventual return to Sierra Leone. Eventually my friend was able to get a message to her brother back in Sierra Leone, and he came looking for her to take her home to her family.[22]

To return to Moinyaha's case, in discussing her departure, villagers focused on the fact that her abductor "said he liked her . . . [so] we gave her to him." I asked whether *she* had agreed, according to the formula customarily employed during marriage negotiations, whereby relatives turn to a prospective bride, point to money and goods brought to the meeting by would-be in-laws, and ask her whether they should accept them. It is the moment closest to what one might define as *consent* in the SCSL's sense of the term, in which a prospective bride moves from being a subject defined by her ambiguously passive acquiescence with the proceedings to having an active voice. On this score, the villagers' responses were vague, and since Moinyaha was not there, I could not confirm or deny their stories.

Other stories of so-called bush wives were less ambiguous: for instance, trial transcripts and postwar interviews by activists and scholars told of women who were swept up in ambushes, raped, and then offered the protection of an exclusive relationship with a particular fighter, whose "woman/wife" they thus became (e.g., Coulter 2009, 1–2). In cases where forced marriages resulted in pregnancy and childbirth, the relationships could last beyond the war, as fathers sought to regularize their positions and hence their claims to their children.[23] In one case, a woman and her abductor sought to formalize their relationship after the war and secure his status as the father of their two children, but her family refused his marriage offer. Having opted for her family's support, the woman separated from her husband, only to have her suspicious relatives still shun and mistreat her, driving her into prostitution to support her children (Coulter 2009).

Though horrible crimes were committed against women during the 1991–2002 civil war, the forced marriages that joined rebels to kidnapped women sometimes ended up being better matches than the arranged marriages that had preceded them in peacetime, particularly because they tended to be between individuals who were closer in age than those selected by families with the intention of improving their socioeconomic prospects. But the homogeneous characterization of all such unions as "crimes against humanity" did not reflect the full range of wartime experiences, which included the transformation of an original violence into a familiar bond. This possibility was addressed by Judge Doherty in the AFRC judgment, though she does not accept the possibility of redemption. She wrote, "A decision to remain in the forced marriage or its transformation into a consensual situation does not retroactively negate the original criminality of the act."[24]

Contrary to the SCSL, where gradations of violence and consent were subordinated to legal arguments for criminalizing forced marriage, the responses to this practice varied across the country at large. In Kailahun near the Liberian border, which was the last place where elements of the AFRC-RUF junta were demobilized, bush wives were less stigmatized, perhaps because there were more of them. But in Pujehun District, where some of the earliest war violence had unfolded, they could be suspected of collusion with the enemy by other fighting factions like the CDF, which occupied the area later, and they risked harm at their hands as well.[25]

A different perspective on forced marriage can be gained from Sierra Leoneans who represented even the most ordinary marriage as a form of aggression, in language that may have been only metaphorical, a gesture toward "culture." Among Mende speakers, wife-takers are called "splitters" (*mbela,* the literal translation of "in-law"), for taking a lineage's women and their future offspring. If a bush husband who was brought back by a woman from her war captivity sought to formalize their union, he would face "wife troubles" (*nyaha monɛ*)—the labor, expenses, and gift-giving to in-laws that accompany marriages throughout their duration. In patrilineages, in-laws, particularly brothers, have a residual hold on their women's progeny beyond the jural rights exercised by the women's fathers and are able to participate in all major decisions affecting their lives. Historically, brothers had the power to place their sisters' children in debt servitude, a condition avoided through matrilateral cross-cousin marriage. Indeed, the rhetoric of slavery and ransom shapes the idiom of matrilateral cross-cousin marriage negotiations to this day in Sierra Leone (Ferme 2001b, 86–88). Thus, an overlooked aspect of customary marriage practices in debates at the SCSL is the extent to which they are informed by contentiousness and explicitly political negotiations even in ordinary times.

Mende speakers refer to wife troubles as an intrinsic aspect of the relationship between wife-takers and wife-givers, and they recognize that on marrying, a man enters a form of lifelong indenture to his in-laws, in exchange for his wife and her future offspring. In a sense, then, even ordinary customary marriage encompasses social transactions centered on reparation for losses. A more nuanced understanding of cultural constructions of marriage and of the political and social negotiations that accompany its arrangement—which is a continuous process rather than a single event—might provide insights into ways of dealing with at least some of the unions formed in wartime, by framing their aftermath within a different logic of punishment and restitution than that governing the incarceration meted out at the SCSL.

## SEX CRIMES IN GENERAL AND CUSTOMARY LAW

Transitional justice institutions, particularly the SCSL and the TRC, became the main context in which Sierra Leonean women could openly testify to being raped, while often remaining silent about the occurrence of rape in ordinary life in local and national legal settings (Nowrojee 2005a, 88). Outside the exceptional conflict scenario of forced abduction—and the legal settings of the SCSL and TRC—denouncing sexual violence remained fraught with stigma and exposed the victims to the further trauma of social exclusion. The fact that victims of forced marriage could testify to it in the RUF and AFRC trials, but not in the CDF one, made even the SCSL an inadequate model for changing local thinking about consent in marriage more generally, not to mention for making rapists legally accountable.

So what is the status of sex crimes in customary law? Litigation cases involving women have long been among the most common in rural Sierra Leone, taking up the bulk of the time and effort of family and chiefly courts at various levels (Little [1951] 1967, 152). But these are not generally cases of sexual violence. Instead, most involve adultery charges made by husbands against other men, sometimes in collusion with their wives, or families seeking damages for the deflowering of their underaged daughters. These have a lasting impact on the woman's chances of making a good marriage. Lodging such charges can be a strategy for older men to secure the labor and "judicial serfdom" of younger men, who, once found guilty of adultery, must pay heavy court fines or do farmwork until the debt is extinguished. Indeed, some believe debt servitude is an important source of the intergenerational grievances that fueled the 1991–2002 civil war and—if not addressed—is a potential source of future conflict in agrarian settings (Mokuwa, Voors, Bulte, and Richards 2011).

In the context of marriage, "sexual violence" in domestic unions is not technically recognized in customary law, but in practice, it can become the basis for divorce proceedings. But customary courts do intervene in cases involving sex with an unmarried virgin, brought by the families of the affected girl, which in Krio—the national lingua franca—are known as "virginating" cases. These are described as rape cases, and during the 1991–2002 civil war, evidence emerged that some combatants deliberately sought out young virgins in order to rape, or "virginate," them (Human Rights Watch 2003, 24–30). But in the cases prosecuted in areas where I did research before the war, this charge could also apply to consensual sexual relations between a man and any girl or woman who had not been initiated into Sande. The fines in such cases were so exorbitant that one prominent member of the village where I was living left the chiefdom permanently to escape the jurisdiction of its courts.

Many of the crimes examined at the SCSL fell within the categories of sex crimes that were familiar in the customary legal landscape of Sierra Leone. However, though the SCSL drew liberally on other areas of "custom," and of "customary law" regulating marriage in debates, the court did not analyze its treatment of marital and sex crimes in those arenas. Perhaps this was because cases involving women in customary law also appeared to reproduce the status of women as passive objects deprived of agency in conflicts over them among men. Nonetheless, because these debates occurred not just for the benefit of this one "hybrid" court, but in a broader jurisprudential context that sought to move international humanitarian law closer to its intended beneficiaries, the opportunity to translate for a broader public the variable implications of prosecuting sex crimes at the SCSL was missed.

## CONCLUSION

A holistic approach to the traumatic consequences of forced marriage over a lifespan—one truly dedicated to understanding the totality of the experience for those affected by it—needs to go beyond seeking justice for its victims and accountability for its perpetrators in courts of law. The fact that after the war, some victims of forced marriage tried to remain with their captors suggests that perhaps over time an original act of violence could be transformed.[26] Labels such as Stockholm syndrome—the bond traumatized victims form with their captors—are not especially helpful in a broader context in which the norm even in peacetime is that women lack consent in marriage (e.g., Gagoomal 2009). Giving attention to temporality—to the aftermath of harms suffered in war—was among the key contributions of the SCSL to international criminal jurisprudence. Particularly useful was the court's focus on the lasting stigma of sexual violence, including the ways in which so-called rebel babies could hamper future reintegration of forced marriage victims into communities of belonging. But even though the aggravating effects of time were explored, its mitigating force was completely overlooked, for instance, in the face of evidence that some wartime abductions had given way to familial and transactional arrangements that offered the possibility of an alternative outcome. There was no single script of what could happen to the victims of forced marriage, especially with respect to the role of the original family of belonging and the society, to which she returned as a bush wife with her husband. There was no presumption of "innocence" or benign welcoming of the victim. The case of the woman shunned and driven into prostitution by a family that refused to recognize her bush husband suggests that further harm is just as likely to result from such erasures as it is from overlooking other aspects of the totality of wartime experiences.

The Mende idiom of wife troubles and ransom brides suggested that customary marriage, evoking as it does relations of indebtedness between in-laws, obligations imposed on husbands, and even the historical legacy of enslavement, may have been fraught with tension in preconflict days. In this, the Sierra Leonean case underscores the relationship among marriage, property transfers, debt, and slavery in African social history. The role of key members of extended families in mediating these relations, which entail labor burdens and the limitation of freedom even as they forge alliances, is at odds with the SCSL's finding that the collectivity's consent legitimates marital unions even against the will of prospective spouses. Harm, restitution, and the balancing of gains (alliances) with losses (a lineage's woman lost to another)—more than love and romance—are part of the conceptual and affective apparatus of marriage in this context. For a woman, marriage choices often center around relative food security, labor exchange, protection, and respectful partnership, especially in the context of urban and rural poverty, where people live on the verge of subsistence. In this setting, submitting a former abductor to the trials of in-law obligations and of wife troubles with the aim of repairing the union with his bush wife might offer more readily recognizable forms of justice to families touched by the war's violence.

At the same time, the case discussed earlier of a young abducted woman who could not refuse to have sex with her captor but did refuse to cook and wash clothes for him suggests that, within the whole field of experiences of sexual enslavement in wartime, there were also spaces in which consent could be denied and minor forms of control exercised. Other women captives, who eventually formed unions with their captors but not under force, were less traumatized by this aspect of their captivity than by the sight of killings and the deaths of close family members. In the end, forced marriage—as a war crime—is best understood as "sexual slavery," given the ways in which its juxtaposition with peacetime unions that also lack women's consent may raise paradoxical implications for women's rights. Even within the framework of the SCSL, litigation seemed to be heading back toward framing this "new" crime within the broader, existing article on "sexual enslavement"—at the final trial, against former Liberian president Charles Taylor. By contrast, the term *forced marriage* is still in active use in the debate among rights-based legal activists and in the human rights jurisprudence focused on underage or arranged marriages in times of peace.

# Inscriptions on the Wall

Chinese Material Traces in the Landscape

Figure 18 is from my own archive—a building in a small Sierra Leonean rural community, with a somewhat "colonial" iconography representing an aging patriarch surrounded by dependents posing in front of it—with the arresting inscription, "Chinese Store." The doors of the store were always shut, the space having been converted years earlier to a bedroom by the large extended family that occupied the house. The reason I found the writing arresting was that there were no Chinese residents in this community in the mid-1980s, when I took this picture. The sign, and the store, disappeared during the war, but analyzing the ways in which different forms of Chinese presence haunted the Sierra Leonean landscape, and point to other forms of postcolonial hauntings, remains useful for assessing the war's role in interrupting processes of remembrance.

In what follows, I focus on the emergence of traces of Chinese presence in the material contours of rural landscapes and in large-scale infrastructural projects. I also briefly consider the circulation of ordinary household commodities and medicinal substances that affected bodily practices in Sierra Leone. Traces are clues that help reconstruct fuller pictures or narratives of sometimes forgotten episodes in history. A focus on the emergent or the overlooked has been central to the discipline of anthropology and to interdisciplinary studies of material culture but is not much in evidence in current scholarship on the Chinese presence in Sierra Leone and Africa as a whole. I view landscapes as historical productions, places that are "constructed out of a particular

**FIGURE 18.** "Chinese Store." Kpuawala, Wunde Chiefdom, March 1985. Photo by author.

constellation of social relations, meeting and weaving together at a particular locus" (Massey 1991, 7; see also Ferme 2001b, 40–47). The emphasis on material traces does not preclude the dynamic quality of these places; rather, it highlights how landscapes are constituted by and through human interactions (Bender 2002, 104), including violent ones, as well as by natural phenomena (Ingold 2007, 7).

Some of the more visible Chinese interventions on the Sierra Leonean landscape are revisitations of earlier agricultural and mining projects, which may have been initiated by them or by others. Others bespeak novel ways in which China is engaging with Africa as a global economic and technological power, particularly in postconflict settings. The palimpsestic revisiting of older projects, their potentiation and duplications elsewhere, are a visible testament to the fact that in many ways we should think of the current engagement of the Peoples' Republic of China (PRC) with African countries like Sierra Leone as a reemergence and reconfiguration of material traces of past encounters. These returns are a kind of re-membering—a process of reconstituting a fragmented archival body by putting together its constitutive parts. This focus on a politics of material traces has methodological implications as well. It calls for the imaginative attention to the significantly small, that which easily can be overlooked, and for a nuanced interpretation of the ways in which clues point to broader histories. It also calls for an attentiveness to the ways in which an environment exists in time, and material forms are only "impermanent by-products" of ongoing processes and relations, including decay (Ingold 2007, 9), and willful destruction. Traces bespeak contingency: they can be easily erased and overlooked in the give-and-take of social practices of historical memorialization. "Memory is played by circumstances, just as a piano is played by a musician, and music emerges from it when its keys are touched by the hands" (Certeau 1984, 87). Similar to the pianist, whose touch on particular keys can produce music, the engaged observer must be able through particular traces to construct a historical narrative.

Among other things, revisiting earlier histories has political purposes in the present. In the case of mutual encounters between China and Sierra Leone, the official rhetoric serves to present political and economic interests in the region as part of a longer history of engagements. As others have argued, it is often only through a "methodological fetishism" of things, always viewed in social and historical contexts, that we can recognize their sociopolitical significance (Appadurai 1988, 5; Pels 1998, 112). Reading traces of China's historical presence allows the nuances and complexities of Chinese-Sierra Leonean relations to come into view. It reveals how what is superficially described as a political and economic relationship between two states is in fact a contested domain with several competing actors and interests, whose dynamics were shaped by a different kind of war, the Cold War, with its own forms of violence.

## "FRIEND-ENEMY" POLITICS IN RURAL SIERRA LEONE

Let us return to the image of the Chinese Store mentioned above (fig. 18). In the mid-1980s, there were no longer traces of a Chinese presence, or of the agricultural inputs, particularly fertilizers, that in the late 1970s had been stored in this space. Indeed, by the end of the 1991–2002 civil war, there was no building either: its mud structure collapsed after years of exposure to the elements without proper maintenance, particularly during the conflict. During that decade, the whole village was abandoned on several occasions, as its population moved to the relative security of refugee, internally displaced persons', or "self-settled," camps in safer locations. The Chinese Store now exists in the social memory of those

**FIGURE 19.** "China-Sierra Leone Friendship" commemorative T-shirts. Freetown National Stadium, February 2013. Photo by Saleem Vahidy.

who once lived or walked by it—an ephemeral gesture within longer and more enduring material sedimentations of history—while some of the materials that once gave shape to it were transformed into something else. A mound of mud on the ground where the building once stood marks its location, whereas other materials were repurposed in newer structures, for instance, the wooden shutters and corrugated metal roofing that were integrated into more recent village housing.

The store was open for a decade, beginning in 1971 with the official establishment of diplomatic relations between China and Sierra Leone (Tarawallie 2011)—an event commemorated on t-shirts given away on its fortieth anniversary, in 2011, which could be seen on Chinese and Sierra Leoneans alike around Freetown, the nation's capital (see fig. 19). Agriculture was the domain in which this early friendship unfolded— a fitting domain, given rice's role as a staple food in both Sierra Leonean and Chinese diets. In 1984, when asked about the genealogy of the Chinese Store in the village of Kpuawala, witnesses recounted the arrival of a four-wheel drive vehicle one day during the late 1970s. The vehicle stopped outside the village, by the rice paddy that the villagers had been taught to clear, and around which they were shown how to improve embankments to regulate the flow of water during the rainy season. Their sole instructor had been a Sierra Leonean extension worker, but that day a foreign-looking "Chinese" man arrived with him, got out, rolled up his trousers, took off his shoes, put on a conical hat made of palm leaf fibers on a pliable reed structure for sun protection, and stepped into the flooded paddy, where he began to transplant rice.

Recalling the event about a decade later, the villagers who witnessed it still marveled at what they perceived as the contradictory, and quite strange, behavior of this particular foreigner. On the one hand he behaved "like one of them," having no fear of stepping barefoot into the paddy and putting in a hard day's farming work under the sun, when most foreigners refused to step in swamps for fear of waterborne diseases. The man even used head protection that looked similar to the broad, conical "Mende t/lebleɛ," as they were humorously called, the "Mende umbrellas" made locally with palm fibers and used by those who could not afford to buy imported ones during the rainy season. These head covers were shaped similarly to those worn by Chinese farmers working in rice paddies, though they differed in construction and materials. On the other hand, the Chinese man did not speak to any of them, or even engage in the perfunctory greetings that other foreigners, such as European aid workers, Peace Corps volunteers, or urban Lebanese traders might offer. Several participants in the conversation marveled that this man had obviously come from very far away, from a country where people behaved very differently.

Pointing to the spot where his vehicle had stopped, they wondered how someone could drive all that distance, and come that close, yet not cover the last few yards to enter the settlement, if only to accept a drink of "cold water"—the ubiquitous first gesture of welcome to strangers in rural communities. The Chinese man had stopped at the creek that marked the symbolic boundary of the settlement—waterways being the place where people accompanying departing visitors take leave of them and the figurative boundaries between the living and the dead in local cultural idioms (Harris and Sawyerr 1968, 26, 32). "The host does not cross water," the Sierra Leonean proverb goes—he or she always accompanies guests to the closest waterway but says goodbye to them on the village side. In this case, the potential guest rendered the issue moot because, by remaining on the opposite shore, he had not fully arrived in the first place. To those who were telling the story, this man's behavior was incomprehensible within the normal parameters of sociability, and his actions were all the more baffling when juxtaposed against his intimate familiarity with rice farming—a central element of local cultural identity and a fact that made him different from other non-Sierra Leonean visitors they had encountered. However, his behavior was typical of the Chinese delegations that sporadically visited Sierra Leone in the years preceding the end of the Cold War. Even when brought to work on projects that required prolonged stays in nonurban, remote parts of the country, Chinese workers, almost exclusively male, lived together, out of sight of the local population, in walled compounds, which they seldom left. They imported all their food and other requirements, and when they left their compounds they did so as a group, accompanied by a Chinese interpreter who spoke English and a Sierra Leonean interpreter who could communicate only with his Chinese counterpart. This earlier presence was less conspicuous in terms of numbers and was mostly restricted to large-scale Chinese, state-owned companies. By contrast, Chinese migration to Sierra Leone—and elsewhere in Africa—in the twenty-first century is larger in number and also includes a more heterogeneous migrant population. Among other things, this new, "granular" presence involves many more small-scale private Chinese businesses, with entrepreneurs often living among the local population and learning to communicate in English or Krio—the country's lingua franca.

Now the Chinese presence in Sierra Leone is more visible: new building, and hydroelectric and road network projects, as well as large-scale mining and agricultural schemes are undertaken by the PRC. But a more nuanced historical approach shows that earlier traces of "Chinese" passages were concealed among competing layers of colonial and postcolonial appropriations. Trade brought Chinese commodities to African markets for centuries. However, these were often introduced to Africa through intermediaries, whose imprint on them shaped their uses and reception, often in the context of consumption and bodily practices framed within the colonial experience. In some cases these objects became associated with their intermediaries, thus deferring knowledge of their Chinese origins among African consumers. For instance, during the nineteenth century, Chinese porcelain was used by northern Nigerian elites, but as prestige "European" objects, which were imported by European traders and therefore not directly linked to China (Platte 2004, 182).

Over time, local rice-farming techniques bore the traces of different Asian influences. Indian experts were brought to the country during the British colonial occupation of Sierra Leone, and later Taiwan (or the Republic of China [ROC]) sent rice-farming experts, who were eventually replaced by emissaries from the PRC. The latter overlaid their own projects onto the earlier Taiwanese inscriptions in order to erase them in the name of the "One China" policy. New projects were initiated as well, such as the expanded Tonkolili mine that resumed operations in 2011 after being dormant for over thirty years, sending its first major iron ore shipment to Shandong Province, PRC (Agence France Presse 2011). This was said to be one of the largest iron ore deposits in the world. Tonkolili was a project of African Minerals, a London-based company formerly known as Sierra Leone Diamond Co., on whose board sat two Chinese nationals (Singh 2009). Among the main shareholders were British, Chinese, and American institutional and private investors—an elegant recapitulation of Sierra Leone's main economic partners in resource exploitation since the nineteenth century, which also pointed to the more complex ramifications of many purportedly "Chinese" ventures. Aiming to become "one of the largest seaborne exporters of iron ore in Africa," the project included renovation of the mining area of Tonkolili, which had stopped production in the 1970s; rehabilitation of a hydroelectric dam at Bumbuna and of the Pepel Port; and construction of a railway to connect the mine to the port (African Minerals Limited 2010b, 30). Chinese firms have been heavily involved in the project, particularly in the construction of railroads, of which a second was planned (Agence France Presse 2013).

The same year in which mining resumed at Tonkolili (2011) saw the fiftieth anniversary of Sierra Leone's independence from British colonial rule, and the fortieth anniversary of the establishment of diplomatic relations with the PRC. Aid projects undertaken jointly by the two countries in the following years explicitly invoked the fraternal spirit of the 1955 Bandung conference, and of the Non-aligned Movement. Decades later, after the Sierra Leonean civil war had come and gone, official PRC rhetoric returned to these material traces of Afro-Asian brotherhood, choosing to upgrade projects that were redolent with symbolism. In Freetown, the Youyi building was rehabilitated and completely recovered in new white tiles (Brautigam 2009, 137). This government ministerial complex was constructed in the 1970s through a PRC aid program and was known in town by its Chinese name (youyi), or "friendship," a fact that was noted by several Chinese residents in Freetown but was unknown to most Sierra Leoneans. The Chinese government also renovated and upgraded the National Stadium, which originally had been completed in 1979 and remained a potent symbol of Chinese aid (Brautigam 1998, 211). Stadiums are an especially popular and politically useful form of infrastructure, and in 2007 the Chinese embassy allocated a grant to construct a second stadium in the provincial town of Bo, even though it had advised that the funds would best be spent addressing more dire development needs (Will 2012, 38). That same year, the Chinese government upgraded the hydroelectric dam it had completed in 1986 at Dodo, in the Eastern Province, to provide electricity to the towns of Kenema and Bo (Brautigam 1998, 211–2; Seibure 2007).

Projects like Tonkolili can change the contours of a landscape—the shape and size of ore-rich mountains and of other physical features—and seem to symbolize the heavy-handedness of the Chinese presence in many African countries today. But even though it is responsible for about 90 percent of the country's export revenues, the mining sector represents only 4.5 percent of gross domestic product in Sierra Leone, while agriculture—most of it practiced at subsistence levels on small farms—constitutes 58.5 percent of GDP (OECD 2009, 562).

Here I focus on less visible material traces that risk being erased by the more monumental scale of projects such as the ones at Tonkolili and elsewhere in Sierra Leone and in other parts of Africa—the improved paved roads, the sports facilities, the government buildings but also the large-scale industrial ventures that are putting the Sierra Leonean environment at risk, potentially creating grounds for future conflicts. I argue that a focus on traces left in agrarian practices on rural landscapes, in the ordinary material fabric of domestic life and in therapeutic practices of healing, enriches our understanding of Chinese-African engagements over time. In the past, these engagements often lacked the direct interpersonal dimension that many Chinese-African ventures have today, and this sometimes made less obvious their distinctive Chinese character, and the meanings with which it was "bundled."[1]

Among other things, this history of prior material engagements is often evoked when new collaborations or accords are announced between the two countries, informing a discourse of "returns" and reactivations, particularly on the Chinese side, whenever new initiatives are announced. Paying attention to this perspective goes some way, I argue, toward decolonizing Sierra Leone's history beyond the Euro-African dynamics that are informed by some two centuries of British hegemony in the region. My focus is on the aftermath of the 1955 Bandung conference in Indonesia, which led to the foundation six years later of the Non-aligned Movement, as most African participants transitioned to independence. These Afro-Asian gatherings offered an emancipatory, alternative vision of mutual aid in a postcolonial future, outside the sphere of influence of former colonial powers, and on the other side of Cold War divides, by which they were shaped in critical ways.

During the Maoist period (1949–76), several African leaders who claimed formal adherence to socialism adopted Chinese development as a model for their own countries (Brautigam 2009, 38). Although Siaka Stevens—prime minister of Sierra Leone from 1967 to 1971 and president from 1971 to 1985—did not seek to establish a socialist regime, his background in union and labor activism brought him to form alliances with such regimes. Under Stevens's administration, diplomatic relations between Sierra Leone and the PRC were officially established in 1971 and resulted in the completion over the next two decades of several projects funded with Chinese aid and completed under the guidance of Chinese technical assistance. These included several rice cultivation projects, construction of the above-mentioned National Stadium—originally named after President Stevens—completed in 1979, and the Magbass sugar complex, completed in 1982, one of the largest sugar-producing plantations in West Africa (Brautigam 2009, 58). During the 1980s, the Chinese government's involvement in Sierra Leone saw a shift from the rhetoric of development aid, which was predicated on an asymmetrical relation, to the discourse of mutually beneficial economic "cooperation." Some of these projects point to the visible impact of a Chinese "monumental" presence—the PRC's engagement in large-scale, durable, often-infrastructural projects that transformed the surrounding landscape. However, these were often symbolic, isolated gestures that did not have an enduring effect on many ordinary Sierra Leonean lives. More impactful on both Sierra Leonean and Chinese lives were the bilateral agreements for joint ventures in fishing and agriculture, signed under President Stevens, and a trade agreement that facilitated the export from Sierra Leone to China of products—primarily coffee and cacao beans—and the importation of Chinese products ranging from machinery to textiles to household goods, which informed culinary tastes, bodily practices, and daily work on both sides of these exchanges (China Internet Information Center 2006).

## SIERRA LEONE–CHINESE AGRICULTURAL ENGAGEMENTS

The history of agricultural engagements reveals a different, though equally nuanced relationship between Chinese and Sierra Leonean actors. In his study of the history of technology transfers in the agricultural sector, Paul

Richards (1986) outlined the complex interactions between British, American, and "Chinese" actors involved in various attempts to import Asian rice cultivation practices to Sierra Leone. West Africa is the only region of the world outside Asia where rice is an indigenous crop (Carney 2001, 32–39), but in response to a catastrophic crop failure in 1918, worsened by the global influenza epidemic, the British colonial government brought to Sierra Leone wet rice cultivation experts from South Asia. They did so through the administrative structure of the Ministry of Agriculture, which, along with its system of extension workers and stations, continued to be the intermediary for delivering farming expertise and inputs to postcolonial Sierra Leone.

World War II and its aftermath saw additional recourses to East Asian farming and water-control techniques. In particular, in the 1950s, diversion of land and labor away from rice-farming areas in order to expand diamond-mining operations made higher-yielding wet rice cultivation an appealing alternative to local "dry" (hillside) farming (see fig. 2), which produced only one harvest per year (Richards 1986, 19). After independence in 1961, a new wave of Asian technical expertise and inputs came along with "Green revolution" projects aimed at building integrated, sustainable farming packages for small-scale farmers. This time also coincided with the era of post-Bandung "south-south" cooperation between select Asian and African countries, though among the latter, priority tended to be given to socialist governments that shared aspects of PRC political ideologies.

Unlike Tanzania or, closer by, Guinea and Ghana, Sierra Leone was not led into decolonization by a socialist leadership, and the politics of Chinese involvement in Sierra Leonean agriculture after independence was not a straightforward matter of ideological solidarity. The "swamp development" mode of rice cultivation, initiated through British experimentation in the 1930s, was promoted in the 1960s by US Peace Corps volunteers in collaboration with the country's Ministry of Agriculture. The system used high-yielding rice varieties engineered by the International Rice Research Institute in the Philippines, along with technology developed in Japanese-occupied Taiwan for the efficient production of *japonica* rice. In 1964, nine agricultural experts from the ROC visited Sierra Leone to conduct a study that demonstrated the successful cultivation of *japonica* rice in irrigated swamps. After this group's pilot work (beginning in December 1972), the World Bank provided a loan to fund three integrated agricultural development projects promoting swamp development (Richards 1986, 16–19). However, these swamp development projects failed to account for local specificities, including the adaptive success of indigenous farming practices, a gendered division of labor that could not be replicated in paddies, and a cultural preference for the taste of upland rice (Johnny, Karimu, Richards 1981, 603). Beyond a select number of showcase paddies, the Taiwanese model failed to be adapted on any significant scale in the rest of the country (Liu 2009, 388), and therefore it had a limited impact on Sierra Leonean rice farming.

The wet rice demonstration team sent to Sierra Leone in 1964 came under the auspices of the ROC's "Operation Vanguard," which was launched in 1961 to provide agricultural aid to developing countries (Brautigam 1998, 79). Indeed, "agricultural aid became a point of battle" between China and Taiwan in the 1960s and 1970s, one mostly played out in developing, relatively new nations of Africa (Brautigam 2009, 237). In the post–World War II years, during which the PRC and ROC struggled for international recognition as the sole legitimate government of "China"—for instance, at the United Nations—alliances with nations that could potentially provide UN votes one way or another were critical to both territorial entities. The Operation Vanguard program was not only a matter of ROC versus PRC interests, though. The US government took note of Taiwan's successful integration of two million refugees from the mainland in 1949—alleged evidence of its superior agricultural techniques—and subsequently provided crucial support for the dissemination of ROC agricultural aid in African countries (Liu 2009, 387).

The PRC displaced the ROC and came to occupy the China seat at the United Nations in 1971, in large part because of votes from the newly independent African nations that joined the UN General Assembly in the 1960s (Yu 1963). In the years leading to this shift, Beijing had promised countries receiving agricultural aid from Taiwan that it would continue projects already in place (Brautigam 2009, 237). China also initiated its own agricultural projects in many African countries during the 1970s, including rice cultivation stations with demonstration farms, new storage facilities, and tools and inputs in Sierra Leone (Brautigam 1998, 81). This was most likely the scheme that accounted for the visit to Kpuawala of the lone Chinese agricultural advisor in the story behind the Chinese Store. Like their ROC predecessors, however, these rice farms had very limited success (Brautigam 2009, 238).

One of the key agro-technical stations, established by the ROC, which was taken over by PRC agricultural advisors in the 1970s, was at Tormabum, in the country's Southern Province. In the mid-1980s, its extensive paddies, established on wetlands near the country's Atlantic coast, were choked by weeds and dotted with the rusting, broken-down relics of large mechanized farming equipment that had become useless soon after it had been introduced, during the previous decade. Farmers included in this and other similar projects worked alongside Chinese extension workers and had access to power-tilling machines, tractors, and other equipment. Though these projects were initially celebrated as successful technology transfers, only a few years after their implementation they began to deteriorate, because the Sierra Leonean Ministry of Agriculture lacked the funds and technical resources to maintain Chinese tractors and power tillers (Brautigam 1998, 89). Ten years later, the Chinese government, however, sent teams of technicians to rehabilitate some of these rice fields, emphasizing their importance in the historical memory of China–Sierra Leone "friendship" (Brautigam 2009, 244).

In a way evocative of a palimpsest, PRC advisors who (re)visited ROC rice cultivation projects in rural areas of Sierra Leone sought to inscribe their own presence on the landscape, while erasing local traces of a different, competing Chinese presence on the world stage. Indeed, the history of Sierra Leonean agriculture in the second half of the twentieth century reveals that it has often been a site for geopolitical Cold War rivalries. As I noted above, the US Peace Corps was one of the main engines for promoting swamp development rice cultivation in the 1960s. This, alongside agricultural inputs from Taiwan, was undoubtedly part of a broader effort to constrain Chinese Communist influence in the context of postcolonial and Cold War politics. In the following decades, the Peace Corps presence in the rural hinterlands of Sierra Leone became one of the largest in the world, in proportion to local population and country size. In 1983 there were 180 volunteers in Sierra Leone, while Mali—a West African country almost twenty times its size, and with about three times its population—had 49. The Philippines, with around 200 volunteers and a population about fourteen times larger than Sierra Leone, was the only country with a larger concentration of Peace Corps volunteers that year (Peace Corps Congressional Submission 1983, 70). In the 1980s, Peace Corps volunteers were virtually the only Caucasians seen in the country's more remote rural areas, and *peace corps* became the generic term there for white foreigners.

I highlight the presence of Peace Corps staff in Sierra Leone only to further emphasize the notion that traces of Chinese involvement in Sierra Leonean agriculture must be read not only as remnants of geopolitical struggles between the two Chinas but also as documented evidence of relationships triangulated by other intervening agents. Just as British-imported, nineteenth-century Chinese porcelain circulated as a sign of European elite taste in parts of colonial Africa—and was not immediately recognized as an example of Asian aesthetic objects or arti-facts—the complexities of Cold War alliances in the postcolony facili-tated the misrecognition of Chinese interventions in rice farming as the contributions of the United States through its young "peace" ambassa-dors. This misrecognition was facilitated by the increase during the 1980s of imported American rice, distributed in fifty-kilogram bags decorated with the American flag and bearing the words "gift of the American people,"[2] on the Sierra Leonean markets, to alleviate the eco-nomic hardships and food scarcity brought about by structural adjust-ment programs. There were political dimensions to this circulation of imported rice within Sierra Leone as well, for its distribution was chan-neled through government agencies, and free or subsidized rice bags were a key element in patronage networks during this decade, especially in diamond-mining areas where land and labor were diverted from farming. Thus, this history underscores how Chinese interventions were not always recognized as such. Instead, as will be discussed further below, they lie in the "underneath" of things, as they become part of the colonial and postcolonial archive.

## BODILY PRACTICES AND ETIOLOGIES OF HEALING

Between decolonization and the end of the Cold War, cheap Chinese goods were ubiquitous in Sierra Leone. Even remote rural villagers or impoverished urban households had access to them—if only through the occasional visits of itinerant traders in the former setting, or through contacts with wealthier neighbors and relatives in the latter—from *Maxxam*-brand toothpaste to Chinese-made kerosene lamps or cotton cloth for bedding. Most domestic units seemed to own at least one hot water thermos and a set of two matching metal food-serving bowls—one for rice and one for the sauce with which it was eaten—in painted enamel, which were also made in China. Virtually every household had at least a large round tray or basin in cheap Chinese enamelware, which was used to share with others the staple meal of rice mixed with sauce and which also doubled as a surface for petty traders to display and hawk their wares: hot peppers in tidy clusters, spoonsful of salt tied in fragments of clear plastic, sugar cubes, small tomatoes or onions, *Maggi* cubes, and so on. These larger, concave containers also carried water and other goods piled high on top of people's (usually women's) heads.

Also pervasive at this time were small tins of Tiger Balm ointment, whose pungent camphor and menthol smell on sick people signaled its use for a broad range of illnesses. It was rubbed on aching or fevered bodies, or drunk as an infusion mixed with warm water for certain stomach ailments. A favorite gift in most households, the small, round and flat cans of Tiger Balm were referred to generically as "mentholatum," itself a brand harkening back to the colonial medicine cabinet. The Mentholatum company website advertises the product as being invented in 1889 by an American, who donated the ointment to church missionaries to support their work abroad. "This is how the product gained entrance worldwide," it states, and the website mentions its popularity in China, where it sold briskly even in the nineteenth century (Mentholatum Asia Pacific Ltd. 2007). Thus though the character for tiger above the animal's image, and the writings and decorations on the container, identify the balm as a Chinese product, the language used to refer to it in Sierra Leone signals its more complicated history and identification with colonial medical practices and consumption habits. Missionary medicine was a critical site for an "ongoing existential and cultural exchange" between Europeans and Africans—encounters in which the racialized segregation of bodies often collapsed in the name of the care for and remaking of a healthy colonial subject, who could also be a provident consumer (Comaroff and Comaroff 1997, 166–217, 323–64). However, similar processes were at work in Asia. Even before the "American" invention of mentholatum, its key ingredients were used for medicinal purposes in Japan and China, a fact that accounts for the product's success in those markets once it was introduced there by American missionaries (A. Taylor 2006, 19, 92).

Similarly to other cases discussed in the previous section, then, in Sierra Leone the Asian origins of Tiger Balm were eclipsed by the introduction of consumers to mentholatum through missionary-colonial healing and trading practices. For local consumers in the years preceding the end of the Cold War, there was nothing self-evidently Chinese about this product, and the packaging's Asian visual cues and writing were eclipsed by its contents. The texture and smell of mentholatum evoked colonial and missionary healing practices that exceeded the more recent exposure to the Chinese version of this Singapore-produced substance. But even as it was assimilated to an earlier and different regime of medical practices, Sierra Leoneans' consumption of Tiger

Balm may be seen as a precursor to the welcoming reception they gave to other Chinese medical treatments decades later.

More recent medicinal treatments are eagerly experimented with precisely because of their novelty on foreign markets. In preexisting arrangements between local healing practices and colonial and postcolonial biomedicine, injections had come to occupy a preferred place (see Bledsoe and Goubaud 1985, 280), their direct infusion in the body of liquid substances being seen as a way to "increase blood," which was the hallmark of good health. By contrast, a wasting, "drying" body, in which blood was not plentiful—among its symptoms being flaky, dry skin—was seen as a harbinger of illness. When given the choice between taking medication in pill or other form or as an injection, most Sierra Leoneans chose the latter. This preference left lasting marks on the bodies of many adult Sierra Leoneans in the rural countryside, where the lack of disposable syringes and proper sterilization in the days of their infancy resulted in infection-related scars at the sites of injections. In Sierra Leonean encounters with Chinese biomedicine, the intravenous drip seemed to promise an even greater therapeutic possibility than the one-time injection of that preexisting healing regime.

In Freetown, the King Harman Road Hospital for years hosted delegations of visiting Chinese doctors. Upon entering the hospital during a visit in 2012, I was struck by the number of patients lying on gurneys attached to intravenous drips from bags of fluid hanging over them—many more than one would ordinarily find in the city's main Connaught hospital or in other medical institutions. When I asked about this, the Sierra Leonean director of the hospital confirmed that Chinese doctors tended to prescribe more "drips" than Western-trained ones, and that these had also been prevalent in Chinese hospitals, where he was trained. It seemed as though in Sierra Leoneans who had developed a preference for the potency of injections, in encounters with colonial medicine, found in the longer-lasting infusion of fluids in the body through intravenous "drips" a recognizable extension of a particular vernacularization of biomedical therapies.

The hospital offered several treatments falling under the category of "traditional Chinese medicine," a designation officially established only after the founding of the PRC in 1949 (Farquhar 1994, 11). Among these, one popular therapy available at the hospital was acupuncture, which, though it involved needles, did not involve the transmission of fluids that made the intravenous drip fit so well within local etiologies of illness and health. Here needles were disconnected from syringes and fluid sacks and did not inject anything into the body. Nonetheless, Sierra Leonean patients found that this therapy provided relief, and they willingly experimented with it. Indeed, one of our Chinese interlocutors in Freetown told us that he once drove the mother of the country's first lady to visit a doctor friend of his, who was a practitioner of traditional Chinese medicine, and that the first lady herself preferred Chinese traditional medicine.

Another side to this site of therapeutic encounters featured the circulation and sharing of medicinal expertise, in addition to the emplacement of imported medicinal practices within a landscape of medical pluralism. Since the 1970s, Chinese medical teams have been dispatched to African countries—a key component of the diplomatic engagements and strategies of "friendship" discussed above (Hsu 2008). The first of such teams came to Sierra Leone in 1973, initially to the provincial towns of Bo and Kenema. Each team of roughly ten-to-twelve doctors spent an average of two years in the country, providing continuous coverage with the exception of the years between 1993 and 2002, when the program was interrupted when the civil war intensified. From the end of the civil war in 2002 onward, they established themselves in the Freetown clinic on King Harman Road (Li 2011, 10), which they helped transform into a full-fledged hospital that was handed over to Sierra Leonean staff, once a large, new, Chinese-built hospital eventually opened in Jui, on the eastern end of the city.

The Chinese medical teams then moved their base in the country to Jui Government Hospital, in a more populous, and rapidly growing part of greater Freetown. The Ebola outbreak of 2014–15 brought from Beijing to Sierra Leone a Chinese military medical team with experience in combating the Severe Acute Respiratory Syndrome (SARS) in the PRC over a decade earlier. This was the first time China had deployed a military medical team for a humanitarian mission, and the team's first project was to rebuild the fairly new Jui hospital to conform with World Health Organization standards for infectious disease isolation and treatment. In another instance of palimpsestic reinscription onto earlier projects, the repurposed hospital was renamed "Sierra Leone-Chinese Friendship Hospital" (Lu et al. 2016, 2).

## CONCLUSION

In this chapter, I have sought to emphasize the historical continuities as well as the qualitative changes in both orientation and scale of Chinese engagements with Sierra Leone, and to explore the ways in which these engagements have shaped collective imaginaries on all sides of these encounters. In Sierra Leone, as elsewhere on the continent, memories of earlier Chinese engagements remain, but their traces on the very landscapes they once helped shape are in some places eclipsed by the marks of the present, or by their palimpsest-like reinscriptions. Small-scale rural farming projects have been replaced in some areas by industrial farms for ethanol production; mining operations are changing the contours of hills and waterways; and infrastructural projects like dams, roads, and buildings are reshaping urban and rural spaces. Individual Chinese entrepreneurs have also begun to open stores and other small businesses in Sierra Leone's capital city, Freetown—an economic niche historically occupied by Lebanese traders, who are no longer as visible in the ground-level shops of their two-story buildings on urban streets. Though some continue to occupy the upper, residential levels of those same buildings while engaging in other kinds of businesses, many have taken advantage of political and economic changes over the past decade to move back to Lebanon or elsewhere. By contrast, many former Lebanese stores in Freetown are now occupied by African traders from across West Africa—some of whom travel to China to purchase their merchandise—as well as by a number of Chinese businesses.

Attention to the material dimensions of everyday life as a constitutive part of China–Sierra Leone relations makes visible more complicated and mediated histories of not only political and economic but also cultural engagements. In the 1980s, the Sierra Leonean rural landscape was being shaped by agricultural practices forged at the intersection of traditional rice-farming practices, colonial and postcolonial agrarian policies, and the political contests of the Cold War. Imported Asian rice varieties had been introduced since the era of colonial swamp-cultivation schemes, and in the postcolonial landscape this was as likely to happen through the mediation of Chinese agricultural advisors—whether from Taiwan or the PRC—as it was through US Peace Corps volunteers and aid projects, or their Sierra Leonean partners in the Ministry of Agriculture. In a similar manner, an already-existing Chinese material presence in African everyday life, from the Maxxam toothpaste used in daily ablutions to the plates on which meals were eaten and goods were carried, shaped tastes in consumption and bodily practices. In some cases, it even sparked curiosity about the language and writing inscribed on these commodities, or about the culture and provenance of elusive Chinese visitors.

The more recent, large-scale Chinese interventions in the rural land-scape of Sierra Leone and other African countries—from mining opera-tions to "the largest agricultural investment in Sierra Leone's history," a $1.3 billion project to develop rice and rubber farmland in the Tonko-lili area (*Agence France Presse* 2012)—may paint an unbalanced picture of the power entailments and economic benefits of this relationship. The material traces I have followed in this analysis, however, indicate the possibility of a different future. After all, the "writing on the wall," or imprinted on objects, books, and landscapes, can conceal as much as it reveals—for instance, an earlier ROC presence interpreted as a uni-form Chinese presence, which especially since the 1990s was overshad-owed by the rise of the PRC as a global power. In order to understand the import of such ephemeral inscriptions, we must not allow the impos-ing physicality of the latest layers in Chinese-African relations to over-shadow the complexities of the earlier material sedimentations outlined in this chapter. Instead, I have argued in favor of a methodological pri-oritizing of the "social life" of ordinary domestic objects and medica-tions, and of the social imagination, in ways that are attentive to both the absences and the intimacies that have variously characterized this relationship. My analysis has shown layers, not only of often-mediated Chinese inscriptions in multiple African landscapes, but also of conver-gences ranging from the cultivation of rice—a shared staple food—to medicinal preferences and even to the preoccupation with male sexual potency (see Ferme and Schmitz 2014).

Though the focus in this chapter has been historical, I suggest that a more complex picture of Chinese-African relations emerges from the imaginative attention to material traces in landscapes where evidence of these encounters may be less obvious. For most of the twentieth cen-tury, Lebanese shopkeepers had been the face of bulk trade in Sierra Leone. But the pacification of Lebanon, the disruptions of the 1991–2002 civil war in Sierra Leone, and the opening up of new economic opportunities elsewhere made many leave the country, or change occu-pations. Trade and shops have become untangled from the "Lebanese" presence, with which they were previously bundled, and now these spaces and activities are occupied by a more diverse range of actors, including some Chinese. But the analysis has also shown that even the category of "Chinese" needs to be scrutinized, because early Taiwanese forays in Africa were revisited with projects and commodities from the PRC. At the same time, I have suggested that well before the spatiotem-poral escalation of present Chinese-Africa engagements—those publicly memorialized in legacy infrastructure or diplomatic friendship agreements, which bring face-to-face, as it were, Chinese and African subjects in multiple ways—other forms of entanglements were already in the making. These were embedded in the social mediation of objects and substances and in the long history of colonial and Cold War rice-farming innovations and therapeutic practices.

# Conclusion

## Surviving and Moving On—Ephemeral Returns

The wounds of the civil war of 1999–2002 discussed in this book reached well beyond the postconflict decade. Sierra Leone was one of the three West African countries struck by the 2014–16 West African Ebola viral disease (EVD) epidemic, the deadliest manifestation of this illness to date. Of the three affected countries (Guinea, Liberia, and Sierra Leone), Sierra Leone had the highest number of cases—14,124 that were labora-tory-confirmed (8,706), suspected, or probable, according to Center for Disease Control statistics. There was some debate about the reliability of the statistics for affected patients and casualties, but what was not dis-puted was the fact that the epidemic peaked in the whole affected region in fall 2014. Also undisputed is the fact that Sierra Leone now has the largest number of survivors from that outbreak. Anthropological analy-sis never seemed more relevant, with online platforms rapidly established to enable information sharing with epidemiologists and health care spe-cialists, such as the University of Sussex–based "Ebola Response Anthro-pology Platform."[1] At some level, the Ebola epidemic, with its disrup-tions to the social world and landscape and the displacement of people, evoked a sense of déjà vu harkening back to the civil war years and their aftermath, but there was a difference Both were emergencies that satu-rated the country with global figures of humanitarianism, its institutions and actors, which were highly politicized and deeply engaged with the interests of neoliberal agendas—as I have suggested elsewhere (Ferme 2013; see also Fassin 2007; Redfield 2013).

They brought in foreign personnel, as had been done during the civil war, but this time both existing hospitals and those set up by organizations like Médecins Sans Frontières had to be reconfigured to isolate patients and protect medical personnel. This was owing to the highly contagious nature of this illness and differed from the way caregiving was foregrounded during the war. As the epidemic intensified, some health facilities were overwhelmed and became places of death, where palliative intervention, as opposed to the prospect of being cured, was the most that could be offered. People were isolated and left to die in these places, rather than being "cured and cared for."[2] Many people who were not affected by Ebola, however, stated that the war was a much worse experience for the country as a whole. For one thing, the total number of wartime casualties was estimated to be between fifty and seventh-five thousand, much higher than the comprehensive numbers for EVD. Additionally, the temporal span of these crises was different: the war lasted more than a decade, while the EVD emergency peaked and subsided within a three-year period. But there were similarities as well. The rhetoric surrounding interventions against the EVD epidemic was military, and at the height of the infection, the state's security apparatus was mobilized to manage the population, shut down the country, and impede mobility, like similar deployments during the civil war.

In the intercrisis period between the end of the civil war and the onset of the EVD epidemic, economic opportunities increased, initially in the interest of rebuilding the country in a "postconflict" landscape, which led to unprecedented rates of growth. However, all this came to a halt with the EVD crisis, which stalled many business ventures and prompted the return of humanitarian organizations, which had saturated the post-conflict landscape. These organizations did hire some local staff, but they were predominantly unskilled public health workers (the "hazmat-suited" figures seen in the media, who ferried suspected cases to treatment centers and worked on burial teams). Other relatively unskilled workers included contact tracers, but their employment was often only temporary. More long-term employment opportunities also increased for youth who had access to a good education. Once security and peace were restored after the civil war, neoliberal business ventures were launched. Among these were consultancies, mining ventures, and large-scale agricultural projects, which together made up a Sierra Leonean iteration of the broader global landscape of "land grabs" that have become a widespread phenomenon on the African continent in particular. Sierra Leone attracted global capital to explore business opportunities and NGOs to ensure that these opportunities were pursued with a modicum of respect for global norms of environmental and human rights protection.

Locally, a well project to provide villagers with safe drinking water, which had often been at the top of the wish list in Kpuawala during the war, had finally materialized with the support of a religious charity, the Church of the Latter-Day Saints. For a few years after the project's completion, a sticker on the well announced the church's support. Thus the "NGO-ization" of the humanitarian landscape brought about by the conflict—the proliferation of a bewildering array of humanitarian organizations, to which I alluded in the Red Cross chapter, which were difficult to distinguish and identify—included religious organizations as well. Eventually the sticker disappeared, as did memories of the organization that had made the well a reality.

The human rights organizations (among them were Namati, Timap for Justice, Green Scenery) that had intervened during the war emergency turned in the postconflict period to environmental causes, the negotiation of fairer commercial farming contracts, or to prisoners' rights. However, the disruption brought about by the EVD crisis in some cases suspended the activities of these organizations, including the negotiations over contracts affecting large land tracts, as well as those affecting employment.

During the NGO-ization phase of the postconflict transition, many Sierra Leonean potential employees addressed this unpredictability through a kind of doubling—secondment from secure but irregularly paid government work to private short-term contract employment with international NGOs, which offered better salaries and benefits. This doubling evoked the practices of "the gift of employment" discussed by Achille Mbembe as being a key feature of the African postcolony (Mbembe 2001). In the aftermath of the Ebola crisis, these forms of short-term employment contracts, whether they worked in parallel to more secure but less remunerated civil service positions or consisted of altogether new positions, have become even more prevalent.

White ambulances with red crosses once again are common sights in villages and urban residential neighborhoods—their familiarity barely eliciting a passing comment as they circulate individually, rather than in convoys, as they did during the war. At the time of the EVD crisis, these vehicles were assumed to be picking up suspected cases, or the bodies of the deceased, for a postmortem determination of the causes of death that was required before the bodies could be properly buried. Indeed, the practice of reporting all deaths to authorities so they could come and handle the bodies, rather than private burials being arranged in a family setting, was becoming established and therefore potentially transformative of the ways in which Sierra Leoneans bury their dead. While the troubling rumors shaped by the civil war about the symbol of the red cross were eclipsed from the social imaginary by this more recent crisis, the Red Cross continued to challenge common perceptions of its task by stepping into the intractable world of death, burials, and mourning that had long been controlled by local institutions.

The presence of Ebola survivors in the post-EVD landscape does raise fears and social anxieties. However, it does not trigger the widespread suspicions regarding concealed motives and loyalties like those cast on Kaikulo and other child soldiers and young survivors during the war. Instead, social anxieties are more about whether or not the bodies of Ebola survivors contain strains of the virus in parts of their bodies where they may remain dormant for long periods before becoming contagious once again, regardless of the hosts' conscious intention or volition. Beyond this local concern about a different kind of future harm, the global biomedical and pharmaceutical community sees the existence of such a large number of survivors of the disease, particularly in Sierra Leone, as offering new opportunities for better understanding the life course of this virus and for developing new vaccines. In a similar manner, new information about humanitarian interventions and jurisprudence during wartime was produced when Sierra Leone became a test case in the deployment and development of the United Nation's larges-cale peacekeeping humanitarian missions. In addition, for a new generation of hybrid international courts for crimes, Sierra Leone was a test case for enriching the global jurisprudence on sexual crimes and on the forced conscription of underage combatants. The Ebola epidemic has brought the country once again to the attention of a global community of actors, media, NGOs, and religious organizations, if only briefly. The advances in virology and rapid-testing abilities, as well as the vaccines developed, will have lasting implications for the way in which the "lurking" of EVD in its human hosts is dealt with by epidemiologists and public health personnel. The unpredictable behavior of the latent virus is, in a way, a kind of land mine, waiting to go off, only it is concealed in body joints, tissues, and fluids, rather than buried in the wartime landscape. Its unpredictability slides across disciplines and areas of interest, mining anthropology, philosophy, and the health sciences with its hidden potentials for disruption. Practices of isolation, internment, administrative and governmental control, and mass burial of victims will be exported to the next large-scale crisis, crossing borders, cultural understandings, and social anxieties.

Survivals take forms other than human, however. They are crystallized in places and objects, which even today can evoke war memories and in so doing elicit narratives of those unstable times. Thus though the number of checkpoints manned by the military and police has once again increased during the EVD emergency, as it did during the civil war, it is only half of what existed during the war. Another difference is that the uniformed personnel there are accompanied by public health workers wearing lab coats and surgical gloves. The "thermometer-guns" that became ubiquitous during the EVD epidemic were pointed at travelers' heads, in a gesture resembling aggression, but they were quickly turned around to display body temperatures, and were followed by offers of hand-sanitizing solutions or injunctions for travelers to get out of their vehicles to wash their hands in chlorinated water. These gun-shaped thermometers marked the threshold between health and illness—another object and technology in the dissemination of global health—rather than being dangerous weapons for dispensing death. Checkpoints were sites where one could see how militarization had given way to securitization—a more general set of technologies and epistemologies of war refocused on the regulation of movements, the management of risk, and the dissemination of biometric data.

The dissemination and mapping of global and local health data mentioned above also take place over the media, and here the Ebola crisis marked another departure from wartime, in that television programming in Sierra Leone juxtaposed the consumer messaging, reporting, and entertainment that had been a feature of that era with animated short stories carrying a didactic intent. Health messages were encapsulated in particular stories to awaken and maintain a permanent sense of vigilance in the population.

Other sites on the postconflict landscape have been repurposed for the 2014–16 Ebola crisis: the physical structures left behind by the Special Court for Sierra Leone became a central coordinating site for agencies, particularly the United Nations Ebola Emergency Response unit, that were intervening in the outbreak, but these had already been shut down before the end of the emergency. What remained was a "Legacy Court" project that continues—for a time—to fulfill its commitment to protect witnesses and victims of the 1991–2002 civil war who had testified at the Special Court, reaching out to them during the Ebola crisis to ensure their well being. The Legacy Court is also developing and maintaining the historical archive of the war, but key elements of this archive have now been deterritorialized and moved to the International Criminal Court at the Hague, or to the digital realm. Its documentation constitutes the core of a law school library that also occupies the court grounds. In Sierra Leone, the proliferation of lawyers, in particular; of the legal profession as a choice; and of litigation as a performative endeavor also point to another enduring legacy of the Special Court for Sierra Leone—namely the reestablishment of the "rule of law," where war crimes had been committed in a context of lawlessness and of the infringement of human rights.

Processes of decentralization that had been deemed essential to curbing central government corruption gradually informed the court system as well, which also met in provincial towns. However, the legal system as a setting for settling conflicts is still characterized by the temporality of deferral—case adjournments and procedural delays. This temporality is shared with local courts and informal moots. In the formal court system, these temporal deferrals are sometimes the result of inadequate staffing—the traveling magistrate or lawyers (mostly based in the capital city) sometimes do not show up at provincial court hearings. Even in Freetown, staffing can be uneven. In one instance I observed, a judge without a stenographer took notes of proceedings himself in longhand, slowing down lawyers who had to dictate their arguments (my notes, 14 October 2015). Thus though an increase in the study and practice of the law as a profession may be among the legacies of the Special Court of Sierra Leone, and though there are now more lawyers in the country, the contrast between the level of efficiency in national courts, compared with the efficient administration, live video streaming and recording, and other high-tech operations that unfolded at the Special Court, is striking.

Dealing with the weight of war memories is key to survivals, and their productive forgetting is an avenue to health (a way of working through traumatic experiences and mitigating their impact on the present). The man from the city, who arrived in the rural chiefdom in the aftermath of the civil war—trapped within the traumatic memories of the loss of his family members—lived in the past and did not survive the present. By contrast, though the rape survivor I met at the Special Court still remembered her wartime experiences some years later, she had moved on, taking advantage of the psychosocial support system that surrounded her testimony at the court and of the material benefits that allowed her to further her education. Unlike the man who had let himself die along the Wunde path, she had managed to work through her traumatic experience and was making plans for her future, even though her iconic status as a witness made her a privileged source for accounts of the war concerning the practice of "forced marriage," and therefore someone likely to be solicited in the future for her story.

The crime of "forced marriage" itself can be said to be a figure of survival: a figure that was defined in international humanitarian jurisprudence and informed indictments for the first time at the Special Court for Crimes in Sierra Leone. It also is a survival in the sense that it places the country, its war experiences, and history within a broader global discourse of jurisprudence that can be used as a precedent in other war crimes litigation. The global military, therapeutic, and humanitarian experimentation in Sierra Leone will have effects across national and international borders, reproducing small- and large-scale techniques produced during both crises—the war and the EVD epidemic. Sierra Leone as a site of experimentation will be embedded in another metonymic relationship, entangled with other realities and politics. What is left in the wake of the global military, humanitarian, and therapeutic passage is a land up for grabs, potentially marked in a permanent way by a sense of insecurity in spite of the radical securitization brought about by these recent emergencies.

The periodic calling of a witness to tell her story in the aftermath of an event and the deployment of an article of jurisprudence, only to have it contested and set aside in later trials—these are examples of a punctuated experience of time. This low-intensity, decade-long civil war was experienced in a similar manner: it flared up in particular space-times, only to leave long stretches of ordinary activity in others. In a similar manner, the Ebola epidemic of 2014–16 unfolded in rural areas, with special force and in highly concentrated spaces and times, of the broader region that encompasses Sierra Leone—affecting large numbers of people in circumscribed areas.

Witnesses, as I discussed when I compared a woman who testified at the Special Court for Crimes with one who suffered similar experiences but did not appear in court, are a particular category of war survivors. The story of my friend in Pujehun was more nuanced, her relations with the captor who became her "bush husband" more ambiguous, than that of iconic "witnesses" produced by the legal performances of courtrooms and trials. But she also did not have to fear stigma as much as the witnesses who had exposed themselves in court—albeit under the cover of identity protection, which sometimes worked only imperfectly. In a similar manner, Ebola survivors are called upon to tell their stories in order to help outreach efforts to stem the spread of the disease, but in the very same act of telling they can expose themselves to stigma.

Wars and other emergencies produce refugees and internally displaced persons, and their emplacement in "self-organized refugee camps, sorting centers, spaces of confinement, and camps for internally displaced persons"—to use Agier's (2011, 39) four-part classification of the camps—shapes new spaces in which time is experienced as a form of permanent "waiting" (for the end of war and the return of security, for the end of isolation to avoid contagion). At one point, the Gondama refugee camp south of Bo, Sierra Leone, could be said to be the second largest city in the country in terms of population and size, whereas today only remnants of it can be seen, thus bespeaking what I call a kind of "biopolitical ephemerality." Ebola treatment centers set up by organizations such as Médecins sans Frontières were established like the internment camps, discussed in the scholarship on biopolitics and the history of "triage," that provide emergency medical care in wartime (see Redfield 2013). Their instantiations, with the modifications required by the fear of contagion, during the civil war were mimicked in the Ebola emergency. Both were ephemeral, as Médecins sans Frontières camps were being dismantled with the waning of the Ebola emergency. They left in place some of the generally applicable triaging practices they introduced, but in Ebola treatment units isolation and separation of contagious patients are the central organizing principles, in contrast with those set up for other emergencies.

The serial deployment of global humanitarian interventions, first in the civil war of 1991–2002, then in the face of the Ebola epidemic of 2014 in West Africa, is leaving behind not just physical infrastructure but also discursive techniques and practices of care that inform particular individuals: the defender of human rights on behalf of war victims, the provider of care to subjects of global health epidemics, the provider of security, who will outlast the crisis. These may be the lasting legacies of war, insofar as they are redeployed in other, similar circumstances, both at home and abroad.

What remains, though in a changed form and with resolutely local—rather than global—appeal are the chieftaincy and other cultural institutions. For chiefs and hunters, too, the war was a transformative event. Sierra Leonean hunters—among the rare legitimately armed individuals outside the military, particularly in rural society—became politicized because over the course of the war they were organized into trained paramilitary forces aligned with the ruling party elected in 1996. They also fit into a regional West African redeployment of organized hunting groups, repurposed for a number of state projects, ranging from security to environmental stewardship. The chieftaincy as an institution of local governance also was implicated in electoral politics, but its historical roots in colonial and precolonial times were deeper. Its legitimacy is rooted in hereditary and dynastic principles that are linked primarily to rural lands.

But the chieftaincy's power is also performative, not only in the substantive socioeconomic and political arrangements a chief oversees but also in the visible emblems of office, which have proliferated since the end of the war. In substantive terms, chiefs publish by-laws, implement national and district policies, and enforce regulations, but they are also now empowered by the national government to negotiate contracts that dispose of their chiefdom's resources with outside interests (mining interests, commercial farming ventures, environmental projects). Thus the chiefship as an institution continues to link the performance of "the law" mentioned above with its more political roles. As the Ebola epidemic was increasing in force, in August 2014, chiefs published by-laws intended to police and fine public behavior in order to stem the spread of disease. These on the one hand fixed in time already-outdated notions of Ebola transmission—for instance, by regulating the sale and consumption of wild animal meat when the global health community already knew that the disease was mostly spread through human to human contact. On the other hand, however, the forced closure of markets and stores on Sundays, which was among the new regulations established by emergency EVD by-laws, may well be a lasting legacy of the epidemic. And as rural communities with large Sunday periodic markets tried to reschedule them on other weekend days that overlapped with neighboring, competing markets, chiefs found themselves embroiled in conflicts and their mediation.

Given the hereditary nature of the chieftaincy, the elections that bring chiefs to power are held infrequently, when a chief dies or is deposed. By contrast, electoral politics on the national or local level unfold more frequently, or every four or five years. This brings about a kind of anticipation, but it also makes for a continuous canvassing in the intervening time and for the periodic enactment of candidate visits, particularly to towns. These events are political, but they are also festive occasions for politicians to give generic speeches about party platforms and development goals.

Just as the end of the civil war witnessed hunters and chiefs being invested with new symbols of power and politicians using party symbols and colors to recruit supporters and sway voters, the war's aftermath saw an increased resurgence and circulation of emblems for public health, development, and humanitarian interventions. Large portions of budgets were devoted both to planning interventions and to their visible markers—posters, messaging, and logos to favor the recognition of particular institutions, such as the new paramount chiefs' emblems and symbols discussed in an earlier chapter. At the same time, the war saw a shift in regimes of care, from a more "developmental" approach to poverty and harm reduction, rooted in long-term planning and advertised by known, familiar brands such as the United Nations, the Red Cross, and other well-established aid organizations, to short-lived humanitarian interventions that proliferated through NGOs.

NGOs are smaller, more mobile, and "private" organizations, both religious and secular, which proliferated after the war. The multiplication of their emblems, along with their complex names, made for confusion among the targets of their interventions, who took to referring to them as generic "NGOs." These, too, were a sort of "chronotope," in the index of biopolitical ephemerality ushered in by the civil war, which was redeployed in the context of the Ebola epidemic and is already moving on with the rest of the "humanitarian international" (De Waal 1997).

While postconflict Sierra Leone has seen a remarkable resurgence of symbols of power, emblems, and forms of humanitarian interventionism, the reality signified by these symbols is still heavily marked by uncertainty and destabilization and is open to political contestation. The scale of brutalities during the Sierra Leone civil war has not vanished in the social memory of this country, nor has the scale of government corruption, which was brought to the redeployment of the chieftaincy—an institution with important historical resonances—and the establishment of more robust, elected district councils. Whether the relationship among chiefs, the councils, and the rural farmers who are being encouraged to turn into "entrepreneurs" will reduce the potential for future conflict remains to be seen. For now, some large-scale, commercial farming projects have already generated conflict, while others have for now adopted innovative partnership models with contracted farmers and may not run into the same problems.[3]

The chieftaincy is more "mobile," as we saw, both in terms of the relative ease of transportation it now enjoys and because of the communication technology that most chiefs rely on in order to attend to their chiefdoms' business. But the chief's mobility in wartime was of a different nature from that in the EVD crisis times. War produced random and unpredictable harms, while Ebola's incidence was more concentrated in space-time, and the advent of cell phone technology and improved communications eventually made the reporting of cases and of public health measures more efficient. Nonetheless, the experience of everyday life and its temporality can only be characterized as being unpredictable over this book's timespan, which is bookended by these two emergencies. What remains are new forms of investment in the political economy, as well as new forms of subjectivities. Among the latter are empowerment models in the legal sphere, where the discourse of rights (or *raiti*) introduced in the postconflict moment shapes the ways in which citizens approach the law. These approaches are more capillary, predicated on more distributed entitlements and on neoliberal models of right-bearing individuals. They are, therefore, potentially more momentous in their impact than the top-down "rule of law" movement represented by the Special Court, with its focus on litigation in formal courts. In a parallel move toward neoliberal forms of subjectivity in the domain of agrarian livelihoods, subsistence producers are being turned into entrepreneurs and encouraged to use a decentralized network of "agricultural business units," which have replaced prewar cooperative models for bringing produce to markets.

Throughout the vagaries of decentralization, however, global capital and political economic interests are reshaping the landscape and the environment, not only in Sierra Leone but also on the African continent as a whole. Africa has the highest incidence of "land grabs" by foreign companies, particularly China, for a variety of mining and farming operations. What the implications of these interventions for food, health, and land security will be, in Sierra Leone and elsewhere, remain to be seen and are a subject for future work. Already evidence from Sierra Leone has pointed to potential conflicts arising from these large-scale land deals, with respect to their impact on the environment and on principles of social justice. In this regard, too, Sierra Leone may be a small-scale test case for broader global phenomena.

# Notes

1. The peace museum is featured in Alain Resnais's film, *Hiroshima Mon Amour,* as a documentary segment in the context of a film being made in post–World War II Japan. Japanese writer Kenzaburö Öe wrote about the traumatized, radiation-exposed doctors who intervened in the aftermath of the atomic bomb (e.g., Öe 1996) but also of the ways in which he coped as a father of a disabled child after his fears and anticipations of the birth (Öe 1969). See too the Japanese graphic stories featuring "Barefoot Gen."

2. Farm plots are first cleared of trees and underbrush, which are left to dry for several days and then burned when weather conditions are favorable. In the absence of fertilizers and animal manure, a good burn and its ashes are the main source of soil nutrients for—and delay weed growth in—the new rice crop.

3. This rhetoric of "flare-ups" has strong parallels with the discourse surrounding the Ebola epidemic, which from the beginning was said to be concentrated in "hotspots," with the difference that "super-spreader" events were at its heart.

4. See Agier (2011, 107–08) on Guéckédou and the plight of refugees in camps in this and other conflicts, and McGovern (2002, 86) for political rhetoric and the ethnicization of Guinean politics during the same period.

5. There is some confusion in the literature surrounding this terminology. I follow here Gberie's, which corresponds to my own understanding of the usage from conversations with Sierra Leonean interlocutors, but the report of Sierra Leone's Truth and Reconciliation Commission inverts the terminology and refers to amputations above the elbow as "long sleeve" and those below the elbow as "short sleeve" (TRC 2004, appendix 5, 8).

6. Interview with a witness (TF1–023), Residual Special Court for Sierra Leone, October 2015.

7. Here I use the notion of space-time not in its phenomenological sense but in the psychoanalytical sense of a time that shapes the sense of place, particularly in the work of memory and trauma, such as in the case of delayed memories. On space-time more generally, rather than in the context of war, images, and traumatic memories, Nancy Munn has written about the importance of a processual approach that links "place-mnemonics and forgetting" (Munn [2003] 2013, 359).

8. Alternative accounts attribute this ambush to elements linked to the National Provisional Ruling Council, which was then in power (Paul Richards, November 2014, personal communication).

9. This concept bears some similarities to Nancy Munn's (1986) concept of "space-time," but it is less indebted to the phenomenological tradition.

10. Joseph Opala, professor emeritus, James Madison University, personal email communication, 31 September 2014.

11. This was underwritten, as we shall see in a later chapter, by the British government, among others.

12. Then as now, the means of transportation also made a difference: during this trip, I was not on public transportation but in a friend's private vehicle, which had no prescheduled stops.

13. For general discussions of the reasons and modalities for this growing interest, see, for instance, Das, Kleinman, Ramphele, and Reynolds (2000); Donham (2006); Feldman (1991); Scheper-Hughes and Bourgois (2003).

14. Postcolonial scholarship has also focused critical attention on methodological and conceptual issues related to the "denial of coevalness" by many anthropological studies in general, and by those focused on Africa in particular (e.g., Fabian 1983). This on a continent distinguished instead by experiences of temporality as emergent, as "time of entanglement" where "the future horizon is apparently closed, while the horizon of the past has apparently receded" (Mbembe 2001, 15–17).

15. The correct phonetic spelling of this word is *kamajɔ*, but scholarly and policy writings about the civil war have by and large adopted the British colonial-era spelling, *kamajo*, followed by a final *h* or *r*. The plural form is obtained by adding "sia" to the singular. Since there are no *r*'s in Mende, and this is a Mende word, I am critical of this practice but use it anyway because it was adopted in Krio and English publications at the national level, as well as in SCSL documents. For example, this spelling was adopted in the displays at the National Museum of Sierra Leone discussed in chapter 3.

**CHAPTER ONE. BELATEDNESS**

1. At its founding, in 1787, by the Sierra Leone Company as a settlement for the repatriation of liberated slaves, and at its 1807 transformation into a Crown colony, Sierra Leone was made up only of Freetown, on the estuary of the Sierra Leone river, and the surrounding peninsula. In 1825, partly to rid the lower reaches of its navigable rivers of slave traders, then-governor Turner annexed to the colony, through treaties, the coastal, Sherbro-speaking strip running from the Freetown peninsula to the Liberian border (Fyfe 1962, 156). Imperri moved under the colony jurisdiction in 1891 (Alldridge, cited in Kalous 1974, 37) but

was transferred to the protectorate in 1898 (Kalous, 46). Uncertainties over jurisdiction and boundaries, and protracted land disputes on the border, made this region insecure well into the twentieth century.

2. There are some inconsistencies in the dating of this chiefly installation. I choose to follow Alldridge's (1910, 269) published writings, which place the event in 1896, but official correspondence from a local chief addressed to him in 1895 mentions "the Coronation of the King Sokang [*sic*]" (cited in Kalous 1974, 41). See Abraham (1976) and Pratten (2007, 344n19) for problems with Kalous as a source, and for the human leopard stories from Sierra Leone as the "stock in trade" of a voluminous body of colonial fiction (Pratten 2007, 17).

3. See E. Valentine Daniel (1998, 70ff.) for a discussion of even more extreme bodily responses to the remembrance of violent attacks in the form of blackouts or "loss of consciousness" suffered by a Sri Lankan survivor every time he was asked about the violence he witnessed.

4. Note that in Sierra Leone it is not common for adult men in any setting to casually expose their genitals. This event was the only time, throughout my several trips to Sierra Leone, when I saw an adult make a public display of his nudity in this manner.

5. I realize that it is problematic to refer to an audience in which I include myself as "us," or "we," presuming shared expectations and reactions across great differences. Other people in the audience may have been familiar with this performance, having witnessed something like it before—though my friend and other members of the audience clearly had not. Those who were more familiar might have reacted to the element of surprise and concealment on display in the performance differently from myself, for whom this experience was completely new. However, it was evident from the way it unfolded that the goal of the performance was to convey to the audience a sense of fear and surprise.

6. I had a backup camera, as I kept one for color film and another for black and white, so I was able to take more pictures during that research trip, which took place in the days of predigital photography.

7. Kema is a common name, given to the chief of a cohort of Sande initiates. This Sande elder was not a party to the audio-taped conversations mentioned above.

8. I had missed an opportunity to have us photographed during a previous postwar visit. Also, she was unwell—I was about to leave and had made arrangements to bring a community health worker and to buy medicines for her. Perhaps my smile was intended, too, as encouragement, and her expression was sorrow.

## CHRONOTOPE ONE

1. Anagnost (1997) has used the term *imposter* to analyze the prevalence of people impersonating party officials in the People's Republic of China (and of rumors about this figure of imposture) as revealing prevailing concerns at a particular time during the post-Mao transition.

2. Other scholars, who focus on the politico-economic sphere, place more stress on the ways in which certain external economic factors sustain these kinds of collusions (Reno 2007, 2010).

3. Evidence that emerged at the Charles Taylor trial at the Special Court for Sierra Leone made it clear that gifts of satellite phones to various RUF field commanders were among the logistical support provided by the Liberian warlord, and later president (Charles Taylor Summary Judgment 2012, 17–18).

4. Kandeh and others, however, argued that even earlier, under then-president Momoh, the army ranks had swelled to fourteen thousand, to help combat the RUF threat (Kandeh 1999; Zack-Williams 1997).

5. Teko Barracks are located in the northern town of Makeni.

**CHAPTER TWO. WARTIME RUMORS**

1. Even after the war, when cell phone technology became more common, the issue of "coverage"—availability of a signal—remained. In theory, cell phone technology allows for communication at will, but in reality its use is predicated on the user's location. In Sierra Leone, coverage even today is often very unreliable. At times of heightened tension, such as during the elections that have taken place since the end of the civil war, rumors have circulated about cell phone towers being turned off by the government to hamper organizing efforts by opposition forces. In 2016, billboards around the country advertised plans to rebuild landline networks in Sierra Leonean towns, finally multiplying the communication options of citizens, who need to carry out important business, and offering opportunities to dispel rumors.

2. The women's Sande society also puts on spectacular displays of silencing audiences and subordinate members who are attending their ceremonies (see Ferme 1994, 33), but for most of their duration, initiations are by and large characterized by an easygoing proximity between the secret enclosure and the ordinary bustle of urban or rural lives unfolding beyond it. Even though men cannot be seen publicly to pay attention to them, the "noises" of Sande songs and conversations within the enclosure easily reach neighboring settlements, while Poro initiation enclosures are usually located in stands of mature rainforest that are well separated from towns and villages.

3. Some studies of rumors point to their proliferation, as an alternative to public discourse (see Turner 1994; Lomnitz 1995, 36), in situations of systemic inequality, but as will be discussed below, wartime rumors are shaped by different dynamics.

4. In his anthropological critique of the humanitarian enterprise and its mediatic dimensions, Jonathan Benthall (1993) discusses cases involving the ICRC, but he does not reach the wholesale indictment of "the humanitarian international" and its political instrumentalization that is offered by Alex de Waal (1997).

5. All translations from the French are my own.

6. Thus, for instance, by the end of the war the head of the International Crisis Group in Freetown had cited security concerns as her reason for driving a leased vehicle with no logos on it (Ero, personal communication, 2002).

7. Telephone interview with M.O.N., 17 August 2011.

8. The fact that the Rebel Cross helicopter story circulated in such a routinized form is explained in part by its repeated iteration on a national radio

program run by the Catholic mission. Recall that a priest had been a key witness of this sighting in subsequent investigations of this event.

9. This number is generally agreed upon. Estimates vary between 5,000 and 7,335, with the latter number having been provided by a senior government pathologist in Freetown, Sierra Leone, who was interviewed in 1999 (Human Rights Watch 1999).

10. The acronym refers to the Economic Community of West African States (ECOWAS) Monitoring Group, a military force set up in 1990 in the absence of other international interventions in the Liberian conflict, which since then has been deployed in several other regional war zones. At the time, this militarization of a regional organization, which had previously concerned itself only with economic and customs policies—a first in Africa—was considered a novel example of flexible responses to new security challenges on the continent.

### CHRONOTOPE TWO. NUMBERS, EXAMPLES, AND EXCEPTIONS

1. For the lower estimates, see the Church World Service 2002 estimates, and those of the British parliament (www.churchworldservice.org/news/archives/2002/07/39.html and www.parliament.the-stationery-office.co.uk/pa/cm200203/cmhansrd/cmo30610/text/30610w16.htm), For the higher ones, see World Hope International (www.worldhope.net/limbs/overview.htm). The Conflict Security and Development Group's March 2003 report, *A Review of Peace Operations: A Case for Change,* cites a figure of four thousand amputees.

2. The fifty-thousand figure comes from the Conflict Security and Development Group, "A Review of Peace Operations: A Case for Change," King's College, London, 10 March 2003, www.google.com/search?q=Conflict+Security+and+Development+Group%2C+March+2003+report&ie=utf-8&oe=utf-8&client=firefox-b-1.

3. This information is available at www.infomanage.com/international/98hdi.htm. The Human Development Index includes figures for life expectancy, education, and per capita income indicators.

4. In his 11 May 2000 address to the UN Security Council, the Bangladeshi ambassador, whose troops eventually made up one of the largest national contingents in the force, argued for the deployment of more troops in the wake of rebel attacks on—and kidnapping of—five hundred peacekeepers in Sierra Leone. At that time, the UNAMSIL contingent was about half the size it reached over the following weeks and months. He argued that "it would be a decisive setback to the credibility of UN peacekeeping if we allow the largest peacekeeping mission ever to fail," and in the process helped ensure that the force would become even larger (see Permanent Mission of the People's Republic of Bangladesh to the United Nations, www.un.int/bangladesh/images/sc/st/11mayoo.htm).

5. Colum Lynch, "Rebels Threaten Collapse of Largest UN Mission in Africa," *Dawn* (Karachi, Pakistan), 8 May 2000, www.dawn.com/2000/05/08/int7.htm. This article appeared as India, Pakistan, and Bangladesh were about to send contingents of thousands of soldiers, who were instrumental in effecting this increase in forces.

6. The sources for these figures are John Prendergast, International Crisis Group, Testimony to the American Congress, 2002, http://intl-crisis-group.org /projects/showreport.cfm?reportid=657); and www.un.org/Depts/dpko/unamsil /;http://www.icrc.org.

7. The hybridity was, in theory, at the level of jurisdiction and legal statutes and in the makeup at all levels of personnel, which included many Sierra Leoneans. The novelty, however, was in the court's being located in the country where the crimes were committed, as opposed, for instance, to the Yugoslavian and Rwandan tribunals of the previous decade, which had been far from the sites of violence. Both generations of war crimes courts now have some connection with the relatively new International Criminal Court in the Hague.

8. Michelle Sieff, "A Special Court for Sierra Leone," *Crimes of War Project* [magazine], May 2001; "Sierra Leone Special Court Approved by UN Security Council," *Crimes of War Project,*
On the News, 27 March 2002, www.crimesofwar.org.

9. "Getting Away with Murder, Mutilation, Rape: New Testimony from Sierra Leone," *Human Rights Watch* 11, no. 3A (July 1999).

10. UK Parliamentary papers, www.parliament.the-stationery-office.co.uk /pa/cm200203/cmhansrd/cmo30610/text/30610w16.htm. I am not claiming that there were not more surviving amputees, including those in camps elsewhere in the country or in the capital city that were more difficult to reach. Among the latter was Grafton, a camp for the displaced of war on the eastern edge of Freetown.

11. I take the concept of "grey zone" from Primo Levi's *The Drowned and the Saved,* as will become obvious later. Here I use the idea only to highlight the fact that there were areas of relative humanity in the midst of generally terrible conditions—in Levi's case, these were in the narrated memories of his concentration camp experiences.

12. "A Review of Peace Operations: A Case for Change," King's College, London, 10 March 2003.

13. For this modest, approximate, and provisional notion of "truth," I am indebted to G. Canguilhem's *The Normal and the Pathological* (1991), especially his analysis of the relationship between physiological and medical forms of knowledge and their different kinds of truth and value—for instance, in their perspectives on the normal, the normative, the average, and the anomaly. As Canguilhem writes, "Physiological constraints are thus normal in the statistical sense, which is a descriptive sense, and in the therapeutic sense, which is a normative sense. But the question is whether it is medicine which converts—and how?—descriptive and purely theoretical concepts into biological ideals or whether medicine, in admitting the notion of facts and constant functional coefficients from physiology would not also admit—probably unbeknownst to the physiologists—the notion of norm in the normative sense of the word" (123).

14. I do not mean here to discount the pragmatic utility of the law and human rights discourse—including human rights tools deployed by humanitarian activists—in attaining justice-as-fairness goals. I merely underscore the fact that, in any situation requiring an appeal to this register of rights and entitlements, justice of a higher order is lacking and generally is not immediately

attained through the law. Seeking it through the law and entitlements may, however, eventually lead to systemic changes that bring justice-as-fairness closer. In conceptual terms, what I call "justice-as-fairness" owes much to a critical debate around questions of justice, of democracy-as-commensurability, and of the philosophical work done by the French notion of *il faut* in Jacques Derrida's *Voyous,* especially "Maîtrise et Métrique" (2003, 67–85), and *Spectres de Marx* (1993, 40); as well as in Di Natale (1999, 92–93).

15. The image and reporting can be found on "Sierra Leone Web" (www .sierra-leone.org/), under the "Archives" tab for the month of July 1999, or at www.sierra-leone.org/kabbaho70799.html.

16. See the RUF manifesto, *Footpaths to Democracy: Towards a New Sierra Leone,* 1995, www.sierra-leone.org/documents.html. The fact that the expression "one hand, one vote" was also intended to educate the voting public in democratic practices, and prevent electoral fraud (multiple votes being cast by an individual voter), only made this appropriation of the slogan by the perpetrators of these atrocities more cynical.

17. On these issues and for a more general critical genealogy of the "humanitarian international," see de Waal (1997, 82–85).

18. For this discussion, I am indebted to the work of Primo Levi in *The Drowned and the Saved.*

## CHAPTER THREE. HUNTERS, WARRIORS, AND THEIR TECHNOLOGIES

1. Mande encompasses a large number of West African peoples and languages, whereas Mende, and its language, designates an ethnic group within that broader family, which is based primarily in Sierra Leone and Liberia.

2. Samuel Hinga Norman emerged as the national leader of the CDF, and after the 1996 elections this position earned him the post of deputy minister of defense.

3. For a detailed analysis of the linkages between war chiefs, or warriors, and hunters in relation to territorialization and deterritorialization processes, see Ferme (2003). For a different use of "war machines" in the analysis of hunter militias, see Hoffman (2011b). Kelsall (2009) wrote about the CDF trial at the Special Court for Sierra Leone, which focused on war crimes and crimes against humanity committed by the hunter militias during the 1991–2002 civil war.

4. See Rodney (1970) for a discussion of the history of this region, the "Upper Guinea coast."

5. Several African conflicts have seen the rise of popular militias endowed with mystical protections by charismatic leaders, who harnessed spiritual powers. Thus David Lan wrote about the key role of particular ancestral figures and their mediums in the context of the 1980 Zimbabwean liberation war, in which the possession by ancestors was a familiar cultural phenomenon (Lan 1985). Carolyn Nordstrom (1997, 57–62, 68–70) has written about the rise of Mozambique's Parama movement—followers of the healer, or *curandeiro,* Manuel Antonio— whose members were provided with magical protections against bullets on condition that they observe specific taboos prohibiting the use of any but white weapons, forbidding the use of firearms, prohibiting looting and raping, and so on.

6. Later, another woman, Mama Munda, became a powerful initiator for the CDF in Mende-speaking areas. The gendered dimension of combat in this region is worth commenting on briefly. One of the key differences between warriors in this region and soldiers in national armies was that the former could harness both male and female destructive powers, whereas the culture of the latter was more decidedly masculine, even when recruitment was opened up to women. See on this subject Ferme (1998, 560–61, notes 8, 9), Leach (2000, 583–84), and Moran (1995, 73–88). However, the taboos imposed on fighters initiated into the hunting societies in order to make them impervious to bullets included ones against sex or any physical contact with women before battle (Leach 2000; McKenzie 1998).

7. Note that Musa, like Braima (or Ibrahim), Mohamed, and other names in this book are very common in Sierra Leone. Their very proliferation is a protection against identification.

8. This is the kind of widespread burial practice that the Ebola epidemic of 2014–15 disrupted.

9. For a perspective on the role of initiation in recruiting young hunter militias in Sierra Leone and Guinée, and for an account of hunters as environmental stewards by international NGOs engaged in development projects and the establishment of protected forest reserves in Guinée, see Leach (2000, 583–84).

10. See Hill (1984) for a political, rather than historical, reading of these stories, developed on the basis of archaeological evidence of village settlement patterns in northern Sierra Leone. Hill's argument is that the generational shallowness of these foundation stories—which places them in a time during the early nineteenth century, when the areas in question were already densely settled—and the changing identities of the founding hunters suggest that these accounts should be taken as political metaphors legitimizing particular chiefly lineages in the present, rather than as sources of historical evidence.

11. Note that here, *sɔlɛ* is more often used literally, to indicate noise, than it is in relation to rumor, as discussed in chapter 2.

12. See Ferme (2001a, 71–74) for more on the distinctions between different forms of hunt. The collective nature of the activity shapes, too, the highly ritualized way in which the prey is partitioned according to formal entitlements. See Hellweg (2011, 81–82) for similar practices among Ivoirian hunters.

13. Andrew Apter (2005) provides a rich analysis of FESTAC in the context of the global boom in oil prices that fueled a Nigerian economic "miracle" in the 1970s, making the festival an opportunity for nation-building in the aftermath of the Biafran war. Apter's analysis shows the ethnic, national, and international politics at work in the cultural displays during this festival, as well as the colonial historical context from which several of its iconic events emerged.

14. At the time, alluvial mining licenses were granted only to Sierra Leonean nationals, and foreigners were not allowed to reside in diamond-mining areas, so these businessmen could only act as "sponsors" in the process, providing food, cash, and a ready market outlet for any gems found. Thus the collaboration of local chiefs was crucial for finding laborers locally, or for granting permission so that men from outside the chiefdom could settle there to carry out this work.

15. See Henry (2000, 47–48). See also Fithen (1999), for details on the transformation of hunter militias in 1996–97.

16. For a more thorough discussion of youth "lumpen" culture and electoral politics during this period, see Abdullah (1997, 45–76) and Abdullah and Muana (1998).

17. For a comprehensive account of the CDF trial at the Special Court for Sierra Leone, see Kelsall (2009, especially ch. 4). The court tried Alieu Kondewa, one of the principal initiators of the *kamajɔ* militias, for his role in a "chain of command responsibility" in which he was not directly accused of any war crimes. Instead, his responsibility was tied to the mystical protections and powers he was believed to possess by those he initiated, who perpetrated crimes under his spell, as it were. This strategy only partially succeeded. For insights into the dissent among judges at the court in matters of culture and belief raised by this prosecution, see Prosecutor v. Moinina Fofana and Allieu Kondewa (Special Court for Sierra Leone 2008).

18. At the time, basic foodstuffs like rice and palm oil cost three hundred and eight hundred leones per cup or pint, respectively. Two thousand leones could supply a decent family meal. Thus spending tens of thousands of leones on a wartime initiation was very burdensome.

19. The trial sentencing phase had set prison terms for Kondewa and his codefendant, Moinina Fofana, at eight and six years, respectively.

20. "Devil" in Sierra Leonean Krio—an umbrella term for masquerades associated with initiation societies. The *Gɔbɔ*—"gorboi" in the trial transcripts—is a masquerade associated with the men's Poro society.

### CHAPTER FOUR. SITTING ON THE LAND

1. After the end of his ambassadorial term in 2000, Penfold became a vocal advocate in British development and government circles on behalf of paramount chiefs, and of Sierra Leone more generally.

2. I use "signature" advisedly—the fact that projects such as the "Tony Blair Academy" are named after him could simply be a tribute to his name, not an intentional endorsement of the actual honoree. Note that in the newspaper article's picture, the new "paramount chief" is surrounded by some of the honorary attributes of chiefship (traditional cloth) but is not holding a real staff of office.

3. Apter (2005, 169–99) offers a genealogy, which is as attentive to the cultural-aesthetic dimensions of this spectacle as it is to the political ones, of the Durbar in its migrations from (British) colonial India to West Africa, by way of Nigeria. He also discusses the ironies and contradictions of placing such icons of colonial rule at the center of nationalist rituals, using the case of the 1977 "Grand Durbar" that took place during the World Black and African Festival of Arts and Culture (FESTAC) in Nigeria.

4. Sometimes this person could be a chiefly messenger who was not necessarily a person in high standing. For a discussion of the aesthetics and logic of power informing the ways in which "big persons" in general, and chiefs in particular, could extend their reach through, among other persons, trusted advisors and substitutes, see Ferme (2001a, 159–86). Even during the civil war, staffs of

offices had this metonymic relationship, as one or other fighting factions could take them away, or even steal them, from chiefs who were thought to have abused their powers.

5. Sources for this chiefdom and family history include conversations with P. C. Dabo II in Gboyama in 1986; the Wonde Chiefdom Consultation report of July 2000 (Action for Peace 2000); the program circulated on the occasion of P. C. Dabo II's funeral (Daboh n.d.); email and phone exchanges in August 2011 with Cillaty Dabo, P. C. Dabo II's oldest son, who was in the United States; and lengthy conversations with Hadji Dabo on 3–4 November 2012 in Berkeley, California.

6. A debate on the weight of this factor emerged among Sierra Leone scholars (e.g., Archibald and Richards 2002; Fanthorpe 2006), which was summarized and assessed by Sawyer (2008).

7. Consultation on Chiefdom Governance Reform Programme, London, June 2002.

8. M. C. Ferme fieldnotes from research in Wunde and Bo, Sierra Leone, May 2008, October 2015.

9. Last minute provisions to the 2004 Local Government Act, subordinating the councils to the resident ministers appointed by the central government, ended up undermining this decentralizing impulse (see P. Jackson 2005, 52). However, the intention of international donors to channel development aid, private investment initiatives, and support for the provision of services through these local councils, once they were fully implemented, has brought "some international agency staff . . . [to predict] the final demise of chiefdom administration as soon as this funding stream reaches the grassroots" (Fanthorpe 2006, 36).

10. See Ferme (2003, 28) for further discussion of this topic and Blair (2007) for reporting on the investiture of former prime minister Tony Blair as honorary paramount chief.

11. Local councils were denominated town councils in urban areas and district councils in rural areas.

12. The three claimants to the Wunde regency were Mualimu Mustapha Sannoh, whose selection resulted from a gathering of chiefdom elders in the presence of a district officer. The choice was not endorsed formally because after the public meeting, a delegation of elders challenged the appointment. The second regent was Karimu Jimmy, who was supported by the late paramount chief's relatives and by written documentation from the Provincial Secretary's Office in Bo—a higher government authority than the district office—appointing him "caretaker" of the chiefdom. Finally, a third regent was mentioned on national radio, but because he "was never brought to the chiefdom people," not even his name is remembered (Action for Peace 2000, 6).

13. Gboyama did continue to be considered the official chiefdom headquarter town, however, and the chiefdom court continued to alternate between there and Fanima. Other chiefdom functions were carried out in Gboyama by the new paramount chief—who at any rate was a relative of the Dabos—or his representatives. His relatedness was itself an aspect of the expansive kinship networks of paramount chiefs, the very same networks that ensured him eventual support.

## CHAPTER FIVE. REFUGEES AND DIASPORIC PUBLICS

1. A later visit to Cairo (2009) provided a fuller picture of this community, which included wealthier members, whose diasporic and transnational existence was no longer framed by the refugee experience because they were legally employed in the Gulf states and had homes in both places.

2. The expression was used by Giorgio Agamben (1998, 174–75) to describe the concentration camp but also to refer to other liminal spaces subject to the suspension of normal rights and legal protections. These include transit centers at airports, where improperly documented immigrants are detained while decisions concerning their status are pending.

3. Michel Agier (2011, 45) uses the expression "out-places."

4. Note that the size of this camp would make it larger than most towns in Guinea. In a similar manner, the refugee camp in Gondama, Sierra Leone, was at one point characterized as "the third largest city" in the country (Kaplan 2001, 8).

5. Better-educated refugees may also bring valuable skills and knowledge that can be put to use in the host country.

6. In this case, the Huaren community itself was a "nonstate" community of belonging, since this network, unlike many others, was not controlled by the Chinese state.

7. For classic work on the place of the media in general to foster a sense of belonging to national communities and the emergence of a critical public sphere, see, respectively, Anderson (1991) and Habermas (1991).

8. See also M'Bayo and Mogkewu (2000). However, Tynes (2007, 500) cites a figure of two thousand users in 2001. For Nigeria, see Smith (2006), and for Ghana, see Burrell (2012).

9. This document defines net migration as the difference between emigrants and immigrants.

10. This author defines the net migration rate as the difference between the population growth rate and the natural population growth rate in one year per thousand inhabitants, but as mentioned in an earlier note, other sources define it as the difference between immigrants and emigrants in a given period. Furthermore, Ammassari's statistics for Sierra Leonean rates of migration to the United States and Great Britain depart from the more conservative World Bank estimates quoted earlier. According to Ammassari, during the five-year period between 1995 and 2000, about 40 percent of Sierra Leonean migrants headed for Europe, the United Kingdom in particular, with the remaining 60 percent going to the United States.

11. On the critical role of Green Book study group leaders in the rise of the Revolutionary United Front, see Richards (2005).

12. There is a rich scholarly literature on the ways in which diasporic experiences radicalized political leaders, who then went on to join emancipatory struggles, from anticolonial to nationalist and other conflicts. See, for instance, Gangal (1992) on Gandhi and his experiences in South Africa in relation to his political life in India.

13. An alternative, perhaps obvious conclusion to be drawn from these directly observed data is that, in more recent years, the Leonenet platform has

been replaced by the plethora of available alternative digital fora and is no longer as important a forum for active political and social participation as it had been during the civil war.

14. In a study of the Internet's role in shaping a public sphere in diaspora communities, Parham (2005) suggests that the "Corbett List," one of several Internet lists focused on Haitian interests, became a "vertical" public that was organized hierarchically to transmit the concerns of the diaspora to the government at home. It also was the site most heavily monitored by members of the Haitian government under President Aristide, who sometimes "lurked" but at other times intervened directly to explain government policies debated on the list (Parham 2005, 360).

15. On the role of Ganda and Gollie in peace talks, see Lord (2000, 45).

16. This was a common tactic for eliminating political enemies in those times of shifting alliances—the National Provisional Ruling Council junta executed twenty-nine Sierra Leoneans in 1994, supposedly for plotting a coup against Valentine Strasser, and in 1990 Vice President Minah was among five purported coup plotters executed under then-president Momoh.

17. For a study of remittances from African refugee diasporas, with a special focus on London-based Somali refugees from the 1990s' civil wars, see Lindley (2009).

18. For an example of the myriad fundraisers among diasporic communities, see Sesay (2012), who discusses a case in Texas.

19. A case in point was the late Reverend Dr. Jeremiah Joe Sinnah-Yovonie Kangova II, who after decades spent in the United States, first as a student and then as a scholar and religious leader, returned to Sierra Leone in 2004 to run for the chiefship. The following year he was elected paramount chief of Kamajei Chiefdom, Moyamba District.

### CHAPTER SIX. CHILD SOLDIERS AND THE CONTESTED IMAGINARY

1. A chiefdom section encompasses several villages, and this particular chiefdom comprised four sections, so there is a nesting hierarchy of rural chiefs ranging from village to section and finally to the highest ranking, or paramount, chief.

2. For a discussion of structural violence and the genealogy of the concept of "the social machinery" that produces inequalities and oppression, see Farmer (2004, 307). Arthur Kleinman (2000, 230–31) expands the scope by including the violence of difficult-to-define, sometimes "bourgeois" ailments such as "stress." He claims that discussing stress as a form of violence offers "a cultural critique of the normal" in modern life.

3. The expression "victim's tale" is from Peter Van de Veer (1997), who uses it to analyze the fate of narratives of individual suffering in the face of national historical accounts of large-scale religious violence in India.

4. These data were drawn from surveys conducted in Canada ("Firearms, Accidental Deaths, Suicides and Violent Crime: An Updated Review of the Literature with Special Reference to the Canadian Situation," Canadian Department of Justice, accessed 2011, www.justice.gc.ca/eng/pi/rs/rep-rap/1998

/wd98_4-dt98_4/p2.html) and in the United States (a 2005 Gallup poll on gun ownership in America, accessed May 2011, www.gallup.com/poll/20098 /gun-ownership-use-america.aspx).

5. AFRC trial transcript, 13 October 2006, 19, www.sc-sl.org/.

6. Ibid., 35–36.

## CHAPTER SEVEN. FORCED MARRIAGE AND SEXUAL ENSLAVEMENT

1. On the role of anthropologists in mediating between such disparate terrains, see, for instance, Merry (2006, 39), and Wilson and Mitchell (2003).

2. See, for example, Scharf and Mattler (2005); Prosecutor v. Alex Tamba Brima, Brima Bazzy Kamara, Santigie Borbor Kanu (henceforth cited as Brima, Kamara, Kanu), SCSL-2004–16-T. Dorte Thorsen was an anthropologist who testified on matters of forced marriage, albeit without country-specific expertise. Hers, therefore, was a necessarily "academic" stance (Joint Defence Disclosure of Expert Report on Forced Marriages, SCSL-04–16-T-535[A] and [B], 26 July 2006). Danny Hoffman bridged the gap between postwar scholarly ethnographic engagements in Sierra Leone and elsewhere and testified as an expert witness in court (see Prosecutor v. Sam Hinga Norman, Moinina Fofana, Allieu Kondewa, SCSL-2004–14-T). Chris Coulter (2009), who focused on the experience of conflict-affected girls and women, was one of several anthropologists who worked in Sierra Leone in the aftermath of the conflict.

3. See also Bunting, Lawrance and Richards (2016) for a historical perspective on the continuities between, for instance, the colonial discourse on slavery and that on "child marriage." Their focus is on the lack of consent in both institutions.

4. Other sources on this topic are Frulli (2008) and Gong-Gershowitz (2009).

5. David Crane, Berkeley, CA, phone interview, 8 March 2011. On the SCSL's advances in sensitizing court staff to gender crimes and establishing new standards for handling witnesses and victims in international law, see Horn, Charters, and Vahidy (2009, 137).

6. Beginning in June 2004 with the Civil Defense Militia (CDF) case in chamber 1, trials unfolded over nine years, concurrently and in staggered order, in two chambers in Freetown, Sierra Leone. Judgments were handed down in the CDF and AFRC trials in 2007, and in the RUF trial in 2009. More information on the sequencing is available on the SCSL website. In 2007, the Charles Taylor trial was relocated to the International Criminal Court at the Hague, and proceedings were streamed live to the SCSL in Freetown over the following years. All trial judgments were followed by sentencing and appeals phases.

7. One notorious case was that of the "laughing judges" in the callous, inept questioning and cross-examination of a rape victim in the Butare trial at the ICTR (discussed in Nowrojee 2005b, 24). [NB: What was so shocking about the Butare case was that the judges themselves, and not just the lawyers and prosecutor, engaged in this callous, inept questioning.]

8. Bangura is discussed by presiding judge Julia Sebutinde in her "Separate Concurring Opinion" to the Brima, Kamara, Kanu Judgment, 20 June 2007, 577. Zainab Bangura's testimony about the stigmatizing aspects of forced

marriage can be found in Brima, Kamara, Kanu (AFRC trial), 3 October 2005, 4 October 2005, and 13 October 2005.

9. See Bélair (2006, 569). Richard Roberts (2016) explores the emergence of the distinction between arranged and forced marriages in early twentieth-century colonial policies in Africa and points to some of the reasons why, in practice, this is a difficult distinction to maintain. This chapter makes a similar argument for contemporary Sierra Leonean marriage practices.

10. Oosterveld (2004) speaks to the enrichment of the jurisprudence discussed in this section in her detailed analysis of the negotiations leading to the adoption of sexual slavery as a crime against humanity at the ICC.

11. See also the Brima, Kamara, Kanu (AFRC) Judgment, 20 June 2007, 578.

12. Ibid., 591.

13. Brima, Kamara, Kanu Appeals Judgment Summary, 22 February 2008, 23–25.

14. See also the Brima, Kamara, Kanu Judgment, 20 June 2007, 580.

15. Brima, Kamara, Kanu Judgment, 20 June 2007, 591.

16. Prosecutor v. Issa Sesay, Morris Kallon, Augustine Gbao (RUF case), trial transcript SCSL-2004-15-T, trial chamber I, October 21, 2004.

17. Brima, Kamara, Kanu, trial transcript, 9 March 2005, 44ff.

18. See Grewal (2010, 66–68) on the history of unsuccessful prosecutions, sometimes owing to the perceived "unreliability" of female witnesses, which failed to bring rapists to justice in domestic courts, as was the case in Rwanda and Yugoslavia.

19. Prosecutor v. Issa Sesay, Morris Kallon, Augustine Gbao (RUF case), trial transcript SCSL-2004-15-T, 21 October, 2004, 14–17.

20. See, for instance, the TRC (2004, 3B:131).

21. Brima, Kamara, Kanu (AFRC case), 4 October 2005, 3 and 13 October 2005, 90.

22. Audio interview with LL by the author, Pujehun District, Sierra Leone, 9 October 2015.

23. Brima, Kamara, Kanu, trial transcript, 3 October 2005, 57–61.

24. Brima, Kamara, Kanu, Judgment, 20 June 2007, 590.

25. Brima, Kamara, Kanu, trial transcript, 3 October 2005, 74.

26. For a similar point about the ways in which violent abductions of women at India's partition in 1947 led to the formation of viable families, as well as about the suffering caused by the Indian state in its insistence on breaking them up many years later, see Das (1995, 82–83).

### CHAPTER EIGHT. INSCRIPTIONS ON THE WALL

1. I take from Keane (2003, 414)—following Munn's (1986) discussion of "qualisigns" of value, in turn borrowed from Peirce—the notion of "bundling" to convey the copresence of different qualities, such as their "Chineseness" or "Africanness," that make up the meanings of particular objects. Qualities such as "redness," Keane points out, are always embodied in particular things, and in that sense become bundled in particular ways with those things' other quali-

ties. Thus, for example, the redness of an apple comes with connotations of spherical shape, light weight, smoothness, and so on, which make it different from the redness of woolen cloth. The implication for my argument here, and in a more extensive article in which this notion is discussed (see Ferme and Schmitz 2014), is that though emergent and perhaps misrecognized, the Chineseness or Africanness of certain substances or objects still does important work in shaping their meanings and uses. The aforementioned work also contains a more sustained discussion of the interface between Chinese and African therapeutic practices and substances in Sierra Leone.

2. These donations were part of the PL480 program, run by the US Agency for International Development.

**CONCLUSION**

1. Existing blogs, such as *Somatosphere,* that have a focus on anthropology and health also attracted contributions focusing on the Ebola crisis.

2. They were isolated in the sense of their having been removed from both their families and from health care personnel—"left to die" because handling the magnitude of the disease was initially impossible.

3. This was the case, for instance, for Lion Mountains Agrico, Ltd., a private venture focused on sustainable rice-farming and crop rotation practices.

# References

Abdulai, A., 2010. "Koroma Swears in 13 Paramount Chiefs in Bo." *Concord Times,* Freetown, 14 April. Accessed 17 August 2011. http://allafrica.com /stories/201004150080.html.

Abdullah, I., 1997. "Bushpath to Destruction: The Origin and Character of the Revolutionary United Front." *Afrique et Développment* 22 (3–4): 45–76.

———, ed. 2004. *Between Democracy and Terror: The Sierra Leone Civil War.* Dakar, Senegal: Council for the Development of Social Science Research in Africa (CODESRIA).

Abdullah, I., and P. Muana, 1998. "The Revolutionary United Front of Sierra Leone: A Revolt of the Lumpenproletariat." In *African Guerillas,* edited by C. Clapham, 172–93. Oxford: James Currey.

Abraham, A., 1976, *Topics in Sierra Leone History: A Counter-colonial Interpretation,* Freetown: Leone.

———. 1978, *Mende Government and Politics under Colonial Rule: A Historical Study of Political Change in Sierra Leone, 1890–1937.* Freetown: Sierra Leone University Press.

Action for Peace. 2000. *Report on the Wonde Chiefdom Consultation.* July. Freetown.

AFRC. 2005a. Special Court of Sierra Leone. Trial transcript SCSL-2004–16-T. 9 March. www.sc-sl.org/LinkClick.aspx?fileticket=a2Ow79yNfnY%3d& tabid=158.

———. 2005b. Special Court of Sierra Leone. Trial transcript SCSL-2004–16-T. 3 October. www.sc-sl.org/LinkClick.aspx?fileticket=ARlWs7fmniE% 3d&tabid=158.

———. 2006. Special Court of Sierra Leone. Trial transcript SCSL-2004–16-T. 13 October. www.sc-sl.org/LinkClick.aspx?fileticket=FVoNnFyANNg%3d &tabid=158.

African Minerals Limited. 2010a. Annual Report. Accessed February 2013. www.bsx.com/AllCompanyDocuments/2010%20Financials/AfricanMinerals%20to%20FYE%2030Dec10.pdf.

———. 2010b. "Tonkolilli Iron Ore Project: 'A World Class Iron Ore Project.'" Analyst site visit 13–15. December 2010.

Agamben, G. 1998. *Homo Sacer. Sovereign Power and Bare Life*. Stanford, CA: Stanford University Press.

———. 1999. *Remnants of Auschwitz: The Witness and the Archive*. Translated by D. Heller-Roazen. New York: Zone Books.

Agence France Presse, 2011, "Sierra Leone: First iron ore shipment in 30 years." 8 November. Accessed 10 April 2014. www.modernghana.com/news/359865/1/sierra-leone-first-iron-ore-shipment-in-30-years.html.

———. 2012, "Chinese Firm Investments $1.3bn in S. Leone Farmland." 18 January. Accessed 10 April 2014. www.vanguardngr.com/2012/01/chinese-firm-investments-1-3bn-in-s-leone-farmland/.

———. 2013. "Sierra Leone, China Sign $8bn Deal." 6 July. Accessed 10 April 2014. www.news24.com/Africa/News/Sierra-Leone-China-sign-8bn-deal-20130705.

Agier, M. 2011. *Managing the Undesirables: Refugee Camps and Humanitarian Government*. Cambridge: Polity Press.

Akyeampong, E. 2000. "Africans in the Diaspora: The Diaspora and Africa." *African Affairs* 99: 183–215.

Albert, I.O. 2003. "The Demise of Traditional Political Authority in Nigeria." Paper presented at the conference on Chieftaincy in Africa: Culture, Governance and Development, Accra, Ghana, 6–10 January.

Alden, C., D. Large, and R. Soares de Oliveira, eds. 2008. *China Returns to Africa: A Rising Power and a Continent Embrace*. New York: Columbia University Press.

Alexander, K.A., C.E. Sanderson, M. Marathe, B.L. Lewis, C.M. Rivers, J. Shaman, J.M. Drake, E. Lofgren, V.M. Dato, M.C. Eisenberg, and S. Eubank. 2015. "What Factors Might Have Led to the Emergence of Ebola in West Africa?" *PLOS Neglected Tropical Diseases* (June 4): 1–26.

Alldridge, T.J. 1901. *The Sherbro and Its Hinterland*. London: Macmillan.

———. 1910. *A Transformed Colony: Sierra Leone, Its Progress, People, Native Customs, and Undeveloped Wealth*. Philadelphia: Lippincott.

Ammassari, S. 2006. "Migration Management and Development Policies: Maximizing the Benefits of International Migration in West Africa." International Migration Papers 72E. Geneva: International Labor Office, 9, table 1. Accessed 15 October 2010. www.ilo.org/public/english/protection/migrant/download/imp/imp72.pdf.

Anagnost, A. 1997. *National Pastimes: Narrative, Representation, and Power in Modern China*. Durham, NC: Duke University Press.

Anders, G. 2011. "Testifying about 'Uncivilized Events': Problematic Representations of Africa in the Trial against Charles Taylor." *Leiden Journal of International Law* 24: 937–59.

Anderson, B. 1991. *Imagined Communities: Reflections on the Origins and the Spread of Nationalism*. London: Verso.

Annan, K. 2000. *Report of the Secretary-General on the Establishment of a Special Court for Sierra Leone.* UN Security Council S/2000.915. Accessed May 2011. www.undemocracy.com/S-2000-915.

Appadurai, A., ed. 1988. *The Social Life of Things: Commodities in Cultural Perspective.* Cambridge: Cambridge University Press.

———. 1996. *Modernity at Large: Cultural Dimensions of Globalization.* Minneapolis: University of Minnesota Press.

Apter, A. 2005. *The Pan African Nation: Oil and the Spectacle of Culture in Nigeria.* Chicago: University of Chicago Press.

Archibald, S., and P. Richards. 2002. "Converts to Human Rights? Popular Debate about War and Justice in Rural Central Sierra Leone." *Africa* 72 (3): 339–67.

Arendt, H. 1951. *The Origins of Totalitarianism,* New York: Harcourt.

———. 1954. *Between Past and Future: Eight Exercises in Political Thought.* New York: Penguin.

Arisenigeria.org. 2018. "Internet Usage Statistics for Africa (Africa Internet Usage and Population Stats)." Accessed 18 February 2018. http://arisenigeria .org/peoples-news/249-internet-usage-statistics-for-africa--africa-internet-usage-and-population-stats-.

Asad, T. 1973. *Anthropology and the Colonial Encounter.* London: Ithaca Press.

Badiou, A. 2008. *Number and Numbers.* Cambridge: Polity Press.

Bakhtin, M. M. 1968. *Rabelais and His World.* Cambridge, MA: MIT Press.

———. M. 1982. *The Dialogic Imagination: Four Essays.* Austin: University of Texas Press.

Bangura, J. 2011. National Conference of Paramount Chiefs, 19–22 April, Hope, Sierra Leone. Accessed 20 August 2011. www.hopesierraleone.org /National_Council_Paramount_Chiefs_Executive_Summary.pdf.

Barajas, A., R. Chami, C. Fullenkamp, and A. Garg. 2010. "The Global Financial Crisis and Workers' Remittances to Africa: What's the Damage?" IMF Working Paper 10/24. International Monetary Fund.

Barnes, S. 1996. "Political Ritual and the Public Sphere in Contemporary Africa." In *The Politics of Cultural Performance,* edited by D. Parkin, L. Caplan, and H. Fisher, 19–40. Oxford: Berghahn.

Barrie, A. 2010. "Njaluahun Chiefdom Amalgamation Saga." *Exclusive Press News Paper* [*sic*], Freetown. Accessed July 2011. http://exclusivepress.net /app/index.php?option=com_content&task=view&id=1334&Itemid=32.

Barrows, W. 1976. *Grassroots Politics in an African State: Integration and Development in Sierra Leone.* New York: Africana.

Bassett, T. 2003. "Dangerous Pursuits: Hunter Associations (*donzo ton*) and National Politics in Côte d'Ivoire." *Africa* 73 (1): 1–30.

———. 2004. "Containing the *Donsow*: The Politics of Scale in Côte d'Ivoire." *Africa Today* 50 (4): 30–49.

Bayart, J. 1993. *The State in Africa: The Politics of the Belly.* Translated by M. Harper and E. Harrison. London: Longman.

———. 2000. "Africa in the World: A History of Extraversion." *African Affairs* 99: 217–67.

Baylis, E. 2008. "Tribunal-Hopping with the Post-conflict Justice Junkies." *Oregon Review of International Law* 10: 361–90.

Baxter, J. 2013. "Who Is Benefiting? The Social and Economic Impact of Three Large-Scale Land Investments in Sierra Leone: A Cost-Benefit Analysis." www.christianaid.org.uk/images/who-is-benefitting-Sierra-Leone-report .pdf.

Bazenguissa-Ganga, R. 1998. "Instantanés au coeur de la violence: Anthropologie de la victime au Congo-Brazzaville." *Cahiers d'Études Africaines* 150–52 (2–4): 619–25.

Bazenguissa-Ganga, R., and S. Makki, eds. 2012. *Sociétés en guerre: Ethnographies des mobilizations violentes*. Paris: Éditions de la Maison des Sciences de l'Homme.

Beattie, K.J. 1915. *Human Leopards: An Account of the Trials of Human Leopards before the Special Commission Court*. London: H. Rees.

Bélair, K. 2006. "Unearthing the Customary Law Foundations of 'Forced Marriages' during Sierra Leone's Civil War: The Possible Impact of International Criminal Law on Customary Marriage and Women's Rights in Post-conflict Sierra Leone." *Columbia Journal of Gender and Law* 15 (3): 551–607.

Bellman, B. 1981. "The Paradox of Secrecy." *Human Studies* 4: 1–4.

Bender, B. 2002. "Time and Landscape." Supplement, *Current Anthropology* 43: S103–12.

Benthall, J. 1993. *Disasters, Relief and the Media*. London, IB Taurris.

Bernal, V. 2005. "Eritrea On-Line: Diaspora, Cyberspace, and the Public Sphere." *American Ethnologist* 32 (4): 660–75.

———. 2006. "Diaspora, Cyberspace and the Political Imagination: The Eritrean Diaspora Online." *Global Networks* 6 (2): 161–79.

Berry, S. 1989. "Social Institutions and Access to Resources." *Africa* 59 (1): 41–55.

———. 2001. *Chiefs Know Their Boundaries: Essays on Property, Power, and the Past in Asante, 1896–1998*. London: Heinemann.

———. 2004. "Reinventing the Local? Privatization, Decentralization and the Politics of Resource Management: Examples from Africa." *African Study Monographs* 25 (2): 79–101.

Besnier, N. 2012. "The Athlete's Body and the Global Condition: Tongan Rugby Players in Japan." *American Ethnologist* 39 (3): 491–510.

Blair, D. 2007. "Sierra Leone Makes Blair 'Chief of Peace.'" *Telegraph*, London, 31 May. Accessed 21 August 2011. www.telegraph.co.uk/news /uknews/1553167/Sierra-Leone-makes-Blair-Chief-of-Peace.html.

Bledsoe C. 1980a. "Stratification and Sande Politics." *Ethnologische Zeitschrift Zuerich* 1: 143–49.

———. 1980b. *Women and Marriage in Kpelle Society*. Stanford, CA: Stanford University Press.

———. 1984. "The Political Use of Sande Ideology and Symbolism." *American Ethnologist* 11 (3): 455–72.

Bledsoe, C.H., and M.F. Goubaud. 1985. "The Reinterpretation of Western Pharmaceuticals among the Mende of Sierra Leone." *Social Science and Medicine* 21 (3): 275–82.

Bledsoe, C. H., and K. Robey. 1986. "Arabic Literacy and Secrecy among the Mende of Sierra Leone." *Man*, n.s., 21 (2): 202–26.

Bloch, M. 1921. "Réflexions d'un historien sur les Fausses nouvelles de la guerre." *Revue de synthèse historique* 33: 2–35.

Bolten, C. 2012. *I Did It to Save My Life: Love and Survival in Sierra Leone.* Berkeley: University of California Press.

Bourdet, Y., and H. Falck. 2006. "Emigrants' Remittances and Dutch Disease in Cape Verde." *International Economic Journal* 20 (3): 267–84.

Bourdieu, P. 1980. *Le sens pratique.* Paris: Ed. de minuit.

———. (1980) 1990. *The Logic of Practice.* Translated by Richard Nice. Stanford, CA: Stanford University Press.

Bourgois, P. 2004. *Violence in War and Peace: An Anthology.* Oxford: Blackwell Publishing.

Brautigam, D. 1998. *Chinese Aid and African Development: Exporting Green Revolution.* New York: St. Martin's Press.

———. 2009. *The Dragon's Gift: The Real Story of China in Africa.* Oxford: Oxford University Press.

Bratton, M. 1989. "The Politics of Government—NGO Relations in Africa." *World Development* 17 (4): 569–87.

Brautigam, D., and X. Y. Tang. 2009. "China's Engagement in African Agriculture: Down to the Countryside." *China Quarterly* 199: 686–706.

Broadbent, E. 2012. *Research-Based Evidence in African Policy Debates. Case Study 4: Chieftaincy Reform in Sierra Leone.* London: Evidence-Based Policy in Development Network.

Brown, W. 2004. "'The Most We Can Hope for . . .': Human Rights and the Politics of Fatalism." *South Atlantic Quarterly* 103 (2/3): 451–63.

Bryce, J., et al. 1915. *Report of the Committee on Alleged German Outrages.* Accessed 15 August 2011. http://avalon.law.yale.edu/20th_century/brycere.asp.

Buechli, V. 2006. "Architecture and Modernism." In *Handbook of Material Culture,* edited C. Tilley, W. Keane, S. Küchler, M. Rowlands. and P. Spyer, 255–66. London: Sage.

Bunting, A., B. Lawrance, and R. Roberts. 2016. "Introduction: Something Old, Something New? Conceptualizing Forced Marriage in Africa." In *Marriage by Force? Contestation over Consent and Coercion in Africa,* edited by A. Bunting, B. N. Lawrance, and R. L. Roberts, 1–40. Athens: Ohio University Press.

Burrell, J. 2012. *Invisible Users: Youth in the Internet Cafés of Urban Ghana.* Cambridge, MA: MIT Press.

Campaign for Good Governance. 2003. "Monitoring of the Paramount Chieftaincy Elections in Dama Chiefdom, Kenema District," Accessed 5 January 2004. www.sierra-leone.org/chieftaincyresults.html.

Canadian Department of Justice. 1998. "Firearms, Accidental Deaths, Suicides and Violent Crime: An Updated Review of the Literature with Special Reference to the Canadian Situation." Accessed May 2011. www.justice.gc.ca /eng/pi/rs/rep-rap/1998/wd98_4-dt98_4/p2.html.

Canguilhem, G. 1991. *The Normal and the Pathological.* New York: Zone Books.

Carey, M. 2006. "Survival Is Political." In *States of Violence: Politics, Youth, and Memory in Contemporary Africa*, edited by E. G. Bay and D. Donham, 97–127. Charlottesville: University of Virginia Press.

Carney, J. A. 2001. *Black Rice: The African Origins of Rice Cultivation in the Americas*. Cambridge, MA: Harvard University Press.

Carroll, J. 2005. "Gun Ownership and Use in America." Gallup. Accessed May 2011. www.gallup.com/poll/20098/gun-ownership-use-america.aspx.

Caruth, C. 1996. *Unclaimed Experience: Trauma, Narrative, and History*. Baltimore: Johns Hopkins University Press.

Cashion, G. A. 1982. "Hunters of the Mande: A Behavioral Code and Worldview Derived from the Study of Their Folklore." PhD diss., University of Indiana.

Castoriadis, C. 1987. *The Imaginary Institution of Society*. Translated by K. Blamey. Cambridge, MA: MIT Press.

Census of Sierra Leone. 1986. *The Preliminary Report on the 1985 National Population Census of Sierra Leone*. Freetown: Government of Sierra Leone. Accessed 24 August 2011. www.sierra-leone.org/1985censusreport.doc.

Certeau, M. de. 1984. *The Practice of Everyday Life*. Berkeley: University of California Press.

Charles Taylor Summary Judgment. 2012. Special Court for Sierra Leone. Trial chamber II. Case No. SCSL-03–1-T 26 April.

Chauveau, J.-P., and P. Richards. 2008. "Les Racines agraires des insurrections ouest-africaines: Une comparaison Côte d'Ivoire-Sierra Leone." *Politique Africaine* 111: 131–67.

China Internet Information Center. 2006. African Member States: Sierra Leone. FOCAC Beijing Summit. Accessed lo April 2014. www.china.org.cn/english /features/focac/183425.htm.

*China Post*. (2008). Agriculture Researchers Make 'African Viagra': Report. 27 March. Accessed 10 April 2014. *www.chinapost.com.tw/taiwan/national /national%20news/2008/03/27/149056/Agriculture-researchers.htm*.

CIA World Factbook. 2013. "Sierra Leone: People and Society." Accessed 10 April 2014. www.cia.gov/library/publications/the-world-factbook/geos /sl.html.

Cissé Y. 1964. "Notes sur les sociétés des chasseurs malinké." *Journal de la société des africanistes* 34 (11): 175–226.

———. 1994, *La confrérie des chasseurs malinké et bambara: mythes, rites et récits initiatiques*. Paris: Éditions Nouvelles du Sud.

Clapham, C. 1998. "Discerning the New Africa." *International Affairs* 74 (2): 763–70.

Clarke, J. I. 1969. *Sierra Leone in Maps*. London: Hodder and Stoughton.

Clarke, K. 2009. *Fictions of Justice: The International Criminal Court and the Challenge of Legal Pluralism in Sub-Saharan Africa*. Cambridge: Cambridge University Press.

Clastres, P. 1989. *Society against the State: Essays in Political Anthropology*. New York: Zone Books.

Clifford, J. 1988. *The Predicament of Culture: Twentieth-Century Ethnography, Literature, and Art*. Cambridge, MA: Harvard University Press.

Comaroff, J., and J. L. Comaroff. 1993. Introduction to *Modernity and Its Malcontents: Ritual and Power in Postcolonial Africa,* edited by J. and J. L. Comaroff, xi–xxxvii. Chicago: University of Chicago Press.

Comaroff, J. L., and J. Comaroff. 1997. *Of Revelation and Revolution.* Vol. 2 of *The Dialectics of Modernity on a South African Frontier.* Chicago: University of Chicago Press.

———. 2006. "Law and Disorder in the Postcolony: An Introduction." In *Law and Disorder in the Postcolony,* edited by Jean Comaroff and John L Comaroff, 1–56. Chicago: University of Chicago Press.

———. 2009. *Ethnicity, Inc.* Chicago: University of Chicago Press.

Cosentino, D. 2005. "Precognition of Civil Violence in Mende Oral Narrative Tradition." In *Representations of Violence: Art about the Sierra Leone Civil War,* edited by P. Muana and C. Corcoran, 11–14. Madison, WI: Twenty-First Century African Youth Movement.

Coulter, C. 2009. *Bush Wives and Girl Soldiers: Women's Lives through War and Peace in Sierra Leone.* Ithaca, NY: Cornell University Press.

Crane, D. 2004. Special Court of Sierra Leone. "Opening Remarks to the RUF Trial." The Prosecutor v. Issa Hassan Sesay, Morris Kallon and Augustine Gbao. Case no. SCSL-04–15-T. Trial Chamber I. 5 July.

———. 2006. "White Man's Justice: Applying International Justice after Regional Third World Conflicts." *Cardozo Law Review* 27 (4): 1683–88.

Cribb, R. 2001. "How Many Deaths? Problems in the Statistics of Massacre in Indonesia (1965–1966) and East Timor (1975–1980)." In *Violence in Indonesia,* edited by I. Wessel and G. Wimhöfer. Hamburg: Abera Verlag.

Daboh, n.d. "Funeral Obsequies in Memory of P. C. Alhaji, M. K. b. Daboh II on Saturday 11th and Sunday 12th July 1998." Unpublished manuscript. Gboyama, Sierra Leone.

D'Alisera, J. 2004. *An Imagined Geography: Sierra Leonean Muslims in America.* Philadelphia: University of Pennsylvania Press.

Daniel, E. V. 1998. "The Limits of Culture." In *In Near Ruins: Cultural Theory at the End of the Century,* edited by N. Dirks, 67–91. Minneapolis: University of Minnesota Press.

Das, V. 1985. "Anthropological Knowledge and Collective Violence." *Anthropology Today* 1 (3): 4–6.

———. 1995. *Critical Events: An Anthropological Perspective on Contemporary India.* Delhi: Oxford University Press.

———. 2007. *Life and Words: Violence and the Descent into the Ordinary.* Berkeley: University of California Press.

Das, V., A. Kleinman, M. Ramphele, and P. Reynolds, eds. 2000. *Violence and Subjectivity.* Berkeley: University of California Press.

Day, L., 1994. "The Evolution of Female Chiefship during the Late Nineteenth-Century Wars of the Mende." *International Journal of African Historical Studies* 25 (3): 481–503.

D'Azevedo, W. 1962. "Some Historical Problems in the Delineation of a Central West African Region." *Annals of the New York Academy of Sciences* 92 (2): 512–38.

Debos, M., 2011, "Living by the Gun in Chad: Armed Violence as a Practical Occupation." *Journal of Modern African Studies* 49 (3): 409–28.

———. 2013, *Le Métier des armes au Tchad: Le gouvernement de l'entre-guer*res. Paris: Éditions Karthala.

De Certeau, M., and L. Giard. 1983. *L'Ordinaire de la communication*. Paris: Dalloz, Ministère de la Culture.

De Waal, A. 1997. *Famine Crimes: Politics and the Disaster Relief Industry*. Oxford: International African Institute and James Currey.

Deleuze, G., and F. Guattari. 1987. *A Thousand Plateaus: Capitalism and Schizophrenia*. Minneapolis: University of Minnesota Press.

Denov, M. 2010. *Child Soldiers: Sierra Leone's Revolutionary United Front*. Cambridge: Cambridge University Press.

Derrida, J. 1993. *Spectres de Marx*. Paris: Editions Galilée.

———. 2003. *Voyous*. Paris: Editions Galilée.

Di Natale, A. 1999. "Decostruzione e Etica (del) Possibile: Percorsi del Testo di Jacques Derrida." In *Saggi su Colli-Spinoza-Derrida*, edited by G Raciti. Catania, Italy: C.U.E.C.M.

Dirks, N. 1990. "History As a Sign of the Modern." *Public Culture* 2 (2): 25–32.

Doherty, T. "Partially Dissenting Opinion on Count 7 (Sexual Slavery) and Count 8 (Forced Marriage)." Special Court of Sierra Leone. AFRC Appeals Judgment. SCSL-2004-16-T. 21 June.

Donham, D. 2006. "Staring at Suffering: Violence As a Subject." In *States of Violence: Politics, Youth, and Memory in Contemporary Africa*, edited by D. Donham and E. Bay, 16–33. Charlottesville: University of Virginia Press.

Dorjahn, V. 1959. "The Organization and Functions of the 'Ragbenle' Society of the Temne." *Africa: Journal of the International Africa Institute* 29 (2): 156–70.

———. 1960. "The Changing Political System of the Temne." *Africa: Journal of the International Africa Institute* 30 (2): 110–40.

Dozon, J.-P. 2000. "La Côte d'Ivoire entre Démocratie, Nationalisme et Eth-nonationalisme." *Politique Africaine* 78: 45–62.

Duffield, M. 1998. "Postmodern Conflict: Warlords, Postadjustment States and Private Protection." *Civil Wars* 1 (1): 65–102.

Dumézil, G. 1948. *Mitra-Varuna*. Paris: Gallimard.

Ellis, S. 1999. *The Mask of Anarchy: The Destruction of Liberia and the Religious Dimension of an African Civil War*. London: Hurst.

Englund, H. 2006. *Prisoners of Freedom: Human Rights and the African Poor*. Berkeley: University of California Press.

Fabian, J. 1983. *Time and the Other: How Anthropology Makes Its Object*. New York: Columbia University Press.

Fanthorpe, R. 2001. "Neither Citizen nor Subject? 'Lumpen' Agency and the Legacy of Native Administration in Sierra Leone." *African Affairs* 100 (400): 363–86.

———. 2004. "Chiefdom Governance Reform Programme Public Workshops: An Analysis of the Facilitators' Reports." *DFID/SSR Research Project R8095 Report*. September. Accessed 10 August 2011. www.dfid.gov.uk/r4d /PDF/Outputs/Mis_SPC/R8095a.pdf.

———. 2006. "On the Limits of Liberal Peace: Chiefs and Democratic Decentralization in Post-war Sierra Leone." *African Affairs* 105 (418): 27–49.

Farmer, P. 2004. "An Anthropology of Structural Violence." *Current Anthropology* 45 (3): 305–25.

Farquhar, J. 1994. *Knowing Practice: The Clinical Encounter of Chinese Medicine.* Boulder, CO: Westview Press.

Fassin, D. 2007. "Humanitarianism As a Politics of Life." *Public Culture* 19 (3): 499–520.

———. 2011. *Humanitarian Reason: A Moral History of the Present.* Berkeley: University of California Press.

Fearon, J.D., and D.D. Laitin. 2003. "Ethnicity, Insurgency, and Civil War." *American Political Science Review* 97 (1): 75–90.

Feldman, A. 1991. *Formations of Violence: The Narrative of the Body and Political Terror in Northern Ireland.* Chicago: University of Chicago Press.

Ferguson, J. 1994. *The Anti-politics Machine: Development, Depoliticization, and Bureaucratic Power in Lesotho,* Minneapolis, University of Minnesota Press.

———. 1999. *Expectations of Modernity: Myths and Meanings of Urban Life on the Zambian Copperbelt.* Berkeley: University of California Press.

———. 2006. *Global Shadows: Africa in the Neoliberal World Order.* Durham, NC: Duke University Press.

———. 2009. "The Uses of Neoliberalism." *Antipode* 41 (1): 166–84.

Ferme, M.C. 1994, "What 'Alhaji Airplane' Saw in Mecca and What Happened When He Came Home." In *Syncretism/Anti-syncretism: The Politics of Religious Synthesis,* edited by C. Stewart and R. Shaw, 27–44. London: Routledge.

———. 1998. "The Violence of Numbers: Consensus, Competition, and the Negotiation of Disputes in Sierra Leone." *Cahier d'Etudes Africaines* 150–52 (2–4): 555–80.

———. 1999. "'Staging *Politisi*': The Dialogics of Publicity and Secrecy in Sierra Leone." In *Civil Society and the Political Imagination in Africa: Critical Perspectives,* edited by J.L. Comaroff and J. Comaroff, 160–91. Chicago University of Chicago Press.

———. 2001a. "La Figure du chasseur et les chasseurs-miliciens dans le conflit sierra-léonais." *Politique Africaine* 82: 119–32.

———. 2001b. *The Underneath of Things: Violence, History, and the Everyday in Sierra Leone.* Berkeley: University of California Press.

———. 2003. "Flexible Sovereignty? Paramount Chiefs, Deterritorialization, and Political Mediations in Sierra Leone." *Cambridge Anthropology* 23 (2): 21–35.

———. 2004. "Deterritorialized Citizenship and the Resonances of the Sierra Leonean State." In *Anthropology in the Margins of the State,* edited by V. Das and D. Poole, 81–115. Santa Fe: School of American Research Press.

———. 2013. "'Archetypes of Humanitarian Discourse': Child Soldiers, Forced Marriage, and the Framing of Communities in Post-conflict Sierra Leone." *Humanity: An International Journal of Human Rights, Humanitarianism, and Development* 4 (1): 49–71.

Ferme, M. C., and D. Hoffman. 2004. "Hunter Militias and the International Human Rights Discourse in Sierra Leone and Beyond." *Africa Today* 50 (4): 73–95.

Ferme, M. C., and C. M. Schmitz. 2014. "Writings on the Wall: Chinese Material Traces in an African Landscape." *Journal of Material Culture* 19 (4): 375–99.

Fithen, C. 1999. "Diamonds and War in Sierra Leone: Cultural Strategies for Commercial Adaptation to Endemic Low-Intensity Conflict." PhD diss., University of London.

Fleming, T. 2005. "The Historian Who Sold Out." George Mason University's History News Network, 8 August. Accessed 15 August 2011. http://hnn.us /articles/1489.html.

Fofanah, M. 2011. "Sierra Leone: Renewed Commitment to Local Government." Inter Press Service, 20 April. Accessed 31 August 2011. http:// allafrica.com/stories/201104210231.html.

Foucault, M. 1994. *Ethics: Subjectivity and Truth.* Vol. 1 of *Essential Works of Foucault, 1954–1984,* edited by P. Rabinow. New York: New Press.

Fox, R. C. 1995. "Medical Humanitarianism and Human Rights: Reflections on Doctors without Borders and Doctors of the World." *Social Science and Medicine* 41 (12): 1607–16.

Freud, S. 1922. *Beyond the Pleasure Principle.* Translated by C. J. M. Hubback. London: International Psycho-Analytical Press.

———. 1939. *Moses and Monotheism.* Translated by K. Jones. New York: Vintage Books.

Frulli, M. 2008. "Advancing International Criminal Law: The Special Court for Sierra Leone Recognizes Forced Marriage as a 'New' Crime against Humanity." *Journal of International Criminal Justice* 6 (5): 1033–42.

Fussell, P. 1997. *The Great War and Modern Memory.* Oxford: Oxford University Press.

Fyfe, C. 1962. *A History of Sierra Leone.* Oxford: Oxford University Press.

———. 1979, *Alimamy Suluku of Sierra Leone, c. 1820–1906: The Dynamics of Political Leadership in Pre-colonial Sierra Leone.* London: Evans Brothers.

Gabiam, N. 2012. "When 'Humanitarianism' Becomes 'Development': The Politics of International Aid in Syria's Palestinian Refugee Camps." *American Anthropologist* 114 (1): 95–107.

Gagoomal, P. 2009. "A 'Margin of Appreciation' for 'Marriages of Appreciation': Reconciling South Asian Adult Arranged Marriages with the Matrimonial Consent Requirement in International Human Rights Law." *Georgetown Law Journal* 97: 589–620.

Galy, M. 1998. "Liberia, Machine Perverse: Anthropologie politique du conflit libérien." *Cahiers d'Études Africaines* 150–52 (2–4): 533–53.

Gambino, C. P., E. N. Trevelyan, and J. T. Fitzgerald. 2014. "The Foreign-Born Population from Africa: 2008–2012." *American Community Survey Briefs.* Accessed 18 February 2018. www.census.gov/content/dam/Census/library /publications/.../acsbr12–16.pdf.

Gangal, S. C. 1992. "Gandhi and South Africa." *International Studies* 29 (2): 187–97.

Gayer, M., et al. 2007. "Conflict and Emerging Infectious Diseases." *Emerging Infectious Diseases* 13 (11): 1625–31.

Gberie, L. 2005. *A Dirty War in West Africa: The RUF and the Destruction of Sierra Leone.* Bloomington: University of Indiana Press.

Geertz, C. 1973. *The Interpretation of Cultures.* New York: Basic Books.

Geffray, C. 1990. La Cause des Armes au Mozambique: Anthropologie d'une Guerre Civile. Paris: Karthala.

Geschiere, P. 1997. *The Modernity of Witchcraft: Politics and the Occult in Postcolonial Africa.* Translated by J. Roitman and P. Geschiere. Charlottesville: University of Virginia Press.

———. 2009. *The Perils of Belonging: Autochthony, Citizenship, and Exclusion in Africa and Europe.* Chicago: University of Chicago Press.

Geschiere, P., and N. Basile. 2003. "Democratization and the Uncertain Renaissance of Chieftaincy: Varying Trajectories in Cameroon." Paper presented at the Chieftaincy in Africa: Culture, Governance and Development conference, Accra, Ghana, 6–10 January.

Gibson, C., and K. Jung. 2006. "Population Division: Historical Census Statistics on the Foreign-Born Population of the United States: 1850 to 2000." Working Paper 81. Washington, DC: U.S. Census Bureau. https://www.census.gov/content/dam/Census/library/working.../POP-twps0081.pdf.

Gilroy, P. 1993. *The Black Atlantic: Modernity and Double Consciousness.* Cambridge, MA: Harvard University Press.

Gong-Gershowitz, J. 2009. "Forced Marriage: A 'New' Crime against Humanity?" *Northwestern Journal of International Human Rights* 8 (1): 53–76.

Goodchild, P. 1996. *Deleuze and Guattari: Introduction to the Politics of Desire.* New York: Sage.

Goody, J. 1971. *Technology, Tradition, and the State in Africa.* Oxford: Oxford University Press.

Gourevitch, P. 2009. "The Life After." *New Yorker,* 4 May, 37–49.

Grafton, A. 1998. *The Footnote: A Curious History.* Cambridge, MA: Harvard University Press.

Grewal, K. 2010. "Rape in Conflict, Rape in Peaxe: Questioning the Revolutionary Potential of International Criminal Justice for Women's Human Rights." *Australian Feminist Law Journal* 33: 57–79.

Griaule, M. (1948) 1965. *Conversations with Ogotemmêli: An Introduction to Dogon Religious Ideas.* Oxford: Oxford University Press. Originally published as *Dieu d'Eau: Entretiens avec Ogotemmêli.*

Gupta, A. 1995. "Blurred Boundaries: The Discourse of Corruption, the Culture of Politics, and the Imagined State." *American Ethnologist* 22 (2): 375–402.

Guyer, J. 2004. *Marginal Gains: Monetary Transactions in Atlantic Africa.* Chicago: University of Chicago Press.

———. 2007. "Prophecy and the Near Future: Thoughts on Macroeconomic, Evangelical, and Punctuated Time." *American Ethnologist* 34 (3): 409–21.

Habermas, J. 1991. *The Structural Transformation of the Public Sphere: An Inquiry into a Category of Bourgeois Society.* Cambridge, MA: MIT Press.

Hagberg, S. 2004. "Political Decentralization and Traditional Leadership in the Benkadi Hunters' Association in Western Burkina Faso." *Africa Today* 50 (4): 51–70.

Hamber, B., and R. A. Wilson. 2002. "Symbolic Closure through Memory, Reparation and Revenge in Post-conflict Societies." *Journal of Human Rights* 1 (4): 35–53.

Hanchard, M. 1999. "Afro-Modernity, Temporality, Publics, and the African Diaspora." *Public Culture* 11 (1): 245–68.

Harris, W. T., and H. Sawyerr. 1968. *The Springs of Mende Belief and Conduct: A Discussion of the Influence of the Belief in the Supernatural among the Mende.* Freetown: Sierra Leone University Press.

Hellweg, J. 2004. "Encompassing the State: Sacrifice and Security in the Hunters' Movement of Cote d'Ivoire." *Africa Today* 50 (4): 3–26.

———. 2011. *Hunting the Ethical State: The Benkadi Movement.* Chicago: University of Chicago Press.

Henry, D. 2000. "Réfugiés sierra-léonais et aide humanitaire en Guinée. La réinvention d'une 'citoyenneté de frontière,'" *Politique Africaine* 85: 56–63.

———. 2005. "Embodied Violence: War and Relief along the Sierra Leone Border." PhD diss., Southern Methodist University.

———. 2006. "Violence and the Body: Somatic Expressions of Trauma and Vulnerability during War." *Medical Anthropology Quarterly* 20 (30): 379–98.

Hill, M. H. 1984. "Where to Begin? The Place of the Hunter Founder in Mende Histories." *Anthropos* 79: 653–56.

Hobsbawm, E., and T. Ranger, eds. 1983. *The Invention of Tradition.* Cambridge: Cambridge University Press.

Hocart, A. M. 1934. *Kings and Councilors: An Essay in the Comparative Anatomy of the Human Society.* Chicago: University of Chicago Press.

Hoffer, C. P. 1974. "Madam Yoko: Ruler of the Kpa Mende Confederacy." In *Woman, Culture, and Society,* edited by M. Z. Rosaldo and I. Lamphere, 183–88. Stanford, CA: Stanford University Press.

Hoffman, D. 2011a. "Violence, Just in Time: War and Work in Contemporary West Africa." *Cultural Anthropology* 26 (1): 34–57.

———. 2011b. *The War Machines: Young Men and Violence in Sierra Leone and Liberia.* Durham, NC: Duke University Press.

Holley, D. 1988. "Chinese Students Bar Traffic, Taunt Police in Anti-African Protest." *Los Angeles Times,* 29 December 2012. Accessed 10 April 2014. http://articles.latimes.com/1988-12-29/news/mn-1285_1_african-student.

Horn, R., S. Charters, and S. Vahidy. 2009. "Testifying in an International War Crimes Tribunal: The Experience of Witnesses in the Special Court for Sierra Leone." *International Journal for Transitional Justice* 3: 135–49.

Howe, H. M. 1998. "Private Security Forces and African Stability: The Case of Executive Outcomes." *Journal of Modern African Studies* 36 (2): 307–31.

Hsu, E. 2008. "Medicine as Business: Chinese Medicine in Tanzania." In *China Returns to Africa: A Rising Power and a Continent Embrace,* edited by C. Alden, D. Large, and R. Soares de Oliveira, 221–36. New York: Columbia University Press.

Human Rights Watch. 1999. "Sierra Leone: Getting Away with Murder, Mutilation, and Rape." *Human Rights Watch* 11 (3), section 4 (July). Accessed
May 2002. www.hrw.org/legacy/reports/1999/sierra/index.htm#TopOfPage.
———. 2003. "'We'll Kill You if You Cry:' Sexual Violence in the Sierra Leone
Conflict." *Human Rights Watch Reports* 15 (1-A): 1–75.
Hymes, D. 1972. *Reinventing Anthropology*. New York: Pantheon Books.
ICG (International Crisis Group). 2003. "Sierra Leone: The State of Security
and Governance," *ICG Africa Report* no. 67. Accessed 29 March 2012.
www.crisisgroup.org/en/regions/africa/west-africa/sierra-leone/067-sierra-
leone-the-state-of-security-and-governance.aspx.
ICRC. 1999. 99/02. Operational Update. 11 March. Accessed October 2002.
www.icrc.org.
*ICRC News*. 1996a. 96/7. Press release. 25 February. Accessed October 2002.
www.icrc.org.
———. 1996b. 96/12. Press release. 27 March. Accessed October 2002 www
.icrc.org.
———. 2001. 01/07. 22 February. Accessed October 2002. www.icrc.org.
Ingold, T. 2000. *The Perception of the Environment: Essays in Livelihood,
Dwelling, and Skill*. London: Routledge.
———. 2007. "Materials against Materiality." *Archaeological Dialogues*
14 (01): 1–16.
Innes, G. 1974. *Sunjata, Three Mandinka Versions*. London: School of Oriental
and African Studies.
International Crisis Group. 2003. "Sierra Leone: The State of Security and Governance." ICG Africa Report 67. 2 September. Accessed 29 March 2012.
www.crisisgroup.orf/en/regions/africa/west-africa/sierra-leone/067-sierra-
leone-the-state-of-security-and-governance.aspx.
Jackson, M. 1982. *Allegories of the Wilderness: Ethics and Ambiguity in
Kuranko Narratives*. Bloomington: Indiana University Press.
———. 2004. *In Sierra Leone*. Durham, NC: Duke University Press.
Jackson, P. 2005. "Chiefs, Money and Politicians: Rebuilding Local Government in Post-war Sierra Leone." *Public Administration and Development*
25 (1): 49–58.
Jaganathan, P. 2004. "Checkpoint: Anthropology, Identity, and the State." In
*Anthropology in the Margins of the State,* edited by V. Das and D. Poole,
67–80. Santa Fe: School of American Research Press.
James, W. 2007. *William James: Essays and Lectures*. Edited by D. Kolak. Lon-
don: Routledge.
Johnny, M., J. Karimu, and P. Richards. 1981. "Upland and Swamp Rice Farm-
ing Systems in Sierra Leone: The Social Context of Technological Change."
*Africa* 51 (2): 596–620.
Joko-Smart, H. 1983. *Sierra Leone Customary Family Law*. Freetown: Fourah
Bay College Bookshop.
Kalous, M. 1974. *Cannibals and Tongo Players of Sierra Leone*. Auckland,
NZ: Wright and Carman.
Kandeh, J.D. 1999. "Ransoming the State: Elite Origins of Subaltern Terror in
Sierra Leone." *Review of African Political Economy* 81: 349–66.

Kaplan, R. 1994. "The Coming Anarchy: How Scarcity, Crime, Overpopulation and Disease Are Rapidly Destroying the Social Fabric of Our Planet." *Atlantic Monthly*, February, 44–76.

———. 2001. *The Coming Anarchy: Shattering the Dreams of the Post-Cold War*. New York: Vintage Press.

Keane, W. 2003. "Semiotics and the Analysis of Material Things." *Language and Communication* 23: 409–25.

Keen, D. 2005. *Conflict and Collusion in Sierra Leone*. Oxford: James Currey.

Kelsall, T. 2009. *Culture under Cross-Examination: International Justice and the Special Court for Sierra Leone*. Cambridge: Cambridge University Press.

Kendall, S. 2009. "Contested Jurisdictions: Legitimacy and Governance at the Special Court for Sierra Leone." PhD diss., University of California, Berkeley.

Khan, A.W. 1996. "The Military-Kamajoh Feud." *For di people*, Freetown, 28 September.

Kilson, M. 1966. *Political Change in a West African State: A Study of the Modernization Process in Sierra Leone*. Cambridge, MA: Harvard University Press.

Kleinman, A. 2000. "The Violences of Everyday Life: The Multiple Forms and Dynamics of Social Violence." In *Violence and Subjectivity*, edited by V. Das, A. Kleinman, M. Ramphele, and P. Reynolds, 226–41. Berkeley: University of California Press.

Koenig, C. 1991. "Observer Status for the ICRC at the United Nations: A Legal Viewpoint." *International Review of the Red Cross* 280. Accessed April 2012. www.icrc.org/eng/resources/documents/misc/57jnwj.htm.

Koselleck, R. 1996. "A Response to Comments on the *Geschichtliche Grundbegriffe*." In *The Meaning of Historical Terms and Concepts: New Studies on* Begriffsgeschichte, edited by H. Lehmann and M. Richter, 59–70. Occasional Paper no. 15, German Historical Institute, Washington, DC.

——— 2004. *Futures Past: On the Semantics of Historical Time*. Translated and with an Introduction by K. Tribe. New York: Columbia University Press.

Kristof, N. 1989. "Africans in Beijing Boycott Classes." *New York Times*, 5 January. Accessed 10 April 2014. www.nytimes.com/1989/01/05/world/africans-in-beijing-boycott-classes.html.

Lan, D. 1985. *Guns and Rain: Guerrillas & Spirit Mediums in Zimbabwe*. Berkeley: University of California Press.

Langwick, S. 2011. *Bodies, Politics, and African Healing: The Matter of Maladies in Tanzania*. Bloomington: Indiana University Press.

Large, D. 2009. "China's Sudan Engagement: Changing Northern and Southern Political Trajectories in Peace and War." *China Quarterly* 199: 610–26.

Leach, M. 1994. *Rainforest Relations: Gender and Resource Use among the Mende of Gola, Sierra Leone*. Edinburgh: Edinburgh University Press.

———. 2000. "New Shapes to Shift: War, Parks and the Hunting Person in Modern West Africa." *Journal of the Royal Anthropological Institute* 6 (4): 577–95.

Legassick, M. 1966. "Firearms, Horses, and Samorian Army Organization, 1870–1898." *Journal of African History* 7: 95–115.

Levi, P. 1989. *The Drowned and the Saved.* New York: Vintage Press.

Levi-Montalcini, R. 2010. *Elogio dell'imperfezione.* Milano: Baldini Castoldi Dalai.

Lévi-Strauss, C. 1950. *Introduction to the Work of Marcel Mauss.* Translated by F. Baker. London: Routledge and Kegan Paul.

Li, A. 2011. *Chinese Medical Cooperation in Africa: With Special Emphasis on the Medical Teams and Anti-malaria Campaign.* Uppsala: Nordiska Afrikainstitutet.

Lindbloom, A. 2005. *Non-governmental Organizations in International Law.* Cambridge: Cambridge University Press.

Lindley, A. 2009. "The Early-Morning Phone Call: Remittances from a Refugee Diaspora Perspective." *Journal of Ethnic and Migration Studies* 35 (8): 1315–34.

Little, K. (1951) 1967. *The Mende of Sierra Leone: A West African People in Transition.* London: Routledge.

———. 1965. "The Political Function of the Poro." Part 1. *Africa* 35 (4): 349–65.

———. 1966. "The Political Function of the Poro." Part 2. *Africa* 36 (1): 62–71.

Liu, P.H. 2009. "Planting Rice on the Roof of the UN Building: Analyzing Taiwan's 'Chinese' Techniques in Africa, 1961–Present." *China Quarterly* 198: 381–400.

Lock, M., and J. Farquhar. 2007. *Beyond the Body Proper: Reading the Anthropology of Material life.* Durham, NC: Duke University Press.

Loëz, A. 2010. *14–18, Les Refus de la Guerre: Une histoire des mutins.* Paris: Gallimard.

Lombard, L. "Navigational Tools for Central African Roadblocks." *Political and Legal Anthropology Review* 36 (1): 157–73.

Lomnitz, C. 1995. "Ritual, Rumors and Corruption in the Constitution of Polity in Modern Mexico." *Journal of Latin American and Caribbean Anthropology* 1: 20–47.

Lord, David, ed. 2000. "Paying the Price: The Sierra Leone Peace Process." Special issue, *Accord: An International Review of Peace Initiatives* 9.

Lu, Y., G. Rong, S.P. Yu, Z. Sun, X. Dong, H. Xia, N. Zhan, C. Jin, J. Ji, H. Duan. 2016. "Chinese Military Medical Teams in the Ebola Outbreak of Sierra Leone." *Journal of the Royal Army Medical Corps* 0: 1–5.

Lubkemann, S. 2007. *Culture in Chaos: An Anthropology of the Social Condition in War.* Chicago: University of Chicago Press.

Lueders, M. 1999. "The Photographer's Diary: Hope and Horror in Sierra Leone." *Digital Journalist,* February. www.digitaljournalist.org/issue9902/diary7.htm.

MacCormack, C.P. 1979. "Sande: The Public Face of a Secret Society." In *The New Religions of Africa,* edited by B. Jules-Rosette, 27–37. Norwood, NJ: Ablex.

———. 1983. "Human Leopards and Crocodiles: Political Meanings of Categorical Ambiguities." In *Ethnography of Cannibalism,* edited by P. Brown and D. Tuzineds, 51–60. Washington, DC: Society for Psychological Anthropology.

Machel, G. 1996. *The Impact of Armed Conflict on Children*. United Nations A/51/306. 26 August. Accessed May 2011. www.unicef.org/graca/.

Maconachie, R., T. Binns, P. Tengbe, and R. Johnson. 2006. "Temporary Labour Migration and Sustainable Post-conflict Return in Sierra Leone." *GeoJournal* 67 (3): 223–40.

Malcolm, J.M. 1939. "Mende Warfare." *Sierra Leone Studies,* old series, 21: 47–52.

Malinowski, B. 1967. *A Diary in the Strict Sense of the Term*. New York: Harcourt, Brace and World.

Malkki, L. 1994. "Citizens of Humanity: Internationalism and the Imagined Community of Nations." *Diaspora* 3 (1): 41–68.

———. 1995. *Purity and Exile: Violence, Memory, and National Cosmology among Hutu Refugees in Tanzania*. Chicago: University of Chicago Press.

———. 1996. "Speechless Emissaries: Refugees, Humanitarianism, and De-Historicization." *Cultural Anthropology* 11 (3): 377–404.

———. 2010. "Children, Humanity, and the Infantilization of Peace." In *In the Name of Humanity,* edited by I. Feldman and M. Ticktin, 58–85. Durham, NC: Duke University Press.

Mamdani, M. 1996. *Citizen and Subject: Contemporary Africa and the Legacy of Late Colonialism*. Princeton, NJ: Princeton University Press.

Marchal, R., C. Ero, and M. Ferme. 2002. "Liberia, Sierra Leone et Guinée: une guerre sans frontières?" *Politique Africaine* 88: 5–12.

Maru, V. 2006. "Between Law and Society: Paralegals and the Provision of Justice Services in Sierra Leone and Worldwide." *Yale Journal of International Law* 31: 427–76.

Massey, D. 1991. "A Global Sense of Place." *Marxism Today* (June). Accessed 11 September 2013. www.aughty.org/pdf/global_sense_place.pdf.

M'Bayo, R.T., and M. Mogkewu. 2000. "Political Authority and the Transformation of the Sierra Leonean Press." In *Press and Politics in Africa,* edited by R.T. M'Bayo, C. Onwumechili, and R. Nwanko, 107–28. New York: Mellen Press.

Mbembe, A. 1992. "Provisional Notes on the Postcolony." *Africa* 62 (1): 3–37.

———. 2001. *On the Postcolony*. Berkeley: University of California Press.

Mbembe, A., and J. Roitman. 1995. "Figures of the Subject in a Time of Crisis." *Public Culture* 7 (2): 323–52.

McCaskie, T. 2003. "KingofAfrica.com: Asante Kingship Now." Paper presented at the Chieftaincy in Africa: Culture, Governance and Development conference, Accra, Ghana, 6–10 January.

McGovern, M. 2002. "Conflit régional et rhétorique de la contre-insurrection: Guinéens et réfugiés en septembre 2000." *Politique Africaine* 88: 84–102.

———. 2011. *Making War in Côte d'Ivoire*. Chicago: University of Chicago Press.

McKenzie, G. 1998. "Sierra Leone's Cult of Killers: Militiamen Tap into Belief That They're Invincible." *San Francisco Chronicle,* 8 December.

McNaughton, P. 1982. "The Shirts That Mande Hunters Wear." *African Arts* 15 (3): 54–58.

———. 1993. *The Mande Blacksmiths: Knowledge, Power, and Art in West Africa.* Bloomington: Indiana University Press.

Mentholatum Asia Pacific Ltd. 2007. *Mentholatum History.* Accessed 10 April 2014. www.mentholatum-ap.com/history.html.

Mercier, M. 1995. *Crimes without Punishment: Humanitarian Action in Former Yugoslavia:* London: Pluto Press.

Merry, S. E. 2006. "Transnational Human Rights and Local Activism: Mapping the Middle." *American Anthropologist* 108 (1): 38–51.

———. 2016. *The Seductions of Quantification: Measuring Human Rights, Gender Violence, and Human Trafficking.* Chicago: University of Chicago Press.

Mokuwa, E., M. Voors, E. Bulte, and P. Richards. 2011. "Peasant Grievance and Insurgency in Sierra Leone: Judicial Serfdom as a Driver of Conflict." *African Affairs* 110 (440): 339–66.

Momodu, S. 1999. "In Bo, Norman Urges Kamajors to Behave Well." *Concord Times* (Freetown), 23 June 1999.

Monson, J., and S. Rupp. 2013. "ASR Forum on Africa and China: Introduction." *African Studies Review* 56 (1): 21–44.

Moorehead, C. 2005. *Human Cargo: A Journey among Refugees.* New York: Picador.

Moran, M. 1995. "Warriors or Soldiers? Masculinity and Ritual Transvestism in the Liberian Civil War." In *Feminism, Nationalism, and Militarism,* edited by C. Sutton, 73–88. Washington, DC: Association of Feminist Anthropologists.

Muana, P. 1997. "The Kamajoi Militia: Civil War, Internal Displacement and the Politics of Counter-insurgency." *Afrique et Développement* 22 (3/4): 77–100.

Munn, N. 1986. *The Fame of Gawa: A Symbolic Study of Value Transformation in a Massim (Papua New Guinea) Society.* Cambridge: Cambridge University Press.

———. (2003) 2013. "The 'Becoming-Past' of Places: Spacetime and Memory in Nineteenth-Century, Pre-Civil War New York." *Hau: Journal of Ethnographic Theory* 3 (2): 359–80.

Nabieu, Eric Sahr. 2007. "Analysis of the Problems and Gains Associated with Rural-Urban Migration, the Sierra Leone Experience." Paper presented at the Fifth African Population Conference, Arusha, December.

Nancy, J.-L. 2000. "War, Right, Sovereignty—Techne." In *Being Singular Plural,* translated by R. D. Richardson and A. E. O'Brien, 100–43. Palo Alto, CA: Stanford University Press.

National Commission for Democracy and Human Rights (Sierra Leone). 2002. "Paramount Chiefs in the Electoral Process." *Voter* 1 (1): 1–2.

National Immigration Law Center (NILC). 2002. "AG Extends TPS for Nationals of Sierra Leone." *Immigrants' Rights Update* 16 (7) (22 November).

Newland, K., and E. Patrick. 2004. *Beyond Remittances: The Role of Diaspora in Poverty Reduction in Their Countries of Origin.* Washington, DC: Migration Policy Institute.

No Peace without Justice. 2004. *Conflict Mapping in Sierra Leone: Violations of International Humanitarian Law from 1991 to 2002.* Sierra Leone Conflict Mapping Program. Freetown: No Peace without Justice.

Nordstrom C. 1997. *A Different Kind of War Story*. Philadelphia: University of Pennsylvania Press.

———. 2004. *Shadows of War: Violence, Power, and International Profiteering in the Twenty-First Century*. Berkeley: University of California Press.

Nowrojee, B. 2005a. "Making the Invisible War Crime Visible: Post-conflict Justice for Sierra Leone's Rape Victims." *Harvard Human Rights Journal* 18: 85–106.

———. 2005b. 'Your Justice Is Too Slow': Will the ICTR Fail Rwanda's Rape Victims?" Occasional Paper 10. Geneva: United Nations Institute for Social Development. www.unrisd.org/80256B3C005BCCF9/httpNetITFramePDF?ReadForm&parentunid=56FE32D5C0F6DCE9C125710F0045D89F&parentdoctype=paper&netitpath=80256B3C005BCCF9/(httpAuxPages)/56FE32D5C0F6DCE9C125710F0045D89F/$file/OP10%20Web.pdf

Ntsebeza, L. 2008. "The Resurgence of Chiefs: Retribalism and Modernity in Post-1994 South Africa." In *Readings in African Modernity*, edited by P. Geschiere, B. Meyer, and P. Pels. Bloomington: Indiana University Press.

Nunley, J. 1982. "Images and Printed Words in Freetown Masquerades." *African Arts*, 42–92.

———. 1987. *Moving with the Face of the Devil: Art and Politics in Urban West Africa*. Champaign: University of Illinois Press.

Nyamnjoh, F. B. 2003. "Chieftaincy and the Negotiation of Might and Right in Botswana Democracy." *Journal of Contemporary African Studies* 21 (2): 233–50.

Oakland Institute. 2011. *Understanding Land Investment Deals in Africa. Country Report: Sierra Leone*. www.oaklandinstitute.org/sites/oaklandinstitute.org/files/OI_SierraLeone_Land_Investment_report_0.pdf.

———. 2012. "Understanding Land Investment Deals in Africa: SOCFIN Land Investment in Sierra Leone." www.oaklandinstitute.org/country/sierra-leone.

Obarrio, J. 2010. "Remains: To Be Seen. Third Encounter between State and 'Customary' in Northern Mozambique." *Cultural Anthropology* 25 (2): 263–300.

Oë, K. 1965. *Hiroshima Notes*. Translated by D. L. Swain and T. Yonezawa. New York: Grove Press.

———. 1969. *A Personal Matter*. Translated by J. Nathan. New York: Grove Press.

OECD. 2009. *African Economic Outlook: Country Notes*. Vols. 1–2. Paris: Organization for Economic Co-Operation and Development.

Ong, A. 2003. "Cyberpublics and Diaspora Politics among Transnational Chinese." *Interventions: International Journal of Postcolonial Studies* 5 (1): 82–100.

Oomen, B. 2008. "Chiefs! Law, Power, and Culture in Contemporary South Africa." In *Readings in African Modernity*, edited by P. Geschiere, B. Meyer, and P. Pels, 80–84. Bloomington: Indiana University Press.

Oosterveld, V. 2004. "Sexual Slavery and the International Criminal Court: Advancing International Law." *Michigan Journal of International Law* 25: 605–51.

———. 2011. "Forced Marriage and the Special Court for Sierra Leone: Legal Advances and Conceptual Difficulties." *International Humanitarian Legal Studies* 2 (1): 127–58.

———. 2012. "Gender and the Charles Taylor Case at the Special Court for Sierra Leone." *William and Mary Journal of Women and the Law* 19 (1): 7–33.

Pandolfo, S. 1997. *Impasse of the Angels: Scenes from a Moroccan Space of Memory.* Chicago: University of Chicago Press.

Parham, A. 2005. "Internet, Place, and Public Sphere in Diaspora Communities." *Diaspora* 14 (2/3): 349–80.

Park, Y. J. 2008. *A Matter of Honour: Being Chinese in South Africa.* Auckland Park, South Africa: Jacana.

Peace Corps Congressional Submission. 1983. "Budget Justification, Fiscal Year 1983."

Pels, P. 1998. "The Spirit of the Matter: On Fetish, Rarity, Fact, and Fancy. In *Border Fetishisms: Material Objects in Unstable Spaces,* edited by P. Spyer, 91–121. London: Routledge.

Person Y. 1968–75. *Samori: une révolution dyula.* 3 vols. Dakar: Memoires de l'IFAN.

Peters, K. 2011. *War and the Crisis of Youth in Sierra Leone.* Cambridge: Cambridge University Press.

Peters, K., and P. Richards. 1998. "'Why We Fight': Voices of Youth Combatants in Sierra Leone." *Africa* 68 (2): 183–210.

Platte, E. 2004. "Towards an African Modernity: Plastic Pots and Enamel Ware in Kanuri Women's Rooms (Northern Nigeria)." *Paideuma* 50: 173–92.

Pratten, D. 2007. *The Man-Leopard Murders: History and Society in Colonial Nigeria.* Edinburgh: Edinburgh University Press.

Prosecutor v. Moinina Fofana and Alieu Kondewa. 2008. Special Court of Sierra Leone. CDF Trial. Appeals Chamber Judgment. 28 May.

Provost, R. 2007. "The International Committee of the Red Widget: The Diversity Debate and International Humanitarian Law." *Israeli Law Review* 40 (2): 614–47.

———. 2012. "Magic and Modernity in Tintin au Congo (1930) and the Sierra Leone Special Court." *Law Text Culture* 161 (1): 183–216.

Putnam, R. 2000. *Bowling Alone: The Collapse and Revival of American Community.* New York: Simon and Schuster.

Rashid, I. 1997. "Subaltern Reactions: Lumpen, Students, and the Left." *Afrique et Développment* 22 (3–4): 19–45.

Rathbone, R. 2000. *Nkrumah and the Chiefs: The Politics of Chieftaincy in Ghana 1951–60.* Athens: Ohio University Press.

Redfield, P. 2011. "The Impossible Problem of Neutrality." In *Forces of Compassion: Humanitarianism between Ethics and Politics,* edited by E. Bornstein and P. Redfield, 53–70. Santa Fe: SAR Press.

———. 2013. *Life in Crisis: The Ethical Journey of Doctors without Borders.* Berkeley: University of California Press.

Reno, W. 1995. *Corruption and State Politics in Sierra Leone.* Cambridge: Cambridge University Press.

———. 1996. "Ironies of Postcold War Structural Adjustment in Sierra Leone." *Review of African Political Economy* 23 (67): 7–18.

———. 1998. *Warlord Politics and African States.* Boulder, CO: Lynne Rienner.

———. 2002. "How Sovereignty Matters: International Markets and the Political Economy of Local Politics in Weak States." In *Intervention and Transnationalism in Africa,* edited by T. Callaghy, R. Kassimir, and R. Latham, 197–215. Cambridge: Cambridge University Press.

———. 2007. "Patronage Politics and the Behavior of Armed Groups." *Civil Wars* 9 (4): 324–42.

———. 2010. "Transforming West African Militia Networks for Postwar Recovery." In *Troubled Regions and Failing States: The Clustering and Contagion of Armed Conflicts,* edited by K. B. Harpviken, 127–49. Comparative Social Research 27. Bingley, UK: Emerald Group.

Rice, X. 2010. "Chinese Archaeologists' African Quest for Sunken Ship of Ming Admiral." *Guardian,* 25 July. Accessed 10 April 2014. www.guardian .co.uk/world/2010/jul/25/kenya-china.

Richards, P. 1986. *Coping with Hunger: Hazard and Experiment in an African Rice-Farming System.* London: Allen and Unwin.

———. 1996. *Fighting for the Rain Forest: War, Youth and Resources in Sierra Leone.* Oxford: International African Institute and James Currey.

———, ed. 2005. *No Peace No War: Anthropology of Contemporary Armed Conflicts.* Athens: Ohio University Press.

Riley, S. 1997. "Sierra Leone: The Militariat Strikes Again," *Review of African Political Economy* 24 (72): 287–92.

Roberts, R. 2016. "Constrained Consent: Women, Marriage, and Household Instability in Colonial French West Africa, 1905–60." In *Marriage by Force? Contestation over Consent and Coercion in Africa,* edited by A. Bunting, B. N. Lawrance, and R. L. Roberts, 43–64. Athens: Ohio University Press.

Rodney, W. 1970. *A History of the Upper Guinea Coast, 1545–1800.* New York: Monthly Review Press.

Roitman, J. 2005. *Fiscal Disobedience: An Anthropology of Economic Regulation in Central Africa.* Princeton, NJ: Princeton University Press.

———. 2008. "A Successful Life in the Illegal Realm: Smugglers and Road Bandits in the Chad Basin." In *Readings on Modernity in Africa,* edited by P. Geschiere, B. Meyer, and P. Pels, 214–20. Bloomington: Indiana University Press.

Rosen, D. 1984. "The Politics of Indirect Rule: Political Leadership among the Kono of Sierra Leone, 1896–1983." In *Sierra Leone Studies at Birmingham, 1983.* Birmingham: University of Birmingham.

———. 2007. "Child Soldiers, International Humanitarian Law, and the Globalization of Childhood." *American Anthropologist* 109 (2): 296–306.

Rubin, E. 1997. "'An Army of One's Own: In Africa, Nations Hire a Corporation to Wage War" *Harper's* 294, no. 1761 (1 February): 44–55.

Samura, S, dir. 2000. *Cry Freetown.* Documentary film. London: Insight News TV.

Samura, S. 2011. "Sierra Leone: Timber! A Story of Corruption That Is Stripping the West African Country Bare." *Aljazeera,* 26 November. www.aljazeera .com/programmes/africainvestigates/2011/11/20111123134340348960.html.

Sawyer, E. 2008, "Remove or Reform? A Case for (Restructuring) Governance in Sierra Leone." *African Affairs* 107 (428): 387–403.

Scharf, M.P., and S. Mattler. 2005. "Forced Marriage: Exploring the Viability of the Special Court for Sierra Leone's New Crime against Humanity." *Case Research Paper Series in Legal Studies* 05–35: 1–24 (October). Case Western Reserve University School of Law.

Scheper-Hughes, N., and P. Bourgois, eds. 2003. *Violence in War and Peace: An Anthology.* Oxford: Blackwell Publishing.

Sebutinde, J. 2007. "Separate Concurring Opinion." Special Court of Sierra Leone. AFRC trial. SCase no. SCSL-2004-16-T. 20 June.

Seibure, B.I. 2007. "Sierra Leone: China to Commence Work on Bo Stadium, Dodo Hydro Project Soon." *Concord Times,* 30 January. Accessed 10 April 2014. http://allafrica.com/stories/200701310724.html.

Sesay, S. 2012. "APC Fundraising Dance in Houston: Al Aziz Says the Time Is Now." *Sierra Express Media.* http://sierraexpressmedia.com/?p=41663.

Shana, E. 2004. "Sierra Leone: The Proving Ground for Prosecuting Rape as a War Crime." *Georgetown Journal of International Law* 35 (4): 873–919.

Shaw, R. 2007. "Memory Frictions: Localizing the Truth and Reconciliation Commission in Sierra Leone." *International Journal of Transitional Justice* 1: 183–207.

Shepler, S. 2014. *Childhood Deployed: Remaking Child Soldiers in Sierra Leone.* New York: New York University Press.

Sierra Leone Chieftaincy Act. 2009. No. 10. Freetown: Government Printing Office.

Sierra Leone Red Cross Society. n.d. *A History of the Sierra Leone Red Cross Society: 1991–2003.* Typescript in author's possession.

Simons, A. 1995. "The Beginning of the End." In *Fieldwork under Fire: Contemporary Studies of Violence and Survival,* edited by C. Nordstrom and A.C.G.M. Robben, 42–62. Berkeley: University of California Press.

Singh, S. 2009. "African Minerals Seeks $2.6bn to Finance Tonkolili Iron Ore Mine." Reuters, 2 July. Accessed 10 April 2014. www.mineweb.com /mineweb/content/en/mineweb-iron-and-steel?oid=85824&sn=Detail.

Sissoko, B. 1995. "Organisations de chasseurs au Mali: quand le chasseur assure la sécurité publique." *Dialogues, propositions, histoires pour une citoyenneté mondiale.* http://base.d-p-h.info/fr/fiches/premierdph/fiche-premierdph-3102 .html.

Smillie, I., L. Gberie, and R. Hazelton. 2000. *The Heart of the Matter: Sierra Leone Diamonds and Human Security.* Ottawa: Partnership Africa Canada.

Smith, D.J, 2006. "Cell Phones, Social Inequality, and Contemporary Culture in Nigeria." *Canadian Journal of African Studies* 40 (3): 496–523.

———. 2007, *A Culture of Corruption: Everyday Deception and Popular Discontent in Nigeria.* Princeton, NJ: Princeton University Press.

Snow, P. 1989. *The Star Raft: China's Encounter with Africa.* Ithaca, NY: Cornell University Press.

Solway, J. 2003. "Charisma and Bureaucracy: Chiefs and the Chieftaincy in Contemporary Botswana." Paper presented at the Chieftaincy in Africa: Culture, Governance and Development conference, Accra, Ghana, 6–10 January.

Spivak, G. 1987. "Explanation and Marginalia." In *Other Worlds: Essays in Cultural Studies*. New York: Methuen.

Staggs Kelsall, M., and S. Stepakoff. 2007. "'When We Wanted to Talk about Rape': Silencing Sexual Violence at the Special Court for Sierra Leone." *International journal of Transitional Justice* 1: 355–74.

*Standard Times*. 2002. Freetown, Sierra Leone, 21 June.

Sullivan, M.J. 1994. "The 1988–89 Nanjing Anti-African Protests: Racial Nationalism or National Racism?" *China Quarterly* 138: 438–57.

Tarawallie, I. 2011. "Sierra Leone: 40 Years of Diplomatic Relations—China Assures More Assistance." *Concord Times*, 15 July. Accessed 10 April 2014. http://allafrica.com/stories/201107201497.html].

Taylor, A. 2006. *Amazing Mentholatum: And the Commerce of Curing the Common Cold, 1889–1955*. La Cañada, CA: Angeles Crest.

Taylor, I. 2006. *China and Africa: Engagement and Compromise*. New York: Routledge.

Tettey, W.J. 2001. "Information Technology and Democratic Participation in Africa." *Journal of Asian and African Studies* 36 (1): 133–55.

Thomas, N.W. 1916. *Anthropological Report on Sierra Leone*. Vol. 1. London: Harrison and Sons.

Thomson S. 2011. "The Darker Side of Transitional Justice: The Power Dynamics behind Rwanda's Gacaca Courts." *Africa* 81 (3): 373–90.

Tostevin, M. 1993. "Sinking to the Depths." *BBC Focus on Africa* 4 (3): 23–26.

Toy-Cronin, B. 2010. "What Is Forced Marriage? Towards a Definition of Forced Marriage as a Crime against Humanity." *Columbia Journal of Gender and Law* 19 (2): 539–90.

Traoré, K. 2004. "The Intellectuals and the Hunters: Reflections on the Conference 'La Rencontre des Chasseurs de l'Afrique de l'Ouest,'" *Africa Today* 50 (4): 97–111.

TRC (Truth and Reconciliation Commission). 2004. *Witness to Truth: Report of the Sierra Leone Truth and Reconciliation Commission*. 3 vols. www.sierraleonetrc.org/.

Turner, P. 1994. *I Heard It through the Grapevine: Rumor in African-American Culture*. Berkeley: University of California Press.

Tymowski, M. 1981. "The Army and the Formation of States in West Africa in the Nineteenth Century: The Cases of Kenedugu and Samori State." In *The Study of the State*, edited by J.M. Claessen and P. Skalnik, 427–42. The Hague: Mouton.

Tynes, R. 2007. "Nation-Building and the Diaspora on Leonenet: A Case of Sierra Leone in Cyberspace." *New Media and Society* 9 (3): 497–518.

US Department of Justice. 1997. "Designation of Sierra Leone Under Temporary Protected Status." *Federal Register* 62 (213) (4 November): 59736.

Van der Veer, P. 1997. "The Victim's Tale: Memory and Forgetting in the Story of Violence." In *Violence, Identity, and Self-Determination*, edited by H. De Vries and S. Weber, 186–200. Stanford, CA: Stanford University Press.

Wallis, C.B. 1903. *The Advance of Our West African Empire*. London: T.F. Unwin.

*West Africa*. 1984. "Sierra Leone: More Malpractices." 21 May.

White, L. 2000. *Speaking with Vampires: Rumor and History in Colonial Africa*. Berkeley: University of California Press.

Will, R. 2012. "China's Stadium Diplomacy." *World Policy Journal* 29 (2): 36–43.

Wilson, R.A., and J.P. Mitchell. 2003. "Introduction: The Social Life of Rights." In *Human Rights in Global Perspective: Anthropological Studies of Rights, Claims, and Entitlements,* edited by R.A. Wilson and J.P. Michell, 1–15. London: Routledge1–15.

World Bank. 2011. *World Development Indicators*. April 2011. Accessed 7 July 2011. https://data.worldbank.org/data-catalog/world-development-indicators/wdi-2011.

*Xinhua.* 2012. "Sierra Leone-China Friendship Hospital Launched as New Fruit of Bilateral Ties." 15 November. Accessed 10 April 2014. http://news.xinhuanet.com/english/china/2012–11/15/c_131974961.htm.

Young, A. 1995. *The Harmony of Illusions: Inventing Post-traumatic Stress Disorder*. Princeton, NJ: Princeton University Press.

Yu, G.T. 1963. "Peking versus Taipei in the World Arena: Chinese Competition in Africa." *Asian Survey* 3 (9): 439–53.

Weber, M. (1956) 1978. *Economy and Society: An Outline of Interpretive Sociology*. Edited by G. Roth and L. Wittich. Vol. 1. Berkeley: University of California Press.

Williams, W.I. 2006. "Complex Trauma: Approaches to Theory and Treatment." *Journal of Loss and Trauma* 11 (4): 321–35.

Zack-Williams, A.B. 1997. "Kamajors, Sobels, & the Militariat: Civil Society and the Return of the Military in Sierra Leonean Politics." *Review of African Political Economy* 24 (73): 373–80.

———. 1999. "Sierra Leone: The Political Economy of Civil War, 1991–1998." *Third World Quarterly* 20 (1): 143–62.

Zemon-Davis, N. 1997. "Remaking Impostors: From Martin Guerre to Sommersby." Hayes Robinson Lecture Series no. 1. London: University of London Publication Unit, Royal Holloway.

# Index

leaders, 143, 145–46, 220, 273n3, 275n17, 279n6 (Chap. 7)

civilians: captured/abducted by rebels, 14–15, 53, 230; gun ownership by, 210; plundered by soldiers, 16, 73; rebels hiding among, 16; as "soldier's affiliates," 211–12

civil society, 188

civil war, Sierra Leonean, 1, 15, 19, 71, 243; agrarian societies disrupted by, 198–99; atrocities on family members, 11; casualty figures, 257; civilian elections (1996) and, 88; civilians preyed on, 71; collusions in, 22, 30; de facto international character of, 81; diaspora and peace talks, 188; Ebola epidemic in relation to, 37; ethnography and, 25–28; film footage of, 40; focus on mutilations, 102; forced marriage issue and, 218; formal end of (2002), 102, 106, 167, 214; generation of children in limbo produced by, 4; Liberia and beginnings of, 203–4; paramount chieftaincy and, 32, 154, 156, 161, 171; as part of regional war, 174, 213; power vacuum as result of, 42, 161–62; Red Cross intervention in, 85–89; temporal disruptions of, 23, 99, 262; UN peacekeepers deployed to end, 23–24

Clastres, Pierre, 56

Coker-Jajua, Chief James Sheriff, 158

Cold War, 22, 23, 87–88, 249; Afro-Asian vision of mutual aid and, 244–45; Chinese–Sierra Leonean relations and, 239, 242, 248, 255; conflicts following, 26, 27

communication, 93–94

community, 199, 208; distribution of aid resources and, 214–15; gestures of welcome to strangers, 241; "local community," 206; re-creation of, 206; religious institutions as component of, 228; SCSL trials and, 226; spatial conception of, 198

consent, 218–19, 225, 232, 235, 236

Cook, Robin, 150

Côte d'Ivoire (Ivory Coast), 91, 182; civil war in, 179; hunting associations in, 116, 118, 119, 122; southern/ Christian–northern/Muslim divide, 122

Crane, David, 208, 220

crimes against humanity, 27, 148, 209; forced marriage as, 218, 219; "hybrid" tribunals and, 34

*Cry Freetown* (CNN documentary, 2000), 51–53

"cyber-publics," 34

Dabo, Chief Ibrahim ("Braima"), 158

Dabo, Paramount Chief M. K., II, 155–56, 276n5

Dabo, Siddiq, 168

Dabo family, 155, 158–59, 168

Davies, Natalie Zemon, 69

death, 8, 10, 236; death toll in attack on Freetown, 82, 94, 271n9; false rumors of, 81; journalists sentenced to death, 94; modalities of death, 106–8; Nazi death camps, 8–9; from "spoiled heart," 108–9, 125; temporality and, 18; Tongo players "cannibal-finding" practices and, 43, 44

decentralization, 32–33, 37, 118–19, 266, 276n9; court system and, 261; international donors and, 121; paramount chieftaincy and, 165

decolonization, 246, 249

defamiliarization, 7

Deleuze, Gilles, 104, 115–16, 118, 171–72, 175

delocalization, 148, 150

demobilization, 25, 202

democracy, 194, 214

deterritorialization, 160, 161, 172, 273n3

de Waal, Alex, 270n4 (Chap. 2)

diamond mining, 45, 64, 71, 79, 89, 121; agricultural land diverted to, 246; diamond-rich areas occupied by rebels, 121; foreign businessmen and, 138, 274n14; Kono region, 79, 89, 96, 178; paramount chieftaincy and, 137–38

diaspora, Sierra Leonean, 26, 33, 168, 169; in Cairo, 34, 176, 195, 277n1; cyber-diaspora, 181–89; formerly diasporic chiefs, 170, 193; internal politics of Sierra Leone and, 173; Leonenet listserv and, 185–87; political economy of diasporic networks, 193–94; refugees as agents of territorialization, 175–81; reterritorialization of, 34, 172; in United States and United Kingdom, 176, 182–83, 188, 193, 277n10

diasporas, 194–95; Africans in the United States, 182; Burundian Hutu refugees in Tanzania, 177, 179–80; Eritrean, 191–92; Haitian, 278n14; Huaren (global Chinese), 180; mobilization of

Internet, 29, 34, 169, 191, 278n14;
advances in digital technology and,
195; chat groups, 174; number of users
in Sierra Leone, 181–82; "virtual
neighborhoods," 187. *See also*
Leonenet listserv
Iran, 174–75, 196
Islam and Muslims, 117, 150
isolation, 7, 24
Israel, state of, 179

Jackson, Michael, 128
Jahn people, 158
Jaiama-Bongor Chiefdom, 9, 127, 130,
135, 137, 155
James, William, 1
Jews, 8–10, 15–16
Jimmy, Karimu, 276n12
Jonah, James, 191
Jui Government Hospital (Freetown), 252
"junta time," 81, 120
justice-as-fairness, 103–4, 272–73n14

Kabbah, President Ahmed Tejan, 27, 32,
144, 191; exile in Guinea, 93, 184, 185;
Kamajor (hunter) militias and, 115;
Malinke (Mandingo) migration and,
118; overthrown in coup (1997), 120,
138; peace process and, 105; press
freedom curtailed by, 190; reinstated in
power, 94, 150, 211
"Kaikulo" (child soldier), 24, 202–8, 214,
259
Kailahun, town of, 9, 90, 91, 123, 232
Kailahun District War Effort Committee,
121
Kallon, Amie, 45
Kamajei Chiefdom, 278n19
Kamajor (hunter) militias, 25, 31, 107,
204–5, 268n15; guerrilla warfare
practiced by, 115, 139; hunting
traditions and, 114–15; identity cards
issued to hunters, 112, 113; institutionalization of, 139–43; modern genealogy
of, 143–45; organized by chiefs, 32; rise
during civil war, 112, 114; Special
Court for Sierra Leone (SCSL) and,
273n3; transition from "cultural"
hunters to, 135–39; "war vests"
(*ronkos*), 110–11, *111*, 121, 137. *See
also* hunting traditions
Kangari Hills forest reserve, 73
Kangova, Rev. Jeremiah Joe Sinnah-
Yovonie, II, 278n19

Kargoi, Chief Mohamed Tshombei, II, *157*,
168
Kema (Sande elder), 65, 66–67, *67*,
269nn7–8
Kenema, town and district of, 92, 140, 158;
Chinese medical teams in, 252;
electricity service in, 36, 244; map, 9
Kilson, Martin, 155
King, Justice George Gelaga, 145–46
King Harman Road Hospital (Freetown),
251–52
kinship: concept of community and, 198;
political ties of chieftaincy, 32, 147,
155, 193, 276n13; SCSL courtroom
discourse and, 200; in victim–perpetrator relations, 43
Kissidougou (Guinea), 91
"Kissy triangle," 8, 9
Kleinman, Arthur, 278n2
knowledge, 4, 81, 170, 219; bearing witness
and, 39–40; chronotopes and, 12; legal,
27; local, 154; loss of, 7, 8
*kɔ mahei* (war chief), 124, 129, 131
Kondewa, Alieu, 119, 143, 275n17; as
"high priest," 145; reputed magic
powers of, 146; sentenced to prison,
275n19
Kono diamond-mining region, 79, 89, 96,
178
Koroma, Salia, 45
Kosselleck, R., 13, 14, 15–16, 17, 21
Kosovo, 99
Kpanga Kabonde Chiefdom, 9
Kpuawala, village of, 240, 247, 258
Krio people/language, 1, 59, 268n15,
275n20; as national lingua franca, 53,
234, 242; Yoruba freed slaves as origin
of, 135, 140
*kugbei* (warrior), 124, 129, 137
Kuranko people/language, 113, 128

Lan, David, 273n5
land: colonial standardization of chiefly
office and, 33; land disputes, 42, 161,
170; "land grabs" by foreign companies,
37, 257, 266; landowning lineages, 7–8;
neoliberal business ventures on the land,
165–67; ownership versus usufruct
rights, 170; paramount chieftaincy and,
154, 161; rights and, 37
language, 13, 70
laughter, fear paired with, 56, 59, 136
law, international, 84, 90, 93, 223
Lebanese shopkeepers/traders, 253, 254

www.ingramcontent.com/pod-product-compliance
Lightning Source LLC
Chambersburg PA
CBHW020456270326
41926CB00008B/635